BRUNEL

Brunel

The Life and Times of Isambard Kingdom Brunel

R. Angus Buchanan

Hambledon and London
London and New York

Hambledon and London
102 Gloucester Avenue
London, NW1 8HX

838 Broadway
New York
NY 10003–4812

First Published 2002

ISBN 1 85285 331 X

A description of this book is available from the
British Library and from the Library of Congress.

Typeset by Carnegie Publishing, Lancaster
Printed on acid-free paper and bound in
Great Britain by Cambridge University Press

Contents

Illustrations

Text Illustrations

Illustration Acknowledgements

The author and publishers are grateful to the following for permission to reproduce illustrations: Brunel University Library, p. 124, pls 13, 16–22; City of Bristol Museum and Art Gallery, pl. 1; National Portrait Gallery, pl. 2. The photographs for pls 7, 10 and 15 were taken by the author.

Introduction

In the autumn of 1998 there was a flurry of interest in the public media of communication about the misuse of a photograph of Isambard Kingdom Brunel. The photograph was the famous shot taken by Robert Howlett, showing Brunel standing against the giant chains designed to restrain the launch of the *Great Eastern*. It presents the engineer, slightly dishevelled but determinedly jaunty, shortly before the first attempt to launch the ship in November 1857. But the feature that caused the recent outcry was the fact that the cigar clasped between Brunel's lips, in a highly characteristic posture, had been erased from the print. It was argued that, as the picture was wanted to promote an educational enterprise, it would not be appropriate in the modern climate of opinion to give publicity to smoking. So out went the cigar.

This event was itself of no great significance but, apart from the misuse of valuable photographic evidence, it suggests a number of observations. In the first place, the incident demonstrates that the image of Brunel has remarkable public resonance. Not many engineers would be so immediately recognized by so many people. Only George Stephenson, whose head has appeared for many years on every £5 Bank of England note, can compete with him in this respect. There is intense interest in Brunel, as an engineer and as a person, and this alone provides justification for another book about him. The interest has been fed, and to a considerable degree generated, by some excellent biographies, but large areas of ignorance remain in our knowledge of the man and of his circumstances, which has encouraged a proliferation of lesser works tending to reinforce the many legends which surround his career. In most of these peripheral studies he has tended to be presented as a spectacular individual outside the norms and constraints of his own time. The result has been a distortion of the general view of Brunel available to the public. At its worst, this has taken the form of presenting him, as in the photograph, as a jaunty little man in a top hat smoking cigars. Alternatively, he has been depicted as a sort of superman, possessing infallible genius and inexhaustible energy. Some sort of case can be made for both these points of view, but to regard them as the whole picture, or even as a significant part of a full portrait, is very misleading. There is thus space for a treatment of Brunel which will place him firmly in his social, political and cultural context, and that is what is attempted in this book.

Brunel's context was that of Britain in the first half of the nineteenth century. He was born in 1806, thirteen years before the future Queen Victoria. As he was already established in his career as a leading railway engineer when she became Queen, in 1837, Brunel was only partially a Victorian. But he was much of an age with John Henry Newman, born in 1801; Edwin Landseer, born in 1802; Benjamin Disraeli and Richard Cobden, both born in 1804; John Stuart Mill, born in 1806; Charles Darwin, Alfred Tennyson and William Ewart Gladstone, all born in 1809; and Charles Dickens, born in 1812. Unlike these great contemporaries, Brunel died at the early age of fifty-three in 1859, and was thus deprived of a distinguished old age in the period of High Victorianism. But he certainly deserves to be regarded as, at least, an Early Victorian. Moreover, as it was precisely this period of early Victorianism from 1837 to 1859 which set the stamp of triumphant industrialism upon the reign of Queen Victoria and endowed it with many of its most enduring characteristics, there need be no reservation about Brunel's right to be considered as one of the most outstanding Victorians.

Victorianism has not always fared well at the hands of the historians. The concept of 'Eminent Victorians' was coined by Lytton Strachey to designate a handful of leading nineteenth-century personalities on whom he turned his trenchant and acerbic wit.[1] The intention, at the end of the second decade of the twentieth century, was a Bloomsbury-inspired debunking of Victorianism, seen as responsible for the attitudes and hypocrisies which had plunged Europe into the holocaust of the Great War in 1914. The implication throughout Strachey's brilliant character studies of Dr Arnold, General Gordon, Cardinal Manning and Florence Nightingale is that their shared assumptions of self-confident progress, in a world where Britain exercised unquestioned leadership and readily adopted the 'White Man's Burden' and responsibility for directing everybody else, created a sort of hubris which led inevitably to catastrophe.

With the further lapse of time, there has been a fundamental rehabilitation of these and other eminent Victorians. They have come to be seen as only part of a much larger transformation of the modern world, in which the Great War, for all its horrors, was merely the first of a series of convulsions which shattered the self-confidence of the European nations in the first half of the twentieth century, for which Victorian attitudes could not properly be blamed. Also the permanent anxiety of living, since 1945, under the shadow of atomic weapons, has produced a tendency to idealize those very qualities which Strachey condemned in his subjects. In particular, the supposedly 'Victorian values' of self-help, hard work, thrift and sobriety have acquired a certain political cachet in our more permissive society. Whether or not these qualities can be regarded as characteristic of Victorianism, there can be little doubt that they received clear articulation in the mid nineteenth century in the works of that quintessential spokesman of Victorian virtues, Samuel Smiles. Smiles drew special attention to the nineteenth-century engineers as representatives of his 'self-help' ethic in the *Lives of the Engineers*, published in 1862. While he did not provide one of his powerful character studies for I. K. Brunel, Brunel can certainly be regarded as one of those figures who epitomized the ethic. Even though he had the advantage of following a brilliant father in the same profession – an advantage which, on Smiles's own account, he shared with his great contemporary Robert Stephenson – Brunel made his reputation as an engineer by his own genius and capacity for hard work, so that in these cardinal respects his career was a product of inspired self-help and a model Victorian success story.[2]

The vision which drove Brunel to create his superlative works of engineering was articulated in iron and stone; in earthworks and tunnels; and in timber, brick and cement. Many of these works survive and have become the focus of much industrial archaeological attention; as such they are a potent source of inspiration and of evidence about the career of their creator.[3] The existence of such evidence has provided an inspiration for this study: the incomparable gracefulness of the iron way from Paddington to the west, with its many cuttings and bridges and fine tunnel porticos, and its surviving station buildings at Bristol Temple Meads and elsewhere; Clifton Suspension Bridge, completed as a memorial to him in 1864; and the miraculously preserved hull of the *Great Britain*. All stand as silent tributes to the talents of I. K. Brunel. When Sir Neil Cossons and I wrote our *Industrial Archaeology of the Bristol Region* in 1969 we observed that: 'one of the most remarkable industrial monuments of the Bristol region' was in the Falkland Islands,[4] but the next year the battered hull was brought home in triumph and is now being lovingly restored to something resembling her original form. Such physical evidence is tremendously valuable as a template for our enquiry, demonstrating the extraordinary nature of the career that has to be explained.

There is another type of visible evidence in the shape of pictures, in drawings, paintings and photographs. The images of both Marc and Isambard were caught in good portraits. There are two of Marc in the National Portrait Gallery, one by James Northcote painted in 1812–13, showing him seated, with high-domed forehead and velvet coat, and with a representation of one of his block-making machines in the background; the other by Samuel Drummond, painted around 1835 and showing the Thames Tunnel in the background. The Brunel family did not like this latter portrait, but Marc was then in his late sixties and the artist felt obliged to recognize that he was no longer a young man. Perhaps it was in response to this that Wyatt painted him in 1836, upright and imposing. There are two portraits of I. K. Brunel, both painted by his friend and brother-in-law John Callcott Horsley, who was a good artist and a Royal Academician. One, of which several copies survive, shows Brunel seated at his desk, in pensive mood with pencil in his hand and papers around him; the other is a full-length painting depicting him standing before a drawing–board. Both were probably composed in the early 1840s, when their subject was at the height of his powers and success as an engineer.[5]

Lady Gladwyn, the great-grand-daughter of I. K. Brunel, went to some pains to emphasize that the Brunels were Normans rather than Latin or 'meridional', and she rejected her mother's view of Isambard's Latin characteristics. This also goes against the description by Charles MacFarlane of Brunel being a small, nimble, dark-complexioned man, but Lady Gladwyn attributes this to him 'writing from memory' and throws doubt on his judgment because he described the sixty-year-old Marc as an old man.[6] As for her mother Lady Noble's claim of Isambard that 'his Latin race had given him glowing dark eyes set in an olive complexion', Lady Gladwyn made the counter-assertion that this was because her mother had herself such Latin colouring, and harboured a belief that the family were descended from the Italian Brunelleschi.[7] Lady Gladwyn settled the matter to her own satisfaction by climbing a ladder in the National Portrait Gallery and subjecting the portrait of the seated Brunel to detailed examination: 'a strong spot-light proved IKB to be fresh-complexioned with keen alert brown eyes with some hazel in them'.[8] It would be unwise to enter too deeply into this disagreement between mother and daughter. Suffice it to say that Marc and Isambard were both men of short stature, and that such Latin features as they might have possessed did not prevent their full assimilation into their Norman-Anglo-Saxon environment.

The matter of skin complexion cannot easily be resolved by black-and-white photography, but we are lucky in other respects that Brunel's career coincided with the introduction of the camera and of permanent photographs, some of which survive to give us brilliant depictions of him and his works. Fox Talbot himself, the effective pioneer of 'negative' photography – taking negatives from which any number of positive prints could be reproduced – appears to have taken photographs of the *Great Britain* as she

awaited fitting-out in Bristol Floating Harbour in 1844, and of the Hungerford Suspension Bridge at Charing Cross about the same time. These two
engineering feats of I. K. Brunel are therefore among the very first objects
of which reproducible photographs are available. A decade later the techniques of photography had improved substantially, and several sets of
photographs were commissioned to record the construction of the *Great
Eastern*. One of these was taken towards the end of 1857, when the first
attempts were being made to launch the ship. It was then that the photo-
grapher Robert Howlett, as we have seen, seized the opportunity to catch
the likeness of Brunel as he stood before the chain-drums which had been
installed to control the launch. He took two pictures, from slightly different
angles, of Brunel in top hat, a dishevelled suit and dirty shoes, with hands
in pockets and cigar in mouth. These pictures have become the most famous
in Brunel iconography, and there is no doubt that they tell a story. It is
not, however, the full story, and the more anxious demeanour of Brunel
with colleagues watching the launching procedures a few days later, also
caught by Howlett, together with the image conveyed by the pensive and
authoritative figure in Marochetti's memorial sculpture on the Thames
Embankment, also need to be integrated into any interpretation of this
complex character.[9]

Intriguing and valuable as they are, it is not so much these visual images
of I. K. Brunel that make him attractive to the historian as the documentary
evidence which survives of his career. He is fortunate among British engineers, not only in having accumulated a large amount of paper work, but also
in having colleagues and a family who valued this documentary material and
ensured that it survived to become an unusually rich archive which has
gradually become available to scholars. The first public donation from this
archive was made in 1909 when Mr (later Sir) Saxton Noble, who had married
Brunel's grand-daughter Celia James, presented a set of letter books and
associated railway papers to the directors of the Great Western Railway, who
had them handsomely bound in sixty-three folio volumes.[10] Then in 1950
Lady Noble, the widow of Sir Saxton and herself a biographer of the Brunels,
made a princely deposit of most of the business papers to Bristol University
Library, where they have been highly prized and carefully preserved. The
remaining papers were generally more personal. These were kept by
the Noble family in their Northumberland home, where L. T. C. Rolt was
able to consult them in the course of writing his biography of Brunel in the
mid 1950s.[11] A subsequent generation of the family became less willing to
allow access to these more personal papers, so that they were virtually
withdrawn from public reach for over twenty years. Then the late Peter
Noble arranged for the sale of a considerable collection of Brunel-related

papers, including the personal and private diaries, and the University of Bristol was able, with help from various funding agencies, to arrange for their purchase. Even more recently, in November 1996, the widow of Sir Marc Brunel Noble placed a further collection of documents for sale at Christie's. Many of these were sadly dispersed, but Bristol University was able to make some useful purchases at this sale, including the desk diaries kept in the Duke Street office and covering most of Brunel's movements in the 1840s and 1850s.

The special collection of Brunel documents in Bristol University Library (referred to hereafter as the 'Bristol Collection') has thus become the fullest archive of Brunel material in the world. Other collections exist, such as those in the Public Record Office (PRO) and the excellent series of Marc Brunel diaries and papers relating to the Thames Tunnel in the archives of the Institution of Civil Engineers, and smaller collections at University College London and elsewhere. But it is the Bristol Collection which has been the major source for this study of I. K. Brunel. The material there falls into several categories. The one 'personal' and four 'private' diaries are in a class of their own, but they only cover the early years of Brunel's professional career. So do the three volumes of his Thames Tunnel journal for the years 1826–29. The collection is dominated by several substantial series of documents: the private letter books, being copies of letters going out of the office from 1834, arranged mainly chronologically in fifteen volumes; the large sketch books and small sketch books, amounting to about fifty volumes altogether, with entries ranging from small doodles to elaborate drawings, all in the delicate pencil hand of IKB; the calculation books, of which several volumes survive; the general note books, with another half dozen volumes; and the broken series of desk diaries. Then there are large collections of correspondence, both from and to Brunel, and many miscellaneous volumes of notes on special projects: the construction of the *Great Eastern*, for example, is covered by a set of letter books devoted to the business of the Eastern Steam Navigation Company and its successor. There are also notable gaps: there is no comparable series for the *Great Britain*, and for the business of the Great Western Railway it is necessary to refer to the collection in the PRO. But even as it stands, the Bristol Collection is a scholar's delight, and the University Library does a public service in making it easily accessible.[12] I have quoted extensively from it, although Brunel's 'stream of consciousness' style of writing rapidly has occasionally required minor adjustments to spelling and punctuation where this has improved the sense, but not altered the content, of the passage.

It must be admitted, however, by anybody seeking to reinterpret the career of I. K. Brunel, that most of the available archival material had been well worked over, even before it was gathered in Bristol, the PRO and elsewhere. In the first place, Brunel's two sons undertook to assemble the material and put it in good order before Isambard composed the text, with the help of notes on engineering topics provided by Henry, and contributions incorporated from several friends and acquaintances. *The Life of Isambard Kingdom Brunel* which resulted from this exercise may be fairly described as an act of filial piety. It is worth remembering that, when it was published in 1870, Isambard was only thirty-two and Henry five years younger.[13] The book does suffer, therefore, from the awe of affectionate and dutiful sons anxious to defend their father from criticism and to represent him in the best possible light. The work does not observe modern standards of scholarly citation, but it is nevertheless one of careful scholarship and it includes valuable verbatim extracts from key letters and reports.

It has been suggested that the young Brunels arranged for the destruction of their father's more personal papers. Although I find this hard to believe, it has to be recognized that there are hints in their text of access to material other than that which can be identified in the existing collections. For instance, there is a reference to 'Mr Brunel's private journal' for 1846,[14] which implies that some potentially interesting material may have been lost because nothing resembling such a journal survives for the years after 1836. It would seem unlikely that their father could have found much time or energy to maintain such personal records in the years when he was most heavily engaged in his professional career. It is possible, however, that he did manage to keep an occasional journal after 1840, as it was part of the discipline of being an engineer that he had learnt from his father. It is also possible that his sons then destroyed such documents in order to protect their father's reputation, as they understood it. The tantalizing possibility of further documentary discoveries remains, but it is not one to be pursued with much hope of fulfilment.

Over sixty years after his sons compiled their worthy account of Brunel, his grand-daughter Lady Noble published *The Brunels: Father and Son*. This is a charming set of recollections, which adds considerable personal information to the rather pedestrian presentation of the first biography. Concerned as she was with both Marc and I. K. Brunel, Celia Noble provided insights through family anecdotes and the documents at her disposal which would otherwise have been lost. The book is therefore a valuable resource for Brunel scholars.[15] On a slighter scale, the same is true of the reflections of her daughter, Lady Gladwyn. These were presented as a lecture to a joint meeting of the Institution of Civil Engineers and La Société des Ingénieurs Civils de France in 1970, and published in the *Proceedings* of the British organization in the following year.[16] A mere fourteen pages in length, this article supplies many perceptive comments on 'The Isambard Brunels' and has become a useful addition to scholarly knowledge.

In between these family works, L. T. C. Rolt made his memorable and highly significant contribution to Brunel studies, published in 1957 as *Isambard Kingdom Brunel: A Biography*.[17] I am already on record as having described this as 'the outstanding work of engineering biography of the twentieth century',[18] and I see no reason to modify this judgment. In the last volume of his autobiography, Tom Rolt tells how he came to write the book, and gives an account of the research which he did at Walwick Hall, the Northumbrian home of Sir Humphrey Noble, and also at the home of Sir Humphrey's mother Lady Noble in the Royal Crescent, Bath, and in the Bristol Collection.[19] He reckons there that he spent eighteen months on the Brunel book, and it is a matter of continuing astonishment to me that in so short a time he managed to cull the best material from all the sources at his disposal to write such a powerful and elegant book. But that he did, and in doing so gave an enormous stimulus to the reputation of I. K. Brunel and to Brunel studies, which have flourished vigorously ever since.

Since then, several further books have appeared on the Brunels, articles have been written, and societies have been formed to perpetuate their memory.[20] None of the new works have discovered any new resources for scholarship, although a few of them have produced some interesting modifications of interpretation, such as Adrian Vaughan's *Isambard Kingdom Brunel: Engineering Knight Errant*, which presents some of Brunel's relationships in a less romantic light than other writers. This is a lively and entertaining book, particularly strong on Brunel's railway works, but like most other modern treatments it does not attempt a scholarly presentation.[21] The one exception in this respect has been the symposium assembled and edited by Sir Alfred Pugsley, *The Works of Isambard Kingdom Brunel*, which tackles some of Brunel's engineering technicalities with new insights.[22] The clear implication of this literature survey is that there is room for a book which aims at a scholarly assessment of the whole of Brunel's career, placing him firmly in the historical context to which he belongs.

It is, then, the aim of this book to present as objective a portrait of Brunel as possible, interpreting him in the setting of his times. Brunel was a man of small stature and enormous energy, so that he acquired the nickname 'the Little Giant'. A precocious genius, whose talents were nurtured by his brilliant father, he demonstrated at an early age his capacity for leadership, his artistic fluency, his vaunting ambition, and his inspired vision of engineering possibilities. By his dynamism and highly articulate enthusiasm he drove himself and his team to works of outstanding creativity and technical brilliance. The object of these pages is not just to tell a familiar story again as much as to relate the key incidents in a way which demonstrates the quality of his vision and the grandeur of his achievement. Above all, this book aims at providing the first fully documented treatment of Brunel, in the sense that the sources of information about him are properly cited and explored. In the process, considerable attention is given to some aspects of his life which have received less attention from previous biographers, including his training, his Bristol connections, his overseas commitments, his comparatively minor works, and his disasters – which were invariably dramatic and instructive. The justification for this emphasis is that these aspects of Brunel's career generated correspondence and other documents that deserve more attention than they have received hitherto and which throw valuable illumination on the main themes. The main themes of railway, bridge and marine engineering are not ignored, but they receive less prominence because there is less of novel interest to say about them. In all areas considered, the subjects are reviewed as far as possible in the light of the documentary evidence. Finally, in the last four chapters, an attempt is made to stand back from the narrative and to assess the role of Brunel in his professional context, in his social and political activities, in his life with friends and family, and in the context of Victorian culture and society. It is hoped that the result is a well-rounded account of I. K. Brunel, both as a person and as an engineer.

IN MEMORIAM

Sir Arthur Hallam Rice Elton (1906–1973)

with gratitude and affection

Acknowledgments

As a Sheffielder, born and bred in the bracing atmosphere of south Yorkshire, I was not exposed at an early age to the fascination of I. K. Brunel. The train numbers which I collected as a boy were those of the LMS and occasionally the LNER: the GWR was to me a remote and rather exotic enterprise. But once I had settled in the West Country at Bristol and Bath I was quickly impressed by the powerful legendary quality of the Great Western and its engineer, and by the surviving bridges, buildings and ships associated with Brunel. When I established the Centre for the History of Technology at the putative University of Bath in 1964, I was befriended by Arthur Elton, Tom Rolt, Rex Wailes, George Watkins, Neil Cossons and others who held Brunel in high esteem. I am grateful to all of them for their support over many years, and especially to Arthur Elton who, as chairman of the advisory council to my centre, did so much to ensure that it had a good start. It was Arthur who, with his infectious enthusiasm for all things to do with Brunel, first put to me the need for a scholarly study of the engineer, and introduced me to the rich Brunel Collection in the University of Bristol Library. It was he who arranged a meeting between ourselves and Norman Higham, then University Librarian, at which we discussed the possibilities of making these treasures more widely available. Arthur hoped that a way could be found to publish the Brunel archive, especially the splendid series of private letter books. Although this has not proved to be practicable so far, the modern media of information technology hold out the promise that it will eventually become an achievable goal. For his devotion to the cause, and for the inspiration which he provided to others, I gratefully dedicate this volume to Sir Arthur Elton.

I have incurred many debts in the gestation of this book, and I cannot hope to do justice to all of them here. There are some, however, which must not be allowed to go without acknowledgment. In the first place, I am particularly grateful to the Bristol University Librarians and to the archivists of the special collections in the Library of the University of Bristol, all of whom have been so consistently helpful to me. When I started work on the Brunel Collection three decades ago, George Maby was the archivist and was engaged on his monumental task of listing all the items in the letter books. As I was anxious to work through the letter books myself, I found that we were metaphorically leapfrogging each other as we tried to work through the volumes in a chronological sequence. When George Maby retired, his place was taken by Nick Lee, who continued the efficient and obliging service of his predecessor. Then, in 1998, when he also retired, Michael Richardson and Hannah Lowery took charge of the Brunel material. They have all been unfailingly patient and helpful as I have burrowed around the interstices of the Bristol Collection.

Other libraries and institutions have been very supportive. I am grateful for the gracious permission of Her Majesty the Queen to quote from papers in the Royal Archives at Windsor. I thank Mr Rod Knight, Family and Probate Service Group Manager of the Court Service, for assistance in securing a copy of Brunel's will. My own University of Bath Library, under the Librarianship of John H. Lamble, became so interested in my research that it acquired the small Hollingworth Collection, which has considerable significance in relation to John Scott Russell and the *Great Eastern*. The high level of helpfulness has been maintained under Howard Nicholson, the present University Librarian. Cambridge University Library has been a home from home over the years. The Bodleian, University College London Library and the British Library have all been of assistance to me. So have the libraries of the Institution of Civil Engineers, the Institution of Mechanical Engineers, the Science Museum and the Royal Society. To the librarians of all of them I give my thanks.

The societies of which I have been an active member have humoured me and encouraged my research. BIAS, the Bristol Industrial Archaeological Society, which I established with Neil (now Sir Neil) Cossons in 1968, has a built-in component of respect for Brunel, which has become all the stronger now that it has absorbed the Brunel Society, a body of which I was the last president. The AIA, the Association for Industrial Archaeology, which we went on to establish at a conference in the Isle of Man in 1973, has also given me considerable moral support. The Newcomen Society has kindly received papers from me on Brunel subjects over the years. ICOHTEC, the International Committee for the History of Technology, of which I was a founder member in 1968, has nobly encouraged a series of presentations from me on topics relating to Brunel studies. Even the Society of Antiquaries of London, for whom Brunel studies are not an obvious priority, has received my offerings most gracefully. Membership of all these bodies has meant much to me, and I am grateful for the friendship and support that I have received from them.

My Centre for the History of Technology has been a valued asset in my research, both through its members and through the functions which it has performed. Several of the early members have already been mentioned, but I would like to repeat the name of L. T. C. Rolt in this context. In addition to being an active and helpful member of the advisory council of the centre, Tom became a personal friend. His empathy with I. K. Brunel, which comes over so powerfully in his excellent biography, remains an inspiration to all students of Brunel. On Tom Rolt's death in 1974, the University of Bath agreed to the establishment of a Rolt Memorial Fellowship, based at the centre, with the objective of encouraging engineers and professional people of mature years to undertake research in aspects of technological history. It has worked well, and the twelve persons who have been members of the fellowship have all brought distinctive talents to their research and produced valuable studies. Only a few of these have had a direct bearing on Brunel studies (especially those of James Richard, David Brown and Derek Portman), but the participation of all the fellows in the regular Seminar in the History of Technology has helped to maintain a high level of discourse, which has been valuable to me when my own bits of Brunelania have been under consideration.

I received help from two research officers, appointed to the centre for three-year terms: Dr Martin Doughty and Dr Helen Bannatyne. Both of them did sterling work on a variety of topics – stationary steam engines, mining history, engineering history, and their own doctoral subjects – as well as useful contributions to my work on Brunel. It was good having them around. Like the Rolt Fellows, they participated in our seminars, and we had valuable contributions over the years from Dr Mark Gray (who was lucky enough to pick up a book with Brunel's annotations in it) and Professor Andrew Lambert (who is very knowledgeable about Brunel's relations with the Admiralty). The contributions of Keith Falconer, Brenda Buchanan and Owen Ward, as Visiting Fellows to the Centre, have also been much appreciated. Trevor Fawcett, Sandy Buchanan, Michael Messenger and Bill and Pauline Hanna, have drawn my attention to details which I would otherwise have missed. Sonia Rolt, Julia Elton and Frank Newby have provided moral support over many years. I have gained from all these friends, and I am grateful to them.

In the same way, I am grateful to my collaborators on Brunel projects: to Sir Alfred Pugsley, and the colleagues with whom he edited *The Works of Isambard Kingdom Brunel*, published in 1976; to Michael Williams, founder of the Brunel Society in Bristol, with whom I cooperated to produce *Brunel's Bristol* in 1981, and his Brunel Society colleague, Keith Hickman; to Stephen K. Jones, with whom I wrote 'The Balmoral Bridge of I. K. Brunel' for *Industrial Archaeology Review* in 1980; and to Stephen again, with Ken Kiss, with whom I wrote 'Brunel and the Crystal Palace', for *Industrial Archaeology Review* in 1994. To these and the editors of *Industrial Archaeology Review* and *Transactions of the Newcomen Society*, I am indebted for permission to draw on my contributions to published material.

Over the years I have given many talks and lectures on I. K. Brunel. These have rarely been one-way performances because I have frequently picked up insights and details of great value to me from members of the audience. Some of these have been virtually anonymous, such as the lady who kindly presented me with a photograph which purports to show the sun shining through the Box Tunnel on Brunel's birthday, 9 April. I never had the heart to point out to her that the picture was taken looking from east to west, but the print retains its curious fascination. Others have had very specific points which they wanted to make. After one lecture, in the National Portrait Gallery, I have a happy memory of Lord Gladwyn cheerfully scribbling out the details of his family tree for me. All such contributions have been gratefully received.

As always in matters of authorship, I take full responsibility for the final shape of this work, with whatever imperfections and blemishes it may turn out to possess. But I would like to conclude with a very special expression of gratitude to my wife, Brenda, who has accompanied me both physically, as I have travelled around giving talks on Brunel (she knows my favourite stories and punch-lines by heart now), and mentally as I have written this book. While pursuing her own pioneering studies on the history of gunpowder, she has been throughout the most admirable research companion.

University of Bath   R. Angus Buchanan

9 April 2001

1

An Age of Revolutions

Isambard Kingdom Brunel was born into a turbulent age. His father, Marc Isambard Brunel, had in 1793 narrowly escaped from the clutches of French revolutionary fury during the Terror, and had only managed to do so by fleeing to the newly constituted United States of America. While still in France, Marc had met and fallen in love with an English young lady, Sophia Kingdom, caught up in the net of hostility towards all monarchists and foreigners. Sophia was the youngest of sixteen children born to William Kingdom, a naval contractor in Plymouth, but he had died when Sophia was still quite young. She had been looked after by a brother, who had unwisely sent her on an educational visit to learn the language in France at this time of great political commotion. She managed eventually to escape back to Britain, and waited for Marc. Six years later, in 1799, he arrived in Britain with a brilliant project for the mass-production of rigging-blocks for sailing ships. Marc and Sophie promptly got married and in 1802 settled in Portsea, a suburb of Portsmouth, to be near the Naval Dockyard where he was supervising the process of equipping the 'Block House' with his machines. It was here in Portsea, on 9 April 1806, that their third child and only son was born, taking the favoured forename of his father and the maiden name of his mother.

When I. K. Brunel was a boy, Europe was reverberating to the heady slogans of liberty and equality, democracy and nationalism, Britain was in the process of establishing a massive lead in the processes of industrialization, and science was reinforcing powerful notions of universal progress. Napoleon had unleashed a devastating series of wars on his continental opponents, in the course of which his armies marched across Europe from Lisbon to Moscow, inflicting humiliating defeats on all the major powers. At the same time, he attempted to impose the Continental System, aimed at bringing Britain to its knees by preventing its trade with Europe. This was Napoleon's only hope of defeating Britain, as, less than six months before the birth of I. K. Brunel, Nelson had won his last great victory over the combined French and Spanish fleets at Trafalgar, thereby securing control of the high seas for the Royal Navy and making sure that Napoleon could not invade Britain. Nevertheless, it is not being overfanciful to see the young Brunel as a child of revolution.

The French Revolution had begun in the spring and summer of 1789 with the calling of the Estates General and the seizure of initiative by the Third Estate. The Estates promptly rejected the authority of the King to dismiss it and converted themselves into a National Assembly which undertook a fundamental reform of French government. The effect of this was to undermine the absolute monarchy in France, and to shatter the delicate stability of relationships between the European powers that had dominated the Continent for the previous century. These developments led in turn to the internal violence which culminated in the execution of the king and queen, and the long series of revolutionary wars with the militant nationalism of the new France pitted against the rest of Europe. One consequence was the emergence of the military genius Napoleon Bonaparte, who became general of the revolutionary armies on the strength of his striking victories on the battlefield, and went on to become First Consul and Emperor, crowning himself in the presence of the Pope in 1804.

The defeat of Napoleon, finally achieved at Waterloo in June 1815, signalled the restoration of as much of the old order as could be salvaged after a quarter of a century of upheaval. As far as France was concerned, this meant the return of the Bourbon dynasty, but their power was curtailed and after fifteen years they were finally sent packing in the Revolution of 1830. This event was observed with some alarm in the Brunel household, but its effect was to consolidate constitutional monarchy in France and affairs quickly settled down again. European political programmes remained constrained by the need to prevent any recurrence of French hegemony, so the other continental powers united behind the conservative policy of the Austrian Chancellor, Prince Metternich, to contain France and to prevent as far as possible any innovations in governments and their policies. But the vast intellectual commotion of the French Revolution was not so easily contained: the great innovative ideas of liberalism and nationalism continued to resound throughout Europe and eventually created tensions which destroyed the conservative Concert of Europe devised by Metternich. Individual governments struggled with varying degrees of success to suppress the disruptive tendencies of nationalism and to deal with demands for liberal constitutions and a democratic franchise. By the middle of the nineteenth century conservatism had been subverted in virtually every country of Europe, even though it was far from clear that the new regimes would be liberal in outlook or would even survive.

Modern nationalism, depending on the mass support of self-consciously nationalistic populations, was a particularly virulent derivative of the French Revolution, and demanded accommodation in mid nineteenth-century Europe. Metternich's conservative hegemony was challenged by the campaign to liberate Greece from Turkey in the 1820s, by the creation of an independent Belgium in 1830, and by the emergence of Serbia thereafter. Even more disruptive were the *Risorgimento*, the movement which culminated in the unification of Italy in 1860; and the Prussian-led campaign to secure the unification of Germany in 1870. Both had been inspired in part by the outbreak of political upheavals which swept Europe in 1848, earning for it the title 'the Year of Revolutions', and evoking once again the events of 1789.[1]

In Britain, the French Revolution had been greeted at first with considerable sympathy, partly because it promised an end to the long tradition of rivalry with the *ancien régime* of the Bourbon dynasty, but also and more positively because it was agreeable to see France moving towards a more constitutional form of government in line with that established in Britain over a century before. To be sure, there were soon signs of hostility, such as the polemic of Edmund Burke in his *Reflections on the Revolution in France*, robustly countered by Tom Paine's treatise, *The Rights of Man*.[2] The initial goodwill soon evaporated, however, as the Revolution was swept into a wave of internal violence and the new revolutionary government rejected any foreign attempts to influence the course of events inside France. Britain became the paymaster for the coalitions of continental states which formed to restrict the spread of revolutionary experiments. While the main continental states – Austria, Prussia and Russia in particular – were all defeated by France, in some cases several times over, Britain managed to preserve its independence through the dominance of the sea by the Royal Navy. From this position of strength, albeit of isolation, Britain continued to encourage its allies to regroup in opposition to France.

In one sense, this implacable opposition to the revolutionary regime in France may be seen as a perpetuation of the traditional anti-French posture of successive British governments, which continued until the beginning of the twentieth century. More significantly, however, it should be seen as the reaction of a conservative government to the new ideas which had boiled up in the French Revolution, and at this level British resistance was less effective than it was in the field of naval and military combat. For whereas French arms were completely defeated by 1815, the principles of liberty, equality and fraternity which figured so prominently in the Revolution had taken a strong hold among sections of British opinion, and survived to animate new radical and reformist movements thereafter. The succession of governments which maintained a conservative domestic policy for over forty

years after the French Revolution came to an end at last in 1832, when the
Reform Act initiated long overdue reforms in the machinery of parliamentary representation. The Whig administrations of the 1830s then put into
operation a programme of far-reaching political and social reforms, including a new Poor Law, the beginning of factory legislation and the liberalization
of municipal government.

Whereas the French Revolution can be precisely dated to 1789 and the
years immediately following, another revolution which did as much to shape
the circumstances of the nineteenth century – the Industrial Revolution –
is much more difficult to fix in time.[3] Some historians, indeed, prefer to
dismiss the concept altogether as implying a sudden once for all transformation of society which did not occur, and which certainly bore no
resemblance to the abruptness of a political coup or revolution. This,
however, is being pedantic, because there can be no doubt either that a
transformation of European society did take place between the mid eighteenth century and the mid nineteenth century, or that it profoundly and
permanently changed the way of life of European populations. Taking a
long view of modern history, these changes certainly amounted to a revolution. And as the changes can most usefully be summed up in the word
'industrialization', even though this should be taken to include demographic,
urban, agricultural and cultural components, there does not appear to be
any reasonable objection to referring to the process as the 'Industrial Revolution'.

The enormity of social change is indicated by the fact that the population
in Britain more than doubled in Brunel's lifetime, from 10,686,000 in the
first national census, held in 1801, to 23,189,000 in the census on 1861.[4] This
increase was unevenly distributed, as the prospects of urban employment
drew people from the countryside to the towns at the same time as
improvements in agricultural efficiency were making them redundant in
the countryside. The expanding population concentrated in the towns and
cities, which had grown rapidly in a largely unplanned manner. In centres
such as London, Bristol, Norwich and Edinburgh there had been a long
experience of town life, so that the increase in size was assimilated with
some success, although even here the traditional modes of water supply
and waste removal were not sufficient to provide for the new needs. But
elsewhere, and especially in the growing new towns of the midlands and
the north – Birmingham, Liverpool, Manchester, Sheffield, Leeds, Newcastle,
Cardiff, Glasgow and others – attempts to deal with the chaotic development were catastrophically inadequate until the prevalence of cholera and
other diseases compelled attention to the basic principles of urban planning.
By the middle of the nineteenth century Britain had become the first

predominantly urban society in the history of the world, and was beginning to come to terms with the social reorganization necessary to accommodate this development.[5]

One other general observation is worth making about the Industrial Revolution: beyond any serious contention it began in Britain, and it can be regarded as a British-led process until the second half of the nineteenth century. It could have been expected to begin in France, which was the wealthiest and most densely populated country in Europe in the eighteenth century. The level of scientific discussion and education was also higher in France than in any other country at that time. But France had internal economic problems that could not be solved without a revolution in its political and social structure, and once that revolution had occurred the country was too preoccupied with national survival and imperial glory to pay much attention to industrialization. For all the intellectual skills and technical expertise available in France in the eighteenth century, the country lacked the vital factor of individual enterprise promoted by the opportunities for social rewards which Britain, its great rival, possessed in abundance. In particular, the newly enriched mercantile and industrial classes of Britain were able to assert a degree of influence in government, and so to secure their own social position, which was without parallel in France.

So the initiative to launch upon the process of industrialization was seized first in Britain. Because of the dislocation of European economic development by the revolutionary wars Britain was able to establish a commanding lead in the process, which was not even seriously challenged until the 1850s. By then Britain had become a fully industrialized society, with a largely urbanized population. In 1851 it celebrated these achievements by presenting itself as the workshop of the world at the International Exhibition held in the Crystal Palace in Hyde Park, and the world came to see and wonder. It went away determined to do likewise, and in the course of the next fifty years Britain was overtaken in some respects by rivals who had grasped the significance of industrialization. But that was after Brunel's time, and it was one aspect of his relatively short life that he left the scene when Britain was still at the summit of its world leadership.

In establishing the revolutionary context to the career of I. K. Brunel, it is important to emphasize a third transformation occurring in the nineteenth century, which must be linked with the political and social revolutions already considered as among the crucial formative influences of the new industrial age. This was the cultural revolution associated with the rise of science which, since the middle of the sixteenth century at least, had been steadily transforming the ways in which people thought and behaved. It may be described as the 'Scientific Revolution', although that term suggests limits which were not strictly applicable because its influence spread beyond science, however that may be defined. It was represented by the gradual displacement of traditional theological assumptions by more secular, rationalistic ideas. This was a complex and subtle process, and involved attempts to accommodate religion to the new patterns of thought and culture which delayed recognition of the comparative decline in the influence of religion. Religion remained important, as it does down to the present day, but its role became increasingly curtailed and some of the most influential realms of belief and decision-making have been removed from its jurisdiction. In its place has come rational analysis and secularization.⁶

This process was already well under way at the beginning of the nineteenth century. The development of scientific thought which had culminated in the work of Isaac Newton had established a new cosmology based on mechanistic principles and the 'clockwork' model of the universe with the sun at the centre. This was generally accepted among the intelligentsia of I. K. Brunel's generation. Brunel conversed freely with astronomers of his time and shared their scientific assumptions. But while space had been secularized, time remained largely in bondage to religious beliefs, and the revolution by which modern society arrived at its virtually unlimited notion of time was only slowly gathering momentum. Brunel had dealings with many of the geologists of his day, often in connection with railway works in which he used their expertise to identify strata or disputed with them about the safety of his tunnels. He had a highly interesting correspondence with William Buckland about the Box Tunnel, and he was aware of the uncomfortable evidence of incredible age associated with the discovery of fossils and observation of the processes of erosion. These were the years in which the long eons of geological time became apparent, and when the slow but sure processes of glaciation and vulcanism began to be understood.⁷ But Brunel was less familiar with the biologists and botanists, and he died a month before the publication of Charles Darwin's *Origin of Species*, so there is no way of knowing how he would have responded to that intellectual bombshell. It is certain, however, that the religious doubts which reverberate in Tennyson's *In Memoriam* and were circulating widely in mid nineteenth-century Britain would have been familiar to him. He was as much a child of the Scientific Revolution as he was of the other great convulsions of his time.

I. K. Brunel was fortunate to flourish in the period when Britain was the foremost industrial power in the world, and to be an engineer at a time when good engineering was essential to success in the operation of new industrial enterprises and transport systems. In terms of British economic and political history, he belonged to the heroic age when Britannia not only ruled the waves but dominated the industrial and mercantile activities of the world, and led the way in promoting political liberalism, constitutional government and assertive nationalism. Of course, it in no way explains the genius of a great engineer to say that he flourished at the right time for his particular talents, because the same advantage was shared by many of Brunel's contemporaries of whom posterity is ignorant. Few men had the ability to respond to the opportunities with which Brunel was presented. But it is important to understand what those opportunities were in order to appreciate fully the quality of his achievements in grasping them and moulding them to the template of his own distinctive talents. Brunel was, first and foremost, a man of his times, and in making full use of the opportunities of those times he showed himself to be a beneficiary of the great revolutions of the first half of the nineteenth century.

There can be no objection to including Brunel in a specifically British pantheon of great engineers. He was British in everything except his name, and he appears to have been so regarded by most of his contemporaries. His father, it is true, had been born, bred and educated in France, and could thus have been regarded as genuinely French. Yet even he, after leaving France as a political refugee to go to the United States, had taken American citizenship. He subsequently became a British citizen and loyally supported his adopted state against Napoleonic France. Marc Isambard Brunel, moreover, showed no inclination to return to the country of his birth after the ending of the wars in 1815, having married a British wife and having adopted her Anglicanism: his great-great-grand-daughter assures us that, having once been impressed by the sincerity of American Protestants, he 'never entered a Catholic church again'.[8] And even though he continued to think and write in French for some time after coming to Britain, his diaries came to be written mainly in English and he happily adopted the social mores of his new home.

Marc became British, but Isambard Kingdom Brunel was British from birth. Incidentally, in referring to the father as 'Marc', in accordance with historical usage and to avoid unnecessary confusion, it should be noted that he actually preferred to be known as 'Isambard', having a somewhat romanticized notion of the importance of the name in his family.[9] As far as the son is concerned, in adopting occasionally the usage 'IKB' we will be following 'those who had the privilege of his intimate acquaintance'.[10] For all their French origins, both Marc and Isambard were fully within the mainstream of British engineering and both, indeed, made outstanding contributions to its tradition. They established one of the great British engineering dynasties of the nineteenth century, a dynasty continued by Henry Brunel, the second son of I. K. Brunel, who served very competently as an engineer in the practice of Sir John Wolfe Barry, and who survived until the end of the century and the end of the reign of Queen Victoria.[11]

The qualities of personality which I. K. Brunel brought to these times were remarkable. Like his father, he possessed a vibrant and vivid personality. He was a natural leader, ready to assert his leadership of any project and to sustain it by an enormous capacity for prolonged hard work. This hyper-activity was reflected in a low need for sleep and in an astonishing capacity to master detail. He once admonished his assistant in Italy: 'You will of course lose no opportunity of ascertaining the prices of everything – work of all sorts and materials, particularly timber of all sorts, bricks, stone and lime',[12] and the evidence of his series of folio volumes of 'Facts', with their many detailed lists of practical information, shows that in this respect he practised what he preached. At the same time, his written reports and volumes of letter books display a robust and well-ordered intelligence, always businesslike and never verbose. His sketch books, large and small, show a finely-honed talent for draughtsmanship with keen aesthetic sensibilities, while his calculation books are the work of a competent mathematician with a good practical grasp of current scientific knowledge. Much of Brunel's writing exhibits a rich exuberance of spirit, expressed in a stream of con-sciousness which sacrifices the clarity of the script to the need for speed. The result is that it is frequently difficult to disentangle the meaning from the flowing handwriting, so that there is a regrettable margin for error in any transcription. It is, however, always worth the effort to establish just what he was saying, because he wrote with high intelligence and was frequently inspirational.

The ends to which this enormous fund of talent was applied are not so easily summarized. Brunel was rarely given to record any self-examination, although when he did, in the early stages of his career, the account is richly informative. This is shown by his personal diary, which he kept in strict secrecy, and in various pre-1836 passages in his private diaries. In these, at a time when the course of his future career was still obscure, he reveals himself as a man of surprising vulnerability and almost maudlin sentimen-tality. The letter to his friend Benjamin Hawes, leaving the personal diary to Hawes in the event of his death, reveals a state of mind bordering on depression.[13] As he gained recognition, however, and the engineering com-missions began to accumulate, his native cheerfulness and good humour reasserted themselves. At the end of 1835 he calculated that the work entrusted to him amounted to a value of £5,320,000 – 'a pretty considerable capital likely to pass through my hands – and this at the age of twenty-nine'.[14] Personal wealth does not seem to have been a prime objective for him, and he declared on one occasion: 'I hate these money discussions about my own accounts'.[15] But he liked wealth and the cultivated, not to say ostentatious, way of life which it brought. Certainly, the wealth came to him, and was duly spent on house, home and family. Yet at the same time, he committed much of it to the undertakings of which he was often the inspirational chief officer; and when, in his final years, the wealth seemed to be slipping away from him in the monumental losses incurred by the SS *Great Eastern*, he seemed more concerned by the suffering of his friends than by his personal financial loss.

While being reasonably objective in his attitude towards wealth, Brunel was likewise detached in regard to most of the other good things of life. He showed no intense pleasure in food or drink, in contrast with his son Henry, whose letters display considerable interest in these subjects. He did, admittedly, have a weakness for cigars, which he smoked constantly, and as a young man he sported a meerschaum pipe when he was with friends.[16] His biographers have looked in vain for any sexual peccadilloes, both his grand-daughter and L. T. C. Rolt finding some vicarious salacity in his relationship with the elderly society hostess Lady Holland.[17] There is some as yet undisclosed romantic interest in his seven-year relationship with the shadowy figure of Ellen Hulme, but that does not amount to much.[18] And when he did marry Mary Horsley in 1836, his marital relationships seem to have provided a model of Victorian propriety.[19] Brunel clearly enjoyed scientific and engineering discussions, taking part in the proceedings of the various professional and learned societies of which he was a member whenever he could. He also enjoyed visits to art exhibitions, going out of his way on one occasion to see Martin's *Fall of Nineveh*,[20] and was always willing to make a detour to visit a church or bridge or any other distinguished architecture. He also attended musical concerts, especially after encountering the aesthetic circle of the Horsleys, into which he eventually married. But his general standard of taste, in terms of paintings and furnishings for his home, was at best conventional.

People reacted strongly to Brunel. The glowing testimonials from family friends and colleagues assembled by Isambard Brunel in preparing the first biography of his father are an eloquent tribute to IKB's energy, his *joie de vivre* and vitality. St George Burke's account of Brunel's device for waking him up to attend to parliamentary business, and George T. Clark's story of Brunel concocting a scheme to convert the Cherhill White Horse into a steam locomotive, catch the timbre of a vital personality.[21] At the same time, however, he expected all his engineering assistants to be as devoted to their tasks as he was, and he had little sympathy with any family or sporting diversions to which they might be prone. Where any professional irregularity or indiscretion was concerned, he could be utterly condemnatory in his judgments.[22] There is an element of ruthlessness here which requires recognition. Leadership calls for both an ability to direct and a determination to prevent any personal matters from obstructing the fulfillment of the project, and Brunel possessed these qualities. The determination could harden into obstinacy, as in the long-standing case of the contractor McIntosh who took the Great Western Railway to court over Brunel's refusal to pay for work performed and who was finally vindicated long after both he and Brunel were dead.[23]

Despite his well-attested capacity for warm friendships it is necessary to remember Brunel's behaviour as a hard taskmaster and disciplinarian. We are told by George T. Clark that: 'His servants loved him, and he never forgot those who stood by his father and himself in the old Tunnel days of trouble and anxiety.'[24] L. T. C. Rolt similarly emphasized the devotion of Brunel's subordinates: 'No strikes and labour disputes marred the building of the Great Western'.[25] But these judgments had little specific justification, and were probably over-generous towards Brunel at a time when any regular employer of labour could expect a high level of obedience from his employees. It is arguable that an attitude of incredulous awe at the fantastic energy and drive of their chief would have been a more accurate assessment of the relationship. It should also be remembered that Brunel quarrelled vehemently with several close colleagues, including William Gravatt, R. M. Marchant, and John Scott Russell, so it is impossible to claim that everything was always sweetness and light in his relationships. On matters of professional etiquette, moreover, Brunel could become almost paranoid and was not beyond rebuking senior colleagues such as Sir Joseph Paxton for consulting one of his assistants rather than himself.[26] Even Robert Stephenson, in many ways Brunel's closest professional friend, found it necessary to be extremely careful in order to avoid causing him offence by some unintended slight.[27]

The vital clue to understanding Brunel's career and achievements is the recognition of the fact that he was a driven man, and that he was motivated not so much by a desire for wealth, or love of family and friends, or even by a desire for personal fame, as by a vision of what he could and should be doing. At first, this vision appears in his personal papers as a romantic and unclear notion of achieving engineering excellence, represented by his imprecisely termed *châteaux d'espagna* – the castles in the sky which inspired his youthful imagination.[28] It stemmed from his natural talents as an artist and engineer, so assiduously nurtured by his father, who, although himself an outstanding engineer, was denied the tremendous opportunities to display his talents which came to IKB. For a few frustrating years the young man's vision appeared to be unrealizable or was made inaccessible by the collapse of the Thames Tunnel and the failure of the 'gaz' experiments, and what seemed to have become a general failure of recognition. But once the opportunity to build a major railway materialized, to be followed closely by the chance to build innovatory ships and bridges, the vision became clear and asserted itself. From the moment when he took his first ride on the Liverpool and Manchester Railway in 1831 and reflected on the possibility of doing better – 'let me try'[29] – the potential of the new railway system becoming the vehicle of his vision for superlative engineering began to mature in his mind. At the same time, his connection with the merchants of Bristol provided him with a perfect opportunity to convert the vision into reality in a railway network for the west of England, and the creation of an international transport system through steam ship services.

The fact that reality frequently intervened to frustrate the complete fulfil-ment of the vision, as over the failure of the atmospheric system on the South Devon Railway and, on an even larger scale, the painful creation of the *Great Eastern*, established a tension in Brunel's life which kept him dispensing a high level of nervous energy, which in turn almost certainly added to his irritability and contributed to his premature physical collapse and death. The vision of engineering excellence is, after all, only partially achievable, and then only for a short time before technological advance renders it obsolete. In terms of building the best railways, ships and bridges, Brunel had constantly to carry proprietors and company officers with him, to find larger sums of money than those demanded by simpler but adequate solutions, and to convince a wider public that his ideas were the best. In the nature of things, he had occasionally to compromise, and this continuing tension between vision and reality became a constant theme in Brunel's career. In the end, his colossal talent and exuberant energy was cut short by his premature death, but he nevertheless achieved more than most mortals could hope to do in a much longer lifespan. By the time of his death at fifty-three in 1859 he had become one of the outstanding figures of British engineering history. Through his engineering works he had con-tributed substantially to the great transport revolution of modern times, permanently changing the British landscape and way of life. In its spirit and its performance, his life was part of an age of revolution.

2

Apprenticeship

Apprenticeship was the traditional method of instruction in any skilled craft. It was essentially a preliterate form of training in which a young man was put in the charge of a master who undertook to look after him for a number of years and to instruct him in the craft in return for a parental payment and obedient service. (It was, until very recently, an almost entirely male system, even though women have always been instructed on an informal sort of apprenticeship in the home.) As a formal system, it developed among the medieval craft guilds of Europe, and the undertakings on both sides were expressed in a contract or indenture between the craftsman and his apprentice. According to such agreements, the young man who success-fully 'served his time' became entitled to practise the craft, and eventually to take apprentices of his own. The continuity of the craft skills was thus ensured, while undesirable recruits could be weeded out and the skills restricted to members of the fraternity.

Alongside the system of apprenticeship, the literate skills as practised by the embryo professional classes of medieval Europe – the skills of the lawyer, the medical practitioner and the cleric – acquired a different status by virtue of book-learning formalized in a university degree course. There was still a strong element of apprenticeship about the procedure for initiating a man into one of these professions, but the component of book learning was regarded as essential and established a clear distinction between the crafts and the professions. One effect of the Industrial Revolution, however, was to generate new skills while frequently making old skills redundant, changing the relative importance of skills and professions. In particular, new skills like those of the architect, the surveyor and the engineer were created by the breakdown and recombination of elements from older skills. Those with these skills aspired to professional status. At the beginning of the nineteenth century there was no immediate prospect of acquiring the equivalent of a university qualification in these subjects, and any such development lay a generation in the future, at least so far as British engineers were concerned. In France the situation was rather different, for despite the failure of French industry to sustain an Industrial Revolution in the eighteenth century, the country had made striking progress in scientific and technological education. Admittedly, the initiative for this was largely military: the several *écoles* of the French higher education system, culminating after the 1789 Revolution in the École Polytechnique of 1794, were designed to train the upper cadres of the French army. But they did nevertheless represent a substantial advance in the theoretical skills associated with engineering, such as practical mathematics, the analysis of materials, and techniques for describing artefacts accurately in drawings. These skills were not generally available to British engineers until well into the nineteenth century.[1]

Engineers in Britain were obliged to rely on the more practical skills from which the profession had sprung. They adopted and adapted traditional apprenticeship as the normal mode for the recognition of candidates as members of their groups. New aspirants were expected to serve time with an established practitioner before setting up in business on their own. This period was normally four or five years, and was frequently formalized with an indenture: such an arrangement was recognized by new professional bodies like the Institution of Civil Engineers as a necessary qualification for admission to its membership. In this way, the skilled brotherhood attempted to maintain control over the profession, but at a time of rapid change in industry this could not be done with any precision, especially when the demand for engineers became too great for the existing fraternity to authenticate the qualifications for all the would-be entrants. Such a situation arose in engineering in the 1830s, with the sudden need for a large number of engineers to undertake railway works.

Apprenticeship had thus become a vaguely determined qualification for British engineering at the beginning of the nineteenth century. Most of the established leaders of the profession had entered it from other skills: Telford had served an apprenticeship as a stonemason, Rennie as a millwright, Watt as an instrument-maker, Mylne as an architect. A few, like Jessop, had served with Smeaton, and a number had worked with Brindley as canal builders, although not specifically as his apprentices. It was clearly an asset to have worked closely with a prominent member of the profession in acquiring commissions of one's own, and it was this sort of association which an engineering apprenticeship or pupilage came to imply. A young man would be employed, at his own or his parents' expense, and frequently on payment of a substantial fee, in the office of an established engineer, in which capacity he could be used to undertake field surveys, to make drawings, to negotiate contracts and land settlements, to supervise operations on behalf of his chief, and generally to participate in the activities which an engineer was called upon to perform. At the termination of the agreed period, he could be retained in the service of his chief on a salaried basis as an assistant or resident engineer. Or more likely, he could take his experience and a reference from his chief to seek employment elsewhere or to set up an engineering practice of his own.

In such an open-ended arrangement it was obviously a great advantage to have friends and to know people. Best of all was to keep the skill in the family, and there were a number of outstanding engineering dynasties in the nineteenth century. Not only the Brunels, but the Stephensons, the Rennies, the Jessops and the Mylnes, and the Stevenson family of Scottish lighthouse builders, ran to two or three generations of engineering excellence. Such dynastic relations were valuable because they ensured a good training from father to son without the need for a formal apprenticeship or the payment of a fee. They also provided a network of contacts for the new entrant to the profession through which new commissions could be sought and engineering prospects pursued. In the case of I. K. Brunel, the advantage of this dynastic arrangement was doubled. Not only did he receive close personal training from one of the best engineers of the period in the person of his father, Marc Brunel, and go on to work as an assistant with his father in tasks which gave him a wide entry into influential sections of scientific and industrial activities; he also received the incalculable advantage of access through his father to some of the benefits of the French system of engineering education.

Although he never served a formal apprenticeship, the young I. K. Brunel was thus prepared for his chosen profession as an engineer in a series of stages that gave him as good a training as any available in Britain at that time. In the first place, he received a sound grounding in engineering principles from his father, supplemented by some conventional school instruction. Then, when he was still a boy, he was sent to France by his father to attend a French academy and to learn at first hand from French engineering experience. Thirdly, he returned to enter his father's engineering practice as an assistant, and immediately became involved in a wide range of enterprises with contacts in science and society. And fourthly, he completed his training by becoming his father's right-hand man in the first stage of construction of the Thames Tunnel, the great enterprise by which Marc Brunel is chiefly remembered in British engineering history, and which won him a knighthood in 1841. The significance of each of these stages is worth considering in turn, beginning with his experience at home with his father, whose own formation as an engineer had taken place in France and the United States of America.

Marc Isambard Brunel had been born into a well-established farming family in Normandy on 25 April 1769. The family had acquired their farm at the hamlet of Hacqueville, between Paris and Rouen, in 1490, and had been *cultivateurs d'Hacqueville* ever since, with a tradition of the eldest son succeeding to the farm while younger sons went into the church, for which the family enjoyed the presentation of a living, or into the legal profession. As the second son of the farmer Jean Charles Brunel and his wife Marie-Victoire Lefèvre, Marc was destined for the church, but it soon became apparent that the gifts of the boy were practical rather than theological. At the age of eight he was sent to the College of Gisors, where he began training as a military officer, and where Marc did well in mathematics and drawing. He was also good at music, and showed rare ability in making his own musical instruments. But his father persisted in his intention of Marc becoming a priest, so that he was sent next to the Seminary of Sainte-Nicaise in Rouen. Here his practical skills were recognized and he was encouraged to do woodworking, in which he excelled, but the Superior realized that he was not a suitable recruit for the priesthood and told his father so.[2]

The result was that Marc was removed from the seminary and sent to live with his cousin Mme Carpentier and her husband, who acted as the American Consul in Rouen. Their friend Professor Dulague undertook to tutor him with a view to securing entry into the navy as an officer cadet. This was an exceptional stroke of good fortune for the thirteen-year-old boy, because Dulague, Professor of Hydrography at the Royal College in Rouen and one of the outstanding French physical scientists of his generation, was associated with the energetic revival of the French navy being undertaken at this time by the Maréchal de Castries, the Minister of Marine. The latter engaged many other highly talented individuals in his enterprise, including the outstanding mathematician Gaspard Monge, who devised the technique of modern mechanical drawing whereby three dimensions are represented on a plane surface. Dulague was greatly impressed by Marc's capacity as a student and made representations on his behalf to de Castries, who nominated him *volontaire d'honneur* to a new frigate, which he joined in 1786 to begin a six year tour of duty. During this he visited the West Indies and America and learnt to speak English. The Revolution broke out in Paris in 1789 and quickly engulfed the whole of France. Marc's frigate returned to Rouen in 1792, and the crew was paid off, just as the new political regime was about to enter its most violent stage.

Marc Brunel had had the benefit of some of the best scientific and technical expertise available at the time. Even though he did not attend one of the traditional *écoles*, his private tutoring and naval experience provided him with outstanding competence in technical drawing, mathematical theory and other practical skills. He maintained these throughout his long life, and in time he passed them on to his son, giving the latter a singular advantage in entering a profession which, in Britain at any rate, had still not developed any formal means of theoretical instruction.

Marc fled from France initially to the United States of America, where he managed to carve out a career for himself, becoming engineer to New York City and being responsible for some of the earliest civic buildings there. He had long cherished an ambition to go to Britain, however, because of its great opportunities for advancement through industry, and this desire had been made stronger by his wish to resume acquaintance with the young English lady, Sophia Kingdom, with whom he had fallen in love. So when he had conceived a brilliant project for the mass-production of rigging-blocks for sailing ships, he decided to sell his idea to the British Admiralty. This was achieved with the powerful backing of Earl Spencer, to whom Brunel had gone with a letter of introduction from Alexander Hamilton, a founding father of the American Republic and First Secretary to the Treasury in President Washington's government. Spencer, who was then First Lord of the Admiralty in the government of William Pitt, was a cultured and discriminating man, anxious to secure improvements in naval administration. He immediately became a firm friend of and patron to Marc Brunel and arranged his introduction to Sir Samuel Bentham, the Inspector General of Naval Works. With Bentham's support the decision was taken to establish a series of machines designed by Brunel in the Naval Dockyard at Portsmouth. Brunel was commissioned to install this equipment, so in 1802 he and his wife, whom he had married on arriving in Britain in 1799, made the move to a house in Portsmouth, within easy walking distance of the Dockyard.[3]

The first two children of Marc and Sophie were both girls: Sophia and Emma, born between 1800 and 1805. Then came Isambard Kingdom in 1806, completing what appears to have been a very close and happy family. They moved to London in 1808 and settled in Lindsey Row, Chelsea, convenient for Marc's interests in a sawmill at Battersea, and for naval commissions at Chatham and Woolwich. A clutch of family stories survives from these years, of nursery games, playing with the neighbours, and swimming in the river, which confirm the impression of a happy and untroubled childhood. Marc took a close interest in the education of his precocious son from an early age. There can be no doubt that Marc was an able and patient teacher, and that Isambard was an attentive and responsive student. Despite the occasional tensions which could be expected to develop between two highly intelligent and strong-minded persons, the relationship between father and son was one of deep affection and mutual respect. According to Lady Noble, Marc taught the boy to draw at the age of four, and instructed him in Euclid at the age of eight. He inculcated the habit 'of measuring and drawing with neat precision any building of interest that he might observe', a habit which Marc regarded as 'the Engineer's Alphabet'. The value of the habit in developing powers of observation and assessment was demonstrated in the almost uncanny ability of both father and son to recognize faults in the construction of buildings and to forecast their imminent collapse. Encouraged by the quick response of his son to everything he taught him, Marc sent the boy to Dr Morrell's boarding school at Hove, where he studied the classics and displayed his talents by undertaking in his spare time a survey of the town.[4]

In 1815 the battle of Waterloo brought to a decisive end the Napoleonic vision of imperial France and restored Europe to a period of peace and stability. Marc Brunel, with the high opinion of French education derived from his own experience, determined to take advantage of peace and the restoration of the French monarchy to send his son to France in order to complete his formal education. So in 1820, at the age of fourteen, Isambard was sent to France and the next three years constituted the second phase of his 'apprenticeship', during which he received at first hand the benefits of the French educational system. He was enrolled first at the College of Caen in Normandy, and then moved to the Lycée Henri-Quatre in Paris, renowned for its mathematical instruction. He moved on to work under the tutelage of Louis Breguet, the famous maker of chronometers, watches and scientific instruments, who is generally regarded as one of the supreme craftsman in the field of horology.[5] In this choice, Marc Brunel recognized the importance of developing to the full the practical skills of his son. An interesting comparison can be made between Breguet, who built up a 'school' of craftsmen, and Henry Maudslay, the toolmaker of Lambeth who made the machines for the elder Brunel's block-making equipment, and who likewise trained up a remarkable body of talented successors.[6] Isambard was certainly fortunate to have been instructed by such a master, and the watchmaker, nearing the end of his life, was clearly impressed by the potential of the young man because he wrote to his father in 1821: 'Je sens qu'il est important de cultiver chez lui les heureuses dispositions inventives qu'il doit à la nature, ou à l'éducation, mais qu'il serait bien dommage de voir perdre'.[7] It is not possible to determine exactly how long the young Isambard spent on each part of his French experience, as the family records are very unspecific about it. His father arranged for him to be presented as a candidate for the prestigious École Polytechnique, but his foreign birth disqualified him, so that, despite his father's wish that he should prolong his stay in France 'pour enricher et mûrir son esprit', he returned home in 1822 at the age of sixteen and began work in his father's office.[8]

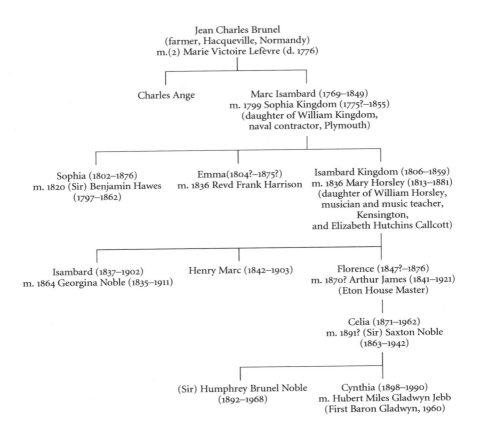

Jean Charles Brunel
(farmer, Hacqueville, Normandy)
m.(2) Marie Victoire Lefèvre (d. 1776)

Charles Ange

Marc Isambard (1769–1849)
m. 1799 Sophia Kingdom (1775?–1855)
(daughter of William Kingdom,
naval contractor, Plymouth)

Sophia (1802–1876)
m. 1820 (Sir) Benjamin Hawes
(1797–1862)

Emma(1804?–1875?)
m. 1836 Revd Frank Harrison

Isambard Kingdom (1806–1859)
m. 1836 Mary Horsley (1813–1881)
(daughter of William Horsley,
musician and music teacher,
Kensington,
and Elizabeth Hutchins Callcott)

Isambard (1837–1902)
m. 1864 Georgina Noble (1835–1911)

Henry Marc (1842–1903)

Florence (1847?–1876)
m. 1870? Arthur James (1841–1921)
(Eton House Master)

Celia (1871–1962)
m. 1891? (Sir) Saxton Noble
(1863–1942)

(Sir) Humphrey Brunel Noble
(1892–1968)

Cynthia (1898–1990)
m. Hubert Miles Gladwyn Jebb
(First Baron Gladwyn, 1960)

1. Family tree of Isambard Kingdom Brunel.

Marc Brunel was an extremely industrious and innovative engineer, but he was not an outstanding businessman, and for three months in the summer of 1821 – while his son was away in France – he was actually consigned to a debtors' prison when his various creditors became particularly pressing. He had been liberated from this 'Misfortune', as the family called the event, by the intervention of Lord Spencer and the Duke of Wellington, who had pointed out to members of the government the value of Brunel's services to the country, both actual and prospective. Back at work, he had immediately become heavily involved in a bewildering range of projects. These absorbed the attention of the young Brunel when he returned to Britain the following summer to commence the third stage of his formation as an engineer. One of his first major jobs was that of supervising the manufacture of the ironwork for two suspension bridges for the Île de Bourbon, now renamed Réunion, in the Indian Ocean. They had been commissioned by the French government, and involved difficulties with the contractors, the Milton Ironworks in Sheffield. There were also plans for German paddle tugs, a Dutch cannon-boring mill, a rotary printing press, various bridge projects, additions to the South London Docks for the Grand Surrey Canal Company, and a swing bridge and a floating pier for Liverpool Docks. Another scheme was a design for a canal at Panama, and Marc also devised a diving bell crane to be used by some treasure hunters in Spain. He collaborated with Augustus Charles Pugin in designing a 'Necropolis of London', which became the Kensal Green Cemetery with the Brunel family tomb in it. His extensive travelling by coach made him sensitive to the well-being of the horses, which were frequently abused by overwork, and I. K. Brunel carried on this keen interest in horses into the next generation.[9]

Possibly the most interesting of all the plethora of bright ideas in which the young Brunel became involved in this period of apprenticeship was the abortive scheme for a 'Gaz Engine'. This derived from a close association with Sir Humphry Davy and Michael Faraday which the Brunel family established through living in Chelsea and mixing with the scientific fraternity of the metropolis. Faraday had managed to liquefy several gases under pressure, including 'carbonic gas' or carbon dioxide. Davy speculated that the small amount of heat required to change liquid carbon dioxide into gas made it a likely candidate for a new type of engine providing power much more cheaply than a steam engine. Marc Brunel was intrigued by this possibility, although he recognized that 'it strikes me to be very difficultly managed'.[10] He and his son struggled for ten years to make the idea work, transferring their experimental equipment from Chelsea to Rotherhithe when they became involved in the Thames Tunnel. Marc took out British Patent No. 5212 in 1825, describing the equipment as 'Gas Engines'. According to the specification, this consisted of five vertical cylinders, with the outer two containing carbon dioxide, transferring changes in pressure through two cylinders full of oil to the central cylinder which contained the working piston. The outer cylinders had long copper tubes running through them, by which the temperature of the carbon dioxide could be alternately raised and lowered, causing it to evaporate and condense in a regular cycle. The Brunels made good progress in the earlier stages of their experiments, encouraging Faraday to devote one of his Friday Evening Discussions at the Royal Institution to it in 1826. He presented it as being particularly appropriate for marine propulsion. But problems with imperfect castings, and with joints which leaked at the high pressures of over 1000 pounds per square inch, slowed the process down and eventually made the construction so intractable that the hoped for economies of the engine began to appear illusory. Sadi Carnot was simultaneously establishing the basis of modern

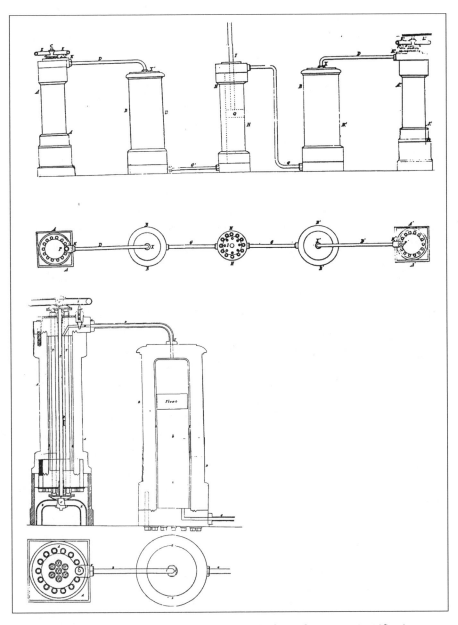

2. The Gaz Engine, British Patent No. 5212 (1825), from the Patent Specification, 1825.

thermodynamics with his theoretical demonstration that an engine could
not give out more power than was put into it, but it took several decades for
this truth to become generally recognized by British engineers. Meanwhile,

however, I. K. Brunel struggled to achieve the chimera of cheap power, until finally abandoning it in 1833.[11] It has been estimated that the Brunels spent about £15,000 on their 'Gaz Engine' experiments, including a grant of £200 from the Admiralty.[12]

Somewhat less colourful, but of more practical consequence, was Marc Brunel's work on the improvement of steam engines, which led to his patent specification for 'Certain Improvements in Steam Engines'. This was a design for a large steam engine system to be used in marine applications: it was described as an 'inverted V' or 'triangle-frame' engine, and it was remarkably advanced for its period. I. K. Brunel subsequently used a form of this engine in the steam ship *Great Britain*.[13]

While still engaged in his father's office, the young engineer became involved in the greatest of all Marc Brunel's projects – the building of the Thames Tunnel. This provided the fourth and last stage of his apprenticeship. The novelty of this enterprise lay in the fact that it was the first scheme for a regular subaqueous passage by the general public. As it was being constructed in London, it received a great deal of public attention and came to be regarded as one of the wonders of the modern world. The work of miners in extracting metals and coal from deep underground was well known, but that had always been conducted at a distance from the metropolis. When it came to mining in London clay and gravel under the Thames, even such distinguished engineers as the Cornishman Richard Trevithick had been defeated. That had been in 1808, when an earlier project for a tunnel under the Thames had been abandoned. The attraction of the scheme was that it promised to provide an alternative river crossing downstream from London Bridge, which was already badly congested by traffic from the populous hinterland on both sides. So when Marc Brunel invented a device for excavating the tunnel safely through the treacherous ground of the lower Thames basin, there were plenty of entrepreneurs prepared to support it.

The device consisted of the 'Great Shield', for which Marc took out a patent on 20 January 1818. He had developed it from careful observation of the ship-worm *teredo navalis*, which was capable of eating its way through the stoutest of ships' timbers. He had perceived that the worm chewed its way through the wood while protecting its head with shells which oscillated to cut the timber at the same time, while its solidified excreta formed a smooth lining to the tunnel to protect its fragile body. Marc simulated this process by designing a cellular structure of cast iron in which workmen could excavate a small piece of the tunnel face at a time. The shield would protect them from any possible collapse of the tunnel roof, and as each section was cleared the cast-iron frame could be jacked forward and the brickwork of the tunnel built up behind it. When he had taken soundings for the route of the proposed tunnel from Rotherhithe to Wapping, Marc modified the design to suit the particular circumstances by substituting a rectangular shield for the circular one envisaged in the patent: this was to permit a dual carriageway within the limits of the band of clay through which he proposed to drive the tunnel. The rectangular shield was made up of twelve vertical frames, within each of which there were three working cells placed one above the other. Every miner worked by removing one or two of the horizontal 'poling boards' that sealed the front of his cell, excavating the ground so revealed, and screwing the poling boards onto the new face. When all the boards in the three cells of one frame had been advanced, the whole frame was jacked forward on its cast-iron feet and the iron staves providing protection at the work-face were moved into the new position. The complete shield literally inched its way forward, and when all was going smoothly it would advance by two or three feet in a week. More usually, however, this rate was curtailed by the necessity to make replacements to worn or broken parts, as well as the need to maintain the supplies of light and air to the workface. That was without reckoning on delays caused by regular influxes of water, both large and small.[14]

The Bill to authorize the Thames Tunnel Company received the royal assent on 24 June 1824, and Marc Brunel was appointed engineer at the first general meeting of the company. The first shaft was sunk at Rotherhithe between March and November 1825, and by the start of 1826 the Great Shield was in place and beginning to crawl under the river. On Brunel's original calculation the work should have been finished in three years. In fact, it took six times as long, being completed in 1843 after a series of calamities, tragedies and epic feats of endurance. Work stopped for seven years after a particularly severe inundation in January 1828, when the young I. K. Brunel, who had been working under appalling conditions, narrowly escaped with his life. He had been involved in much of the preparatory work, and began on the tunnel as assistant to his father. The man appointed as resident engineer, William Armstrong, broke down under the strain in 1826, and I. K. Brunel was promoted to replace him. Shortly afterwards, three other assistants were appointed, Beamish, Gravatt and Riley. Riley soon succumbed to the deadly atmosphere of the tunnel and died, but the other two became stalwart colleagues of Brunel, and when Marc was obliged through illness to curtail his activities, the Herculean task of driving the tunnel forwards fell to his son and to Richard Beamish and William Gravatt.

Richard Beamish, an Irish gentleman aged twenty-eight, had served in the army with the Coldstream Guards, but had resigned his commission in order to study engineering independently. He was brave and unimaginative, serving the Brunels with great loyalty. It must have been difficult for him to concede professional seniority to the young Brunel, but he seems to have done so with only the mildest reservations. He went on to write a sound but pedestrian biography of Marc Brunel. William Gravatt was even closer to I. K. Brunel in age, being a couple of months younger. He had received an excellent engineering training from his father, a colonel with the Royal Engineers, and had served an apprenticeship with Bryan Donkin, the London mechanical engineer who was also a director of the Thames Tunnel Company. He was a very competent mathematician, and Marc Brunel made him responsible for the management of the Great Shield. He was fearless and outspoken, and possessed few social graces, but for eighteen months he was, with Beamish, the intimate colleague of I. K. Brunel in conducting the construction of the Thames Tunnel. Marc continued to give overall direction to the operation, but he was encumbered with logistic arrangements of supplies for the work, and with maintaining difficult relationships with a board of directors that grew increasingly impatient with every delay in the tunnel's progress. Being in his late fifties, moreover, his own health was beginning to fail, so that he was obliged to leave most of the underground work to the younger men.[15]

The weight of the responsibility which thus devolved upon the shoulders of the young Brunel at the age of twenty is difficult to imagine, and would have crushed most engineers of more mature years. But I. K. Brunel stepped into the office of resident engineer in January 1827 with tremendous energy and complete authority. His energy quickly became legendary. He required little sleep, and was constantly on the move, underground and on the surface of the site. He rallied the motley crew of Somerset miners and Irish labourers working on the shield; he supervised the bricklayers and checked the incoming supply of bricks, occasionally sending back a load as being below standard; he dealt successfully with labour disputes, even when the directors obliged him to reduce wage rates; and he kept a watchful eye on the steam engine which was essential to pump water out of the Tunnel and to remove excavated spoil. He lived on the job for most of the time, sharing a cabin with Gravatt at Rotherhithe, where they managed to make themselves comfortable. They worked twelve-hour shifts for six days a week, and frequently found that there were things to be done on Sundays also. Even so the young Brunel found energy to socialize when he was not on duty, going to concerts and dinner parties, and finding time to pursue mild flirtations.[16]

Under his vigilant direction, the shield drove forwards, slowly but surely. Beamish records that in one week of 1827 it actually advanced by three feet in one day, and that the average progress became thirteen feet a week, while the number of men employed had risen from 180 in October 1826 to 467 in March 1827.[17] By 1 May 1827 the shield had advanced 540 feet, approaching the half-way point on the 1200 feet march under the river to Wapping. But in February Riley, a well-qualified assistant engineer, died, and Beamish was afflicted with partial blindness in one eye. Both were victims of the dreadful conditions of poor ventilation and noxious effluvia under which all the underground workers laboured, and these only got worse as the tunnel lengthened. The directors had imposed economies in the provision for draining the workings and for adequate fresh air and lighting, and the need to conduct all services through the Rotherhithe shaft imposed hazardous bottlenecks on operations. Then, on 18 May, came the first of the serious inundations that had long been feared by Marc Brunel. The tunnel was completely flooded, but with vigorous life-saving activities by Gravatt and Isambard no lives were lost, and it was subsequently found by risky operations in a diving bell that the river bed had collapsed over the shield. This was remedied by dumping bags of clay into the hole, so that the tunnel could be pumped dry again and work resumed.

The directors of the Tunnel Company were a fractious group, who made life difficult for their engineers. The necessity for economies was reasonable enough, considering the very narrow margins left on their estimates within the available capital, and they had good cause for anxiety over the construction delays and the inundation of the tunnel. But they added the pressure of a piece-work system of payment for the bricklayers, which led to disagreements between them and the miners about the relative speed of their labours, and called for special precautions by the engineers to ensure that work was not unduly hurried. The directors also had the idea of raising funds by opening the tunnel, unfinished and crowded as it was, to visitors. Marc Brunel complained bitterly, but the younger Brunel accommodated himself cheerfully to showing round various political and social dignitaries, from home and overseas. He arranged a special visit for his family, and conceived the brilliant publicity stunt of holding a dinner in the tunnel. The first such event, in December 1826, was a small affair for himself and nine friends, but on 10 November the following year he staged a magnificent dinner under one of the arches with some fifty guests, while 150 workers were entertained under an adjacent arch. There were enthusiastic toasts and speeches, and Beamish arranged for the band of his old regiment to provide a musical accompaniment while an artist was commissioned to commit the event to canvas. It is not explained how the filthy and stinking conditions of daily work in the tunnel were ameliorated for these social events, but they appear to have passed off without complaint.[18]

Two months after this splendid occasion, on 12 January 1828, with half the tunnel excavated to about 600 feet from the Rotherhithe shaft, the second disastrous inundation occurred. This time there were casualties, six workmen losing their lives, and Brunel himself came within a hair's breadth of being drowned, with only prompt action by Beamish rescuing him from the swirling water as it rushed up the shaft. His leg was injured, and he sustained internal injuries for which, beyond being bled and having leeches applied, there was no adequate medical treatment. He certainly became very seriously ill, being absent from work for many months. He was sent off to Brighton to recuperate, but the illness recurred and Beamish was sent down to bring him home, where he languished until the spring. Meanwhile, work on the tunnel came to a standstill. The company had exhausted its capital and the directors considered various expedients to rescue the project, of which the most promising was a grant or loan from the government. Less promising was the possibility of changing their engineer, but under the petulant chairmanship of William Smith MP, they considered several options. Fortunately for Marc Brunel, they needed him to remain in post in order to preserve the hope of government aid. Smith was eventually outmanoeuvred, a handsome government loan was received, and a more cooperative board established. But from the point of view of the young Brunel, the project effectively closed down for seven years. He thus found himself, after several years of superhuman work on what was arguably the major engineering work in the country, out of work.

Work did start again, with a Treasury loan of £270,000, and with a new shield which was installed in place of the damaged original, and from 1835 to 1842 this resumed its slow crawl under the Thames, surviving further inundations and accidents, to break through into the shaft prepared to receive it at Wapping. I. K. Brunel had no part in this phase of the work, being fully engaged by this time on his own enterprises, although he continued to help his father whenever he could. Nevertheless, the Thames Tunnel played an important part in his practical apprenticeship. As his father's resident engineer and the man continuously on the site, Brunel carried tremendous responsibilities and exercised authority in crucial decisions affecting the life or death of the men working under him. It was a hard and exacting training, and one which prepared him admirably for the leading role in major engineering operations. Most particularly, the experience demonstrated his qualities as a leader, an administrator, and an expert in public relations.

I. K. Brunel's qualities as an administrator and a public relations expert have already been illustrated, but it is worth emphasizing the discovery of his capacities as a leader because these helped to shape his subsequent refusal to share responsibility for any of his engineering enterprises. He had seen his father being pressurized into compromising his engineering judgment in order to satisfy the demands of his board for economies, and he resolved that he would never submit himself to such bullying: 'N.B. never *will* I then be prevailed upon by others to do what I think imprudent'.[19] It was clearly gratifying to him to see how easily he had assumed the role of a leader of men. Beamish, who might have had reason for envy towards him, eloquently records the unanimity with which everybody turned to the young Brunel for direction at a critical moment underground in the tunnel:

> We gazed on one another with a feeling not to be described. On every countenance astonishment, awe perhaps, was depicted, but not fear. I saw that each man, with his eyes upon Isambard Brunel, stood firmly prepared to execute the orders he should receive with resolution and intrepidity.[20]

Isambard Brunel had emerged from having been an eager but light-headed young man into a mature engineer, resolute and decisive in manner, and with a personal charisma that aroused the respect and loyalty of those who worked with him. The Thames Tunnel was far from being finished in 1828, but it had finished his training. Henceforth, through frustration and success, disaster and triumph, he was his own man.

3

Castles in the Sky

The Thames Tunnel was completed, although not to Marc Brunel's full specifications, by March 1843. Marc had originally provided for gently graded descents at both ends, which would have made possible vehicular access to the tunnel. Without these, it remained only a foot-tunnel, and it was not until it was integrated into the London Underground railway system in 1865 on the line linking Whitechapel to New Cross that the tunnel found a use commensurate with its cost and engineering excellence. Queen Victoria was among the first of two million people who walked through the tunnel in its first year: she had already conferred a knighthood on Marc for his achievement in 1841. The practical importance of the tunnel was disappointingly slight, but it had great symbolical significance. It demonstrated the ability of engineering to overcome some of the most intractable conditions in the natural world and, in particular, it represented the genius and indomitable resilience of its creator, Sir Marc Isambard Brunel.

While the elder Brunel was completing his great work on the tunnel, his son was making his own transition to the career of an independent professional engineer. But this did not happen immediately after the break-down of the tunnel project in January 1828. There were, first, five difficult and frustrating years while the younger Brunel recovered from the injuries sustained in the tunnel and thrashed around for alternative applications for his talents and energy. It was in these years that he established the connections with Bristol which prepared the way for his major works and the fulfilment of the vision which had been maturing in his mind. This is also the one period of his life for which we possess a personal account in the shape of the diaries which he kept at this time. It was partly owing to his father's influence that the young Brunel tried hard to keep a regular diary. Marc Brunel regarded it as a professional duty to keep meticulous records of his practice, both in personal diaries and in other written accounts, and his son modelled himself on this practice. Three parallel diaries by I. K. Brunel survive from these years: the three volumes, 1826–1829, of his Thames Tunnel journal, which contain plenty of entries not confined to tunnel business; the four volumes of private diaries; and the single slight volume of personal diary. The autobiographical content of these diaries is of uneven value. They cover only a small part – albeit an important and formative one – in the career of their author, and most of the commentary is perfunctory. But they also contain some intensely interesting reflections, and even the shortest notes are useful in building up a picture of their author's commitments and preoccupations.[1]

The first two volumes of the Thames Tunnel journal contain much information about managing the tunnel enterprise, showing concern with mechanical and technical problems such as broken plates in the shield, slipped staves, the quality of brickwork, problems with plugging leaks, arranging for diving bells, and overcoming difficulties with the board of directors. They also include items on dealing with labour disputes over pay (3 March 1827), and attending the funeral of the unfortunate Riley, who had been taken on by Marc as an assistant engineer: 'Breakfasted after which Gravatt and I dressed to attend Riley's funeral ... He certainly was an amiable young man and intelligent but no energy of character and certainly not fit for our work nor likely to have become so.'[2] There are also many entries which show that Brunel managed to maintain a social life even when under great pressure from these commitments. On one occasion he visited Dulwich Gallery with 'Sophia, Benjamin and Mr Beamish', being critical of most of the art exhibited except *Tragedy* by Sir Joshua Reynolds.[3] On another occasion, he dined with Gravatt and 'engaged with him in discussing the merits of a most absurd perpetual motion invented by the ever scheming Sir W. Congreve proposing to obtain a power by the weight of water rising in capillary tubes'.[4]

The third volume begins in October 1827 and soon reaches 12 January 1828, for which the word 'WATER' is written prominently in the margin: 'Went below little thinking how I should come up again.' Thereafter, the journal becomes an outline of his activities, through convalescence and a gradual return to work until August 1829, when it comes to an end. It took him over six months to recover from his injuries, and his condition caused serious concern amongst family and friends. He went down to Brighton to recuperate at the end of January, but after a fortnight he was so unwell that Beamish was sent down to bring him home: 'the journey however brought on a return'.[5] A month later, he was still not well: 'Mr Travers bled me – and he and Mr B. prescribed sugar of lead – felt much better after bleeding'.[6] Friends, particularly D'Eichthal and John Hulme, went out of their way to visit him, and the latter, in particular, seemed to have welcomed the opportunity to exchange personal writings and other confidences.[7] In July Brunel departed on a holiday, sailing to Plymouth in a crowded cabin on the *Thames*, and encountering bad weather on the way.[8]

The boat put into Plymouth on 17 July and he immediately arranged to visit the breakwater, where he made several drawings.[9] But that day he received a letter from his mother urging him to return home because his father needed help. The journal resumed at home on 31 July, but then he was taken ill again and spent another fortnight in bed.[10] His parents went off to France for a holiday at the end of August: the tunnel had been blocked up on 14 August; even though negotiations to raise money in order to resume operations continued, they obviously felt that this was an opportunity to take a break.

Brunel was left in charge at home, and to judge from the paucity of journal entries he became bored with little to do: 'Went in the evening to see Kean in Shylock – disappointed.'[11] It seems that, on his parents' return, he also took a break in France, and did not return until 'one cold, raw February morning' in 1829.[12] He boarded a coach from Paris to Calais, taking his preferred seat on top where he was joined by another British young man, a cadet from Woolwich, with whom he got on famously and had an hilarious journey. Another Briton, who heard their jollity from inside the coach, decided to join them, and the three made up a very lively party, calling for more hay at every stop in order to keep themselves warm. Their good-humoured fellowship continued on the ferry, and then on the coach from Dover to London. They gave each other nicknames, and it was only towards the end of the journey that they declared their identities. The cadet was called Orlebar, and the man who joined them from inside the coach was Charles MacFarlane, an antiquarian and traveller, who subsequently wrote a vivid account of the journey. This included a beautiful thumb-nail portrait of Brunel whom he described as: 'A little, nimble, dark-complexioned man with a vast deal of ready poignant wit'.[13] When they reached London, Brunel gave an invitation to his co-travellers to dine at his parents' home in Bridge Street. Although nothing more is known about Orlebar, MacFarlane accepted the invitation and came to know the family well.

The Thames Tunnel journal resumes on 10 February 1829, when Brunel checked the work on the new London Bridge ('all centres slacked') and 'went to the Engineers paid my fee'. Two days later, 'William and I went to the Royal Society – Mr Babbage conversing on Log Tables';[14] and then 'Dressed and went to R. S. Lecture on Mr Browne's new discovery of moving mole-cules'.[15] The next week he was making drawings of geological strata for Davies Gilbert, and explaining them to him two years before Gilbert was persuaded to place Brunel's drawings first in the Clifton Bridge competition;[16] and dining with Michael Faraday.[17] An entry for 23 February reads: 'MacFarlane, Street and Benjamin to Breakfast – very merry'. The next day he went to 'the Engineers' ('McNeale on roads') and the Society of Arts ('nothing').[18]

Then in March he accompanied his father and Woolaston to seek Lord Althorp's support for a grant to revive the Tunnel: 'Long conversation – he seemed to form a very sanguine opinion of the Tunnel *hopes* – undertook to think over the matter and see the Duke *alone* – much better'.[19] On his twenty-third birthday Brunel went to the Royal Society with his father (he did not become a member himself until the following year). Even though Marc was not well and left early, 'A. and I stopt very late talking to Mr Babbage and D. Gilbert'.[20]

The round of visits to societies, conversations with distinguished scientists, and rapid journeys continued. On Wednesday 22 April he took the mail coach to Northampton and then on to Macclesfield and Manchester, on unspecified business although it seems likely that he would have called on the Hulmes: then he returned by mail coach on the Monday morning. On 1 May 1829, he 'went to the Geological in the evening – very interesting – Pr. Buckland etc.' and three days later, 'went to Humane Society Dinner'.[21] Then he:

> went to Clements examined and understood Babbage's machine – went to Maudslays about panoptic glasses – went to Mr Faraday's. Dined with him. Memo about block making returned saw *Pandemonium* (humbug) to Rotherhithe.[22]

On 8 May, he went to the Royal Society 'to hear Lecture on block making' (the speaker is not named, but it could have been his father), and on 17 May he had a narrow escape when conducting an experiment in the course of which the bottom fell out of a pot as it was removed from the furnace. This was only one of many tricky experiments conducted by I. K. Brunel in the course of his work on the Gaz engine, designed to test pipes under pressure and to devise suitable sealants: bursting pipes and mercury running around the workshop were among the hazards. A wistful entry on 19 May says: 'my father gone to Smeatonians' – a select group of senior engineers to which the younger Brunel was not admitted. On 15 July, 'Mendhelsohn [sic] came – went to St John's Church – where he played on the organ'; on 6 August, MacFarlane came to dinner with Gravatt and others; and on 12 August he reported 'Poor Faraday low spirited and unwell'. This brought the third volume of the Thames Tunnel series to an end.

The private diary series begins on 22 April 1824, when Brunel, at the age of eighteen, was employed by his father in making preparations for the Thames Tunnel. On that day he reported: 'Took my Theodolite down to Rotherhithe to take the Level of the ground where we are boring.' Not much more was said about the tunnel until 2 March 1825, when the first bricks were laid. Meanwhile, he was involved in experiments with the Gaz apparatus;[23] drawings for a treadmill;[24] and a drawing for 'a Mausoleum for the necropolis',[25] including a reference to: 'A Mr Pugin an architectural draftsman called at Necropolis of which he is to make a Bird's eye view'.[26] There were references to staying with Benjamin Hawes and at his parents' house at No. 30 Bridge Street;[27] to 'My father and mother and Emma went to Brighton';[28] to taking tea at Sophia's (his sister, wife of Benjamin Hawes);[29] and to calling on Mr Faraday – 'nothing particular'.[30] His father featured as calling on Mr Telford[31] and going to the Smeatonians.[32] He responded cautiously to: 'A French or German engineer' who called 'to see all our models, drawings, etc.'[33] For three months, from 9 September to 31 December 1824, he ran a line through and pencilled in 'Illness and Idleness'. There were many other gaps, and in 1826 he began a second volume with good intentions: 'I fully intend, having once more begun my journal, to continue.'[34] He reported on 'Gaz' the same day: 'the Scotch patent is already taken out'. There followed a note on the Tunnel: 'about 10 ft of Brickwork completed – not much', and on the South London Dock: 'My father appointed Engineer, I am afraid we shall want money'. But most of this second volume was left blank.

Any fellow diarist can sympathize with this determined but hyperactive young man in his struggle to keep a regular account of his life, and can understand his decision, after the erratic performance of his early private diaries and tunnel journals, to try a new approach. In October 1827 he began a more reflective journal, which is referred to here as the 'personal diary'. It consists of a mere thirty-six pages of script, including some fascinating reflections on life, love and the tunnel. The document gives a concentrated insight into Brunel's mind in these years. There are valuable descriptive passages on the tunnel work, and dreams of *châteaux d'Espagne*, his castles in the sky, which he hopes will bring him fame and fortune. He was even prepared to see himself in a military role:

> My ambition or whatever it may be called (it is not the mere wish to be rich) is rather extensive: but still am not afraid that I shall be unhappy if I do not reach the rank of hero and Commander in Chief of his Majesty's forces, in the steam (gas) boat department. This is rather a favourite castle in the air of mine. Make the gas engine, fit out some vessels (of course a war), take some prizes nay some island or fortified town, get employed by government, construct and command a fine fleet of them and fight; in fact, take Algiers or something in that style.[35]

In a different mood, he expressed anxiety about defects that he perceived in his character:

> My self conceit and love of glory or rather approbation vie with each other which shall govern me. The latter is so strong that even of a dark night riding home

when I pass some unknown person who perhaps does not even look at me I catch myself trying to look big on my little pony.[36]

At other times, he reflected in considerable detail on the sort of daily routine which made make him most efficient, and devised the regimen of early rising, sparse dining and hard work that characterized so much of his working career.

Then he meditated repeatedly on the question of his marriage prospects: 'Q – shall I make a good husband – Am doubtful.' Of his feminine acquaintances: 'EH is the oldest and most constant now however gone by. During her reign (nearly seven years!!!) several inferior ones caught my attention.'[37] Self-revelation clearly reached its limits here, because despite the disguise of some rather primitive shorthand, part of page 12 was subsequently cut away. The 'EH' of this passage is Ellen Hulme, and the claim to have known her since 1820 is surprising, especially as her family appear to have been Mancunians. It seems likely that the 'J. Hulme' who appears as a friend, visiting him in London when he was convalescing after the tunnel inundation, was Ellen's brother.[38] When Brunel visited Manchester in 1831 in order to take his first ride on the Liverpool & Manchester Railway, he 'spent the day at the Hulmes – John is now established at Mansfield',[39] although Ellen was not mentioned on that occasion. She had, however, been mentioned by name in an entry in the personal diary made early in 1828: 'Ellen it seems is still my real love.'[40] But as he could not see how he could afford to marry her he had written to her to detach himself from any commitment: 'I have had long correspondence with Ellen which I think I have arranged well. I may now consider myself independent.'[41]

These reflections on what seems to have been an unsatisfactory love-life come at the end of the volume. He began the last page on 16 April 1829: 'Why the lock's almost grown rusty so long since I opened this book – a new mode of dating I see too – march of the intellect.'[42] But it did not persuade him to resume his mode of free commentary, and he brought the volume to an end. Having done so, however, he added an introductory letter and a codicil. Both were addressed to his friend Benjamin Hawes, and the letter was dated '8th April 1829 4 am', so that it was almost a reflection on his twenty-third birthday. It consists of three pages declaring his friendship and affection, and leaving Hawes the journal as part of his will. He signed off melodramatically: 'Adieu my dear Fellow, Yours in death I. K. Brunel'. One can only speculate about the reasons for these maudlin sentiments, out of character with the dynamic figure of successful activity that became so well known to a wide public. Presumably the enforced idleness brought on by his personal disabilities following the accident in the tunnel, and the virtual closure of the works thereafter, had served to depress him, as had the dismal prospects of his career and love life. He was still less than cheerful two years later when he added the codicil of one page declaring his own faults: 'Ben I have a painful conviction that I am fast becoming a selfish cold-hearted brute ... I'm unhappy, exceedingly so – the excitement of this election came just in time to conceal it.'[43] This refers to the post-Reform Act election of September 1832 in which Brunel busied himself in support of his friend's candidature for the seat at Lambeth, which he won.[44] So far as we can tell, Hawes never received the document 'willed' to him, which remained among Brunel's personal papers and so survived. From 1832 onwards the careers of the two friends diverged, although they remained in touch, as did their families. It is doubtful whether Hawes, who became a moderately successful parliamentarian and junior statesman, ever had any indication of the lugubrious sentiments addressed to him in the personal diary, even though he lived to 1862.[45]

In 1830 Brunel returned to a more conventional form of diary, with two further folio volumes of the private diary which contain a reasonably well-maintained account of his activities from 7 March 1830, when he visited the sea walls at Tollesbury, to 11 November 1833, after which extreme pressure of work finally overcame the best intentions of the diarist. The two volumes break at September 1832 but may be regarded as a single work, cover the greater part of a crucial four years in the life of their author. They begin with frequent trips to Bristol, to meet Guppy and other friends,[46] and thereafter to explore the Clifton Bridge site at Leigh Woods,[47] to call on William Beckford in Bath,[48] to win the support of the Clifton Bridge Committee, 'unanimous in favour of Egyptian',[49] to promote 'bridge business' at Bath Races and elsewhere,[50] and to take an active part in the Bristol Riots, although unfortunately for posterity most of this entry consists of three blank pages with only marginal notes – 'Bishop's Palace' and 'Riots' – intended for completion at some moment of leisure which never arrived.[51] Other entries for 1830 and 1831 include an account of a trip to Birmingham, armed with a letter of introduction from Babbage, to call on Mr Whateley, solicitor to the project for a Bristol & Birmingham Railway, who enquired: 'whether I would undertake under certain conditions the survey for the Birmingham and Gloster Railway – whether I felt competent etc etc of course after due consideration I accepted'.[52]

Nothing came of this encounter, but a year later Brunel made a more extensive journey north, in response to a request for advice on a new dock scheme at Sunderland. On 16 November 1831 he set out: 'Travelling all day, breakfasted at Grantham dined at 4.40 at York ... arrived at Newcastle at 2.30'. The next day he went by chaise to Sunderland and met the Docks

Committee – 'a set of deuced clever fellows – but a rum set'. This was a productive meeting, because Brunel won the commission to do the work and went on to design the Monkwearmouth Dock. In the following days he visited the Scottiswood Bridge, Hartlepool, Beverley, and Hull, and then went on to Manchester to visit the Hulmes and to ride on the Liverpool & Manchester Railway, only just over a year after its opening. He wrote a note while the train was in motion (sadly, the handwriting looks just about normal) and stuck it into his diary opposite the words: 'I record this specimen of the shaking on Manchester Railway – the time is not far off when we shall be able to take our coffee and write while going, noiseless and smoothly, at 45 miles per hour – let me try'.[53] This is a significant moment in Brunel's career, because it marks the kindling of his enthusiasm for railways, and shows his immediate vision of smooth high speed transport which became such a powerful inspiration when he was appointed Engineer to the GWR. He returned to London via Chester, where he: 'examined bridge attentively – a most beautyfull [sic] bold and grand work'.[54]

Brunel's return to base was marked by the word 'TUNNEL' in a black frame, and the comment:

> Tunnel is now I think DEAD ... The commission have refused on grounds of security – This is the first time I have felt able to cry at least for these ten years ... it will never be finished now in my father's lifetime I fear. However nil desperandum has always been my motto – we may succeed yet – *perservation*.[55]

There were other disappointments in these years. The Gaz experiments were pursued whenever the opportunity occurred, but in May 1832 Brunel 'met with an unexpected difficulty in the existence of an intermediate state ... between liquid and vapour. This obstacle is very likely to create a delay serious with consequences'.[56] By the time he came to review his commitments at the beginning of 1833, he had at last acknowledged the failure of the experiments, and reflected ruefully on ten wasted years so far as Gaz was concerned.[57]

There are some frustrating lacunae in Brunel's diaries during these years. For one thing, there are surprisingly few references to Bristol, although there appears to be a reference to 'going to Redcliff' (a central district of Bristol) in the personal diary in the summer of 1828.[58] There are no Bristol references in the private diaries before March 1830, when he reported: 'heard from Guppy – all going as well'.[59] The young Brunel's bid to be considered as engineer for the Newcastle & Carlisle Railway, reported by his biographers as occurring in January 1830, appears to have slipped into the gap between the two series of private diaries. There are also no references to that intriguing item of Brunel's career – his only publication (apart from his engineering reports), which dates from these years. This was his contribution to a treatise on *The Horse* published in 1831 for the Society for the Diffusion of Useful Knowledge.[60]

The 1843 edition of this book was a substantial work of 563 pages appearing under the name of Willliam Youatt. The section at the end written by Brunel is 'A Treatise on Draught', consisting of forty-five pages of closely-printed text and line-drawings. It is devoted to an 'investigation of the subject of draught by animal power',[61] although in practice it deals only with the horse, making a very sensible and practical analysis of its power as a draught animal. The essay goes on to consider various applications of this power, especially in road transport, giving detailed attention to the design and construction of wheels and carriages. The whole treatment employs the minimum of technicalities and mathematics, and is careful not to take even basic facts for granted. The subject may seem a curious one for Brunel, but it appears to have been a response to a specific commission and came at a point in his career when he had time to consider matters of apparently peripheral importance. It also reflects a personal fondness for horses which he shared with his father. In its treatment of resistance, such as that encountered by barges being hauled through canals, the thinking anticipates that which he was subsequently to apply very effectively to problems of oceanic steam navigation. The editors of the tract tried hard to persuade Brunel to revise his text for later editions, but once he had finished working for his father and had embarked upon his independent career he refused to do so and only managed to find time to make a few superficial changes in the edition of 1843.[62]

An exploit which was well-documented in the private diary was the commission to build an observatory at the Kensington home of Sir James South. Brunel had already shown an amateur interest in astronomy, taking 'the Transit of several stars'[63] and discussing astronomical matters with his friend Sir John Herschel.[64] On 5 October 1830 he took the dimensions of the dome required for South's telescope, and by the following spring it had been erected, as he reported: 'Lionised it till 6 – sat down forty-five people, a good dinner on the lawn'.[65] However, all did not function well at the new observatory. In the autumn:

> Sir James made a long and wandering tirade full of false assertions as to his prognostications my statements of what it would cost ... It was conceded that the Dome was without fault – The plan of the Shutters good – and their not fitting the only fault.[66]

Two days later Brunel called on Sir James who: 'immediately on shaking hands informed me that he had received two accounts which compelled

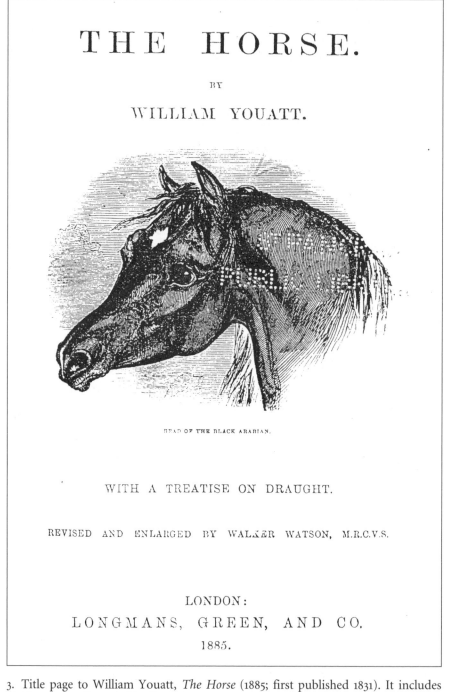

THE HORSE.

BY

WILLIAM YOUATT.

HEAD OF THE BLACK ARABIAN.

WITH A TREATISE ON DRAUGHT.

REVISED AND ENLARGED BY WALKER WATSON, M.R.C.V.S.

LONDON:

LONGMANS, GREEN, AND CO.

1885.

3. Title page to William Youatt, *The Horse* (1885; first published 1831). It includes 'A Treatise on Draught' by Brunel.

him to withdraw all confidence from me'.[67] It appears that there were objections both to Brunel's design for the shutters and to his charges. These were echoed in an article in the *Athenaeum*, a copy of which was carefully inserted into Brunel's diary. Under the heading 'Kensington Observatory' this anonymous article described the dome and criticised the arrangement for the central opening:

> It is not easy to imagine any arrangement more ill-judged than the chax or opening ... and the shutters by which it is attempted to close it ... In fact, this absurd project has no other object than the display of a *tour de force*, and was an effort to produce effect on the part of the architect.[68]

The article gives the original estimate as £504, rising to an actual sum greater than £1700, with the shutters estimated at £40 and costing more than £500. Charles Babbage, a good friend of the Brunels, expressed his anger at this report and advised a libel action.[69] But Brunel took more cautious advice and decided that 'it would not be prudent to notice it'.[70] The subject of Sir James South and his observatory then disappeared from Brunel's diaries, but the tone of exasperated clients, complaining about unanticipated expenses, was to become familiar to Brunel in his subsequent career.[71]

Not all events noticed in these years covered by the diaries, however, were disappointments or causes for depression. A more cheerful item occurred in June 1832: 'After Church I went to Kensington called at the Horsleys and Mr Callcutts walked about the Gardens went to the Athenaeum as I came home. Got something to eat returned home dressed and went to Mr Cartwright's – beautiful music.'[72] This may have been the beginning of Brunel's close relationship with the Horsleys, leading to his marriage to Mary Horsley four years later. Not inappropriately, it is the first entry showing any musical appreciation. In the following weeks he was heavily committed to Hawes's election campaign, which figures prominently in the diary entries. But he also managed to fit in trips to Bristol to review the condition of the Floating Harbour, and he submitted a report on this to the Bristol Docks Company on 3 September 1832.

At the end of January 1833 Brunel surveyed his prospects in tones which were considerably more upbeat than those of his rather morbid secret letter to Hawes of only a few months earlier: 'Having got clear of Election ... etc. I must now seriously attend to business and my journal.'[73] Even the fact that on the Clifton Bridge there was 'nothing doing', and other schemes like that for the Monkwearmouth Dock were in temporary abeyance, did not subdue a sense of hopefulness. While he regretted the years wasted on the Gaz experiments, he was still 'examining some of the more *curious* features and qualities of the gaz with the view of writing a paper for the

Royal Society'. And the Bristol Docks figured with the comment: 'I am still waiting with *expectation* of something being done.' But even more than he anticipated was in the offing. When he went down to Bristol in February to examine the harbour during one of its periodical drainings, he was approached by Roche, his friend on the Merchant Venturers and Dock Company, with a proposal for a railway survey. This appeared for the first time under the abbreviation 'BR' for 'Bristol Railway' in Brunel's diary, as he asked himself: 'How will this end?'[74]

In this way the Great Western Railway was launched. Brunel immediately undertook a preliminary survey of the route from Bristol to Bath, and 'returned to town by mail' on 26 February. But on 1 March he was back in Bristol for the crucial committee to which he presented his views on the proposed railway. Then back to London again for a few days before he 'started outside mail for Bristol' on 6 March to be present for a meeting on 7 March at which he was appointed engineer to the project.[75] Apart from a few engagements elsewhere – to Lincoln in March to examine the Fossdyke Navigation;[76] to Boston in April;[77] to Swansea in July;[78] to Ramsgate with Babbage in August;[79] and to Chelsea Waterworks in November;[80] – much of the rest of his diary consists of brief notes regarding his feverish activity on the route of the railway from Bristol to London. Other items, hurriedly reported, included the marriage of William Hawes, younger brother of Benjamin;[81] the Peckham Reform Dinner;[82] and the start of the work on the improvement of the Bristol Docks.[83] But the railway became all-pervading. It was named as the 'Great Western Railway' in August, with a note assessing 'Mr Saunders an agreeable man'.[84] It dominated the life of Brunel to such an extent that his diary writing came to an end. There are blank pages and a few fragmentary references for 1834 and 1835, but only at the end of the latter did he manage to make a reasonable entry: 'What a blank in my journal! – and during the most eventful part of my life'.[85] He went on to list his engineering commitments and added up their capital value as amounting to £5,320,000 – 'a pretty considerable capital likely to pass through my hands – and this at the age of twenty-nine'. There are a few scrappy entries thereafter, for 1839 and 1840, but for all practical purposes that was the end of Brunel's career as a diarist.

While the decline of Brunel as a diarist is regrettable from a biographical point of view, it is clear that this literary falling off coincided with the ending of the years of preparation and the embarkation on his years of maximum engineering creativity. The diaries and other accounts available from these years demonstrate the emergence of an exceptionally able and independent-minded young engineer. His father continued to help him, with the designs for the Clifton Bridge and even with the early survey drawings for the GWR.

But Marc had his own anxieties with the tunnel, and he knew better than to interfere with the plans of his talented son, and accepted gracefully the role of a proud father. By 1833 I. K. Brunel had fully worked his passage to professional status and independence. St George Burke, Brunel's legal colleague in the early years of the GWR, provided a vivid memoir of him at this time:

> I believe that a more joyous nature, combined with the highest intellectual facilities, was never created, and I love to think of him in the character of the ever gay and kind-hearted friend of my early years ... I believe at that time he scarcely ever went to bed, though I never remember to have seen him tired or out of spirits ... I have never known a man who, possessing courage which to many would appear almost like rashness, was less disposed to trust to chance or to throw away any opportunity of attaining his object ... In the character of a diplomatist ... he was as wary and cautious as any man I ever knew.[86]

Brunel's own reflections, in his personal diary, demonstrate his need for attention, a certain vanity, an enormous ambition, and a tremendous capacity to dream dreams, to have visions of castles in the sky. But they were qualities that animated his restlessness, and set him constantly searching for self-improvement and the achievement of grander schemes. These were the qualities of character which he brought to the profession of engineering, enabling him to carve out a brilliant career for himself.

The five years between the inundation of the tunnel and his appointment as Engineer to the GWR were undoubtedly of considerable significance in his formation as an engineer. The opportunities of practice in his father's undertakings, and most particularly the precocious responsibility thrust upon his youthful shoulders by the Thames Tunnel project, had given him formidable experience in managerial problems, and self-confidence in his own abilities. Easy access to business, scientific and aristocratic circles, provided by his father's reputation, had given him enviable social connections. He numbered leading aristocrats and influential politicians amongst his friends. He mixed freely with the leading London scientists and engineers of his day. He attended learned societies and became a member of several of them. He maintained a vigorous social life, whereby he established the social and personal relationships which led to his marriage. He travelled extensively in search of commissions, taking every opportunity to observe engineering and architectural works as he went around the country. And he made his first encounters with the railways which were to become his gateway to professional success, and his means of transforming his visions of 'castles in the sky' into magnificent works of engineering. All this served to shape the mind and character of the young man and to give him most extraordinary advantages in entering upon his chosen career. The timing could not have been better than in was for him. At the precise moment when he was ready for it, the demand for railways presented him with the opportunity to make a unique contribution to the transport revolution. He seized the opportunity with confidence and enthusiasm.

4

Bristol

Bristol played a crucial part in the career of I. K. Brunel. The city provided him with the vital springboard from which he launched himself upon his first steps as an independent bridge builder, harbour engineer, ship constructor and creator of a railway system. He was drawn to the city in 1829 by the competition for the Clifton Bridge, and he found the company of the merchants and industrialists whom he met there very congenial. He made several enduring friendships amongst them, and found their support immensely helpful at several critical moments in his career. But he never became a Bristolian. Born in Portsmouth and brought up in London, his attitudes were always those of a metropolitan man. When, in the prime of his professional life, he began to think about acquiring a country estate, he chose one much further west than Bristol, at Marychurch near Torquay, although when he died the house he designed there had still not been built. He came, in retrospect, to be regarded as a Bristolian, but this was by affectionate adoption rather than by any claim of birth or domicile. Even then, an element of ambiguity about his relationship with Bristol persisted, because an undertone of disgruntled prejudice against what was seen as his recklessness with the funds of shareholders was widely expressed in the late nineteenth century.[1] But more positive sentiments have prevailed, so that in more recent years Brunel has come to be regarded as one of Bristol's favourite sons.

There is a problem about the precise circumstances that brought Brunel to Bristol. Previous biographers have taken the view that he must have come in the summer of 1828, in the course of recuperating from the injuries which he sustained in the Thames Tunnel inundation in January of that year. There is no doubt about the seriousness of the accident, nor about the initial response of the family to send him to Brighton, nor about his subsequent trip to Plymouth in the summer. All this is recorded in his journals, covering the years 1826–29, but there is no entry relating to Bristol before 1829, except for a brief and cryptic reference in the personal diary, which appears to anticipate a visit to 'Redcliff' in June 1828.[2] It is impossible to tell whether other biographers possessed sources of information in personal documents or family gossip, or were just rounding off inadequate information in a reasonable way. It seems most likely, however, that Brunel received notice of the competition for a new bridge at Clifton from his father, and managed to visit the site in order to make the drawings which he submitted by the deadline on 19 November 1829. Presumably his father made a visit also, as we know that Marc had a hand in the drawings.[3] We may assume that they stayed in a hotel. Brunel subsequently explained, in describing the best procedures to be pursued by a professional engineer, that it was necessary to avoid staying with friends in the course of business visits because this disrupted the work one should be doing, and it is reasonable to consider that this was his normal practice.[4] There is a curious confirmation of this practice in the notebook of the census enumerator for 1841, recording the presence of 'I. K. Brunel, Civil Engineer', at the Lion Hotel, High Street, Bath, on census night, 7 June 1841.[5] But this procedure occasionally makes it difficult to plot the movements of the Brunels when they were away from home.

By the beginning of 1830 there was certainly a bustle of activity in Bristol with which Brunel was involved. The Clifton Suspension Bridge Company had issued a prospectus on 23 January 1830, in which the chairman, Philip Protheroe, had announced that 'none of the Plans delivered in consequence of the Advertisement were suitable for adoption' and that further proceedings would be necessary.[6]

Thereafter frequent diary entries record visits to Bristol by Brunel as he engaged in relationships with a widening range of prominent citizens in the course of acquiring significant engineering commissions in the city. It is clear that he liked the city and the people to whom he referred as 'the spirited merchants of Bristol'. But this raises another enigma about the relationship because, in the judgment of some modern historians, Bristol was deficient in 'spirit' in the nineteenth century. It has been represented as being in the grip of a long-term decline, resulting from its own previous success and complacency, and showing little initiative in breaking out of this trend.[7]

There can be no doubt that Bristol was in comparative decline by the 1820s. For several centuries it had enjoyed the status of being one of the greatest cities of the kingdom, with a major port and large industrial hinterland dominating the western part of England as London dominated the east.[8] From the beginning of the eighteenth century, however, the city had gradually lost this favoured position as other urban centres, and especially Liverpool, had risen in importance and challenged it for trade and markets. The rivalry of Liverpool was felt particularly acutely because, like Bristol, it had good access to the Atlantic trade routes and the lucrative trade in African slaves. Bristolians had established a flourishing interest in this notorious 'Africa trade' in the eighteenth century, with its concomitant industries in tobacco and sugar products, but had given little attention to developing the commercial potential of their port. The merchants of Liverpool, on the other hand, had promoted an astonishingly dynamic development in commercial activities and port facilities that carried on throughout the nineteenth century and overtook Bristol in practically every aspect of urban growth.

Bristol made a belated attempt to retrieve lost ground by ambitious schemes for harbour improvement at the beginning of the nineteenth century. This took shape in the enclosed river-courses of the 'Floating Harbour', so called because ships which had previously been stranded on the tidal river beds twice in every twenty-four hours were now able to remain afloat all the time in what had become in effect an enclosed dock. The new harbour design was constructed under the direction of the great canal and harbour engineer William Jessop between 1803 and 1809, and seemed to give Bristol a chance to catch up with Liverpool.[9] Development languished for another twenty years, however, so that when Brunel arrived on the scene the port was once again badly in need of improvement, and the mercantile community of Bristol was in need of inspiration.

Whether or not Brunel deserves the credit for providing such new energy, there is a remarkable coincidence between his arrival and the spirited commercial revival that occurred in Bristol in the 1830s and 1840s. There were enterprising developments in a wide range of industries such as sugar, soap, tobacco, cocoa, tar distilling and paper processing. The cotton industry established a dramatic new factory on the northern model, naming it the 'Great Western Cotton Factory'. The railways came to Bristol in the elegant shape of the Great Western Railway. And the first transatlantic steam ship service was inaugurated from Bristol by Brunel's *Great Western*. Quite suddenly, Bristol appeared to have re-emerged under the 'Great Western' banner as a serious contender for its lost role as metropolis of the west and second city of the realm. Liverpool took the challenge seriously enough to take steps to retain its advantage, successfully snatching the lead again in transatlantic trade. But several forces, including substantial vested interests and inertia, worked against Bristol. Even as the optimism of the 1830s had been associated with the arrival of Brunel, so the renewed pessimism of the 1850s was linked to his effective withdrawal from Bristol affairs. It is imprudent to be dogmatic, however, in denying the possibility that, with slightly more favourable circumstances, Brunel and his Bristol contemporaries could have achieved a more distinguished industrial record in the second half of the nineteenth century.[10]

Whatever the precise circumstances of Brunel's arrival in Bristol, he was busy in the city from at least 1829, and was immediately involved in the competition to design the new bridge proposed to span the Clifton Gorge. This quickly brought him into the closely-knit circle of the mercantile community in Bristol, where he appears to have been made welcome and where his talents were recognized. The fact that he won the competition, after considerable altercations, and subsequently benefited from the personal support of his friends amongst the Bristol merchants in his port, railway and ship-building projects, indicates the value of this 'Bristol connection' to him. Organized in a self-perpetuating guild as the Society of Merchant Venturers, the leading figures of the Bristol mercantile community were wealthy and well endowed with lands and possessions. Many of the merchant families had made fortunes from the transatlantic slave trade and the industries associated with it, and had acquired substantial estates close to the city. Amongst their leading representatives were the Smyths at Ashton Court, the Eltons at Clevedon and the Brights at Hanham. As mayors and sheriffs and members of the city council, they ran Bristol as a closed corporation and there was some ambiguity in the relationship between their self-interest, which tended to prefer as little change as possible, and their attitudes as City Fathers in a community which needed to change in order to maintain its status. Brunel was befriended by leading members of this group, who then persuaded their colleagues to accept him as their engineer for their bridges, docks, railways and ships. He served them well in all these respects.

The idea of a bridge over the Clifton Gorge had been promoted by William Vick, a Bristol merchant who had left £1000 for the purpose in his will in 1753, with the instruction that when it had accumulated to £10,000 the plan should be put into effect. By 1829 the sum had reached £8000. Inspired by the recent completion of Telford's Menai Suspension Bridge, the Society of Merchant Venturers announced the competition which fired Brunel's imagination. Of the twenty-two designs submitted by the deadline on 19 November 1829, four were by Brunel and were presented in a series of beautifully executed sepia sketches illustrating different schemes for suspension bridges. Brunel's drawings and those of four other contestants were short-listed for adjudication by Thomas Telford, the elderly President of the Institution of Civil Engineers and the outstanding engineer of his day. But Telford faulted all the schemes submitted. Experience at Menai with lateral wind resistance had convinced him that 600 ft was the maximum possible span for a suspension structure. As Brunel's designs varied from 870 ft to 916 ft for their main span, Telford dismissed them as impractical, despite Brunel's careful engineering calculations to show their feasibility. As a result,

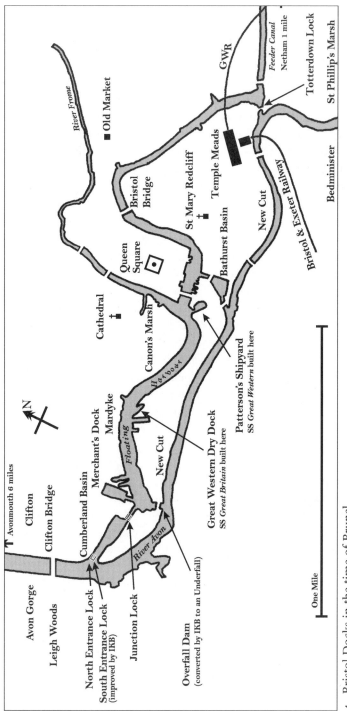

4. Bristol Docks in the time of Brunel.

Telford was invited to submit a design of his own, which he did. But, as this involved the construction of two massive piers from the bottom of the Gorge in order to reduce the central span to one which the engineer regarded as safe, it made the scheme prohibitively expensive as far as the Society of Merchant Venturers was concerned.[11]

The Bridge Trustees attempted to escape from their dilemma by deferring a decision until Telford's scheme had been assessed, alongside some of the best designs in the competition, by a new adjudicator, the scientist Davies Gilbert, assisted by the marine engineer John Seaward. Brunel duly submitted a modified design in which he compromised with the cautious attitude expressed by Telford by reducing the projected main span to 630 ft, with a massive abutment on the Leigh Woods side of the Gorge. Gilbert and Seaward met at Blaise Castle, on the edge of Bristol, on 17 March 1831. They deemed Telford's plan to be too expensive for the funds available, and politely dismissed it. They found fault with the four remaining entries, but after representations from Brunel – who knew Davies Gilbert in the London scientific community, and had attended his *soirées* – they accepted his explanation of his calculations and made his design their first choice. The trustees immediately appointed him 'Civil Engineer for the construction of the Bridge'.[12] A month later they agreed on a prospectus and on terms for Brunel, which were to pay him £2500, being 5 per cent of the estimated cost of erection (£50,000), plus £500 expenses, £800 for a resident engineer, and £400 for an assistant resident engineer.[13] It is not clear how much of these sums was actually paid out, as the bridge was unfinished at Brunel's death, but they seem generous enough as initial terms. After the acceptance of his design, Brunel wrote in high spirits to Benjamin Hawes:

> I have to say that of all the wonderful feats I have performed since I have been in this part of the world, I think yesterday I performed the most wonderful. I produced unanimity amongst fifteen men who were all quarrelling about the most ticklish subject – taste.
>   The Egyptian thing I brought down was quite extravagantly admired by all and unanimously adopted; and I am directed to make such drawings, lithographs, etc. as I, in my supreme judgment, may deem fit; indeed, they were not only very liberal with their money, but inclined to save themselves much trouble by placing very complete reliance on me.[14]

The reference to the 'Egyptian thing' shows that Brunel had converted the Gothic style which he had adopted for most of his earlier designs and that the conception of the bridge had reached a form recognizable as the familiar shape which survives today. There were some further modification, mainly in order to effect economies. The decorative ironwork planned for the piers was abandoned, and the engineers who completed the bridge in 1864 added a third chain to the two designed by Brunel on either side in order to make it stronger than he had intended. In all its leading features, however, the Clifton Bridge was completed as intended by Brunel, although not in his lifetime. It survives as an elegant monument to the talents of its designer.

Having at last agreed to a plan, the bridge trustees of the Merchant Venturers were anxious to begin work quickly. The first sod was turned on 21 July 1831, in a ceremony at which Sir Abraham Elton and Lady Elton of Clevedon Court played a leading part. The recorded account of Sir Abraham's address closed on a prophetic note, as he drew the attention of the assembly to the young engineer who had designed the work:

> The time will come when, as that gentleman walks along the streets or as he passes from city to city, the cry will be raised: 'There goes the man who reared that stupendous work, the ornament of Bristol and the wonder of the age.' [15]

Little immediate progress was made, however, as there were legal difficulties about the approaches on the Leigh Woods side of the Gorge, and it was clear that barely half the estimated cost of £52,000 had been subscribed. So the project faltered. When it was overtaken by civic commotion in Bristol in October it was shelved for five years. A new start was made in 1836, the Marquis of Northampton laying the foundation stone of the Leigh Woods abutment on 27 August during the proceedings of the British Association for the Advancement of Science, which was being held that year in Bristol. The piers were completed in 1840, and a contract was agreed for the iron chains which were duly delivered to the site. But in February 1843 it was announced that the sum of £40,000, including the original Vick legacy, had been spent and that another £30,000 would be needed in order to finish the project. This sum was not forthcoming until after Brunel's death, so that the bridge remained incomplete for twenty years. The chains prepared for the bridge were sold on to the South Devon Railway and were incorporated in the Saltash Bridge, leaving two functionless piers to show to the world at Clifton.[16]

The Bristol Riots, which interrupted the work of bridge building in the autumn of 1831, were a great shock to the *status quo* and constituted one of the worst outbreaks of urban rioting in Britain for over fifty years.[17] The centre of the city was engulfed in a frenzy of arson and violence at the end of October, with the civic buildings around Queen Square and the new city gaol on Prince Street being particular targets. At least twelve rioters died, in addition to those who were later hanged, and the troops called in to quell the disorder acted indecisively and ineffectively. It is not clear precisely what caused the riots, although the national agitation for parliamentary reform at this time, leading up to the Reform Act of the following year, must have been partly responsible. Inevitably, there appear to have been many local issues regarding the conduct of city business by the closed mercantile oligarchy which were felt as grievances at this time, as one of the strangest facts about the events in Bristol was the extraordinary detachment from the turmoil shown by the well-to-do middle classes in the city, at least for the first two days. Much of the initial hostility was directed against the Recorder, Sir Charles Wetherell MP, who had distinguished himself in local affairs as a bitter opponent of parliamentary reform, and there was a sense in which many Bristolians thought that he received his just desserts in the protest. But Wetherell easily slipped away from Bristol, while the momentum of the agitation increased. The mob began to attack property belonging to the corporation in Queen Square, and their indignation was fired further by drink obtained from the well-stocked cellars of these buildings. Colonel Brereton, the officer in charge of the soldiers brought in to restore order, seems to have reflected the ambivalence of Bristol citizenry, because it was only after two days, and after the rioters had moved on to destroy private property, that he gave the order to intervene, with the result that the rioting was quickly terminated. Brereton was subsequently court-martialled for his dilatoriness and took his own life.

One historian of the disturbances has recently concluded: 'There can be no doubt that it was the fate of the Corporation, and not that of the Reform Bill, which was really at issue in Bristol in 1831.'[18] Several modern studies have explored the social psychology of the Bristol Riots in order to explain the outbreak of violence and the slow reaction of the civil and military authorities. These have established that, although the agitation for parliamentary reform provided a general context of social unrest, the immediate causes were indeed of a more local nature. In particular, the agitation derived from the 'decades of widespread loathing for Bristol's executive' in the shape of the oligarchic corporation which exercised in its own interest an effective monopoly over all the institutions of local government.[19] The corporation was dominated by a few dozen rich mercantile families, who had come to exert a dead hand over new enterprises and industrial development. Manufacturers and most of the new professional groups were largely excluded from this self-selecting ruling group, but they had established the Bristol Chamber of Commerce in 1823 in order to oppose the corporation and to seek the removal of restraints on trade. Many influential citizens thus stood aside when the headquarters of the corporation, the Mansion House in Queen Square, came under attack. Only when private property elsewhere in the square was sacked did the mood change. Respectable middle-class citizens then combined to bring the Bristol Riots of 1831 to an end.

The end of the riots provided no immediate relief to the oligarchic control of the city by a mercantile clique. This did not come until 1835, and then only partially, with the passage of the Municipal Corporations Act, which established in Bristol, as in urban government elsewhere, the principle of an elected council with effective powers to organize a police force and to perform other vital functions. These reforms were an important step towards the liberalization of trade and expansion of industry envisaged by Brunel and his close friends. At the same time, it has to be recognized that several of Brunel's friends were themselves members of the commercial oligarchy of which the powers had become a matter of public grievance. His circle of influential acquaintances included both members of the corporation and members of the chamber of commerce. It says much for his native diplomacy that he was able to retain support from both the opposed parties in this divided city.[20]

Brunel arrived in Bristol on Sunday 30 October 1831, the second day of the riots, and reserved space in his diary for an account which was never written. He subsequently gave evidence at the trial of the mayor, Charles Pinney, who like the military was deemed to have behaved ineffectively in the crisis. Although Brunel was thoroughly involved in the disturbances, it is impossible to document fully his part in the affray. He appears to have spent much of the time with his friends Alderman Hillhouse and Nicholas Roche, who were both prominent members of the dominant oligarchy. Before abandoning his diary account he reported:

> Having dressed went down to Bristol heard that there had been some fires and that the 14th were gone – could hardly believe it – went to the Mansion House – found it nearly deserted – it had been broken into again and sacked – armed myself with a chair back and found the guard – Alderman Hillhouse and Mr Roache busy getting the pictures and plate by the roof and through the custom house.[21]

It is probably because he was so much the professional engineer, shunning political involvements, that he managed to retain the friendship of men from a variety of different points of view. But in so far as the Bristol Riots posed a general threat to property, Brunel's reaction to them was the same as that of the property-owning classes whose attitude he shared. However much he enjoyed the excitement, the violence had to be brought under control.

In the aftermath of the Bristol Riots and the cessation of work on the Clifton Bridge, Brunel's prospects appeared to be at a standstill in the first half of 1832. But then, in August of that year, he was introduced to the directors of the Bristol Dock Company by his friend Nicholas Roche. He had met Roche in the Mansion House during the riots and already knew him as a trustee of the Clifton Bridge. Although not directly involved in Brunel's appointment, as he only became a trustee of the Bridge Company in June 1831,[22] Roche quickly formed a high opinion of Brunel's abilities and supported him with the Dock Company and over the nomination to become engineer to the Bristol Railway project in 1833. His illness at the end of that year, and his subsequent retirement to Pembroke, was thus a set-back for Brunel, but by that time Roche had probably already done all he could for his friend.[23]

In 1832 Roche's intervention led to Brunel receiving a commission from the Dock Company to report on the deterioration in the condition of the Floating Harbour, where severe silting was interfering with its operating efficiency. The company was a cumbersome body set up under the terms of the Bristol Docks Act of 1802 to undertake the construction of the Floating Harbour and to manage the affairs of the improved port facilities. It consisted largely of representatives of the Society of Merchant Venturers and the city corporation, and it had been inhibited from the outset by the fact that the harbour works had cost twice Jessop's original estimate, so that the company had adopted a policy of charging high port dues in order to recoup its losses. This proved to be counter-productive, as it drove yet more trade towards Liverpool. Despite the ingenuity of Jessop's conception, the Floating Harbour also encountered problems of pollution and silting which he had badly underestimated, so that within twenty years of its completion it was experiencing persistent operating difficulties. Jessop had maintained high water in the River Avon and the River Frome, around their confluence in the centre of Bristol, by building a dam at Rownham in Hotwells, and he had diverted the high tidal flow in the river into an artificial 'New Cut' running more or less parallel to the Floating Harbour. The harbour was fed from upstream on the River Avon, where another dam at Netham diverted a supply of fresh water into it through the 'Feeder Canal', and excluded the tidal waters in the old course of the river. This system had worked reasonably well at first, but by the 1820s the harbour was being fouled by sewage brought down by the River Frome, and by sandbanks accumulating in its almost stagnant water. Much of the sewage was removed by a culvert from the Frome into the New Cut, with a marked improvement in the atmosphere in the city. But the shoals continued to accumulate, and became a hazard to shipping in the harbour.[24]

This was the situation in which the Bristol Dock Company turned for assistance to the young engineer whose brilliant talents had impressed at least one of its directors. Brunel applied himself energetically to the task of preparing a report, and delivered it on 31 August 1832. He understood at once that the main problem of the Floating Harbour was one of water supply, and that the solution was to maintain a constant flow of water through it:

> A constant stream, though nearly imperceptible in its motion, will carry with it the lighter particles of mud which form the principal part of such deposits [the shoals in the harbour]. If the whole of the River Avon were at all times running through the Float, and which I have no doubt Mr Jessop originally intended should be the case, such a stream might generally be obtained.[25]

Brunel was probably being overgenerous to Jessop on this point, because the original scheme allowed for a considerable overspill from the Netham Dam into the tidal flow of the New Cut. Nevertheless, it led him directly to his main recommendation, which was to raise the height of the Netham Dam and so increase the volume of water passing through the harbour. In addition, he recommended the construction of sluices through the Rownham Dam at the bottom end of the harbour, so that deposits of mud could be scoured out into the New Cut each time the tide fell in the latter. This would have the effect of converting the dam from an 'overfall' weir into an 'underfall'. Brunel recognized that both these recommendations were long-term measures which would keep the Floating Harbour in good condition once it had been cleaned, but that more drastic short-term measures were necessary in order to remove existing shoals. To this end he devised a 'drag-boat', capable of winching itself across the harbour while dragging a spadeful of mud into the middle, from which it could be removed by sluicing.

With characteristic irresolution, the directors of the Dock Company delayed acting on Brunel's recommendations, and then, when they did act, accepted only one of the major proposals deferring any modification to Netham Dam. The conversion of the Rownham Dam from an 'overfall' to an 'underfall' arrangement, with sluices running through its base, and the introduction of a drag-boat, were both carried out under Brunel's supervision in 1833–34, and produced an immediate improvement in the condition of the harbour. He saw that this was a mixed blessing, for when he next made a report to the company, in 1842, he observed that his various short-term measures had been '(perhaps unfortunately) found so effective as to induce a hope that they might be depended upon solely for the removal of the evil; the permanent interests of the Port were, I cannot but think, sacrificed to temporary convenience'.[26] On this occasion he insisted on the need to increase the height of the Netham Dam, and also recommended the construction of a drag-boat to work in the upper parts of the harbour, and these works were completed by 1844. The new drag-boat, which came into use that year, became known as 'BD6' (Bristol Dredger No. 6) and had an exceptionally long working life, as it survived in full working order to the 1960s.[27]

Despite these outstanding services to the Port of Bristol, effectively keeping its harbour in working order for another hundred years, relations between Brunel and the Dock Company became strained in the 1840s. His first two steam ships were built in the Floating Harbour, but both caused problems with the port authorities. The *Great Western* was constructed at William Patterson's shipyard and launched in 1837. When the ship began the following year to operate regularly between Bristol and New York, the Dock Company was less cooperative than it might have been. As a paddle steamer, she was too broad in the beam to work through the entrance locks of the Floating Harbour without dismantling the paddle wheels. As this was too laborious a practice to adopt on every visit to her home port, she took to using berths in the river outside the harbour, eventually using Kingroad near Avonmouth. Yet the company continued to insist on the full payment of harbour dues.[28]

The friction thus generated between the Great Western Steamship Company and the Bristol Dock Company was accentuated when the SS *Great Britain* was floated out of her dry dock into the harbour in 1843, and it became apparent that she was too wide to pass through the entrance lock at Cumberland Basin. Brunel had expected that improvements would have been made at the entrance lock by the time that the ship was ready to leave the harbour, but he did not calculate on the extreme unwillingness of the Dock Company to spend any money on improvements. So he was obliged to bargain with the company in an unseemly manner in order to obtain permission to remove a course of masonry from the side of the lock so that the ship could squeeze through. Once this had been done she never returned to the Floating Harbour until her battered hull was brought home in triumph in 1970.[29] As far as the Port of Bristol was concerned, the ship was a gift to its main rival as it operated for most of its long working life out of Liverpool. When the Steamship Company was wound up in 1848, even the SS *Great Western* was sold off, and spent the rest of her working life based in Southampton.

The moral of these experiences, that the Floating Harbour was becoming inadequate to deal with the large new vessels coming into service in the mid nineteenth century, was abundantly clear to Brunel, but he was unable to persuade the Bristol Dock Company to take measures to deal with this critical situation. They did eventually commission him to build a new entrance lock – and then criticized him for doing so too slowly – but the directors persistently refused to consider the necessity of preparing new deep-water facilities at the mouth of the River Avon. There were several reasons for this. One was the problem of changing the prejudices of Bristol merchants, who were deeply attached to their traditional land-locked river harbour, some eight miles from the open sea. This was compounded by the fact that strong vested interests in warehousing and other dock-side facilities had developed in the Floating Harbour resisted any down-river movement of resources. More particularly, however, the Dock Company had come under strong pressure by the 1840s from a party among the city merchants who objected to its high rates and poor service and sought a remedy through a local government take-over of the harbour. The company was so preoccupied with these criticisms, and so short of capital for new developments, that it was unable to take seriously ideas for a pier to receive transatlantic traffic at Portishead, as promoted by Brunel, or a dock at Avonmouth, both to be served by new railways from the city centre.[30]

There was little change in these respects when the reformers were successful in 1848 in winding up the Bristol Dock Company and replacing it by the Docks Committee of Bristol Corporation. The new committee bustled into action to the discomfort of Brunel, who had still not completed the new entrance lock, but it proved to be as committed as its predecessor to keeping the Floating Harbour as the centre of Bristol port activity rather than preparing for a shift of the port facilities downstream to Avonmouth. Brunel came sadly to the conclusion that Bristol was incapable of making the imaginative jump of envisaging its port as one equipped to meet the trading needs of the future. As early as 1844, when submitting his proposals for the reconstruction of the south entrance lock, he had said: 'I have recommended these dimensions because I believe they would be sufficient to accommodate all ordinary Steam Boats built for the Irish Trade – and this I now think is sufficient for the Port of Bristol'.[31] It was an ominously dismissive attitude for Brunel. He was virtually writing out Bristol from his vision of transoceanic steam ship navigation.

In addition to the change in control of the port of Bristol and the continuing difficulties in operating large steam ships from the Floating Harbour, several other factors combined to worsen Brunel's relations with the port authorities. The most important of these was that, with his extremely heavy commitments on railways and other projects, he certainly did take a long time on the construction of the south entrance lock. He had resolved that the job should be well done, having written to his friend Captain Claxton: 'I think of recommending a thoroughly good lock',[32] and tackled the design with his usual panache. It included novel single-leaf iron caisson gates, one at each end of the lock, which became almost buoyant at high water so that they could be easily winched into the recesses prepared for them in the masonry on the southern side of the lock. Work began in 1844, but was still not complete when the Docks Committee took over control four years later. In fact, it was not until the middle of 1849 that it came into regular use, and even then there were further delays with the installation of the innovative swing bridge over the lock. All sorts of difficulties were encountered with the building work, and Brunel's chief assistant engineer, John Hammond, who had been seconded to the task, died on the job. Altercations between Brunel, the contractors and the Docks Committee dragged on into 1852 before a final settlement was reached. All of this served to sour what had been a creative and mutually beneficial relationship, so that Brunel did no further substantial work for the port of Bristol.

When Brunel had made his first report on the condition of the Floating Harbour, he was actually in a mood of deep despondency about his career, as none of the projects in which he was involved appeared to be making much progress. When plans for a railway link between Bristol and London began to stir at the end of that year, however, they initiated a general revival of activity which quickened in the following years. Between 1833 and 1848 Bristol was the scene for a remarkable burst of political and commercial activity. The reform of municipal government gave the new industrial middle classes enlarged say in local affairs, although this only slowly affected the composition of local leadership. The national agitation for free trade, which reached a crescendo with the repeal of the Corn Laws in 1846, was echoed in Bristol by the movement to encourage trade in the Floating Harbour by reducing dues. And the railways arrived in force. The Great Western Railway was established in 1833, to be closely followed by the Bristol & Exeter Railway in 1836. The Bristol & Gloucester Railway came next, being built in stages and opened in 1844. It was controlled by the GWR until 1844, when the Midlands Railway acquired a majority shareholding and drew it into the narrow gauge network. Amongst other important links, the Bristol & South Wales Railway was promoted in 1845, but not completed to New Passage Ferry until 1863. Brunel played a dominant role in all these Bristol-centred railway enterprises.

Brunel's vision of a railway system involved a novel service of high-speed passenger transport.[33] He came to mastermind one of the largest railway empires in the country, and this was made possible by the Bristol connection, because it was the same enterprising merchants of Bristol, who had already employed him on the Clifton Bridge and on docks improvement who then engaged his professional skills on the new railways. They included Robert Bright, John Cave, Henry Bush, C. P. Fripp, Peter Maze, George Gibbs, John Harford and T. R. Guppy, to most of whom Brunel was already an admired acquaintance. In the case of Guppy at least he was shortly to become a close personal friend. It is hardly surprising, therefore, that when Nicholas Roche suggested him as their engineer, they were ready to accept him, even though he insisted that the quality of the engineering should not be compromised by financial economy. With this Bristol support, Brunel got the job and undertook his masterpiece, the Great Western Railway.[34]

In the early years of the GWR the directors confronted shareholders in Bristol for one of the two half-yearly meetings. These meetings became increasingly difficult as the railway boom of the 1840s collapsed with the fall of George Hudson's Midland Railway empire. At the meeting of the GWR shareholders in August 1849, the directors proposed a reduction in the dividend from 4 per cent to 2 per cent. The oratory of Charles Russell and C. A. Saunders, the chairman and secretary respectively, appear to have carried the day on this occasion. It is not clear whether or not Brunel was required to intervene, but the local newspaper noted disparagingly: 'little Isidore [sic] Brunel, creeping into a corner, laughed securely behind Lord Barrington's shoulder'.[35] Recalling the same incident twenty years later, in connection with the publication of the biography of Brunel by his son, the same newspaper commented more favourably under the heading 'Isambard Kingdom Brunel and the Old Railway Days':

> Though the 'little giant', as some one called him, has been 'gone from our gaze' about thirteen or fourteen years, we can still see him in our mind's eye sitting 'calm as the halcyon' behind the row of Directors at the stormy half-yearly meetings at Temple Meads ... He contemplated the hurly burly before him with the composure of a philosopher and the quiet enjoyment of a humourist, even though his own 'extravagance' was the subject under discussion.[36]

Brunel's presence was certainly regarded as essential to the smooth running of any GWR meeting in those formative years.

As early as October 1835 the GWR board of directors took the decisive step towards extending their railway from Bristol to New York by way of a steam ship service, although it is not certain whether the original idea was Brunel's or Guppy's. The decision gave Brunel another Bristol opportunity, and one which extended substantially his vision of creating a fast and convenient transport service. He seized the opportunity and thereby revealed his genius as a marine engineer. There had been no anticipation of such a development, apart from his general engineering interest in engines, materials and construction techniques encouraged by his father, but without further specialized training he embarked on the design of three strikingly innovatory ships which contributed significantly to the modern transport revolution. As the first two were built in Bristol, their story has become part of the history of the city, so that it is appropriate to consider their significance here.

The *Great Western* and the *Great Britain* were built by the Great Western Steamship Company, which was set up by the GWR in 1835 to undertake the construction of steam ships. Peter Maze, a Bristol merchant with interests in railways and the cotton industry, was its first chairman, and Christopher Claxton was appointed its managing director. Claxton was a retired naval captain who had acted as Quay Warden for the Bristol Dock Company, where Brunel got to know him and found his expertise most useful in several matters relating to the docks. Brunel remained slightly guarded in his relations with Claxton, whom he described obliquely on one occasion as 'a warm friend but changeable and very capable of being a devil of an opponent'.[37] But he found Claxton a valuable source of information on all maritime matters and a most reliable colleague in the construction of his Bristol ships.

The first ship, the SS *Great Western*, was a timber-hulled paddle steamer designed by Brunel and built by William Patterson in his yard at Prince's Wharf. Maudslay and Field provided the power unit with a pair of side-lever steam engines. While the ship was being built, in 1836, the British Association met in the city and Dr Lardner gloomily prophesied that the venture was bound to fail. Lardner was a popular scientific lecturer who made a valuable contribution to statistical knowledge about railways, but who also had a penchant for dogmatic statements about subjects with which he was less familiar. He demonstrated to his own satisfaction that transoceanic steam navigation was not feasible because no steam ship would be able to carry sufficient fuel, in addition to a useful cargo, to make it a commercial success. Brunel was present and responded, but unfortunately no record survives of the exchange.[38] He had considered the mathematics of this problem and had formulated the principle that, while the carrying capacity of a hull increases as the cube of its dimensions, its resistance increases only as the square of those dimensions. In other words, the need for fuel to overcome the resistance and drive the ship forwards increases at a lower rate than the total capacity of a ship, so that as the vessel is made larger the proportion of space devoted to fuel may be safely decreased. Mastery of this principle enabled Brunel to design a hull of sufficient size and correct shape to undertake efficient transatlantic navigation, refuting Lardner and the received consensus of opinion among marine engineers.

In designing the wooden hull of the *Great Western*, with a length of 236 feet and a displacement of 2300 tons, Brunel aimed at securing the maximum possible longitudinal strength. It is clear that he consulted the Admiralty for advice on this subject. The company report of March 1838 declared:

Your Directors cannot allow this opportunity to pass without publicly acknow-
ledging their deep obligation to the Board of Admiralty, by whom an earnest
interest has been shown in your undertaking. Not only have the plans, drawings,
and calculations of her Majesty's Steam Service been readily placed at the disposal
of your Directors, but they are indebted to Sir William Symons for important
suggestions, and to Mr Lang, the able, practical builder, in the Royal Dockyard
at Woolwich, for continual communications of the most valuable character.[39]

This is particularly significant in view of the persistent legend that Brunel
was always at loggerheads with the Admiralty. It shows instead that the
Royal Navy was showing a keen interest at this time in the development of
steam navigation, and that they were prepared to help generously any project
from which they could learn useful lessons themselves.[40]

Construction went ahead smoothly and the ship was duly launched on 19
July 1837, and was taken to London to be fitted out. She was ready to make
her maiden voyage in the spring of the following year, but was delayed by
a fire in her engine room in which Brunel again almost lost his life. The fire
was soon extinguished, but Brunel fell off a ladder of which the rungs had
been charred, and it was fortunate for him that his fall was broken by Claxton,
who was standing underneath. But Brunel was sufficiently badly injured to
be carried off the ship, and he was unable to accompany the maiden voyage
across the Atlantic. She sailed to Bristol on 31 March 1838 and departed for
New York on 8 April, arriving fifteen days and five hours later. She was
narrowly beaten for the honour of the first westward steam-powered Atlantic
crossing by the *Sirius*, an Irish packet boat hastily adapted for the purpose
by rivals in Liverpool. But whereas the *Sirius* had struggled desperately to
keep up steam by burning anything combustible, the *Great Western* arrived
in New York with 200 tons of coal in reserve.[41]

The *Great Western* triumphantly vindicated the skills of her engineer and
the confidence of her supporters, for she went on to become a great
commercial success and quickly came to require a sister ship. The Great
Western Steamship Company recognized the importance of such a sister
ship with which it could hope to conduct a shuttle-service across the Atlantic
and secure the remunerative mail contract. In the event, they did not move
quickly enough, because their rivals in Liverpool grasped more swiftly the
way things were going and had already commissioned new steam ships
for the Atlantic traffic. It was thus Cunard which acquired the mail contract
for Liverpool and which quickly developed a reliable shuttle-service across
the ocean. The Bristol company was further delayed by problems nearer
home. Work had begun on the new ship by July 1839, with Brunel being
commissioned once again to design it. But it immediately became clear
that the vessel conceived by Brunel would be too large for Patterson, so the

company undertook its own construction and acquired a dry dock for the purpose. Claxton remained as manager of the ernterprise, while Guppy became involved as 'Directing Engineer', the two making a very effective team with Brunel. T. R. Guppy was a manufacturing engineer in Bristol. He came from a prominent Bristol merchant family with interests in the copper trade. He worked harmoniously with Brunel and the two came close to establishing a formal partnership, to judge from the surviving correspondence between them.[42]

Brunel could not rest with a repetition of his earlier success, but designed a ship, the SS *Great Britain*, which was not only much larger than its predecessor, but was also the first large ship to be built in iron and, after a change in plan in the course of construction, the first large screw-propelled ship. Brunel had the major responsibility not only for the hull, which was – and remains – a brilliant piece of technical perfection, but also for the engine and the screw. It is unfortunate that only fragments of the documentary material about this work have survived. Brunel adopted his father's idea for a large marine engine, with four inclined cylinders driving upwards to a common crankshaft on which was mounted a wide drum carrying four toothed chains which drove the propeller shaft. The engine developed an indicated horsepower of 1500 at eighteen revolutions per minute, and was the largest marine propulsion unit of its day. The design of the propeller also demonstrated Brunel's innovative genius. The device was so new that it had received no large-scale testing, and Brunel contrived with the Admiralty to adapt a naval ship, HMS *Rattler*, to conduct a series of tests from which they both benefited. The inventor of the screw propeller, Francis Pettit Smith, was not so fortunate, although his innovation came to be generally adopted for marine propulsion.[43]

The ship was floated out of her dry dock on 19 July 1843, at a lavish ceremony over which Prince Albert presided. The *Great Britain* was 322 feet long and had a displacement of 3018 tons. She was fitted out in Bristol City Docks, but was then trapped there for eighteen months until Brunel could negotiate her release with the Bristol Dock Company. This was achieved with great difficulty on 11 December 1844, and late that night Brunel wrote to the directors of the South Wales Railway apologizing for his inability to attend their meeting the next day:

> We have had unexpected difficulty with the *Great Britain* this morning. She stuck in the lock. We *did* get her back. I have been hard at work all day altering the masonry of the lock. Tonight, our last tide, we have succeeded in getting her through but being dark we have been obliged to ground her outside, and I confess I cannot leave her till I see her afloat again and all clear of our difficulty here. I have as you will admit much at stake here and I am too anxious to leave her.[44]

Having left Bristol, the new ship proceeded to Liverpool to complete her fitting out and to begin her long operating career from that port. She did not return to Bristol until her rusting hull was brought home from the Falkland Islands in 1970.[45]

The *Great Britain* was substantially larger than her predecessor, for which she did not provide a realistic sister ship. She was, nevertheless, an extraordinarily innovative ship and had an exceptionally long and successful operating life. This was despite almost coming to grief in 1846 when she ran aground in Dundrum Bay on the coast of northern Ireland and spent the winter exposed to storms which would have broken up any other ship. Her rescue on that occasion produced an astonishing frenzy of activity by Brunel, who castigated his colleagues for abandoning her 'like a useless saucepan' on the beach and directed them in providing her with a protective sheath so that she could be salvaged successfully the following spring. The ship was refloated and found to have suffered only minimal damage, but the episode brought the Great Western Steamship Company to liquidation and the ship was sold. She went on to operate for other owners on the North Atlantic, as a troopship in the Crimean War, and then for many years on the long run to Australia. The great strength of her hull made possible several drastic refits with new engines and additional decks, and she remains today a tribute to the skill and vision of her designer.[46]

In addition to the Clifton Bridge, the harbour improvements, the railways and the first two of his three ships, all of which demonstrated the astonishing virtuosity of his engineering talents, Bristol provided Brunel with a context for various other engineering tasks. Amongst these, the project for a deep-water pier at Portishead, with a railway connection to Bristol, was the most significant. It led to the establishment of the Portbury Pier and Railway Company with a capital of £200,000 in 1846, and it would have enabled Bristol to maintain a stake in the transatlantic steam trade. But it was abandoned before completion in 1852, even though a very similar scheme was undertaken and finished in the following decade. Brunel was also instrumental in setting up the engineering works for the Clifton Water Works in the 1840s, with a pumping station in the Clifton Gorge, but these were absorbed into the much larger undertaking of the Bristol Waterworks Company. Again, Brunel contributed marginally to ecclesiastical architecture in the city by responding to an invitation from the Dean of Bristol to examine some defects in the fabric of Bristol Cathedral by proposing: 'to give a couple of hours for a cursory inspection to form some opinion of the subject ... I can be at the Cathedral at 5 o'clock on Tuesday morning next, having to leave Bristol by train to Exeter at 7.50.' We must assume that the Dean kept the appointment, as Brunel went on to make an examination and presented a report, although he did not recommend any immediate action.[47]

By the end of the 1840s, the group of intimate friends on whom the success of Brunel's relationship with Bristol depended had begun to disperse. Roche had already long since gone into retirement in Pembroke. Guppy removed to Italy in 1849 after the collapse of the Great Western Steamship Company, apparently for health reasons, and established a successful engineering business in Naples. Claxton remained involved in Brunel's enterprises, but left Bristol to live in London. So the bonds of personal affection which had tied Brunel closely to Bristol and made him proud to describe himself as 'a Bristol man' were loosened, and other preoccupations were borne in upon him which removed him still further from the affairs of the city. To the end, however, he retained his interest in Bristol and proclaimed his readiness to assist 'the spirited merchants of Bristol' in any worthwhile enterprise.[48]

It is tempting to speculate that, with a little more support in Bristol for his conception of a new terminus for transatlantic liners at Avonmouth, the city could have arrested the long secular decline in which it found itself in the nineteenth century. This solution certainly seems to have worked a generation after Brunel, when the development of dock facilities at Avonmouth ensured the prosperous recovery of Bristol in the twentieth century. There can be no doubt, however, that Brunel and Bristol served each other well: Brunel enabled Bristol to retard the process of decline, while Bristol provided Brunel with the essential launch-pad for the consummation of his vision of a modern transport system. Voices were raised in Bristol, then and subsequently, against his rashness and extravagance, but posterity has decided more generously in his favour so that Bristolians are now generally glad to regard I. K. Brunel as an adopted citizen. This is a happy end to a great creative partnership.

5

The Great Western Railway

Isambard Kingdom Brunel was a visionary. He had an extraordinary capacity for seeing the possibilities of a good idea, for working out in detail the implications of putting it into practice, and for realizing in substantial form the shape of his 'castles in the air'. This faculty did not always contribute towards his success as an engineer, because it led him to undertake projects which were sometimes beyond the imagination of his contemporaries to accept, in circumstances in which more routine solutions to the engineering problems were easily available. But it did give a distinctive quality of ingenuity and excitement to everything he did. That is why it is important, in making any assessment of the engineering work of Brunel, to look beyond description and the fulfilment or otherwise of contractual requirements, and to seek to understand the vision which they encapsulate. This is particularly appropriate with those works which were central to his vision of a transport revolution bringing fast long-distance travel within the reach of everybody who could pay for it. The outstanding examples of such works are the railways of the Great Western Railway system.[1]

Once Brunel had become the Engineer to the GWR, his vast resources of energy, which had been underused since the collapse of the Thames Tunnel project, were turned to realizing the vision of an integrated railway system. He continued to attend to other projects, such as harbour works and bridges, but for over ten years the main focus of his activity was the GWR and its subsidiary lines. From the moment when he had taken his first ride on the newly opened Liverpool & Manchester Railway in 1831, he had conceived the notion of a new type of transport system and sought a way of bringing it into reality. He had to wait another fifteen months before his chance came but then, in March 1833, he received the commission to undertake the huge work that became the Great Western Railway. He was then only twenty-seven, but this had not prevented him from telling the directors that he was not prepared to consider an inferior or penny-pinching solution to what he immediately envisaged as a design requiring vision on a grand scale. When it became clear from the questions put to him by the appointing committee that they were seeking an economical fulfilment of their project, Brunel rebuked them:

> You are holding out a premium to the man who will make you the most flattering promises, and it is quite obvious that he who has the least reputation at stake, or the most to gain by temporary success, and the least to lose by the consequent disappointment, must be the winner in such a race.[2]

Thanks to his vision and personal charm he got the job, although only by a narrow margin, as several of the directors preferred more conventional candidates. On reflection after his interview, Brunel felt that he had run it too close for comfort, and that the opposition had almost defeated him. But once installed he immediately applied all his remarkable energy to the first of his grand designs.[3]

The Great Western Railway was one of several major railway projects that were under construction in the mid 1830s. Opening in 1830, the Liverpool & Manchester Railway is generally regarded as the first of the modern railways, in the sense of offering a fully timetabled service for goods and passengers, and its immediate success encouraged entrepreneurs and investors elsewhere to explore the possibilities of the new transport system. From being a somewhat despised provincial figure, working in the colliery districts of Tyneside in north-east England, George Stephenson had come to win reluctant admiration from would-be railway promoters, who were now inclined to take seriously his notion of a national network of railways linking all the main districts and urban centres. It seemed natural to begin by linking the Liverpool & Manchester line with London and the south through the Grand Junction Railway, launched in 1833, and the London & Birmingham Railway, started in the same year. George Stephenson himself was engaged to build the former, although in the event most of the work was directed by Joseph Locke. The engineer of the London & Birmingham was Robert Stephenson, making his first independent step into civil engineering (as distinct from mechanical engineering, although the distinction had not yet been institutionalized). The London & Southampton followed in 1834, with Locke as engineer. Then came the Great Western Act in 1835, and the Eastern Counties, subsequently the Great Eastern, in 1836. And in addition to these trunk routes there appeared the first of a gigantic flood of railway schemes, especially for lines in and around the metropolis, as the vogue for railway construction in Britain rapidly gathered momentum.[4]

It is not easy to recall, after a hundred and seventy years of experience of this mode of transport, what was expected of these early railways. We can be fairly certain, however, from the recorded views of George Stephenson, that his expectations and those of his followers amongst the engineering community were primarily directed towards the carriage of goods at modest speeds all over the country: their emphasis was on accessibility rather than speed, and the possibility of passenger transport was regarded as a welcome bonus rather than as a primary objective. We can be reasonably sure that nobody at the time could have conceived the profound effect that the railways were to have on the economies of all the industrializing nations in the decades which lay ahead. In their concentration of unprecedented amounts of capital; in their stimulus to the coal, iron, steel and engineering industries which provided their essential fuel and equipment; and in their galvanizing effect on every industry which benefited from their vastly improved transport services, the railways were revolutionary. They transformed, first, the economic and social life of Britain, and thereafter the economic systems of Europe, America and the rest of the world. This was a development without precedent in either its scale or its far-reaching consequences for life in industrial societies.

The role of I. K. Brunel in designing the Great Western Railway has to be seen against this background in order to appreciate the magnitude of his achievement. Unlike most other railways, the GWR was conceived as a whole, like a work of art, with the mind of the artist establishing the guiding principles and ensuring that every detail harmonized in the overall pattern. This was to be no work of minimal engineering, cutting all possible corners in order to save the pockets of its investors. The GWR provided Brunel with the opportunity to express in full and in detail the comprehensive ideas which he had framed for an ideal railway. It was to be the best of all possible railways, 'the finest work in England', designed in all respects to achieve the highest standards available to the best engineering practice of the time.[5] He seized the opportunity to undertake a major creative work, well prepared by his training in engineering principles and practices, and tempered by his experience of persuading colleagues and leading a varied team of men.

Brunel's vision for the GWR departed from what was then the standard view of railway construction in two important respects: he envisaged a system, first, which was primarily devoted to the movement of passengers; and, secondly and following from this, one which would achieve high speeds in order to reduce journey times. These criteria determined his integrated approach to the design of the railway, which he saw as a system of interdependent parts, the efficiency of each being essential to the smooth operation of the whole. The creation of any such system required a series of stages. The first stage was the promotion of the project, in which support was canvassed and necessary legislation acquired. Secondly, there was the survey, to secure the best possible route for the railway. Thirdly, came the construction stage, in which the vital civil engineering works were performed. Fourthly, the operation of the system required provision of the necessary locomotives, rolling stock, stations and signalling to be in place. Fifthly, measures of consolidation were needed, to prepare the sub-structure of workshops, offices and accommodation which would guarantee the permanence of the enterprise. And sixthly, there was the further development of the railway to be considered, whereby long-term modifications and extensions could be introduced, and viable relationships established with neighbouring railways. These stages were not entirely chronological and overlapped in time: the work of surveying the route began while the essential Act of Parliament was being promoted, and the railway began to operate in instalments as stretches of new line became available. They were all essential parts of a cumulative process, and Brunel took a leading part in each of these stages in the creation of the GWR, supervising the whole process and taking all the major engineering decisions.

The promotion of the scheme involved making an initial survey and acquiring an Act of Parliament, and this in turn meant preparing the necessary legislation and submitting it to parliamentary enquiry. From the moment of his appointment as Engineer, Brunel threw himself into these tasks. He was not, of course, the only active promoter, and in particular he was powerfully supported by Charles Alexander Saunders (1796–1864), the secretary of the London committee of directors, who subsequently became the first secretary of the whole company. MacDermot claimed of Saunders that he 'was destined to do more towards founding the Great Western Railway system than any other single individual, Brunel himself not even excepted'.[6] But Saunders's role in promoting the enterprise was concentrated on raising individual and financial support for it, whereas Brunel was fully responsible for determining the route, and establishing the necessary engineering works. Saunders frequently relied on Brunel's support in order to persuade a wavering investor to risk his capital, and the two must have made a formidable team. Nevertheless, they had enormous difficulty raising sufficient funds to make possible an application for parliamentary powers, and even then they did so by curtailing the enterprise to the more accessible stretches at the two ends of the projected trunk route. Brunel meanwhile undertook the preliminary survey that selected the route, choosing the northerly option through the Vale of White Horse rather than the southerly one through Newbury and the Kennet valley. This choice provided easier overall gradients, and ensured better access to Oxford, Gloucester and the north. At the two ends, there were simpler choices: the route from London to Reading was straightforward, apart from some indecision about the terminus before Paddington was selected; and from Bristol to Bath Brunel quickly established his preference for the Avon valley route, rather than one already developed to serve the collieries of the Bristol coalfield swinging northwards through Kingswood and Bitton. The initial survey was thus achieved by a rapid inspection of the alternative routes conducted almost entirely by Brunel, and it equipped the two committees of directors, one in London and the other in Bristol, to prepare the Bill which was submitted to Parliament in November 1833.

This was then submitted to detailed scrutiny at the committee stage in the House of Commons, a process that began on 16 April 1834 and occupied fifty-six days, during eleven of which Brunel was subjected to close cross-examination in which he demonstrated his comprehensive knowledge and authority. His legal colleague, acting on behalf of the company, was St George Burke, who was tremendously impressed by Brunel's natural skill as a witness. Burke told charming anecdotes about Brunel, such as his description of Brunel's device of a string carried across the road from Burke's apartment to ring a bell and wake him up in order to get them both to the committee meetings on time.[7] Although Brunel's skilful advocacy helped to overcome the opposition to the Bill in the Commons, it was thrown out by the House of Lords at the end of July 1834. But it was resubmitted in the following session, and this time the chairman of the Commons committee was Charles Russell, MP for Reading, who was in favour of the Bill and helped to get it through with less difficulty than the previous measure. A few years later, Russell became chairman of the GWR, and it was his deft control of the business that made him, together with Saunders and Brunel, one of the triumvirate of powerful figures who led the company through its early years. Brunel had to defend his decision to build a long tunnel at Box before the committee, but he did this with his usual panache and the Bill was passed once more in the Commons. It then went to the Lords, where Lord Wharncliffe was chairman of the committee responsible for its examination, and he steered it through to a satisfactory conclusion. Objections to the Box Tunnel received another airing, as did the opposition of Eton College to having the proposed line in close proximity. The Bill was then passed and received the royal assent on 31 August 1835, and the Great Western Railway Company was at last incorporated.

While these parliamentary engagements were being conducted, the project required promotion in other respects because it was essential to raise the initial capital of £2,500,000, and to placate, as far as possible, the many parties who felt their interests threatened by the proposed railway. These measures demanded the constant attention of Brunel, who was called upon to persuade potential investors to become shareholders, and to mollify people who objected to the proposal to carry the railway across their property. There could be no compulsory purchase until the Act was passed, but the more landowners who could be pacified in advance, the easier the passage through Parliament. The most vociferous objections, such as those of Eton College already mentioned, reached the parliamentary committees, and it was not until the trains were operating on the line that Eton changed its mind and recognized that the GWR posed no threat to the morals of its pupils. But for most small-scale objections it was desirable to make settlements in advance of completion, and Brunel travelled extensively in the course of such negotiations.[8]

When the GWR Act became law, the detailed survey of the whole route from London to Bristol got under way. By this time Brunel had acquired a team of assistants, who set to work under his close supervision. J. R. Hammond was put in charge of the eastern end of the project, while G. E. Frere took over the Bristol end. Both were appointed as resident engineers, and both had two or three assistants. None of them, however, were encouraged to take any initiatives on their own: Brunel saw them as extensions to his own eyes and ears, and expected them to fulfil his directions in every detail. His constant personal supervision was made possible by his acquisition of a specially constructed horse-drawn carriage in which he could travel the course of the proposed line, sleeping and writing in it to save time returning home or to his London office. He spent many weeks on the go in this britzska, nicknamed the 'Flying Hearse' by his staff and the contractors, who must have watched its regular arrival with some apprehension as it brought Brunel with his next whirlwind of instructions and incisive criticisms. Writing to Hammond on one occasion when he was not able to see him in person, Brunel observed: 'Between ourselves, it is harder work than I like. I am rarely much under twenty hours a day at it.'[9] But thanks to his dedication, the line was surveyed with consummate skill and thoroughness, and the myriad negotiations for access and purchase were conducted with diligence.

Construction could thus begin over a well-prepared route. Brunel masterminded every detail of the civil engineering works. The most distinguishing feature of the new line was the novel track bed with broad gauge lines set on continuous baulks of timber. Brunel argued persuasively that this was necessary in order to achieve the sustained high speeds which he envisaged for his trains. The Stephenson-style permanent way of 4ft 8½ ins gauge – the 'narrow' or 'standard' gauge for colliery tramways on Tyneside and extrapolated thence over the rest of the national system by the success of Tyneside engineers – with iron rails laid over stone blocks, was regarded as inadequate by Brunel for the sort of speeds which he intended to introduce. So while other railways adopted the narrow gauge as a matter of course, Brunel managed to avoid a commitment to a specific gauge in the legislation and then, in a masterful piece of special pleading, persuaded his directors to adopt a wider gauge. In a report presented in September 1835, he argued in favour of a broad gauge which would permit a lowering of the centre of gravity of the rolling stock, the adoption of larger wheels, and the diminution of friction. By thus expressing the engineering advantages of the broad gauge, he indicated his intention of securing high operating speeds as a matter of routine practice on the new railway.

Brunel considered the possible objections to this scheme, but the only one which in his view constituted a 'real obstacle to the adoption of the plan' was 'the inconvenience in effecting the junction with the London and Birmingham Railway'.[10] He regarded this problem as capable of being over-come by providing an additional rail for mixed-gauge working, but he did not envisage the more general inconvenience which would be caused by the break of gauge. The directors were impressed by Brunel's reasoning, and adopted his proposal. He went on to devise his innovative and controversial 'broad gauge' of 7 ft, with the rails firmly bedded on longitudinal sleepers which were themselves fixed by piles driven into the ground beneath. In fact, he made the permanent way too firm, so that it gave passengers an uncom-fortably 'hard' ride, and he had to remove the piling in order to restore some flexibility. But the objective was secured, namely, the provision of track that was sufficiently firm and stable to take trains travelling at very high speeds.[11]

The problem of discomfort caused by over-firm piling of the track was quickly recognized and dealt with. Other problems of the broad gauge line were not so easily accommodated. The greatest of these was that of the break of gauge as traffic moved between the GWR and other railways. Although he was aware that this presented difficulties, Brunel played them down in his reports to the directors. He appears to have thought that other railways would adopt the broad gauge once its merits had been established. He also envisaged his railway dominating such a large segment of south-west England and Wales that there would be little need to transfer to other railways operating on a narrow gauge. But he was not consistent in this view, as he used the narrow gauge himself for some of the 'feeder' lines into the GWR, such as the Taff Vale Railway, which created a need for transfer between gauges within his own system. It seems likely that he simply underestimated the problem in so far as it involved relationships with rival, and sometimes hostile, companies.

Work went ahead rapidly from both ends of the railway, with a special team engaged on the Box Tunnel, the largest engineering work on the line, linking the east and west ends. Difficulties with the tunnel delayed the opening of through-running from London to Bristol until 30 June 1841, but long before that partial-running had been extended gradually from both ends as the track was completed. The first section, from Paddington to Maidenhead, had opened on 4 June 1838, incorporating the splendid brick Wharncliffe Viaduct, for the construction of which the first GWR contract was issued. The days of the large-scale contractor, able to undertake commissions to build a whole railway, had not yet arrived, and the GWR negotiated contracts with a host of small operators, most of them with local businesses. Some of these proved themselves to be efficient and reliable, but in many cases there were serious breakdowns of contractual responsibilities, so that the railway was obliged to complete many of them itself. The contract for the Wharncliffe Viaduct, with its eight semi-elliptical arches across the Brent valley at Hanwell, went to Messrs Grissel & Peto, who were subsequently to emerge as a very large business.

Brunel had commissioned some locomotives to be ready for the opening of the first stretch of line. He had attended to the specifications for these engines and all other aspects of a fully operational system, but he came close to disaster when his locomotives behaved erratically and failed to give reliable service. For all his great gifts, Brunel was not an outstanding steam engineer, and his designs for these machines were defective in several respects.[12] He was narrowly saved by two strokes of good fortune. First was his success, in July 1837, in securing the services of Daniel Gooch (1816–1889), a young engineer from the north of England devoted to the idea of high-speed passenger traffic operating over a broad gauge track. Gooch wrote to Brunel in July 1837 hoping for a post, and when they met for the first time a few weeks later Brunel immediately appointed the twenty-one-year old Gooch as Chief Locomotive Assistant to the GWR. His enthusiasm and capacity for hard work were straightaway applied to the task of making Brunel's remarkable set of locomotives function effectively.

The second piece of good fortune was the availability of an excellent locomotive from Robert Stephenson's workshops on Tyneside. This was *North Star* which, adapted to broad gauge service, arrived in November of the same year and became the most reliable engine available when the first stretch of line opened the following summer. The combination of Gooch's diligence and the supply of excellent Stephenson locomotives which followed *North Star* enabled the GWR services to recover from a shaky start, and thereafter Gooch's skill in building a fleet of superb locomotives made it possible to fulfil the aspirations of himself and his chief. It was typical of Brunel's approach to the enterprise that, with the line approaching completion throughout, he wrote a New Year letter to Daniel Gooch in 1841:

I look forward with considerable anxiety to the period now fast approaching when we shall have to conduct a concern of most unusual magnitude and scattered over great distances and throughout which we have undertaken to obtain results at least equal nay superior to others. While from the number of trains we run and the speed to be maintained our difficulties are greater ... I feel that an extraordinary degree of *system* and *method* will alone enable us to succeed.[13]

He enclosed a paper setting out the system, and showing how his mind ranged over the whole field.

One feature to which Brunel gave considerable attention was the method of signalling, and the apparatus installed for this purpose. Signalling in general was extremely haphazard on the early railways, and the GWR seems to have relied on railway policeman to make appropriate hand-signals to passing trains when the first stretches of line were opened. But by 1841 Brunel had devised the 'disc-and-crossbar' signals which were then installed throughout the broad gauge system, and did good service for many years. He also designed capstans for working points, and a system of coded lights for night operations. Brunel took a pioneering interest in the 'Electric Magnetic Telegraph', which was being promoted in the 1830s by Cooke and Wheatstone, and installed it on the line from Paddington to West Drayton in 1839. It won fame in 1845 as the means by which a murderer taking a train from Slough to Paddington was apprehended, but once this excitement was over the system seems not to have been extended and fell into disuse. Not until 1850 was a satisfactory arrangement made for the general extension of the telegraph over GWR lines.[14]

The pressure of maintaining close supervision over all these activities, in promoting, surveying, constructing and ensuring the efficient operation of the new railway system, implied an astonishing work-load for Brunel, and he came close to collapsing under the strain. Even though he recruited some excellent officers and received consistent support from the leading directors of the company, there were times, particularly in 1837 and 1838 when the first parts of the line were opened to traffic, when the problems inherent in Brunel's innovations brought poor initial performance and enraged a significant opposition amongst the 'Liverpool Group' of shareholders to demand his replacement by Stephenson or some other more conventional engineer. The directors, at both the Bristol end and the London end, held firm in their support, but it was a close thing. George Henry Gibbs, who was chairman of the London Committee from 1833 to 1840, and a firm friend to Brunel, confided his misgivings to his private diary in the summer of 1838:

With all his talent he [IKB] has shown himself deficient, I confess, in general arrangement; I mean in arranging his work in his own mind so as to enable him to proceed with it rapidly, economically and surely. There have been too many mistakes; too much of doing and undoing.[15]

The directors conceded to the opposition to the extent of calling for reports from two other engineers, Nicholas Wood and John Hawkshaw. Wood made a long-winded and non-commital report, only risking a strong statement of opinion in relation to the over-piling of the track. Hawkshaw, a young engineer five years junior to Brunel, was more outspokenly critical of the broad gauge. He described all the serious problems associated with the break of gauge and concluded that it was necessary to abandon the broad gauge and to conform with general practice in the nation. But Brunel recovered his composure and fought back. Aided by Daniel Gooch and the supply of fine locomotives from Robert Stephenson, the situation improved and the operation became profitable. Once the line had opened throughout, in June 1841, Brunel's position was secure, and Hawkshaw's report was quietly shelved. Even though Brunel's salary was reduced when the major works were completed, he retained his post as Chief Engineer to the GWR to his death in 1859.[16]

The opening of the line from London to Bristol in June 1841 was only one of a succession of such events. After the first section, from London to Maidenhead, came into service in June 1838, the line pressed on westwards. The completion of Brunel's Maidenhead Bridge, with its gracefully elongated main arch, which aroused criticism of his design but which has been vindicated by continuous heavy use, enabled the railway to be opened to Twyford in July 1839. Then the formidable two-mile cutting at Sonning Hill, sixty feet deep at the middle, opened the way to Reading by March 1840. This linked with work already under way through the Goring Gap, including two more crossings over the River Thames, to be opened to passenger traffic as far as Faringdon Road station, beyond the modern Didcot junction, in July of the same year. The long stretch through the Vale of White Horse to Hay Lane at Wootton Basset was open by December 1840, passing to the north of the small town of Swindon which was about to be adopted by the GWR as the base for its main workshops. There were heavy earth-works beyond Wootton Basset, where the line dropped down to Chippenham in the upper Avon valley, and this was opened on 31 May 1841. An imposing masonry viaduct over the main road into the town then took the line out towards the long cutting which approached the eastern end of the Box Tunnel.

Meanwhile, the line was being pushed eastwards from Bristol with equal vigour. Brunel had met some of the promoters of the railway in March 1833, the month when he was appointed engineer, and claimed to have 'frightened them a little about the difficulties and expense of the Bristol end'.[17] This was because of the need to construct two short tunnels, and then a longer tunnel under Brislington, before hugging the River Avon upstream to

1. Portrait of I. K. Brunel, seated at his desk, painted about 1844 by J. C. Horsley. (*City of Bristol Museum and Art Gallery*)

4. Clifton Suspension Bridge, completed as a memorial to I. K. Brunel in 1864, and still carrying a considerable volume of suburban traffic.

5. Hungerford Suspension Bridge, shown in an early Fox Talbot photograph of about 1844.

3. Mary Horsley, who married I. K. Brunel in 1836: the sketch for a portrait by her brother, J. C. Horsley.

4. Clifton Suspension Bridge, completed as a memorial to I. K. Brunel in 1864, and still carrying a considerable volume of suburban traffic.

5. Hungerford Suspension Bridge, shown in an early Fox Talbot photograph of about 1844.

1. Portrait of I. K. Brunel, seated at his desk, painted about 1844 by J. C. Horsley. (*City of Bristol Museum and Art Gallery*)

2. Portrait of Marc Isambard Brunel, painted about 1835 by Samuel Drummond, with the Thames Tunnel in the background. (*National Portrait Gallery*)

6. The SS *Great Britain* in Bristol Floating Harbour in 1844: another early Fox Talbot photograph.

7. The SS *Great Britain*, now undergoing restoration in the Bristol dry dock in which she was built. (*R. A. Buchanan*)

12. A photographic portrait of Brunel probably taken about 1855.

10. The Cumberland Basin swing bridge, shown here below the modern fly-over, was one of Brunel's first experiments in wrought-iron bridge construction. (*R. A. Buchanan*)

11. The Royal Albert Bridge over the Tamar, completed in 1858, was the largest of Brunel's wrought-iron bridges.

12. A photographic portrait of Brunel probably taken about 1855.

6. The SS *Great Britain* in Bristol Floating Harbour in 1844: another early Fox Talbot photograph.

7. The SS *Great Britain*, now undergoing restoration in the Bristol dry dock in which she was built. (*R. A. Buchanan*)

8. A broad gauge locomotive emerging from the Box Tunnel in J. C. Bourne's engraving of 1846.

9. Temple Meads Station, Bristol: the original train shed as depicted by J. C. Bourne in 1846.

Keynsham. Thereafter, there was a cutting and short tunnel in Saltford and a brush with an unexpected Roman villa site in Newton Meadows (Frere and his assistant engineer, T. E. M. Marsh, were allowed a short time to remove the tessellated pavement), and so by another short tunnel into Twerton and by stretches of viaduct into Bath. The railway remained south of the River Avon through Bath, except for Bath Spa Station itself, which was approached by river-crossings from both ends. That from Bristol was by a skew bridge of laminated timber arches over a pier in the centre of the river. The eastern crossing, by St James's Bridge, was a more conventional masonry structure. The line from Bristol to Bath, with it fine covered station and neo-Jacobean façade, was opened to traffic on 31 August 1840. Brunel's route described an elegant S-bend out of Bath, following the line of the Kennet & Avon Canal and cutting a theatrical swathe through Sidney Gardens. Then it crossed the Avon again and followed the valley of the By Brook up to the portal of Box Tunnel, with a short tunnel under a shoulder of hill as it approached the main tunnel.

The Box Tunnel, the major engineering work on the line, remained the final link to be completed before the route from London to Bristol could be opened throughout. Over a mile and three-quarters in length, this was driven in a straight line on a falling gradient of one in a hundred from the Chippenhan end westwards towards Bath. Work had begun on sinking the six permanent shafts from which the tunnel was excavated in September 1836, and contractors were then appointed to undertake the main work. These were George Burge of Herne Bay, who excavated the western mile and a quarter, which was lined with brick; and two local teams under Brewer and Lewis, who received the contract for the other half mile at the eastern end. This section was through a thick bed of greater oolite which has subsequently been mined in large quantities as a source of Bath stone. Brunel left this unlined. He appointed his assistant engineer William Glennie to be in charge of the work. It was a huge undertaking, involving a labour force of several thousand navvies, apart from the use of gunpowder and the assistance of several hundred horses and steam pumps to remove spring water which threatened to flood the tunnel, entirely by human hand power. It has been estimated that a hundred of them perished during the construction of the tunnel. Even with all this effort, all the rest of the line was finished before the tunnel was complete in June 1841, and on the last day of that month a special train left Paddington and arrived in Bristol Temple Meads four hours later.

As soon as the railway was operating, the next stage was the consolidation of the enterprise by providing a sub-structure of workshops, offices and other necessary services. Brunel gave much thought to the arrangement and architectural details of his main stations. His first preference was for single-sided stations, as he considered that these better suited the convenience of passengers, but the inconvenience of bringing trains across the tracks in order to reach the platform militated against the arrangement so that most stations adopted the now-conventional two-sided form. Brunel equipped some of these, such as Bristol and Bath, with wide timber roofs to provide a canopy over all the platforms. The original terminus of the GWR survives at Temple Meads Station in Bristol, with its elegant mock-hammer-beam roof supported on cast-iron columns, but it is now converted to other uses. It did not remain a terminus for long, because the need for a link with the adjacent terminus of the Bristol & Exeter Railway involved the construction of an inter-connecting curve of rail, and the construction of the present Temple Meads Station in 1878 recognized the importance of this link by realigning the building around it.[18]

Special attention was given to the London terminus. At first, the directors had considered joining the London & Birmingham Railway at Kensal Green and running into Euston Station, but the divergence of gauges put an end to those negotiations, and the GWR established its own terminus at Paddington. A series of temporary platforms and sheds was installed, but by 1851 it had been decided to build a show-piece station and Brunel wrote in some excitement to Matthew Digby Wyatt, with whom he was then collaborating in preparations for the Great Exhibition. Clearly inspired by Paxton's Crystal Palace design, Brunel prepared a plan for an iron and glass shed in three interconnecting pavilions with cross-transepts. He invited Wyatt to join him as his assistant in order to attend to 'the detail of ornamentation':

> Now in this building which *entre nous* will be one of the largest in its class I want to carry out strictly and fully all those correct notions of the use of metal which I believe you and I share (except that I should carry them still further than you) and I think it will be a nice opportunity. Are you willing to enter upon the work *professionally* in the subordinate capacity (I put it in the least attractive form at first) of my *assistant* for the ornamental details? [19]

He stressed the urgency of the commission: 'Do not let your work for the exhibition prevent you. You are an industrious man and night work will suit me best.' They went on to construct together the splendid terminus to the GWR, which survives intact except for additions and superficial modifications.

Brunel was also responsible for the construction of the complex of workshops and the provision for a new community of railway workers at Swindon. He was greatly helped in this by Gooch, who, as Superintendent of the Locomotive Department, was sent by Brunel to select the best site for railway workshops and chose Swindon, at the junction with the Cheltenham and Gloucester line, and near the point where the long easy gradient from London changed to the more heavily graded section to Bristol. Gooch reports in his diary: 'Mr Brunel and I went down to look at the ground, then only green fields, and he agreed with me as to its being the best place.'[20] That was in 1840, when Gooch's first locomotive, *Fire Fly*, was already demonstrating his prowess as an engine designer. The following year the directors accepted the proposal, and work went ahead immediately on the workshops, which were in regular operation by the beginning of 1843, with Archibald Sturrock as the local manager. The workshops quickly became a hugely successful operation, catering for all the locomotive construction and maintenance of the GWR, and much of its other engineering requirements. Here, in 1846, Gooch began to build the powerful 4–2–2 locomotives with 8 ft driving wheels which incorporated his experience of broad gauge engines and made possible the achievement of Brunel's vision of reliable high-speed transport. The best known of this class was *Lord of the Isles*, built in 1851 and shown in the Great Exhibition that year.

Meanwhile the neat terraces of houses for the workshop staff, together with a church and various other public buildings, had been set out in the community which became New Swindon. The building of the station and houses, as usual, was done by a local contractor, but Brunel 'was personally responsible for the layout of the new settlement'.[21] Provision of refreshments at Swindon station was put out to a contractor on generous terms, but became the subject of constant complaints about the quality of the coffee and other goods, provoking Brunel's famous quip: 'I did not believe you had such a thing as coffee in the place; I am certain I never tasted any.'[22] But generally the creation of an operating sub-structure for the GWR went forward smoothly and efficiently.

While all these overlapping stages in the establishment of the GWR were being fulfilled, Brunel began to consider the implications of the long-term development of the system and to undertake new projects which developed from it. The need to keep at bay the narrow gauge track of neighbouring rival companies encouraged the GWR to adopt a vigorous expansionist policy from the outset so that it could claim to serve the whole of a large area, thus spreading its influence into south-west England and the midlands, and into Wales and Merseyside. The main rival in the south was the London & Southampton Railway, becoming the London & South Western and promoting the line from Basingstoke to Exeter in 1851 in order to make a narrow gauge bid for business in Devon. In the north, the London & Birmingham amalgamated with the Grand Junction Railway to form the

London & North Western in 1846, while George Hudson's enterprising amalgamation of several lines to form the Midland Railway in 1844 led to a successful bid for the Bristol & Gloucester Railway in the following year. This predatory act secured the conversion of the line to narrow gauge, which was carried through into Temple Meads Station in Bristol by 1854, after overcoming legal objections from the GWR.

The effect of this stringent competition from narrow gauge railways placed severe constraints on the field of operation of the GWR broad gauge system, and encouraged it to secure its interests by promoting its own extension through subsidiary broad gauge companies that soon amalgamated with it. The first was the Bristol & Exeter Railway, established in 1836 with a capital of £1,250,000 by a different group of Bristol merchants from that which had taken the initiative with the GWR. The B & ER immediately invited Brunel to be their engineer, and he accepted, sending William Gravatt to survey the route. Under his guidance, the directors naturally accepted the broad gauge, and it was only a mater of time before the two companies combined to run trains over the route from London to Exeter. The first section, from Bristol to Bridgwater, was opened on 1 June 1841, with a branch to Weston-super-Mare two weeks later. The line through from Paddington to Exeter was opened on 1 May 1844, when Daniel Gooch drove the *Orion*, one of his 2–2–2 'Firefly' class, pulling a special train which did the journey exactly in the five hours scheduled. Tensions arose between the two companies, however, from the need of the GWR directors to promote a 'direct' route to Exeter on the Newbury-Kennet valley line in response to the projected L & SWR line from Basingstoke to Exeter. Even though the GWR extension was not pursued beyond Newbury in Brunel's lifetime he felt that the clash of professional interests obliged him to resign from the B & ER. Nevertheless, the B & ER was rapidly assimilated into the GWR system.

Similarly, the Cheltenham & Great Western Union Railway, also founded in 1836, with a capital of £750,000, was merged fully into the GWR in 1844. It diverged from the GWR near Swindon, crossing the Cotswold plateau and descending through the Stroud valleys to Gloucester and Cheltenham. The South Devon Railway, established in 1844 with a capital of £1,100,000, extended the broad gauge from Exeter to Plymouth, while beyond the Tamar the Cornwall and West Cornwall Railways, both founded in 1846, with capital of £1,600,000 and £500,000 respectively, came strongly under GWR influence from the outset because it was a major shareholder in all these extensions. So did the Wiltshire, Somerset & Weymouth Railway, set up in 1844 with a capital of £750,000, which opened up a line southwards from Bath, through the Limpley Stoke valley to Westbury and beyond. Brunel was appointed engineer to all of these railways.

Meanwhile, the need to ensure access to the enormously profitable trade of the South Wales coalfield, and to the possibility of a link with the Irish traffic beyond, led to the promotion of the South Wales Railway, set up in 1845 with a capital of £2,800,000 as a GWR subsidiary. It was soon merged into the parent company, with which it was physically linked via a line through the Forest of Dean to Gloucester. Brunel had his men out surveying the line in 1844, when they disturbed his old Bristol friend Nicholas Roche in his Pembrokeshire retirement home,[23] but it was some years before serious work began. The estuary of the River Severn created an awkward barrier for the GWR system, although Brunel was confident that this was not an insuperable engineering problem, suggesting a bridge at the site of the Old Passage near Aust in 1854: 'I believe firmly that before fifty years are over there will be one (or a tunnel)'.[24] But the Severn Tunnel was not opened to traffic until 1886, and Brunel had to settle for the Bristol & South Wales Union Railway, opened through Filton to New Passage, for the ferry over to Portskewett, although this was not finished until 1864.

Several other important lines, including that to Oxford and beyond, came under the GWR umbrella from an early date. The Oxford Worcester & Wolverhampton Railway had a particularly troubled history, with construction problems and bitter opposition from narrow gauge interests. It was eventually completed as a standard gauge railway, but it nevertheless established an important link through to Birmingham and Birkenhead. Despite problems at the periphery of the broad gauge empire, therefore, the railway lines constructed in the south west in the 1830s and 1840s were largely dominated by the GWR and its engineer, who was able to supervise the creation of a cohesive broad gauge system. Brunel was the mastermind in weaving this gigantic fabric, being involved in virtually every stage in the development of every one of these railways.[25]

In the event, of course, the GWR monopoly was never as complete as the desideratum of avoiding break of gauge problems required, and with rival companies challenging it to both the south and the north west the problems became an all too frequent feature of railway operation. The period from 1844, when difficulties of transshipment at Gloucester and elsewhere began to arouse public complaints, until the end of the 1840s has become known in British railway history as the period of the 'Gauge War'. The controversy was waged through vigorous debate in the newspapers and pamphlets, various government committees and commissions, a competition between locomotives of broad and narrow gauges, and an Act of Parliament. A Royal Commission was appointed in July 1845 to consider the situation. It consisted of Sir Frederick Smith, who had been an early Inspector General of Railways, together with G. B. Airey, the Astronomer Royal, and Peter Barlow, Professor

of Mathematics at Woolwich. Brunel was examined at length, and assured
the commissioners that if he had the chance again he would have chosen
an even wider gauge than he had done. But he showed that this was a
rational rather than a dogmatic decision by defending his choice of the
standard gauge for several of his lines in Britain and abroad on empirical
grounds of local requirements.[26]

Brunel suggested that the merits of the two gauges should be submitted
to a practical test by conducting trials over similar sets of rails and subject
to agreed conditions. The commissioners agreed, and tests were arranged
between Brunel and G. P. Bidder, a fellow railway engineer and a close friend
of Robert Stephenson. Gooch chose *Ixion*, one of his seven-foot locomotives
of the 'Firefly' class, built in 1841. It made three round trips between
Paddington and Didcot, a distance of fifty-three miles, hauling trains of
eighty, seventy and sixty tons at an average speed of 50 mph. Bidder equipped
two locomotives for the narrow gauge party. The best of these was a brand
new Stephenson machine referred to as 'Engine A', which managed an
average speed of 53¾ mph hauling a train of only fifty tons on a single run
over forty-four miles between Darlington and York. Despite this convincing
demonstration of more consistent and reliable performance by the broad
gauge, it is significant that the narrow gauge supporters were managing to
improve their performance with better track than that originally mounted
on stone blocks, and with ever more powerful locomotives. The long-term
advantages of the broad gauge were already dwindling, and it is not surprising that the commissioners reported in favour of the narrow gauge. They
were convinced of the need for uniformity over the main national routes,
and they decided that, as the narrow gauge system was already eight times
larger than the broad gauge, and as it was much easier – and cheaper – to
convert broad to narrow than vice-versa, all track should be standardized
as narrow gauge.

The broad gauge party did not accept this conclusion, and campaigned
vigorously to ensure that its provisions were not incorporated into legislation. The subsequent Gauge Act of 1846 failed to resolve the dispute
because, while ruling that new lines must all conform to the narrow gauge,
it permitted the continued existence of the broad gauge and allowed extensions to its system. But the collapse of the 'Railway Mania' in 1847, and
the subsequent period of retrenchment which brought hard times to all
the national railway operators, caused a diminution in the agitation and
the rival systems settled down to work alongside each other as smoothly
as possible. With the help of his locomotive engineers, and especially
Daniel Gooch, Brunel had dramatically vindicated his choice of the broad
gauge by achieving consistently high speeds for his services. Nevertheless,

the narrow gauge proved itself to be adaptable to higher speeds, by the construction of sounder track and by improved suspension of the rolling stock, so that the outstanding advantage of the broad gauge in the early years of operation was soon eliminated. For all Brunel's vehement argument in reports to the directors of the GWR and to anxious shareholders, and despite all his brilliant ingenuity in creating a smooth-running railway system, the result was that the broad gauge came very soon to be recognized by all except the most devoted loyalists as being an expensive luxury which set the GWR at odds with every other railway in the country.

Even if the broad gauge is deemed to have been ultimately a costly failure, the civil engineering of the railway won widespread admiration, including the approval of George Stephenson.[27] Once Brunel had determined the route of his great iron road to Bristol and the west country, he and his surveyors achieved an exceptionally level course – nicknamed 'Mr Brunel's billiard table' – with the only noticeable gradients being between Swindon and Bath, where the line drops into the valley of the Bristol Avon. Along this route, the stations have been substantially modified and in some instances rebuilt, the signalling has changed out of all recognition, and the permanent way has long since been converted to standard gauge with conventionally placed cross-sleepers. But the long straight stretches, the gentle curves, the elegant bridges and viaducts, the impressive cuttings and embankments, and the dramatic tunnels with ornamented porticoes stand as an enduring testimony to the brilliance of their designer.

Beyond Exeter, and into South Wales, the terrain provided plenty of exercise for engineering ingenuity. For one thing, the gradients had to be steeper, even though Brunel sought to avoid them as far as possible by adopting coastal routes, as in South Devon, and by constructing lofty timber viaducts, such as those built in Cornwall.[28] The greatest of these engineering *tours de force*, however, were the two large iron bridges constructed by Brunel at Chepstow, to link the South Wales Railway with the line from Gloucester over the River Wye, and at Saltash, where the Royal Albert Bridge was built to link the South Devon Railway with the Cornish lines across the estuary of the Tamar. Brunel's earlier railway bridges had usually been masonry and brick structures, as in the Maidenhead Bridge and other crossings of the Thames, where his artistic eye and careful attention to materials had achieved such graceful shallow arches that contemporaries commented critically on their safety. He had also used laminated timber for the skew bridge across the Bristol Avon downstream from Bath Spa Station but, unlike the brick bridges, which continue to do good service, this was replaced by the present girder bridge in the 1870s. Brunel generally avoided cast iron, and when Robert Stephenson's Dee Bridge at Chester collapsed in 1847, his suspicion of this material for railway bridges seemed to have been justified.[29]

Cast iron was known to possess great strength in compression, so that the road and canal engineers of the early nineteenth century had been encouraged to use it increasingly in their bridges, and it has continued to be useful in pillars and foundations. The first railway engineers adopted the same practice and built a number of cast-iron bridges, some of which developed faults as a result of the relative weakness of cast-iron girders when in tension, such as that to which they were subjected by railway working. The most serious failure was that of the Dee Bridge, which had been a composite structure of cast and wrought iron and which collapsed disastrously when a train was passing over it. This experience convinced the engineering fraternity generally that it could not be regarded as a safe material for large span railway bridges, and set them searching for suitable alternatives. The result was the rapid evolution of wrought-iron bridges in various forms, of which the lattice-girder bridge – with many different varieties soon appearing – was acknowledged as being the best available. Before this conclusion was reached, Robert Stephenson and I. K. Brunel both produced highly novel and robust solutions to the problem. Stephenson's solution was the box girder, built up of wrought-iron plates and with the permanent way passing through (or potentially over) the box. This was the design which was dramatically vindicated in the Britannia Bridge over the Menai Straits and the smaller bridge over the Conwy estuary.[30]

Brunel's solution to the same problem was also a tube of wrought-iron plates, but he used it as a truss to support the carriageway rather than as a beam providing its base. He experimented with a truss of this type in the small road bridge designed to swing over his entrance lock to the Cumberland Basin in Bristol, completed in 1849. This bridge, which happily survives alongside the modern entrance lock, consists of two longitudinal trusses carrying a web of wrought-iron plates which support the road surface.[31] He immediately proceeded to scale up this design for the large railway bridge at Chepstow, where the parallel trusses supported an open lattice framework of wrought iron below them to carry the railway high over the River Wye. This structure was completely replaced by the present bridge in 1962, but the fullest expression of Brunel's innovative bridge design survives in the Royal Albert Bridge at Saltash. Completed in 1859, the year of Brunel's death, this consists of two arched elliptical trusses arranged in series over one central column, the ends of each arch providing the anchorage for a pair of wrought-iron chains. This arrangement creates two rigid independent units from which the railway track is suspended and connected up with masonry viaducts at each end. The construction of the central pier in the River Tamar was particularly difficult, requiring dangerous working conditions under pressure in a diving bell. Brunel sent his chief assistant, R. P. Brereton, to supervise the operation.[32] He attended himself to the delicate task of floating the first truss into position in a coordinated manouevre requiring military precision which he conducted with impressive efficiency. He and Stephenson had devised this procedure in order to get the huge components of their major bridges into position.

Although these essays in wrought-iron bridge design by both Stephenson and Brunel were inspired masterpieces which established the viability of the material for the purpose of large bridge construction, and determined stringent new standards of scientific testing for bridge safety, neither of them provided a model which was widely adopted. The trouble with both designs was that they were elaborate and expensive. When it was demonstrated that the lattice-girder design provided equal safety at much less expense, both the box girder and the wrought-iron truss were unable to compete with it. Brilliant though they were, the future lay with the much more anonymous lattice-girder in all its many forms; but it should be remembered that Brunel contributed directly and substantially to the emergence of this standard design in his robust bridges at Windsor and Balmoral. The former still carries the railway branch from Slough over the Thames, and the latter survives as the road bridge over the River Dee at the entrance to Balmoral Castle.[33] The box girder has, of course, been restored to engineering popularity in many modern road bridges, for which it has shown itself to be particularly well suited, but Brunel's conception of the wrought-iron truss has enjoyed no such revival. It remains, therefore, as a brilliant innovative design, showing an inspired grasp of the potentiality of what was essentially a new material for large-scale applications, but as one which is unique in the sense that it has no descendants.

The achievement of creating the Great Western Railway system constitutes the outstanding success of I. K. Brunel's engineering career. It made an imaginative quantum leap in the expectations of people to be able to travel, and to be able to do so at speed and in relative comfort over distances which, only a generation before, would have seemed quite impossible. Other pioneers, and especially George and Robert Stephenson, also made invaluable contributions to the transport revolution of the nineteenth century. But Brunel set the visionary stamp of his own creative genius on the way in which the national railway system developed. The vision was never completely realized. For one thing, it cost much more than had been allowed for in his original estimates, and proprietors complained about continuing claims on their resources and diminution in dividends when times became harder after 1847. For another thing, the GWR made no attempt to open up its high-speed passenger facilities to anybody except those sufficiently affluent to be able to pay first or second class fares, until obliged to do so by government cheap fare legislation. Brunel preserved to the end the support of his board of directors, who retained him as their chief engineer and made a presentation to him of a massive silver feature to adorn his dinner table.[34] But many others were bemused or disgruntled by Brunel's success, and hints of this occurred at shareholders meetings and in public commentaries. Many of his striking innovations would, in time, have been achieved without him, but the manner of their coming and the form which they took owe much to his vision. Brunel made his mark, in a very substantial and tangible form, on the transport revolution of the nineteenth century, contributing personally, in a way in which very few individuals have a chance to do, to framing the structure of modern society.

6

Overseas Projects

The fact of British priority in railway construction meant that for three decades, from 1830 to 1860, British expertise in railway engineering was not merely unrivalled – it was a virtual monopoly. The result was that any country in Europe or America wishing to embark on a programme of railway building was obliged to turn to British engineers for leadership, and most of the senior engineers of this period undertook such overseas commissions. The advice of these engineers was critical in determining not only the route of the railways, but also the source of their rails, the contracts for equipment, and even the availability of capital. In the USA, British experience was speedily copied and replaced by home-grown American talent as the railroads took off on their prodigious expansion to cover the continent with a network or iron tracks. In France, also, the domestic engineers were soon able to dispense with British support. But elsewhere in Europe reliance lasted longer; and in some parts of the world it continued into the twentieth century.[1] Brunel's involvement in this veritable diaspora of British expertise was established first by his work in Ireland, and then by his projects in Italy, India and Australia. His biographers have had little to say about any of these activities, but that is a pity because their geographical remoteness made it necessary for Brunel to commit himself to written advice and instructions in a way which was largely avoided in his domestic commitments by his 'hands-on' supervision and regular meetings with his assistants. They are also worth considering for their more general significance, as a substantial contribution by Brunel to the internationalization of British engineering.

Although so near mainland Britain, Ireland can properly be regarded as a subject of overseas activity as far as railway works were concerned. After three centuries of bitter conquest, partial settlement and religious bigotry, the whole of the country had been brought under direct control from Westminster in 1800. The authority of the central government was imposed through various commissions and boards, amongst which was the Public Works Board, with the distinguished Royal Engineer Sir John Fox Burgoyne as chairman from 1831 to 1845. Burgoyne did much to stimulate railway building in Ireland, and he was also responsible for the organization of the first professional association for engineers there in the form of the Civil Engineers Society of Ireland in 1835 (it adopted the title 'Institution of Civil Engineers of Ireland' in 1844). Under Burgoyne's guidance, as 'a sort of engineering proconsul',[2] the Public Works Board promoted railways by commissioning surveys and by direct funding, dividing the country into Northern and Southern Districts. Sadly for Ireland, this policy of vigorous government intervention in public works, which ran counter to the prevailing *laissez-faire* ethos of the consensus of British public opinion, did not survive Burgoyne's departure from the country in 1845 and was not available to assist in the years immediately following when the potato blight led to the Great Famine, with its tragic loss of life and the desperate resort to mass emigration.

It was during these years that Brunel struggled to extend his railway empire to Dublin. He only partially succeeded in achieving this objective, which seemed to be a logical step from the South Wales Railway reaching Pembrokeshire to continue, via a ferry service, to establish a fast link between London and Dublin. Brunel made at least two visits to Ireland in the early 1840s, to examine amongst other things the experimental stretch of atmospheric railway constructed by the Dublin & Kingstown Railway, opened in 1843. He was there at the end of October and the beginning of November 1843,[3] and again in November of the following year.[4] It is a reasonable inference that he used these occasions to lay out a route which would link the projected ferry, from Fishguard to the point which eventually became Rosslare, and so on to Dublin. After negotiations with existing local companies, Brunel was engaged as engineer by the Waterford, Wexford, Wicklow & Dublin Railway (the 'Three Ws'), and he took on an assistant engineer, Gibbons, to work on the line from Dublin to Wexford. But he was obliged to tell Gibbons in November 1844 that the project had collapsed because of the withdrawal of the major supporters.[5] Some work must have proceeded, however, because we find him writing again to Gibbons at the end of the month: 'I have in vain endeavoured to get more hands to send you, but the wet the fogs and the dreadful press of work has prevented me.'[6] This was at the height of the Railway Mania in mainland Britain, when it was exceptionally difficult to find staff of sufficient quality to work in Ireland. Nevertheless, work did begin on parts of Brunel's scheme for a line between Dublin and Wicklow, anticipating an extension of the coastal route southwards to Cork, between Cork and Youghal, but everything went into abeyance during the Famine.

Brunel was in Ireland again in December 1846, to advise on the protection of the stranded steam ship *Great Britain* in Dundrum Bay,[7] but work on the railways did not revive until 1853, when Brunel had his assistant Hughes working on the Cork to Youghal line.[8] This was virtually complete by the summer of 1855, when Brunel reported it as 'only requiring sober steady management to become a very important and largely paying line'.[9] Meanwhile the Dublin to Wicklow section, for which Brunel had chosen the difficult coastal route round Bray Head, had made some progress under the resident engineer, W. A. Purdon. It was eventually opened to Bray in July 1855 and to Wicklow in October 1855.[10] But substantial gaps still remained in Brunel's arterial route when he died, by which time the ambitions of the GWR and its subsidiary the South Wales Railway for extensions into Ireland had dwindled almost to extinction. It was many years before the line to Fishguard was constructed and before the Rosslare ferry came into operation.[11]

Brunel undertook two Italian projects between 1841 and 1848, one in Piedmont and the other in Tuscany. The former was abortive, at least as far as Brunel was concerned, and the latter was quite a small line. Neither absorbed a large proportion of his time and energy. They are illuminating, however, because an unusually complete record of Brunel's instructions survives in the letter books. It does not appear from Brunel's Italian correspondence that Italy was one of the epicentres of European nationalism, rebellion and violence in these years, culminating in the 1848 Year of Revolutions. Despite his silence on these matters, it is necessary to keep in mind the political condition of Italy at the time in order to make sense of the difficulties which plagued Brunel's projects. Italy was, in short, an area of great political confusion in the middle decades of the nineteenth century.[12] Ever since the sixteenth century – if not, indeed, earlier – the Italian peninsula had been dominated by its powerful neighbours, Spain, Austria and France, and there had been little sense of national unity amongst the many small states into which the country was divided. When Brunel's negotiations with the Piedmont promoters of the Genoa Railway project began, in 1841, there were eight such states, ranging from the large and populous kingdom of the Two Sicilies (also known as Naples) in the south, ruled by an autocratic Bourbon monarchy, to the small duchies of Tuscany, Lucca, Modena and Parma in the north. These latter were under strong Austrian influence, while Austria ruled Venetia and Lombardy directly. French influence was strongest in the Papal States, in the centre of the peninsula, and in the kingdom of Piedmont and Sardinia, which had been enlarged at the end of the Napoleonic Wars by the acquisition of Genoa and Savona, giving it for the first time strong maritime and industrial interests. From 1831 to 1849 Piedmont was ruled by King Charles Albert, who pursued a policy of vacillating conservatism which involved him in war

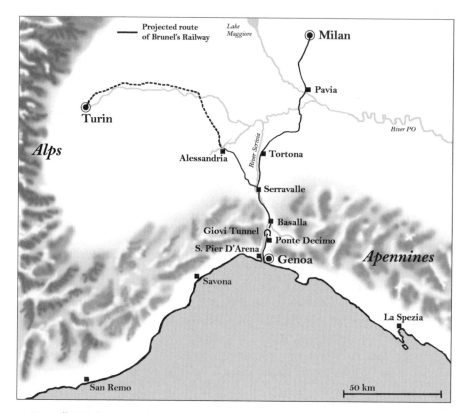

5. Brunel's Piedmont Railway.

with Austria in Lombardy when the multiple revolutions of 1848 included the overthrow of Austrian rule in Milan. As a result, a state was set up uniting the provinces of the north Italian plain under the kingdom of Piedmont.

Unfortunately for the interest of Italian unity, this state only survived for a few days. The Austrian army regrouped, the revolutions were crushed, and King Charles Albert was obliged to abdicate in favour of his son, who became King Victor Emanuel II, and who managed to come to terms with the Austrians in a way which preserved the constitutional monarchy in Piedmont. In the 1850s the new king was well served by his chief minister, Count Cavour, who made Piedmont into an economically flourishing state around which the new spirit of Italian national unity – the *Risorgimento* – could crystallize into a modern nation state.[13] In view of the disturbed nature of Italian political life in these years, it is remarkable that any railways were built. To some extent they began as an expression of inter-state rivalry, so it was some time before the new railway lines crossed any national frontiers. The first railway in Italy was built (under the direction of Robert Stephenson) in Naples, which also had the distinction of possessing the first steam ship and the first iron bridge in the peninsula, despite the reactionary nature of its monarchy.[14] The attempt to link Turin, the capital of Piedmont, with its port at Genoa by a railway was in large part a patriotic project pursued with the support of the government. Cavour was one of the directors of the society commissioned to build it, at a time before he was in the government himself but was active in various agricultural and industrial promotion schemes. It is not clear what contribution he made to the Genoa Railway project, but he was certainly much involved in supporting railways in Piedmont at the time.[15] The project was of considerable strategic significance because Austria was at the same time promoting railways in Lombardy and developing links with dependent duchies such as Tuscany, and a plan for a north-south railway running the whole length of the Italian peninsula was being canvassed by the Austrian authorities. In the event, Brunel became involved in both these major projects: first, with the Genoa-Alessandria-Turin Railway, with a link projected to Milan, and then with the short length of the Maria Antonia Railway north east from Florence, which was promoted by Austria as part of the north-south route. Both projects fell foul, to a greater or lesser degree, of the political instability of Italy in the 1840s.

Brunel was approached with the invitation to build the Genoa Railway through a solicitor, Edwin Gower. He responded cautiously but positively:

> I have hitherto invariably declined any foreign engagements for which of course I have had many proposals partly on account of my engagements here and partly, I may say principally, because of the difficulties of satisfying myself of the perfect respectability of parties, without more trouble and enquiry than I could devote time for, and also the similar difficulty of obtaining any redress or of clearing myself should the direction change hands and the promoters adopt any course towards myself or in the conduct of their affairs which I disapproved of.[16]

Having been reassured on these points, Brunel proceeded to discuss terms with Gower. In December 1841 he set out the conditions on which he was prepared to act. These included an undertaking to visit Italy to examine the line of the proposed railway, spending at least twenty-one days in the service of the company. Brunel was 'to be considered as principal engineer and first authority on all engineering matters', and to be paid ten guineas a day, from the time of leaving London to his return, plus £166 10s. 0d. for travelling expenses with further additions for expenses incurred in surveying and ten guineas a day when engaged on company business elsewhere. £100 was to be paid on account as an indemnity, and there were to be arrangements for compensation. Finally, the terms were assumed to be between Brunel and Gower: 'Mr Brunel undertaking to perform ... the professional duties required of him in the manner in which a professional man in England would consider himself bound to perform these duties', and Gower was to ensure that Brunel was: 'treated in all respects as professional men are treated by gentlemen engaged on similar undertakings in England'.[17] A few weeks later Brunel wrote again to Gower pointing out:

> as it is so long since I travelled anywhere out of England that I can form no estimate of the expenses ... I am always obliged to have a confidential clerk, or a pupil or some person who takes charge of my papers etc and copys any letters and documents which I may require (and for which I make no charge except his expenses)

Moreover, he would be obliged to stay in hotels: 'As I find it quite impossible to *work* as I ought to do (where my time is paid for by others) if I am enjoying the comforts and subject to the customs and conveniences of a private house'.[18]

With the acceptance of these terms, Brunel embarked on the first of his Italian projects. The operation fell into three phases. The first phase culminated in Brunel's report on the Genoa Railway scheme, and was completed in December 1843. The second phase lasted through 1844, from the response of the Piedmont government to the report and through some haggling over terms to Brunel's appointment as engineer to the project in December. The third phase lasted through 1845, involving Brunel and his team in some detailed design work before he eventually withdrew from the project in disgust at the end of the year. Although he made two visits in person, most of the work was done through his staff in Piedmont. The first members of this team were a veteran British railway surveyor and a young assistant engineer. The surveyor was W. Johnson, to whom he held out the prospect of surveying a total of some eighty miles: 'Roughly fifty miles is dead flat which one man could survey at a great rate – thirty miles is very like the Stroud Valley which I think you did for me.'[19] Johnson duly made the survey between August 1842 and April 1843. Brunel's assistant engineer for most of the project was Benjamin Herschel Babbage who, at twenty-eight, was only nine years younger than Brunel, who always treated him with a certain guarded affection. It seems likely that Brunel was doing a favour for his friend Charles Babbage by employing his eldest son in this capacity, and it is more than likely that the young Babbage accepted the commission with alacrity because it helped to liberate him from the dominating presence of the 'irascible genius' who was his father.[20] Babbage set out for Italy with his wife in March 1842 and spent little time in Britain thereafter. His work on the Genoa Railway seems to have been diligent but somewhat slow: if anything, he suffered from being over-conscientious, but he was an excellent engineer and Brunel never had any cause to regret the confidence he had placed in him.

Scarcely had Babbage arrived on the job before Brunel made his first visit to the area. After making his first assessment of the projected route, he felt able to write to the 'President and members of the Royal Railway Society from Genoa to Piedmont' telling them that: 'I am convinced the line now under consideration may be constructed at a very moderate average expense compared with any of the English railways.'[21] In the next few months Brunel wrote a dozen letters to his assistant, setting out detailed instructions for the conduct of his duties. He told Babbage to write to him weekly, keeping a memorandum book to jot down any notes of items which should be passed on. He gave particular orders about the nature of the drawings he wanted to receive from Babbage, and told him to check carefully all work done previously by Italian engineers:

> these details must be worked from straight lines set out on the ground in the manner practised in England – and nothing must be plotted that is not measured on the ground ... remarkable trees ... edges of cliffs, of rock – water courses – buildings, walls etc etc must be laid down perfectly correctly ... It must be clearly understood that *nothing* whatever is *sketched* in by the eye.[22]

The next letter to Babbage introduced him to Johnson as 'an excellent surveyor and in every respect a good man for the purposes', and expressed the hope that Johnson would be joining him in Italy very soon. Meanwhile, Brunel approved of Babbage's insistence on high quality amongst the Italians being recruited to help in the work:

> let no fear of the consequences induce you to employ *anybody* whom you have not perfect confidence in as *competent to the professional duties required of him and unlikely by his character or previous conduct to induce any belief that he will occupy himself otherwise than simply in the duty of following your directions*, and you may quote these words as my positive instructions.[23]

With the approach of winter, Brunel expressed some concern about the ways in which his assistant could be gainfully employed:

> Much will still depend upon the chance of the weather you may have for the next month and what you find you can do in the winter ... You will of course lose no opportunity of ascertaining the prices of everything – work of all sorts and materials, particularly timber of all sorts – bricks, stone and lime – and you will by this time have learnt the necessity of closely cross examining every evidence to make perfectly sure that each party understands the other as to the terms used for *dimensions* or price or quality of material.

He went on to direct Babbage on the need for close and detailed meas-
urements of winter floods in the streams on the route: 'In case of violent
floods it would be very desirable to have hourly or even more frequent
notes to show the wave of the flood if there be any. I will send you two or
three Massey's logs for measuring the velocity.' He suggested that it would
be useful if a rough dam could be built across the stream to be measured,
and sections taken of the river bed on either side of it. Winter, in short,
was not to be a time of relaxation.[24]

Three months later, in early March 1843, he regretted that 'those acquainted with the locale' had not yet decided on the route over the plains
to the north of the mountains, and gave Babbage some subtle engineering
advice on this part of the line:

> In going over these plains, you must wind about to seek easy levels. *Long* undu-
> lating country like this is just that in which the best engineers fail. But if you bear
> in mind that the lead becomes so great and everything must go to spoil, and
> embankments be formed from side cutting while the value of land is excessive,
> earth-work thus costs at least *double*, and yet the plain is our only resource for
> *economy*.[25]

But with Johnson having completed his survey, Brunel realized that he
needed to write up a report promptly, so he recalled Babbage to Britain to
help in this task.[26]

Babbage was back in Britain by the end of April, where Brunel packed
him off to Wales to study the Taff Vale Railway, especially the inclined
planes, and to Yorkshire to look at the Woodhead Tunnel then under
construction.[27] Brunel was preoccupied with other commitments, including
the Irish negotiations which we have already noted, so that the Piedmont
report did not receive immediate attention, and by September Babbage
was back in Italy. He must have given his chief a very upbeat account of
the situation there, because Brunel thanked him for his 'very satisfactory'
account, although he went on to warn him against 'the consequences of a
sudden rush of such very fair wind. I have always found that nothing tried
more seriously one's prudence and judgment and nothing involved greater
risk of difficulty from the slightest imprudence than a run of easy smooth
agreeable weather'.[28] It is not apparent whether or not Babbage's euphoria
survived this application of cold water, but in view of what was to come
the warning was not inappropriate.

Brunel delivered his report to the directors of the Genoa, Piedmont &
Lombardy Railway in the middle of December 1843. Running to twenty-five
manuscript pages, it set out the whole extent of the enterprise, even though
Brunel insisted on the need for more detailed survey work before precise

estimates could be prepared,. Nevertheless, after lecturing the directors at some length on the general principles of railway construction and operation, he outlined the main engineering works which would be necessary along the route and pronounced confidently on its feasibility and economic advantages. This was to be a line devoted to freight rather than high speed passenger traffic, so he recommended the standard 4ft 8½ins gauge and opted for inclined planes on the steep gradients out of Genoa, which he reckoned could be economically operated by water power. He also recommended double track throughout. He estimated the whole line of 120 kilometres and double track could be built in three and a half years for '40 million' – presumably pounds sterling, although if so it would appear to have been strikingly expensive by British standards.[29]

The submission of this report marked the completion of the first phase of Brunel's involvement with the Piedmont Railway project. He followed it up immediately by a personal visit to Italy in the first three weeks of 1844, but this served to convince him of the slowness of progress as he found the Genoa men 'unprepared to make any arrangement or even to mature their own financial scheme as they had actually not made as yet any written proposal to the government. I think I put this part in train and that matters will now begin to assume some more positive shape than they had done as yet.' [30] In the event, it took the greater part of a year to reach a decision, so that the second phase of the operation, which lasted throughout 1844, consisted of prolonged waiting and protracted wrangles about details of the scheme. The first positive reaction came in July, when an abstract of comments on Brunel's report became available, causing him to write to Babbage:

> Your letter promises some movement I hope we may not be disappointed ... Of course any suggestions such as those contained in the abstract of the report must be met temperately and even if possible by concession ... Keep me just at present constantly informed upon everything doing.[31]

But as details of the Italian response began to reach him, Brunel found it difficult to follow his own advice about meeting them temperately: 'I will read the report and if I have patience I will answer it ... I have read enough to feel great contempt for the production.' [32] And a fortnight later:

> I have read the report and having cooled upon it will write a short answer ... It is all so contemptibly childish that it requires some patience to answer it ... they go to work as if I had been an operative employed by *them* to furnish sections and plans of the various lines of country for them to select and direct – instead of the case being that I was called as a person assumed to be *more experienced* and *more competent* than they are, and their business only to see on the part of the Government that the proposed line is acceptable.[33]

It is unfortunate that the terms of the response which caused Brunel's indignation are not available, but it is clear that they did not recognize the status to which Brunel felt that he was entitled as an engineer, and raised queries which reflected upon his engineering competence. However, the company despatched an agent to London to reassure him of their confidence,[34] and at last the Piedmont government took a more direct interest in the project when Brunel was invited by the King of Sardinia's ambassador in London, Count Pollan, to undertake: 'the direction of the works of the proposed railway from Genoa to Alessandria'. Brunel replied by setting out his conditions: he wanted full cooperation from the government in awarding contracts; one year's salary to be paid in advance, at £1200 a year as a retainer, with twenty guineas a day in addition when Brunel was attending to works in Italy; a principal assistant at £800–900 p.a. with £500–600 p.a. for each of two second assistants, all to be British; and an insistence on close liaison with neighbouring projects in order to ensure 'a whole and complete system of railway'.[35]

Presumably these conditions were accepted, because Brunel wrote to Babbage in June: 'I have arranged everything with the Government for the construction of the line from Genoa to Alessandria', so that the third and final phase of Brunel's involvement with the project could begin. He urged Babbage to stir himself into activity and listed the tasks which required immediate attention, including the summit tunnel. And he added: 'I think of bringing Brereton over for you at the tunnel – he has had more experience than any man I have and as I suppose he will take his wife he will be a great addition to your circle.'[36] But there was a snag. Partly with Brunel's connivance, Babbage had been approached by another Italian railway project, and he had decided to throw in his lot with this, so that Brunel was obliged to write apologetically to the Count:

> I have been somewhat embarrassed in my arrangements by losing the assistance of Mr Babbage who under the advice of his friends has determined to accept an offer made to him for directing the construction of certain other railways projected in Italy and particularly one in Tuscany, his father being I believe well known to the Grand Duke.[37]

The planned despatch of Brereton and other assistants did not provide a remedy for this situation. R. P. Brereton was shortly to become Brunel's chief assistant, and was a most diligent and careful engineer. He reached Genoa in July, so that he was already established when Brunel made his third visit to the project in August and September, travelling on this occasion in the company of his wife.[38] There is no record of what Brereton did on the project, nor on any impressions formed by Brunel as a result of his visit, but clearly matters did not go well because the next relevant entry in the letter books heralded the end of the enterprise, at least as far as Brunel and his team were concerned. In mid-November he wrote to Count Pollan withdrawing from the Piedmont Railway on account of the excessive interference and officialdom which had been encountered: 'My assistant, a peculiarly energetic persevering young man writes to me declining to remain as feeling disheartened at the constant interference with every detail – and at the entire absence of confidence.'[39] There were a few loose ends to tie up, and then he wrote to Brereton telling him to arrange the transfer of papers with the minimum of inconvenience and to come home – 'the sooner you come the better'.[40] The project thus came to an ignominious end: after all the surveying and waiting it fizzled out without any track having been laid. It seems likely that, when the line from Genoa to the north was eventually built, some of Brunel's plans may have been used. But he and his team had nothing more to do with the project.[41]

This was not the end, however, of Brunel's Italian commitments. Even before the third phase of the Piedmont project had come to an abrupt halt, he had become involved in the Florence Railway project, with which he remained engaged from the end of 1845 to the summer of 1848. This was the undertaking to which Babbage had already moved, so that the old relationship was resumed. The directors of the Maria Antonia Railway – being an Austrian enterprise, it was named after a Habsburg princess – had already asked his advice about Babbage's salary, as well as about systems of propulsion.[42] At the beginning of December 1845 he was able to report on his survey of the Florence-Pistoia route, made in the course of his autumn visit, and to ensure the authorities that it contained no great engineering difficulties.[43] The subject of these negotiations was a short stretch of railway running north west from Florence through Prato to Pistoia. Although short, it was a significant link in the grand design for a north-south railway down the Italian peninsula promoted by Austrian interests and supported by British capital. Whereas Brunel's correspondence about the Piedmont Railway was preoccupied with the civil engineering aspects and never got down to constructional details, that about the Maria Antonia Railway went almost immediately into such details. This may be because, having arrived somewhat late on the scene, the main points about the route had already been determined. With none of the heavy gradients through mountainous country encountered on the Piedmont line, the engineering was also more straightforward. Brunel's main contribution to the discussion of the route was a rather truculent letter to Babbage complaining about the penchant of the Italian engineer, Bonfil, for long stretches of straight line.[44] He pointed out that any determination to apply such 'arbitrary rules' to railway construction

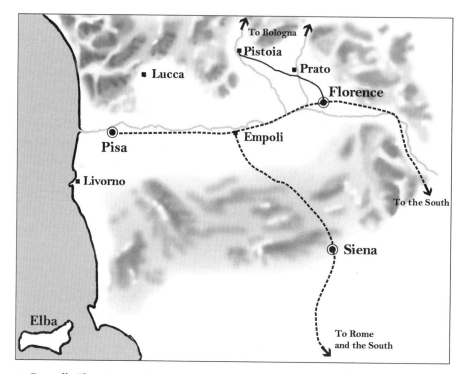

6. Brunel's Florence to Pistoia Railway.

would mean that: 'a very large portion of the traffic will be sacrificed'. But it seems that Brunel was resigned to leaving the setting out of the route to Bonfil, who continued to loom large in the project as the 'Government Engineer', and who eventually acquired the title of 'Count St George'. On the other hand, for eighteen months from June 1846 a stream of instructions left Brunel's office, mostly directed to Babbage, and many of them through Brereton, containing detailed guidance on almost every aspect of railway construction and equipment – quantities and qualities of rails and machin-ery;[45] dimensions of bridges, girders and timber viaducts;[46] the preservation of timber;[47] commissions for locomotives and tools;[48] the design of stations;[49] and the use of guard timbers 'to protect the girders against anything that may get off the lines and strike them sideways which has been alleged as the cause of the accident at Chester of which you have probably heard and which has alarmed the Government and the Country against Cast Iron Bridges'.[50] He returned to the theme on a later occasion: '[Cast iron] is a horrid metal at best and never used by Mr Brunel to carry heavy loads if he can help it.'[51]

There can be little doubt that Brunel kept his Italian team busy in this period, until the Maria Antonia line was complete and operations had begun. He was able to write to Babbage in February 1848: 'I am glad to hear that you are at last running an engine', and went on to give advice on operating practices.[52] By this time the team was already dispersing, but the running down of the project produced formidable financial problems for Brunel and his staff, as the Austrian authorities were reluctant to settle any of the outstanding accounts. Brunel turned to Bonfil for help:

> My Dear Bonfil – Are you aware that your Company owes me £2150 for moneys advance in salaries to Babbage etc and for my own. It has been a most shocking piece of carelessness on my part to allow such an arrear accumulating but in the midst of a pressure of business it has occurred and I appeal to you individually to get this debt discharged.[53]

And a month later he wrote again to Bonfil, now elevated to his new title, expressing anger at the dismal state of affairs:

> Indeed the whole is a most unprofitable business and I will never again enter into such concerns and managements – and for this reason I am willing to make some further sacrifice and even to sustain a loss to get quit of it ... If therefore the company will at once reimburse me that which *I have paid for them* – with the interest as they must have done to any banker or merchant making £1438 – I will make them a present of more than *all* the *profit* upon my charge of £750 – namely the half of this sum or £375 ... I hate these money discussions about my *own* accounts.[54]

There was more haggling, but Brunel appears to have settled for a payment of £1028 on his own account, although there is no confirmation of this in the letter books, and there is no indication of the settlement of the other outstanding accounts. As this was a moment of maximum inconvenience as far as the governments of Tuscany and Austria were concerned, with revolutions and conflicts blazing all around them in the summer of 1848, it is probably fortunate that Brunel achieved any financial settlement at all.[55]

It was on this unsatisfactory note that Brunel's direct involvement in Italian railway projects came to an end. There is no indication on his part of any sensitivity towards Italian nationalism or the severe political embarrassments of his clients in these operations, and all the signs are that he regarded them only as an extension of his British practice, expecting the same sort of treatment from government agencies as he received at home. But Italy remained attractive to him, and there are some later echoes of his interest in the surviving correspondence. In 1852, for instance, he corresponded with John Field and S. M. Peto about possible backing for a railway from Rome to Ancona, and a year later he was approached about the chances of building a railway from Alessandria to Piacenza, which led to him trying to lure Johnson out of retirement in order to undertake the survey.[56] He made a final visit to Italy in 1859, when returning from his 'convalescent' holiday in Egypt. But there is no hint in the surviving records that he undertook any further professional commitments in Italy after 1848.

Promoters of railways and other parties involved in overseas projects continued to approach Brunel in the 1850s. In 1853 he compiled a 'Memorandum of Data Required in Reference to the Crossing of the Berwick Creek', giving technical advice on pile-driving to an American client acting for the New Orleans and Great Western Railway.[57] At the end of 1855, in response to a request from Robert Stephenson, he wrote to the Grand Trunk Railway in Canada, commenting on the proposal for the dramatic box-girder Victoria Bridge across the St Lawrence River: 'After much consideration of the "Victoria Bridge" my impression is that a considerable saving could be effected by increasing to a moderate extent the spans and the weight of iron and diminishing the number of piers.'[58] In 1858 the directors of the Ceylon Railway sought his advice on a suitable engineer, and Brunel thought they 'cannot do wrong' if they secured the services of any one of four men short-listed – Ward, Burke, Fuller and Doyne. He placed Doyne last because he was not personally acquainted with him and stated a preference for Ward. Doyne got the job, and went on to important commissions in Tasmania and New Zealand.[59] Of rather more substance than any of these affairs, however, were Brunel's involvements in Indian and Australian engineering.

Indian railways were being promoted in the 1840s, and the first line to be completed was the twenty mile section of the Great Indian Peninsula Railway from Bombay to Thana, opened in 1853. The chief engineer of this line was J. J. Berkeley, who had served under Robert Stephenson.[60] Other lines followed quickly elsewhere in India, but the programme of railway construction was severely interrupted by the Indian Mutiny of 1857–58. John Brunton, after completing his work for Brunel on the Renkioi Hospital, and having helped to sell off the surplus equipment when he returned to London, had taken a post in India as chief engineer of the Scinde Railway between Karachi and Kotru, only to arrive in India in the middle of the Mutiny.[61] He and his wife stayed with the Berkeleys in Bombay until it was safe to go into the interior again. There was then a vigorous resumption of railway work, and it was at this point that Brunel made his contribution to engineering in the subcontinent.

Brunel had been consulted about railways in Bengal as early as 1855, because at the end of that year he felt empowered to offer an engagement of twelve months in India to W. A. Purdon at 1000 guineas plus expenses in order to investigate the possibility of a railway running 150 miles north

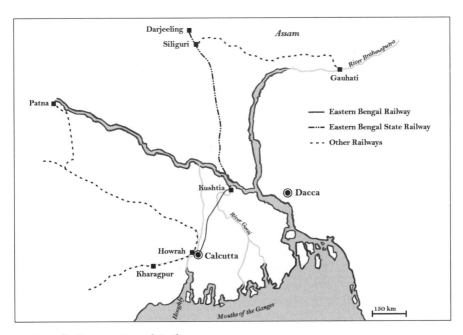

7. Brunel's Eastern Bengal Railway.

from Calcutta.[62] Purdon accepted, but it was over a year before he received his instructions on departing for Calcutta, when Brunel stressed the import-ance of taking soundings in the Hoogly, and of making sure that any confidential matters were expressed in personal letters rather than in official company business.[63] It was another year before Brunel reached an agreement with the Eastern Bengal Railway, when he wrote – in the middle of the Mutiny – setting out 'the position I should hold if acting as Engineer to the Eastern Bengal Railway Company and my professional and other charges and also with reference to the staff I should recommend and the salaries of the principal members'.[64] The terms he stipulated were £3000 p.a. for Purdon as Chief Engineer; £1500 for a Second Engineer; £800–1000 for each of four Resident Engineers; and wages for eighteen to twenty craftsmen, to include some bricklayers. For his own professional services he asked £1200, although, when he learnt that it was intended to direct the operation from India rather than from London, he reduced this figure to £750 for advice to the English board.[65]

It is not clear whether or not Purdon made a preliminary survey between January 1857 and the acceptance of these terms in September 1858, but it seems likely that he did because Bennett wrote to Brunton in India then:

I daresay that you have heard that the Railway called the Eastern Bengal Railway has been progressing so well that Purdon goes out with a staff on the 20th of this month. I am sorry that we have not been able at present to do anything for you in the way of Assistants – we were obliged to secure Glennie which we did in May last ... We have considerable difficulty in securing good men and it is thought that in future the Company must offer higher salaries if they wish to secure efficient officers ... Everything here in the Railway world of construction is flat and but little prospect of advancement.[66]

Brunel took a lively interest in the development of the Indian project, but his powers were waning and at the end of 1858 he was obliged to leave his work and take a holiday. Before departing for Egypt, on his last foreign expedition, he wrote to Purdon: 'I am definitely ordered by my medical men as absolutely necessary to spend the winter in Egypt. I leave here on 4 December. I did talk of the possibility of my *running over* to Calcutta I don't think this is likely.' But he did ask Purdon to send duplicates of his letter from India to await him in Cairo, so that he could keep an eye on the business.[67] Of course, in his poor health the idea of a trip to India was never realistic, and little evidence survives of Brunel's activities in the affairs of the Eastern Bengal Railway thereafter. But one of his last letters was written to Purdon in August 1859 to express his concern at what seemed to Brunel the 'unyielding' attitude of that engineer and his subordinates to the authorities in India:

Remember that the Local Government *is your master* ... You must remember also that we have a very peculiar direction here men having no experience whatever in the conduct of works – an unlimited confidence in themselves, with an amount of suspicion of motives in others which I never met with before – amongst *gentlemen* – and from them you will get nothing but distrust.[68]

It is unrewarding to speculate about the reasons for this intriguing reflection on the quality of the directors of the Eastern Bengal Railway, but clearly Brunel was anxious to avoid rocking the boat and to get the job done with the minimum trouble. The Mutiny had been a traumatic event for the British in India, and it is possible that Brunel was sensitive to the increased government intervention in railway building which was part of the complex reaction stimulated by it. The indirect rule of the East India Company was replaced by direct action from the British government, thus initiating the period of the British Raj which culminated in the 1870s with Disraeli having the Queen crowned as 'Empress of India', and Victoria herself regarding India as the fairest jewel in her crown. Brunel was one of those practical men who helped to make this development possible.[69]

Unlike India, Australia was regarded as an empty continent when the First Fleet under Admiral Phillips arrived off Botany Bay in January 1788. The intention was to establish the first white settlement in the land which Captain Cook had called 'New South Wales' when he had explored the coast twenty years before. The British government had no great expectations of the colony: it was a penal settlement, intended as a sump to receive domestic criminals when it was no longer possible to send them to America and when it had become inconvenient to keep them in hulks in British harbours. After a difficult start the colony had settled down, with a steady stream of voluntary immigrants joining such ex-convicts who had served their time and chosen to remain in Australia moving out into the hinterland to explore it and to establish farms and townships. By the middle of the nineteenth century urban communities were thriving in Sydney, Melbourne, Brisbane, Adelaide and Hobart, and the first tentative stretches of railway were being projected. These developments then received an enormous stimulus from the discovery of gold in the bush inland from both Sydney and Melbourne.[70]

The new state of Victoria was created in 1850 in response to the rapid acceleration of economic activity accompanying the gold rush into Melbourne. The first railways in the state were built inland from the city to Ballarat and other mining centres, and round Port Phillip Bay to Williamstown and on to Geelong.[71] Brunel appears to have been consulted by the Colonial Office about aspects of these railways in the mid 1850s, but there is little surviving evidence of these negotiations in the letter books. Towards the end of 1858 a letter headed 'Victoria Railways' asked for a payment on account from the Victorian government,[72] and shortly after Brunel's death the following year Bennett submitted another account for his services as 'Inspecting Engineer for the Government of Victoria', amounting to £2063.[73] He also wrote to Gooch asking him to remain 'the paid professional adviser' on matters referred to the office by the Victoria Railways in Melbourne.[74] The pattern seems to have been that colonial governments tried to secure the support of well-established engineers to advise them on professional matters such as the appointment of contractors, the determination of tenders, and the provision of materials and equipment, rather than to secure detailed engineering designs from them. Brunel was prepared to give such support to the authorities in Victoria, and on some matters of bridge design he went further and provided specifications.

We know this because after Brunel's death his executors wrote to the Duke of Newcastle, then Secretary of State for the Colonies, requesting an arrangement in order to complete the fourth and fifth of a series of contracts for the Victoria Railways. From this it can be shown that the first contract had been completed about two years before, and the appointment of R. P. Brereton was suggested to supervise the completion of the contracts because he: 'has been upwards of twenty-three years in Mr Brunel's service,

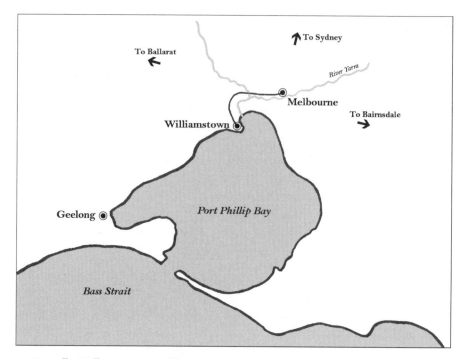

8. Brunel's Melbourne to Williamstown Railway.

and for some time past has been chief of the Engineering Staff and he has
under Mr Brunel had charge of the former contracts for the Victorian
Railways.'[75] It is probable that most if not all of these five contracts would
have been for bridges and other works on the line from Melbourne to
Williamstown, as this was being actively pursued at the time of Brunel's
involvement. This was a stretch of about ten miles crossing flat marshy
ground west of Melbourne, intersected by some substantial creeks. One of
these, Saltwater Creek, was crossed by a wrought-iron girder bridge similar
to Brunel's Balmoral Bridge, and was designed in his office. The deck of
this bridge has long since been replaced to cope with heavy suburban traffic,
but the abutments on both sides of the Saltwater, in tough black local stone,
are almost certainly authentic Brunel designs.[76] These are the only genuine
Brunel relics known to survive in Australia, although the service of the
Great Britain, which visited Melbourne regularly for many years, enriched
the Australian population by conveying boatloads of immigrants to the
expanding antipodean colonies.[77]

Perhaps the most lasting contribution of Brunel to Australian engineering
was an indirect one, through the work of other engineers who had worked

under him. The most interesting of these men from our point of view was B. H. Babbage who, as we have seen, had worked diligently as Brunel's principal assistant on his Italian railway projects. When the funds for these finally expired in the summer of 1848, Babbage returned to Britain and found work, amongst other things, in advising local authorities in Lancashire about their water supplies.[78] Then, in 1851, he had gone to Adelaide, on the invitation of the South Australian Government, to build the first railway there linking the capital city with its port. Thereafter he made his home in the state and spent the remainder of his life on engineering and survey work.

The sum total of Brunel's overseas projects is unquestionably slight in comparison with his huge engineering achievements in mainland Britain. But the fact that they were conducted at a distance from Brunel's head-quarters in London meant that they generated much more recorded correspondence than was the case with his domestic commissions, which gives them a greater interest than their substance suggests. In the last resort, however, Brunel's overseas projects are significant not so much for their substance as engineering works as for what they represent in the development of British engineering as a worldwide activity. In this context, they were an aspect of the universal dependence on British expertise in the age of massive railway, ship and general engineering construction that had arrived in the middle decades of the nineteenth century. They stand at the zenith of British industrial and political leadership, and on the cusp of a new wave of intense nationalistic and imperialist sensitivities. Although these did little to touch Brunel personally, his engineering services overseas helped to prepare the way for the flowering of British imperialism which followed the Crimean War, the Indian Mutiny, the opening up of Africa, and the *Pax Britannica* during which British naval superiority made it possible for British industrial and commercial enterprise to flourish all over the world.

7

Disasters

For all his great achievements, the career of I. K. Brunel was distinguished by some astonishing engineering disasters, and it is a remarkable tribute to the excellence of his successes that his reputation has been able to endure blows which would have overwhelmed most engineers. The largest of these disasters were the collapse of the atmospheric system on the South Devon Railway, and the extraordinary series of problems which accompanied the attempts to build, launch and fit out the *Great Eastern*. But there were several other near-disasters in Brunel's engineering career, such as his failure to provide satisfactory steam locomotives at the opening of the Great Western Railway. At a more personal level, there were the accidents in which he almost lost his life in the Thames Tunnel in 1828, and in the engine room fire on the *Great Western* in 1838. Such episodes demonstrate that his career was not unblemished, and an examination of them should distinguish the qualities of the man as a risk-taker with outstanding faculties of resilience and recovery.

The more personal disasters incurred in Brunel's professional life need not detain us long because they, like the occasion when he swallowed a coin in the course of performing conjuring tricks for the amusement of his own children, were the results of high spirits or the immediate recognition in a crisis that his leadership involved a readiness to be where the trouble was, even if it entailed real risk to life and limb. Such was the case when he responded immediately and boldly to critical situations in the Thames Tunnel, particularly to inundations when the river broke in. Another such incident occurred a few years later, when the basket carrying him and others over the Avon Gorge by the preliminary cable jammed, and he climbed out of the basket to remove the impediment.[1] Brunel's natural bravery and even foolhardiness was never in doubt, and so long as he was not physically overwhelmed by events his inventiveness in devising means of overcoming a problem was striking. The same qualities were apparent in his engineering failures, but in these cases it was his initial judgment in design and policy-making which has to be questioned.

Even L. T. C. Rolt, who was reluctant to find any cause of censure in Brunel's life and works, said of the specifications which he required for the first GWR locomotives that they 'represent the greatest and most inexplicable blunder in his whole engineering career'.[2] In asking for a standard speed of 30 mph with a piston speed not exceeding 280 feet per second, and a maximum weight of engine (including fuel and water) of ten and a half tons on six wheels or eight tons on four, Brunel made it virtually impossible for his locomotive builders to provide fast and efficient machines. Narrow gauge locomotives were already being built of much greater weight and piston speeds. In obliging his manufacturers to opt for larger wheels with a short piston stroke, the weight of the wheels led them to compensate by reducing the size of the boiler, with the result that most of these early locomotives were underpowered. Other builders met the axle-loading requirements by separating the boiler from the motive unit, but this proved to be too cumbersome an arrangement for easy operation.

When the GWR began to run regular train services in 1838, it was therefore equipped with a remarkable assortment of underpowered and inefficient locomotives, for which Brunel was fully responsible, as they had all been designed to his specifications. Breakdowns were frequent, and the directors began to lose patience with their engineer. Without some help, it is possible that his career as a railway engineer might have come to a premature end. Fortunately for Brunel, help was at hand in the shape of the young man whom he appointed on 9 August 1837 at the age of twenty as his chief locomotive assistant, Daniel Gooch. Gooch recognized the inadequacies of Brunel's locomotives, and persuaded his chief to purchase a machine from Stephenson on which he had worked himself and which, with some adaptation, could be made suitable for broad gauge working. This was *North Star*, which was duly delivered to the GWR and came into operation in May 1838. Joined by *Morning Star* soon afterwards, these locomotives with their seven-foot single pair of driving wheels became the workhorses of the new railway as it opened up in stages to Maidenhead and beyond to Reading and the west. By 1840 Gooch had developed his own class of seven-foot flyers in the shape of *Firefly* and its successors, the first of which, with its larger boiler and fire-box than *North Star*, was capable of sustained high speeds of 50 mph. Brunel's reputation had effectively been saved by the success of Daniel Gooch, and the future of steam locomotion on the GWR was secure.[3]

This episode, even though happily resolved, has some bearing on the next significant disaster in Brunel's career, because it demonstrates that he was uneasy about the steam locomotive in the late 1830s and that, in this respect, his eye for good design failed him. This may have encouraged him to look for substitutes, of which the atmospheric railway was the most dramatic. The atmospheric system was a pneumatic device using the pressure difference in a tube from which the air had been partially evacuated to propel a piston or a capsule along the tube. By attaching the piston to a wheeled vehicle it could be made to propel a carriage or a train of carriages and thus become the motive power for a railway. The snag about this arrangement was that the arm connecting the driving piston to the carriage required a longitudinal slot along the tube so that it could move freely in response to the pressure differential inside the tube; and to maintain the working pressure in the tube it was necessary that this slot should be tightly sealed except at the moment when the arm connected to the piston passed through. The efficiency of this seal, or rather the impossibility of securing its efficiency, was the most troublesome feature of the atmospheric system and contributed substantially to its ultimate failure.

Credit for the invention of the system is generally given to George Medhurst, a manufacturer of scales in Soho, London, who took out a patent in 1799 for a method of transporting goods and mail at high speed through an iron tube, apparently intending to use a mixture of compressed air and atmospheric pressure as the motive power.[4] He was followed by John Vallance and John Hague, both of whom patented pneumatic devices in the 1820s, and by Henry Pinkus, an American living in Britain, who took out a patent in 1834 and launched the prospectus for the National Railway Association in the following year. Nothing of substance came from any of these initiatives, but in 1838 the gas engineer Samuel Clegg, in partnership with the marine engineering and ship-building brothers Jacob and Joseph Samuda, took out a patent (no. 7920) for 'a new improvement in valves, and the combination of them with machinery', which promised to overcome the problem of achieving an air-tight seal on the longitudinal valve. They set up a successful working model at the Samudas' workshop in Southwark in 1839, and the following year they laid out a half mile of full-scale test track at Wormwood Scrubs, with carriages drawn along by a piston in the tube mounted between the rails. The demonstrations which they put on there received widespread attention and were taken very seriously by the leading railway engineers of the day. It is true that some locomotive pioneers, including the Stephensons, were unimpressed and remained committed to steam traction. George Stephenson described it as a 'great humbug', and Robert Stephenson pointed out the problems which would arise from any failure at the pumping stations.[5] Several prominent engineers, however, were persuaded that the atmospheric system had operating advantages of which they could make use. They included Charles Vignoles and William Cubitt, as well as I. K. Brunel, all of whom recommended the Clegg-Samuda atmospheric system on lines for which they were responsible.

As far as Brunel was concerned, it is significant that this interest in atmospheric railways coincided with his disenchantment with steam locomotives in the first years of operation of the GWR, but it must also be remembered that locomotive steam power was still in its formative development stage in these years. Although it went on to become one of the outstandingly successful innovations of the nineteenth century, it had started inauspiciously with attempts to make high-pressure steam engines mobile only progressing slowly until 1829. In that year the Rainhill Trials vindicated the confidence of the Stephensons in steam propulsion for the new Liverpool & Manchester Railway, but even after the *Rocket* had demonstrated its viability for most duties of railway traction, doubts lingered about the capacity of the steam locomotive to cope with steep gradients or to maintain high speeds over long hauls, so that engineers continued to show keen interest in alternative systems which could offer superior performance over heavily graded routes. Not until well into the 1840s did steam traction become sufficiently mature to win general confidence. By this time the so-called 'Railway Mania' was in full swing, with its extraordinary crescendo of capital investment in railways. A corresponding wave of hyperactivity by entrepreneurs, surveyors and engineers built and equipped the new transport system. Parliament passed 650 Railway Acts between 1845 and 1848, authorizing the construction of almost nine thousand miles of track.[6] In these conditions, any idea capable of encouraging the further expansion of railways was sure to receive a warm response.

The atmospheric railway was such an idea, and it was taken up with enthusiasm by several engineers and their railway companies. In only four cases, however, was it actually adopted, and one of these – the Nanterre to St-Germain railway – was in France. The first to be built was the Kingstown & Dalkey Railway, on the outskirts of Dublin. It was only one and three-quarters of a mile long, with a single engine house at the uphill (Dalkey) end of the track, so that trains were drawn up the incline by atmospheric power and returned under gravity. The line was designed by Charles Vignoles and was opened in March 1844. It attracted great interest among the engineering fraternity, all of whom were anxious to see how the system worked in regular passenger service. Its initial success did much to encourage the next two ventures, both of which applied the system to full-scale main-line operation.

William Cubitt had been one of the pioneers of railway engineering in Britain, being responsible for several important lines in the south east. As part of one of these, the London, Croydon & Epsom Railway, he recommended the installation of atmospheric working on the stretch from New Cross to Croydon. This was authorized in 1844 and the first section was opened in January 1846. The line was about five miles long and was single track, equipped with four Gothic engine houses which provided the power for trains in both directions. The service of commuter traffic had teething troubles, especially when it was shown to be underpowered as a result of having adopted a size of tube which was too small for the load required. It appeared to have settled down remarkably well, however, until there was a failure in Samuda's improved valve which caused a serious shut-down of services. As a consequence of this, Cubitt was prevented from recommending any extension to the system, and in May 1847 the whole line was converted to conventional locomotive propulsion.

Like Cubitt, Brunel had been impressed by the demonstrations of the atmospheric system at Wormwood Scrubs and on the Kingstown & Dalkey Railway. On his own Great Western Railway, through-running had commenced between London and Bristol on 30 June 1841, and his Bristol & Exeter Railway had opened on 1 May 1844. Thanks largely, as we have seen, to the application of Daniel Gooch's skills, steam locomotives were running efficiently throughout this system. But as the GWR broad gauge empire spread westward, Brunel saw the opportunity of benefiting from the advantages offered by the atmospheric system. He had been appointed engineer to the South Devon Railway, established by Act of Parliament in July 1844, to take the line on from Exeter to Plymouth, and at an early meeting of the directors he warmly recommended the atmospheric system:

> Gentlemen: I have given much consideration to the question referred to me by you at your last meeting – namely that of the advantage of the application of the atmospheric system to the South Devon Railway . . . I have no hesitation in taking upon myself the full and entire responsibility of recommending the adoption of the atmospheric system on the South Devon Railway and of recommending as a consequence that the line of works should be constructed for single line only.[7]

Brunel was conscious of the fact that the terrain was becoming more difficult as his line swept westwards, and he judged that the atmospheric system would allow him to adopt stiffer gradients than any considered suitable for the steam locomotives of the early 1840s. His point about the 'single line' was that, as the atmospheric tube could be made to draw a train in either direction, it would be possible to dispense with the double lines of track which had already become normal practice for major railways, and thus lead to significant economies in construction. This argument, however, was disingenuous and the 'advantage' was misleading, because the reversion to single-line operation meant that any stretch could be used only for trains in one direction at any one time.[8]

On Brunel's recommendation, the directors of the South Devon Railway undertook to lay fifteen miles of single track on the atmospheric principle from Exeter St David's Station to Teignmouth. It was later extended a further five miles to Newton Abbot. All this stretch was fairly level, much of it running by the seashore. It was intended to apply the atmospheric system all the way to Plymouth, as well as on the branch to Torquay, and Brunel designed some unusually steep gradients on the assumption that they would be operated in this way. Although some preliminary work had been done on the track and engine houses, the atmospheric system on these extensions was abandoned at an early stage. Nevertheless, eight engine houses were brought into working order, and the construction of this first stage of the system kept a team of Brunel's engineers and Joseph Samuda busy in Devon from 1844 to the opening of the first section of atmospheric track in September 1847. The Newton Abbot section followed on 10 January 1848. But on 5 September of that year the whole system was abandoned. Brunel, who for all his visionary qualities was a realist in matters of practice, advised his directors that the longitudinal valve had been a failure. In a long report he reviewed the catalogue of problems and concluded: 'From the foregoing observations, it will be evident that I cannot consider the result of our experience of the working between Exeter and Newton such as to induce me to recommend the extension of the system.'[9] As Samuda and the contractors were not prepared to carry the cost of a complete replacement of the valve, the line was immediately converted to locomotive operation.

By the end of 1848, the two largest excursions into mainline atmospheric practice had thus been abandoned, leaving the Dalkey line as the only British exponent of the principle. The Nanterre to St-Germain line had been opened in Paris in April 1847, but this was like the Dalkey line in being less than two miles in length, with only one engine house and capable of operating under atmospheric pressure in one direction only. Like the Dalkey line, it was also modestly successful in terms of carrying passengers regularly and reliably, and it remained in operation until 1860. The Kingstown & Dalkey Railway itself was converted to locomotive traction in 1854 as part of the rationalization of Irish railway lines. This was the end of passenger transport by the atmospheric system. Except for some pneumatic devices for the underground transport of mail and for the central receipt of cash payments in certain big department stores, it was also the complete end of atmospheric propulsion. The problem is to explain the sudden rise and collapse of this striking innovation and, in particular, to account for the readiness of I. K. Brunel to commit his reputation to it.

If the initial enthusiasm for the atmospheric system can be explained partly in terms of the euphoria engendered by the Railway Mania in Britain, it is not unreasonable to account for its collapse, in part at least, in terms of the sharp drop in the crescendo of railway promotions in 1847. By this time all the atmospheric schemes had been launched, only to encounter constraints and anxieties which made both the public and the directors of companies critical of performances which, in more favourable circumstances, would have been given more opportunity for improvement. The climate of railway promotion in Britain thus changed dramatically in 1847, and quickly became hostile towards innovations which did not produce satisfactory returns on their investors' capital. In this situation, technical success alone was not sufficient to guarantee survival, and as it happened the atmospheric system was not even able to demonstrate unequivocal technical success.

In practice, the atmospheric system encountered severe technical problems, some of which could have been anticipated while others were unexpected. Among the unexpected difficulties was the poor performance of the pumping engines. These were without exception very conventional specimens of well-tried steam technology by reputable manufacturers, and it was a matter of genuine surprise and irritation to Brunel that they did not perform well. The makers grumbled about the unevenness of the loading, in that the engines had to be kept ready for action at any time in order to exhaust the tube, and would then be expected to work very hard for a few minutes before coming to a halt again. It is difficult to understand why they should have caused Brunel so much vexation, although it seems likely that, like Cubitt's Croydon Railway, the pumping engines were seriously underpowered as a result of errors in estimating the loads they would need to carry.[10] Similarly, Brunel complained about the poor communication between engine houses, which led to inefficient and sometimes unpredictable bursts of pumping activity, even though the line was supposed to be equipped with the latest Cooke and Wheatstone electric telegraph facilities. The GWR had pioneered the use of this equipment between Paddington and Slough, but its extension had been delayed by formidable problems in maintaining the efficiency of the insulating materials, and it was not until the 1850s that the electric telegraph became widely used for railway signalling. Again, it is difficult to understand the reluctance of the South Devon Railway to promote the electric telegraph more rapidly, but the delay certainly impeded the smooth introduction of atmospheric operation.[11] It may be that Brunel was using these problems, to some extent, to deflect attention from more fundamental failures.

Among the anticipated problems of the atmospheric system were its inflexibility and the performance of the longitudinal valve. One of the economies of the system was that it depended upon a single line of track. This had weighed heavily with the directors of the South Devon Railway, faced with the expense of some difficult engineering and steep gradients. But any single track involved considerable inflexibility in operating two-way traffic, in addition to the irritation encountered by all atmospheric operations in relation to points, level crossings, sidings, transfer of rolling stock, and other conditions of what had already become normal daily railway working. All these difficulties could be overcome – and were – but at the cost of undesirable extra labour and passenger inconvenience. Given sufficient time, and with Brunel's characteristic ingenuity for solutions to such problems, there is little doubt that the system could have been made to work satisfactorily, if these had been the only problems.

The longitudinal valve, however, posed a problem of a different magnitude. This had been recognized as a critical weakness in the system, and the significant breakthrough by Clegg and the Samudas had been to devise what promised to be a workable valve. Moreover, Joseph Samuda – his brother had been killed in an accident in 1844 – went on improving the valve until the closure of the working lines. The problem could not be solved quickly enough for the South Devon Railway, and it is likely that it was insoluble with the materials available at the time. The valve depended on a leather flange or flap, fixed to the tube on one side of the longitudinal gap and fitting into a recess lined with some form of sealant on the other side. The flap was reinforced with metal strips above and below, providing both the weight necessary to bring it back to the sealed position and some protection against the piston arm which pushed it up every time a train passed along the line. In addition to heavy treatment from every passing train, the valve was also subject to the vagaries of the weather, especially to being soaked by rain and frozen by frost. According to South Devon legend, the leather of the flap also suffered from the depredations of rats which took a fancy to the wax applied to keep it supple. For one reason or another, the valve of the atmospheric section of the South Devon Railway became weakened or was damaged, with a consequent loss of vacuum in the tube and hence persistent inefficiency. One railway historian has described it wisely as a case of 'demand defeated by an insufficient technology'.[12] In the last resort, it was the failure of the development process to overcome this problem in the time available which led to the abandonment of the system.

With the benefit of hindsight, and the modern acceptance of the necessity for exhaustive testing before bringing any invention into commercial development, there can be little doubt that the move to introduce the atmospheric system by Brunel and others was overhasty and mistaken. Engineers have learnt to insist that every innovation should be subjected to prolonged examination under working conditions before admitting it to the development process. But in the conditions of the 1840s, when new ideas were

available in abundance to railway engineers, and when the whole conception
of a national railway network was itself relatively untested, engineers were
under great pressure to make use of promising inventions; and in some
instances – the electric telegraph is a good example – their initiative in doing
so paid off handsomely. After all, at the same time as he was experimenting
with the atmospheric system, Brunel was introducing the novelties of iron
construction and screw propulsion to marine engineering, and he has been
praised for doing so because they were conspicuous successes. It is not
surprising, therefore, that some engineers – particularly the more visionary
ones like Brunel – were tempted by the advantages that the atmospheric
system appeared to offer (light trains, high speeds, freedom from smoke,
and easy running over gradients which would be difficult or impossible for
locomotive traction in its contemporary stage of development) and who,
after carefully assessing the available evidence, took the bold decision to
adopt it. In the circumstances, the decision proved to be costly for shareholders on the South Devon Railway and for the reputation of their engineer,
although it is probably true to say that posterity has forgiven Brunel his
lapse, and the directors of the company appeared to have borne him no
grudge.13

There were other factors which could not have been anticipated in the
early 1840s, but which provided the *coup de grace* for the atmospheric system.
In the first place, the remarkable development of the steam locomotive over
the next hundred years quickly made some of the purported advantages of
the atmospheric railway obsolete. The Stephensons, it is true, did have
confidence in the possibilities of steam traction, but they were outstanding
engineers who made distinctive contributions themselves to the development
of the technology. Brunel, on the other hand, although in many respects an
engineering polymath, was not himself a steam locomotive engineer and, as
we have seen, his essays in this field were almost disastrous for the GWR
and himself. It is easy to understand the anxiety and alarm with which
Daniel Gooch, who had rescued Brunel on that occasion, must have watched
his chief plunge into the untried technology of atmospheric propulsion.
Gooch recorded in his *Memoirs* his agreement with Robert Stephenson's
dismissal of the system, and concluded: 'This is certainly the greatest blunder
that has been made in railways.'14

Not even the Stephensons could have anticipated the eventual replacement
of steam locomotives by electric traction, which provided the most successful
alternative to steam in the twentieth century. Electric traction is like the
atmospheric system in that it provides the power of movement from outside
the train, with all its attendant savings of weight on the track, but it does
so through a simply maintained extra rail or overhead wiring instead of

through a long tube with a dubious and easily damaged sealing device. It is possible, with the application of rubber or plastic materials, that a suitably resilient seal could have been made for an atmospheric railway; but it is difficult to see how this could have been competitive with the highly flexible system provided by electric traction. In the long run, as well as the short, Brunel was therefore mistaken in gambling on the success of the atmospheric railway. In particular, he made a costly misjudgment in committing the South Devon Railway to a form of propulsion which was, at best, untested in mainline passenger service, and technically unproven. Such a procedure appears virtually inconceivable to modern management practice, where the comparative costs of alternative innovations are carefully calculated and thoroughly tested. Brunel had a well-honed imaginative intuition, which he used to assess the best engineering solution to each new situation; and when he had made his judgment he could be an eloquent and effective spokesman for the solution he had chosen. In the highly volatile world of railway building in the 1840s, boards of directors were frequently persuaded by his enthusiasm and undoubted authority, and in many cases they were well rewarded for doing so. But in the case of the atmospheric system Brunel made a serious misjudgment about its practical viability, and one which proved to be an expensive failure for the South Devon Railway. His vision of high-speed passenger transport remained substantially correct, however, and in relation to this his failures to anticipate the complications of the atmospheric system, or the capacity of the steam locomotive continuously to improve its performance, these were minor but costly errors.

8

The Great Ship

Brunel's career underwent a significant change around 1850. For the greater part of twenty years he had applied his enormous energy to fulfilling his vision of a high-speed passenger transport system in the part of the country dominated by the Great Western Railway. That vision had achieved impressive reality, but the collapse of the 'Railway Mania' and the subsequent demands for retrenchment had involved cutting back on new developments and the distressing task of dismissing young engineers who had been recruited during the period of rapid expansion. There was still railway work to be done, and Brunel delighted in the opportunity to build the new GWR terminus at Paddington, and in tackling the challenge of large bridge construction with his great iron truss bridges at Chepstow and Saltash, and his ingenious wooden viaducts in Cornwall. But his attention began to turn to other things. He bought the estate at Watcombe in Devon, where he made plans for a house and garden. He became heavily involved in the Great Exhibition in 1851, and in the same year he engaged in the 'Battle of Mickleton Tunnel' on the troublesome line from Oxford to Worcester and beyond. Most important of all, however, was the increasing interest with which he applied himself to the problems of long-distance sea transport. His vision of better transport assumed a global scale, and began to take the form of a huge iron ship which would be capable of carrying its own fuel to the Antipodes and back. The shape of what was to become the SS *Great Eastern* began to appear, in a variety of forms, in Brunel's sketch books.

The story of the *Great Eastern* is the most contentious feature of Brunel's engineering career, as historians have debated at length the clash of personalities between the engineer and John Scott Russell, the shipbuilder who built the ship. This became a running conflict throughout most of the construction and launch of the ship, and its subsequent fitting out. Brunel's family collected the documents that presented his side of the controversy, and incorporated them in the account published in the biography by his son. At that time Scott Russell was still alive, so there was no explicit hostility towards him, although his role was played down. Then L. T. C. Rolt, writing almost a century later, used the same selection of documents and convinced himself that Russell had played a demonic role in attempting to subvert the vision of Brunel. This view was forcibly and eloquently expressed, so that it was widely accepted by a generation of readers. It distorted the role of both main participants, however, and it took a new biography of John Scott Russell by George S. Emmerson to give his point of view. Both the case expressed by Rolt and Emmerson's response seem overly partisan. The truth probably lies somewhere between them.[1]

While it is not necessary to recapitulate these rival arguments in full, it is important to make an assessment of what really went wrong in the saga of the *Great Eastern*, which came close to becoming an epic disaster. The fact that the ship was completed, and that she was a considerable technical success, can only partially offset the tremendous financial liabilities incurred by those who invested in the enterprise, and the commercial failure of the vessel in operation. Perhaps most disastrously, the troubles of the ship were intimately related to the decline of Brunel's physical and mental powers and to his premature death. It would be going too far to claim that the *Great Eastern* killed I. K. Brunel, but the continuous anxiety and labour associated with her construction was spread over the last five years of Brunel's life and contributed significantly to the undermining of his hitherto buoyant constitution. The construction of the *Great Eastern* was Brunel's last great accomplishment; but even though he averted complete public catastrophe by delivering the ship, he could not prevent it from becoming the ultimate personal disaster for himself.

Several special factors in the story of the construction of the ship deserve consideration. First, Brunel showed exceptional sensitivity and possessiveness about the ship from a very early point in the project. As early as November 1853, before a plate had been laid, he had written two agitated letters to Charles Manby, the Secretary of the Institution of Civil Engineers, about a notice to discuss problems of large ship construction at the Institution:

> I assure you that I find no fault with the discussion or with anything that I have heard of as said. It was the *printed* invitation to come and see the fun and promise of a set to between fancy Sam and bloody Bill, one of whom at any rate never wished to fight and has a wife and family dependent on his keeping off the stage, that I complain of – if it is to be a practice. It is not my vanity that makes me believe that everybody understands the 'proposed large steamer' to mean 'Brunel's absurd big ship', but I will bet you any odds that out of any hundred men going into the room of whom you would ask the question, ninety-five would not dream of any other meaning. And this I say if it is to be a practice will make our meetings nuisances and drive everybody away who has anything new and difficult in hand.[2]

Although cast in a slightly whimsical mode, there is an element of irritability here which is surprising. It recurred in a stronger form about a year later, when the *Observer* published an article about the work on the ship on 13 November 1854. Brunel reacted with surprising sharpness to this article, apparently convinced that either Russell or Yates, the Secretary to the Eastern Steam Navigation Company, had commissioned it, and that it did less than justice to his contribution to the project. He wrote to Russell:

> My Dear Sir, I have actually read through twice that long article in the *Observer* and little as I generally regard newspaper notices I am annoyed by it, and inasmuch as it has the *appearance* of authority, particularly as I understand copies of it have been circulated by Mr Yates which will give it the character of authenticity, I want to take some means of correcting or altering the impressions that might be produced by it. But before determining either whether I shall do so or how I want to know its origin and whether it is (it does not look so) by a friendly hand who would himself rectify what I consider the errors in it.[3]

At the same time he wrote to Yates, making more specifically the points about the article which he found objectionable:

> A writer wishing success to our enterprise would not have omitted to mention that I had claim to public confidence on this occasion by the reason that I was the principal adviser in those previously successful attempts [in building steam ships].[4]

Neither Russell nor Yates appear to have offered Brunel much help with this enquiry, and the matter was soon dropped. But without trying to read too much into the tetchiness displayed about what was a very ordinary newspaper report, the incident provides a possible danger signal about Brunel's state of mind regarding the Great Ship project. While Brunel welcomed public esteem as much as any ambitious man, he abhorred the inquisitiveness of public opinion, and he found it difficult to handle the enormous public interest in the ship. It made him suspicious of those who sought information about it, and undermined his confidence in colleagues whom he suspected had at least connived in seeking publicity. This possessiveness had not been apparent in any of Brunel's previous projects, and it hardened into a sort of paranoia that sharpened misunderstandings and engendered conflict.

Secondly, it is worth emphasizing both the scale and novelty of the operation, because they raised problems of management with which neither the company nor the engineers were well equipped to deal. No ship even vaguely approaching the *Great Eastern* in size or complexity had been built before, yet she was commissioned to be built in a traditional shipyard, albeit by a shipbuilder of outstanding reputation in the shape of John Scott Russell.

The managerial style of Russell seems to have been non-interventionist: he told his staff what he wanted and left them to get on with it, and they tackled their responsibilities like conventional shipbuilders, relying on well-tried techniques for laying out a ship. The company, moreover, seems to have made no special provision for the organization and safety of the large labour force required, nor for the supply of the huge number of metal plates and other special materials, nor for the security of all the materials and equipment under its nominal control. Without detailed evidence of the managerial structure of the enterprise it is unreasonable to press these apparent inadequacies too strongly, but such evidence as is available tends to confirm the view that the deficiencies, however understandable, were real enough. Brunel did what he had always done to monitor the quality of the goods he purchased and posted assistants with the firms preparing iron plates and forgings for the ship, who reported regularly to their chief.[5] But what happened when supplies reached the shipyard and came under company control was less subject to personal supervision by Brunel and his team. He relied at this point on the cooperation of Scott Russell. When this was not forthcoming he became deeply frustrated.

Thirdly, Brunel and his partners and colleagues in the construction of the *Great Eastern* were trapped in an enterprise which laboured under crippling financial constraints. Not only was a great deal of capital locked up unprofitably in the towering hulk which rose up beside the River Thames, but the prospect of ever getting any return on this investment seemed to become increasingly remote. Meanwhile, the enormous costs of wrought-iron plates and steam engines, of labour and shipyard accommodation, had constantly to be met. Scott Russell was pressed to vacate the site when he became virtually bankrupt, and passed on the pressure to the company, while the owners of adjacent properties objected to obstructions and blockages. Little is known about John Yates, the secretary to the Eastern Steam Navigation Company, but he had a thankless task and was constantly harassed by the problems of paying accounts. While worried by a shipbuilder who was unable to account for large quantities of material and other costs, he was also understandably unsympathetic towards a chief engineer who behaved occasionally with excessive sensitivity, and on one occasion at least told him so.[6] He must also have had anxieties about the labour force. Much of it was organized through sub-contracting of various sorts, but it can scarcely have been under a thousand strong, so that the deployment and supervision of this large body with only a minuscule staff at his service must have been a permanent headache for the secretary. Despite this, the supervision appears to have been reasonably efficient, as there was never any serious question about the quality of the finished work.[7] But delays in construction ensured that the whole operation was hopelessly undercapitalized, causing the ruin of one company and continuing financial problems to the company which acquired the still unfinished ship.

With such crippling financial constraints there should be no wonder at the anxiety of the directors to recoup marginally on their investment by securing a small income from visitors to the site, and by promoting such activity through newspaper articles and other publicity. The crowds which turned out to witness the launch of the ship in November 1857 had responded to this publicity, even though their presence was a great nuisance to Brunel. He felt that they compromised his own personal control of the operation, involving the coordination of complicated tasks over considerable time and distance. This response suggests a fourth and last general observation about the Great Ship project. This is the fact that the *Great Eastern* provided the first engineering feat to become a massive public attraction. In spite of Brunel's dislike of intrusive publicity, the project made a profound impression on the public mind from the moment when construction started on the Isle of Dogs. Newspapers sent correspondents to describe it, magazines employed illustrators to draw it, visiting dignitaries came to look at it, and the great British public turned out to marvel at its growing bulk. As the leader writer of *The Times* surmised, the ship incorporated an enormous amount of national pride and expectation, even to the extent of justifying the British claim to 'the moral supremacy of the world'.[8] Nothing quite like this had happened before: new bridges had won local attention, but there had always been other bridges; the railways had been fascinating novelties, but there were many of them. The *Great Eastern* was different, and it was unique: there was nothing else like it in the world of maritime transport, or anywhere else for that matter. The only possible engineering precedent was Marc Brunel's Thames Tunnel, only a couple of miles up river, which had been a great novelty and pulled in crowds of visitors, but the tunnel lacked the spectacular quality of the Great Ship. Neither the company nor their engineer had bargained on this publicity factor, and the former tried to cash in on it, while the latter was embarrassed by it. For those working in the Thames-side shipyard, it made a difficult life much more complicated.

On Brunel's own account, he began work on the idea of the Great Ship towards the end of 1851: 'to make long voyages economically and speedily by steam [which] required the vessel to be large enough to carry the coal for the entire voyage at least outwards and unless the facility for obtaining coal was very great at the out port – then for the return voyage also'. He also believed that: 'vessels much larger than now built could be navigated with great advantages from the mere effects of size'.[9] From the outset, he

envisaged an iron ship, double-skinned below the water-line and compart-
mentalized by ten lateral bulkheads, with longitudinal bulkheads running
the length of the ship. Power would be derived from two sets of steam
engines – one to drive giant paddle-wheels and the other to power a screw
propeller: 'I propose both paddles *and* screw because the limited draft does
not give screw power enough and also as giving a very great increased
command over the ship under many circumstances.' The final form, with
five funnels and six masts for ancillary sail-power, 692 feet long and with a
gross register of 18,915 tons, soon began to appear in Brunel's sketch books.[10]

Early in 1852, Brunel persuaded the Eastern Steam Navigation Company,
which had been recently formed with the intention of competing with the
Peninsular and Orient line for the Indian traffic, to undertake construction
of one or two ships of these dimensions. It was necessary to raise firm
commitments to subscribe half the £800,000 estimated for the project before
work could begin, and Brunel became heavily involved in negotiations to
get together the resources and personnel to make a start. Some of Brunel's
professional colleagues, including most directors of the GWR, backed away
from any financial commitment, but others supported him and he found
sufficient friends and persons with confidence in his leadership to provide
the essential financial basis for the operation. He also established a working
relationship with John Scott Russell, who agreed to undertake the actual
building of the ship in his London shipyard. Both Brunel and Russell were
strongly supported by Charles Geach, the Rotherham ironmaster whose firm
supplied much of the ironwork for the ship. His death early in the project
was a serious loss to both men, and removed a moderating influence in
their relationship.[11]

Russell was a long-standing advocate of the 'wave-line' theory of ship
construction designed to give maximum speed and stability in all seas. He
and Brunel had known each other at least since 1836, when they had met
at the British Association for the Advancement of Science meeting that year
in Bristol. As that was the occasion when Brunel had been obliged to defend
himself against the ultra-conservative views of Dr Lardner regarding the
feasibility of ocean-going steam ships, he must have been grateful for the
support of Scott Russell. They later worked together on committees in
connection with the 1851 Exhibition, and there is every reason to believe
that the two men had a high regard for the talents of each other. So much
so that Brunel seems to have deserted the principle of a lifetime of refusing
to undertake any professional project of which he was other than in complete
control. The relationship between Brunel and Scott Russell in the project
to build the *Great Eastern* (to give the name by which the Great Ship
eventually became known) appears never to have been precisely defined, or

at least they were able to interpret it differently. Brunel believed that he had written in his usual insistence that he should be in total control of the engineering side of the project. But Scott Russell, as an established and successful shipbuilder, expected some latitude to build the ship according to his usual methods, which did not always coincide with Brunel's engineering ideas. This weakness was to prove almost fatal to the project.

Like his railway enterprises, Brunel's Great Ship project needs to be seen as a system, depending for its successful outcome on the smooth integration of a large number of interdependent parts. The marshalling of the materials and the labour force were formidable tasks, requiring management skills which were in short supply in the company. The actual construction, depending upon the riveting of a huge number of wrought iron plates and beams in a most innovative form, was beyond the competence of all traditional shipbuilders at the time, and depended heavily on the expertise available in Scott Russell's shipyard. The lateral launch, which was determined on by Brunel from the outset, was an untried procedure, calling for careful preparation. And the equipment of the ship with a wide range of new navigational gadgets figured prominently in Brunel's correspondence with contemporary scientists and craftsmen. There is a poignant indication of Brunel's concern for the total management of the project in his 'Memorandum on the Management of the Great Ship'. This arose out of the need to consider the appointment of a commander of the vessel who, Brunel observed, would require special qualities: 'The question of the principles to be followed in the use of this new Machine for such it must be considered and the character and the qualification of the man to whom it is to be entrusted ... have long been subjects of deep and serious consideration with me.' Good seamanship alone would not be enough: the commander needed also to be free of prejudice, aware of the novelty of his situation, and able to give oversight to a complete system. 'Finally, the Commander's attention must be devoted exclusively to the general management of the *whole* system under his control and his attention must not be diverted by frivolous pursuits and unimportant occupations ...', such as those encountered in running a large hotel.[12]

At about the same time – October 1855 – Brunel jotted down a series of 'Memoranda for my Own Guidance' regarding the 'Steam Ship':

1. Must provide a washhouse and large *Icehouse* ... Lamp and Candle room, Spirit stores, and inflammable stores-room. Of course the best possible place would be aft – and above deck – can this be?

2. It would be a good thing to have a railway let into the deck on each side along which a truck can carry dinner etc etc from the Kitchen to each saloon ...

3. To see what room can be gained into the inner side of the Paddle box as a gangway down to the Kitchen: also for urinals etc from the deck ...

4. A poop for a smoking room and bar ...

5. Ventilation and drainage ...

6. Gas ...

7. By constant observation to lay down position and course of ship: and correct compasses ...

8. The Captain's Cabin to be before the mainmast, with a bridge close in front of the mast ...

9. A principal entrance through one of the loading ports, and a good staircase ...

10. Second Tunnel to communicate fore and aft ...

11. Make the chimneys oval.

12. To steer by Semaphore from forward with a loud bell to call attention. Such steering however is only for emergencies: the ordinary steering will be as usual by a binnacle compass ...[13]

All this detail is reflected in Brunel's correspondence, for instance in his consultations about navigational details with Professor Airy, the Astronomer Royal, and with Piazzi Smyth, urging him to prepare some gyroscopic equipment.[14] From the beginning, the Great Ship was conceived in Brunel's mind as a huge system, over the details of which he constantly reflected, frequently changing his mind. His mental restlessness did not make him an easy colleague.

The actual construction of the ship can conveniently be described in three stages, of which the first began in February 1854 and lasted for two years until February 1856. Quite early in this period, the directors expressed concern at the burden of responsibilities which Brunel had undertaken, and resolved to appoint a full-time resident engineer. But instead of expressing gratitude for some relief from overwork, Brunel chose to stand upon his dignity. He protested to Yates: 'I have received your letter ... with great surprise', and reminded the directors of his 'stake of professional character not merely pecuniary risk [which] must ensure on my part an amount of anxious and constant attention to the whole business of the Company which is rarely given by a professional man to any one subject ...'[15] He made it clear that he wanted no partnership in his control over the enterprise, even though he had found it convenient to appoint resident engineers on most of his other projects. It was not a good portent for working relationships on the *Great Eastern*.

Very substantial progress was made on the hull in this first stage, but relations between Brunel and Scott Russell became increasingly acrimonious, at least on Brunel's side, because Russell generally managed to maintain a suave public face. It is not easy to understand just what went wrong, although the partisans of both men have developed elaborate justifications and conspiracy theories to explain the quarrel. Basically, there seems to have been a clash of temperaments exacerbated by conflicting interpretations of their managerial functions. The immediate cause of tension was the apparent laxness of Scott Russell, from Brunel's point of view, about procedures for supervising the allocation of valuable supplies. What happened to the ironwork when it reached the shipyard and came under the jurisdiction of the company or Scott Russell caused Brunel particular exasperation because he considered that no proper oversight was maintained. He wrote at the beginning of 1856, when struggling to avert the collapse of the enterprise:

> My Dear Russell, It is impossible that I can feel otherwise than greatly alarmed at the appearance of the state of things as regards 'stock'. There are 2400 tons to be accounted for. If my fears should prove too well founded let me entreat you as a sincere friend to meet the thing openly and to trace up the explanation and to give it plainly ... [16]

Considering the long tradition of petty pilfering from Thamesside operations Brunel had good justification for his anxiety, and Russell's bland replies to his entreaties were quite unsatisfactory. When Russell persisted in answering his precise requests for information about the projected weight of the ship in vague approximations, he eventually lost his temper:

> How the devil can you say you satisfied yourself of the weight of the ship when the figures your Clerk gave you are 1000 tons less than I make it or than you made it a few months ago. For *shame*, if you are satisfied. I am sorry to give you trouble but I think you will thank me for it. I wish you *were* my obedient servant, I should begin by a little flogging. [17]

Such language left little room for diplomatic manoeuvre, and as personal relationships broke down so the possibility of improving the overall management of the work declined. By February 1856 the situation had become so serious that Brunel had suspended payments to Russell. Russell, facing imminent bankruptcy, dismissed many of his staff and brought work on the ship to a standstill. The hull was taking substantial shape, with its ten transverse bulkheads creating water-tight compartments, and two longitudinal bulkheads and double iron skins, with a cellular construction in the base and top deck modelled on that of the Britannia Bridge. But it languished for several months until the formidable managerial and financial problems could be sorted out.

There followed a second stage, also lasting for about two years, during which the company struggled to keep its creditors at bay and Brunel managed to assert his personal control of the project and to resume building work. Russell, meanwhile, did not go away: the ship, after all, was in his shipyard, and his bid to provide the paddle-wheel engines for the ship had been accepted by the company. His shipyard, it is true, had been mortgaged to his bank, but his personal estate had survived and he struggled to recoup his financial solvency with other projects, while supervising the resumption of work on the ship in May. Personal friction remained, causing paranoia and bitterness. A letter from Scott Russell to the directors demonstrates the extent of his continued involvement in the project in the summer of 1856:

> Gentlemen: It is now more than three months since I had an interview with the Board, at which they proposed that I should undertake to organise the recommencement of the Works on the Great Ship, and to superintend the completion as fast as possible of the Iron Hull of the Ship, and her Paddle Engines, in order that she might be launched early in the spring of 1857 ... the whole of the Iron Hull is now in a state of rapid progress and so completely planned and organised that the workmen under the Foreman can proceed with it during my absence without further instruction.

He went on to detail other arrangements he had made before going off on holiday, which hardly coheres with the picture of an heroic Brunel managing the project unaided during this second period.[18] But Brunel seized the opportunity to tighten up on the management, turning his attention on the unfortunate Yates: 'Pray get a storekeeper and lock up your stores. I assure you the rivets walk off at a great rate besides being a means of amusement to the boys – three of whom I caught playing with them on the floor.'[19] Yates clearly felt that Brunel was undermining his position as secretary to the company, and responded with some gusto: 'I feel strongly that from your having failed in your attempt at a quarrel with Mr Russell you appear determined if it be possible to seek an occasion of one with me.'[20] And he continued in similar vein a few days later: 'You have repeatedly put me down when venturing to advise the Directors ... as something beneath their notice from a 'mere Secretary' ... but I will not be constantly subject to your misrepresentations, or to be trampled upon by you or any other man.'[21] Some of this could be attributed to tiredness in trying times, but it does suggest that Brunel had become a difficult man to work with.

Work went ahead, however, and the ship reached a sufficient stage of completion for a launch to be attempted in the autumn of 1857. This was bound to be a tricky operation as Brunel had determined to make a lateral launch into the River Thames, instead of a conventional stern-first launch. He made this decision, initially with the concurrence of Scott Russell, because the width of the river at Greenwich was little more than the length of the ship, and it was necessary to avoid interfering unduly with the normal heavy traffic. Another reason was the inconvenient height at which the bow would have been built if a more conventional procedure had been adopted. Once the commitment had been made, the keel was laid parallel to the river, with the bows pointing out to sea. The ship was built in two huge timber cradles, mounted at the top of a carefully designed and piled slipway, down which it was meant to glide easily into the water when the moment came. Brunel had insisted on a controlled launch, so that the movement of the ship could be controlled by a set of restraining chains, to prevent any possibility of damage. He had also taken great pains to calculate the trim of the ship, so that it could be moved easily off its cradles once it was in the water. Russell's reluctance to provide him with the necessary data for these calculations had been an intense irritation to Brunel.

The first attempt to launch the ship, made on 3 November 1857, was a failure. The directors had strong financial reasons for hurrying Brunel to make the launch, but he had not managed to make all the meticulous preparations he normally prepared for such an operation, and was then extremely annoyed to find that the site was full of paying visitors when the time came to begin the launch. When the first pressure was applied, the cradles carrying the ship could not be moved. Then they gave a sudden jerk that killed a worker on one of the winches. Brunel suspended the operation in order to deal with this tragedy and reassess the situation. The expectant but disappointed public considered that the launch procedure had failed and volunteered remedies. But Brunel believed that only more power was necessary, and it was after the installation of a battery of hydraulic presses that the ship was successfully pushed into the river on 31 January 1858.

One result of the tremendous warmth of support from people wishing the project well was amply demonstrated when the first launching attempts were abandoned in November 1857. The company immediately began to receive from the public a stream of helpful suggestions about how the launch could be successfully concluded. A substantial batch of these arrived around Christmas 1857, and it is possible that they were a response to a specific request for advice. Yates passed on the packet to Brunel with the note: 'Although I do not know who put the advertisement in the *Builder*, I enclose several answers.'[22] Rolt's expostulation that: 'half the cranks in England plagued Brunel with their idiotic notions' is understandable, but it is misplaced.[23] They were not all from cranks but came from a broad cross-section of informed British opinion, almost as if the nation was willing the ship into the water. Twenty-three of them seem to have arrived in two days, 21 and 22 December 1857, and received a circular acknowledgment from

9. The *Great Eastern* moored in the River Thames after the successful launch in January 1858. (*Brunel University Library*)

Bennett on 24 December. Two more arrived after Christmas, on 27 December and 7 January. Most of these twenty-five, which may conveniently be treated as a representative group, seem to have been written by professional people – doctors, clergymen, architects and businessmen – and one of them was a distinguished physicist and a Fellow of the Royal Society. Their helpful suggestions range over a diverse field, from shaking the mass of the ship through blows from cannon reactions or more direct uses of gunpowder, or by building up vibrations through tramping soldiers; to applying levers to the inert hull and improving the slipways by ball-bearings or other devices; and to introducing an armada of tugs or excavating new tidal approaches up to the ship.

Several of the suggestions, such as that from Thomas Wright, are worth recalling:

> I ... suggest that a body of soldiers, five hundred or more of the guards should fall in, say four abreast, on the deck close to one side, and when the purchases are upon the full strain, that the men should start off at the double, or jog trot, to the music of a drum or fife (to ensure their keeping in step) round the ship.[24]

This was not as silly as it sounds, because it was generally agreed that the ship had become stuck after the aborted launch efforts in November, and that the crucial problem was that of overcoming the inertia of 10,000 tons of iron sitting in two massive timber cradles at the top of the slipway. A Manchester physicist, J. P. Joule, suggested applying a modest force 'to pull on the cradles alternately, using the other as a pivot', with the recoil from a 'few small cannon' helping to overcome the resistance.[25] The only response which seemed to have aroused Brunel to irritability was that of G. Thornton, who coyly refused to commit his brilliant idea to paper, evoking the answer:

> the difficulties are clear enough to me, and the remedy, and the only remedy, is clear enough and I can hardly imagine the cleverest man in the world who is not *acquainted with all the particulars* suggesting anything useful. Still, I shall pay great attention to anything you may say, particularly if you will tell me what is the difficulty you have assumed to exist.[26]

No specific suggestion from Thornton is recorded.

It is clear that Brunel did not welcome any of the suggestions he received, because he had no part in inviting them and had already decided what needed to be done:

> after full consideration of all the circumstances and assisted by the best advice I could call to my aid – namely that of my friend Mr R. Stephenson – I considered that the only mode of proceeding and one which there appeared no reason to

doubt would succeed was to apply considerably more press power ... to double
what we had.[27]

And so it was: at first light on a bleak winter's day at the end of January
1858, and with a much smaller crowd than hitherto, the Great Ship was
pushed into the river by a greatly augmented bank of hydraulic engines.
Brunel had convinced himself that the fault, such as it was, lay with the
economy measures forced upon him which had reduced the power available
to him at the first launch attempt, and Stephenson supported him in this
conclusion. The remedy was thus comparatively simple, though expensive:
increase the battery of presses to do the job. So his assistants were sent
round the country to secure hydraulic presses, and many firms such as
Tangye Brothers of Birmingham benefited from this request.[28]

The correspondence regarding methods of launching the ship failed to
produce any ideas which were of genuine use to Brunel. It is significant,
nevertheless, because it demonstrates the keen national interest with which
the construction of the *Great Eastern* was being followed, and the strength
of the goodwill towards the project. Once in the water, the third stage of
construction lasted from the launch until September 1859, and was concerned
with fitting out the ship as she lay moored in the Thames. For much of this
period Brunel was absent owing to the illness which was to prove fatal: from
May to September 1858 he was obliged to take a family holiday in South
France, and then from December 1858 to May 1859 he was again dispatched
by his doctors to Egypt and Italy in an attempt to recover his failing health.
In his absence Scott Russell secured the major contract for fitting out the
ship. A new company had been formed after the launch to acquire the
unfinished vessel. Even though Brunel did his best to urge on the new
proprietors the unique qualities of their acquisition, the critical condition
of his health made it impossible for him to monitor the operation. Before
he departed on his enforced 'rest cure', however, he wrote to Thomas
Brassey, one of the new directors:

It is generally said that the new company are buying this ship under the impression
that they are embarking only on a speculation similar to that of buying very cheap
a large and costly but ordinary building in which no expense has been spared but
which is not quite finished and that all they have to do is to call in a few ordinary
tradesmen, upholsterers and painters and finish it off and let it at a large profit ...
Now if that is the belief in which the leaders of the new company embark in the
matter they will find when too late that a very great mistake has been made ...
The mercantile success of the undertaking depends first entirely on the perfect
mechanical success of the ship as a machine and though great progress has been
made in the construction of the machine the buyers will find that it is not quite
such a simple straightforward business to finish it and make it work efficiently

and profitably. Like a half-finished chronometer it may be capable as I believe it is of being made into a perfect machine and then into a profitable one, but it will be much easier to spend a great deal of money and time and make it a total failure. I have no doubt there are many men in England quite as competent as myself to have originally designed the whole, but there are few if any who could now take it up and learn all the difficulties and what may be called the weak points – and make the thing a success.[29]

It is unlikely that the directors were unaware of the previous disputes but it is probable that, in Brunel's absence, they turned to Scott Russell because his knowledge of the ship and its requirements was second only to that of Brunel. Scott Russell, moreover, was engaged in the installation of the paddle-wheel engines, so that he had a lively interest in the completion of the ship. Under his guidance, the fitting out appears to have been done with reasonable efficiency and punctuality. It is impossible to determine whether or not Brunel's return to the scene for the last hectic months made any significant difference in these respects. In any event, by the beginning of September 1859, the ship was ready to make her first voyage.

Like most of the major organs of British public opinion in these years, *The Times* took a continuing interest in the affairs of the *Great Eastern*. In a leading article published about this time, it mused on past difficulties and future prospects:

> It is only the other day that thousands were flocking to see the *Great Britain*, then the largest ship afloat. There are now more than a dozen larger than she is. It is only a question of size, and that is a question of money. The undertaking had to do everything for itself, and those who have contributed to the work have paid heavily for their generous confidence in the powers of nature and of man. But the work survives, and will shortly be put to the proof ... [30]

As it turned out, the 'proof' was ambiguous: within a few days, a disaster on her first voyage and the death of her creator brought a renewed loss of confidence in the ship, even though she sailed well and appeared to fulfil all the design specifications of her builders. The events of these September days provide an important footnote to the story of the construction of the *Great Eastern*, because they encapsulate many of the factors that had brought her so close to complete disaster. They so epitomized the problems of the vessel that it is worth reviewing them. Although technically complete and seaworthy at the beginning of the month, neither set of engines (the paddle-wheel engines and the screw engines) had been tested or given proper sea-trials, even though Scott Russell was later to protest that the paddle-wheel engines had been tested within the terms of his contract. The ship, moreover, still had no licence to carry passengers. It was proposed, therefore, to carry out tests as the ship sailed to Holyhead via Weymouth, by which time it was hoped that the necessary certification would be complete and that the ship could depart on its maiden voyage carrying passengers to New York. Meanwhile, only specially invited or paying guests and members of the press were present with the crew on board the ship. She moved off from her moorings on Wednesday 7 September and sailed down the Thames. Two days before, while inspecting the ship, the ailing Brunel had been afflicted by the stroke which was to prove fatal, and had been taken to his home for the last time. For a few days he remained conscious and continued to wait for every communication from the voyage.

There were two unusual features on this first voyage. Not only was the ship itself an outstanding innovation in marine technology, it was also crammed with novelties, many of which had sprung from the fertile brain of Brunel, but all of which required new routines and procedures from members of the crew to whom they were completely unfamiliar. Among these was Brunel's ingenious scheme for preheating the water before it entered the boilers, and it was this which was to be the major cause of trouble on the voyage. The second remarkable feature was the anarchy that prevailed on the ship. The autocracy of the ship's captain, traditional in the British merchant marine as in the navy, was suspended on this occasion by the need of the company to permit the engine builders and other contractors access to their equipment, and also, it would seem, by the anxiety of the company to win the approval of a favourable press coverage, and possibly also to earn some income, by allowing representatives of the press and a selection of privileged individuals to become passengers. The emergency, when it occurred, revealed the lack of clear lines of command on responsibilities amongst the crew.

The Great Ship spent the Wednesday night off Purfleet, and on Thursday 8 September moved down to the Nore, where the compasses were checked. Then of Friday 9 September she set off down the English Channel, gradually building up the speed of her engines. She proceeded with astonishing smoothness, as the accounts of passengers and journalists subsequently demonstrated. But then, just after 6 pm, as she was cruising off Dungeness Light, there was a terrific explosion. The first of her five funnels was hurled into the air, together with a large section of the deck and forward saloon, and a stream of scalding water cascaded into the paddle-engine boiler room, inflicting terrible injuries from which five stokers died. The explosion, which would have destroyed a smaller ship, had little effect on the progress of the *Great Eastern*. Although the paddle-engine boilers were immediately closed down, Brunel had arranged for either set of engines to draw steam from the supply of the other set if necessary, so that the ship was able to carry on smoothly with both paddle-wheels and screw operating. The next morning, about 10 am, she drew into Portland Harbour near Weymouth, where the inquest into what had gone wrong began almost immediately.

There was, first, the formal inquest into the cause of the deaths of the five stokers, but beyond this there was also a more general enquiry about the safety of a ship which appeared to be accident-prone. The legal inquest began promptly on Monday 12 September when Mr H. Locke, the coroner for the district of Weymouth, assembled a jury of fifteen men in the town hall. Journalists from London covering the inquest expressed surprise at the small amount of public interest which it generated, and the Special Correspondent of *The Times* commented critically on the jury: ' The *nonchalance* of these gentlemen seemed to excite considerable surprise among those present [as they] occupied themselves throughout the greater part of the day in reading country newspapers.'[31] Presumably it would have been acceptable if they had been reading *The Times*, but one is bound to wonder how frequently the eligible citizens of Weymouth were called upon to perform this sort of onerous duty for accidents at sea. In any case, the enquiry got off to a muted start because several important people, including Scott Russell, were unable to be present on the day. But evidence was taken from James Briscoe, junior engineer of the paddle-engine department; Dr Slater, the ship's surgeon; and R. P. Brereton, the chief of Brunel's staff. The jury was then taken to Portland Bay to view the ship, and the coroner adjourned the proceedings until the following Saturday. The first reports of the enquiry appeared in the press on Tuesday 13 September. Two days later Brunel died, throwing his staff into grief and perplexity. Brereton made a competent witness, but in the circumstances it is hardly surprising that many questions went unanswered, or even asked, at the inquest. Proceedings were resumed on Saturday 17 and on Monday 19 September, ending late in the evening of this third day. The inquest took evidence from the entire senior engineering staff and several of the distinguished passengers, including Scott Russell and his son Norman, and ended with the evidence of the captain, William Harrison. The jury then came to a verdict of accidental death, although they were critical of the engineers for not using 'sufficient caution' and implied that there had been some negligence by those who should have performed specific functions. Unfortunately, it was not able to determine what those functions should have been, or who should have been responsible for them. As virtually every person who gave evidence seemed anxious to disclaim responsibility, the jury had an impossible task.[32]

The point at issue was who should have opened a particular stop-cock. This was on a pipe providing a vent from the feedwater tank which encircled the lower part of the front funnel. The tank was intended to provide pre-heated water to the paddle-engine boilers and, incidentally, to keep the saloon cool. It was quickly established that the explosion had been caused by the build-up of steam in this tank when, after some mechanical difficulty with the donkey-engines pumping water into the boilers, the engineers had cut out the supply from the feeder tanks in favour of a direct supply. If the stop-cock on the vent-pipe had been open, as was the intention of the designer, this procedure would have caused no danger. But it was closed, even though witnesses testified that it had been open earlier in the voyage. The implication was that somebody had deliberately closed it on the day of the fatal accident, taking the necessary spanner and getting to it in a cabinet behind a closed door. But who and why? Nobody would admit to having done so and, more seriously, nobody would accept responsibility for having to attend to it. The stop-cock was one of the many detailed innovations on the ship which seemed to have fallen outside the remit of both the crew and the engineers.

The situation generated conspiracy theories. The enemies of Scott Russell convinced themselves that it had been his malign hand on the stop-cock which had caused the disaster. But this is preposterous, because not only is it unthinkable that he should have risked his own life and that of his son by such an act of spite, but also he had simply nothing to gain from any failure of the *Great Eastern.* His reputation was as much involved with its success as that of Brunel. On the other hand, Russell's disclaimers of responsibility at the inquest were out of keeping with the role he had played since the beginning of the voyage, as several observers were prepared to confirm that they had seen him quite incontrovertibly giving orders for the management of the paddle-wheel engines. Russell did not deny this but claimed that, as the contractor for the engines, he had made himself available for advice when called upon. He was insistent that, as he had fulfilled the terms of his contract, the engines were no longer technically his responsibility, but had been handed over to the company.

It seems likely that there had been some loose drafting of contracts, which allowed Scott Russell to get away with this interpretation. He was able to claim that he had performed the required test runs on the paddle-engines, even though Brunel had protested that at least one of these had been held in the middle of the night, when nobody other than Russell's men had been present to observe it, and none of them had been conducted while the ship was in motion. One of Brunel's last instructions to McLellan, the chief engineer for the company, had been on no account to accept the engines until they had been given a proper sea trial, which would mean by the time the ship reached Weymouth at the earliest. This was certainly the understanding of the team from James Watt & Co. who had installed the screw-engines, and it is difficult to understand how Russell could have avoided the same interpretation of his responsibilities for the paddle-engines. In this, as in other matters, he displayed a crafty evasiveness which did not endear him to the other parties to the disaster.

At the end of the inquest, the coroner observed: 'The real question was, whether Mr Russell, Mr Dixon, or Mr Arnott was in charge of those paddle wheels, and if they were in charge, whether their conduct was such as to render them liable to a charge of manslaughter.'[33] Dixon and Arnott had both been employed by Russell, although the latter was able to claim that, at the time of the accident, they were in the pay of the company. Both, needless to say, like Russell, denied any responsibility. The coroner professed himself unable to come to a positive conclusion on the first question, so that the jury was not able to apportion blame. But in pinpointing command over the paddle-wheel engines as the key issue, he inferred that the responsibility for the stop-cock on the feed-water tanks to the boilers of those engines was located there. The most informative evidence, amongst all the usual evasions which were such a feature of this enquiry, was that of John Arnott. Although formerly one of Russell's team, he had been employed for a three-month period by the company, and represented himself as being answerable to McLellan, the company engineer. He appears to have been in charge of the paddle-wheel engines at the time of the explosion. He was asked by the coroner if he had taken any action regarding the stop-cock: 'After the accident occurred witness did not send Mr Patrick to open the cock or any other syphon. He told Mr Patrick there was a cock, but he did not know they were shut.'[34] There seems to have been no pursuit of such statements by rigorous cross-examination at the inquest. But it was fortunate for all concerned that if in fact the workman Mr Patrick only received such an oblique instruction, at least he acted on it promptly and averted a further disaster by opening the stop-cock on the second funnel which, like the first, had been equipped with a feedwater jacket.

In the circumstances, the coroner and jury at Weymouth were probably correct in refusing to find any person responsible for the tragedy. The real responsibility lay with the anarchy which characterized the first voyage of the *Great Eastern*, with its uncertainty about contractual liabilities and lines of command. It was the sort of situation which was anathema to Brunel, who would have wished to be in charge of and responsible for the whole operation. If he had been present, there is of course no guarantee that the oversight or error which led to the closure of the stop-cock would not have occurred. But at least the lines of command would have been clearly defined, and everybody would have been put on their mettle to perform efficiently. He was not there, however, and in the resulting power vacuum chaos reigned. It was a situation in which disaster was waiting to happen. This is not to exonerate the company or its officers or Scott Russell, all of whom contributed to the confusion with which a novel and highly complicated technological system was put into operation. But the failure shows how badly prepared the participants were to carry through Brunel's plans when the master was not himself present. It also shows the administrative inadequacies whereby an accident of this magnitude was allowed to pass without anybody insisting on a full-scale independent legal enquiry.

The first voyage of the *Great Eastern* did not end at Weymouth. After three weeks of repairs and modifications, which included the removal of the ill-fated feedwater tanks and the replacement of the funnel, the ship proceeded on its way to Holyhead. There she was welcomed by various civil and national dignitaries, and survived a ferocious storm. But the company felt that it was then too late in the year to commit their vessel to a maiden voyage across the Atlantic, and instructed Captain Harrison to bring her back to Southampton Water for the winter. Further disaster struck there, when the captain was drowned while going out to his ship, and it was well into 1860 before she was ready to depart for New York under a new captain and with very few passengers. The misfortunes of the first voyage had made their mark, and the travelling public awaited reassurances, which were not forthcoming. Except for her service as a cable-laying vessel, the ship was never a commercial success, and it seems likely that the volume of trade available did not justify a vessel of this size at that time. Forty years later there would have been ample traffic, but in this respect, as in some of his other undertakings, Brunel's vision was premature. *The Times*, which maintained a close interest in the ship and its misadventures, summed up the discords which surrounded the first voyage and set such a poor precedent for her future prospects:

> The immense vessel was a microcosm with internal politics as diverse as those of the United States on the eve of a Presidential election ... We should like to know who the engineers were whose want of caution is vaguely indicated by that jury as the cause of a catastrophe which has consigned several of our fellow-creatures to a horrible death, and has cast a great gloom over the inauguration of an enterprise which our hopes, and sympathies, and pride had made national, and which we had accepted as an exponent of the vigour, enterprise, and grandeur of conception, that justify our claims to the moral supremacy of the world.[35]

It cannot be claimed that Brunel derived any great encouragement from public sympathy with his endeavours, and in the end the triumph, such as it was, was his own. The last six years of his life were devoted to the construction of the *Great Eastern*, and in these he showed the same sense of driving vision and willingness to commit himself to an engineering 'hunch' which had characterized so much of his career. With the Great Ship project, as with the broad gauge, longitudinal sleepers for his railway, iron ships, screw propulsion and the atmospheric system, he adopted and persuaded others to support him in pursuing what he believed to be the correct engineering solutions to specific problems. Iron ships and screw propulsion were generally accepted and Brunel's vision widely applauded. The broad gauge and longitudinally mounted rails came to appear as costly diversions from economical practice, and were abandoned for financial rather than engineering reasons. The atmospheric system was an unqualified disaster, and Brunel was driven to recommending its abandonment. The Great Ship came close to becoming another disaster, and helped to drive its author to an early grave, even though, from an engineering point of view, it was a remarkable technical success. In all this, Brunel's career showed an outstanding continuity of vision: he was an engineer of brilliant perceptions who had the courage and persistence to act upon his perceptions. In his failures as in his successes, Brunel tended to do things with a spectacular flourish that confirmed his image as a distinguished engineer and an esteemed public figure. But as the final episode in his career, the construction of the *Great Eastern* left an ambivalent impression. It had the majesty and towering technical achievement of all his great works. At the same time, it demonstrated an overweening self-confidence, amounting almost to megalomania, in his determination to take complete control of the operation. In his prime, he might have managed it. By the mid 1850s, however, failing powers and impending mortality made it a close call, only narrowly avoiding complete disaster.

9

Other Significant Works

In addition to all his great works on railways and ships, Brunel spent much of his time on less demanding undertakings, even though they were frequently substantial commissions and had considerable significance as engineering achievements. Once his inspired vision of a worldwide transport system had begun to take shape, however, Brunel tended to treat other tasks as routine and unchallenging, so that these comparatively minor works definitely occupied a subsidiary role in the hierarchy of his interests. As early as 1835 he spoke dismissively of his project to build the Hungerford Suspension Bridge across the Thames at Charing Cross. To him, it was merely a modified version of his Clifton Bridge design, and not worth a lot of thought: 'I have condescended to be engineer to this,' he wrote in his journal, 'but I shan't give myself much trouble about it.'[1] It seems probable that this was his attitude to his harbour work in Sunderland and Plymouth, and to most of the modest bridges, waterworks and drainage schemes to which he made a contribution. Some of these lesser works, however, throw a useful light on Brunel's methods of working, when sufficient documentary evidence survives, and serve further to illustrate the range of his talent and the diversity of his design styles.

Any perusal of the series of sketch books in the Bristol Collection, or study of the surviving artefacts of his engineering career, demonstrates that I. K. Brunel was an enthusiastic rather than a discriminating stylist, distinguished by the eclecticism of his designs rather than by any stylistic consistency. In the course of his career he worked through a bewildering variety of styles, employing each in turn with skill and panache, but not committing himself for long to any one choice. He characterized his first successful design, which won the competition for the Clifton Bridge, as 'the Egyptian thing', but went on to design most of his early railway buildings for the Great Western Railway in an ebullient Gothic style, with Romantic Tudor embellishments. Then in the 1840s he developed a taste for the Italianate style which became popular at that time, passing on in the last decade of his life to design ships and bridges which expressed a more functional style. In all this variety, it is curious that the one style which he does not appear to have adopted on any scale, with the exception of the western portico to the Box Tunnel, was Classicism. In this he was probably reflecting the Victorian reaction against the Palladian Classicism of the eighteenth century. This raises the interesting question of the degree to which Brunel's styles mirrored the taste of his contemporaries, or helped to formulate them.[2]

Egyptology was certainly a fashionable vogue in Europe in the 1830s Promoted partly by Napoleon's Egyptian campaign of 1799, and by the 'discovery' of the Middle East by wealthy young men making the Grand Tour, there had developed something of a cult for objects and styles representing the ancient traditions of the pharaohs. It was expressed in the spectacular linen mill built in Leeds by John Marshall, and on a more domestic scale by the Egyptian House in Penzance. Both these buildings survive from the 1830s, and there were many more ephemeral features in houses and gardens of the period which were influenced by the fashion. Brunel was certainly aware of it when he entered the Clifton Bridge competition. His winning drawings incorporated tapered towers capped by Egyptian-style sphinxes. Not all the detailing could be described as Egyptian, because he planned to clad the towers with cast-iron plates displaying a frieze showing all the phases of construction of the bridge. These were abandoned on grounds of economy, so that it is almost true to say that, minus the sphinxes which were abandoned for the same reason, the surviving design is more authentically Egyptian than Brunel intended. He made little subsequent use of this style, although the fact that he chose to convalesce in Egypt in the last year of his life suggests that it remained an interest to him.[3]

Once he had been appointed chief engineer to the GWR in 1833, Brunel became absorbed for a decade in the enormous task of setting up a major railway system, and every detail of this enterprise bore the hallmark of his exuberant workmanship. The style, however, was not consistent, so that every station and tunnel portico tended to be different, although the dominant theme was a sort of Romantic Gothicism. The Gothic Revival was still in its infancy, but Brunel was a friend of the elder Pugin, the talented but eccentric architect who did so much to popularize the Gothic style, and who had collaborated with Brunel's father on a scheme for a London Necropolis to ensure a seemly burial for its dead citizens.[4] It is probably true to say that the Pugins' Romantic vision of a medieval ecclesiastical style being adopted for everyday secular and domestic purposes was the most powerful single influence on Brunel's style. This was not the High Gothicism of Barry's rebuilt Palace of Westminster, with internal details by the younger Pugin, or of Scott's St Pancras Station Hotel, but the inspiration was much the same. The romanticized neo-Tudor façade of Temple Meads Station, and the rusticated and castellated porticoes on the tunnels between Bristol and Bath, stand as monuments to this early Gothic Revival. The façade of Bath Spa Station is particularly revealing because here, where Brunel might have been expected to defer to the ubiquitous Palladianism of the city's style, he chose instead to embellish it with a form of cottage Gothicism. However much it was overlaid by subsequent styles, this was the original pattern of the GWR, and many specimens survive throughout the system.

Brunel first visited Italy in the 1840s, in the course of supervising his railway projects in Piedmont and Tuscany, and he subsequently incorporated many Italianate features into the architectural aspects of his engineering style. The best examples of this were the eight engine houses which he designed as the pumping stations for the atmospheric system of propulsion on the South Devon Railway. These were the engine houses which were completed before the abandonment of the system in 1848, and two of them survive today. Their Italianate features, such as their massive campanile-like chimneys, gently pitched roofs and overhanging eaves, still contribute a distinctive quality to the Devonian landscape. The style became very popular in the second half of the nineteenth century for large chimneys in mills, such as the monumental structure at Listers' Mill in Bradford, and in water-pumping stations, although in the chimney of Brunel's own excursion into water-pumping engineering – the Clifton Water Company in Bristol – he adopted a subdued Gothicism which received some local ridicule. The Bristol chronologist John Latimer, always disposed to be critical of Brunel, described the building of 1845 at Black Rock in Clifton Gorge as having been 'mistaken for a seamen's church'.[5]

Brunel achieved his mature engineering style in the 1850s. It was a sort of functionalism, presenting engineering efficiency with elegance but minimal decoration. He had already anticipated such functionalism in the austere but graceful bridges and viaducts on the GWR between London and Didcot, and his intimate experience of ship design also provided a firm discipline in the functional tradition. In its fittings and furnishings there was plenty of High Gothicism about the *Great Eastern*, but as far as its marine engineering was concerned it was built for strength and maximum functional efficiency in any sea or weather conditions. Brunel's strikingly successful use of wrought iron in the *Great Britain* and the *Great Eastern* demonstrated his mastery of this material, and he applied the same skill in his later bridges.[6] One such bridge of distinctly functional design was the Balmoral Bridge, to which we will return shortly. Like other expressions of engineering functionalism, however, it aroused criticism from exponents of High Gothicism in mid- and late Victorian Britain. The new generation of wrought-iron girder bridges which brought railways over the Thames to termini in the heart of the metropolis, in particular, were subject to strong aesthetic protests on account of their perceived 'ugliness'. One of these, into Charing Cross Station, replaced the Hungerford Suspension Bridge for pedestrians which Brunel had built in the 1840s. It incorporates the piers of the Brunel bridge.[7] This sort of criticism continued through the later decades of the nineteenth century and came to a crescendo in the tirade of William Morris against the new Forth Bridge when it opened in 1890. But it was a controversy in which Brunel was only present for the first salvo, and we can only guess that he would have added strength and elegance to the functionalist tradition.[8]

Perhaps Brunel's outstanding service to engineering functionalism was his design for Paddington Station as the London terminus of the GWR. He had served on the Great Exhibition Building Committee in 1850, when the organizers of that ambitious event were working to a daunting timetable in their attempt to devise a suitable building to house it. Brunel had himself prepared a design which sported a large cast-iron dome, but which was otherwise undistinguished, and like his colleagues he had been immediately impressed by the breathtaking design submitted by Joseph Paxton. This was essentially an extension of the successful conservatory which he had constructed for the Duke of Devonshire at Chatsworth, being conceived as a structure which could be erected speedily from mass-produced iron sections, panes of glass and pre-cut timber. It was an ideal functional solution to the problem of housing the Exhibition in Hyde Park. It was also extremely graceful, and quickly endeared itself as the 'Crystal Palace' to the thousands who flocked to visit it when it was opened to the public in May 1851.[9] Brunel became an enthusiastic supporter of the scheme and a personal friend of Paxton, and he was undoubtedly much influenced by the Crystal Palace when he came to design the great train shed at Paddington. He employed an architect, Digby Wyatt, to attend to the detailing, but the overall conception was Brunel's, with its three parallel arched corridors, carried on rows of cast-iron pillars and with elegant transepts, all glazed to give the maximum possible amount of light to the platforms below. It broke away from the bleak sheds of the earliest termini and stations, like the original Euston platforms, although it was at Euston that Philip Hardwick provided for Robert Stephenson the quintessential Greek Temple as a decorative *motif* in the form of the Doric portico which stood at the entrance to the station.[10]

Brunel's association with the Crystal Palace did not end with the Exhibition of 1851, as Paxton, now knighted as Sir Joseph in recognition of his spectacular success, called on him to help in the reconstruction of the building on its new site at Sydenham. This became one of the two lesser works of Brunel in the 1850s on which it is possible to assemble from the documents an instructive account of his procedure. Already, in the summer of 1851, Paxton had produced a scheme for the retention of the Crystal Palace in Hyde Park as a 'Winter Park and Garden under Glass'. When this scheme was turned down he busied himself in forming a company to purchase the building and with finding a site on which to re-erect it. The site he chose was a country estate of two hundred acres at Sydenham Hill, Croydon, a few miles south of London. The palace was dismantled and removed to this new home between 1852 and 1854, and the Queen reopened it on 10 June 1854. Paxton was able to use the site to great advantage, placing the palace at the top of the hill with wonderful prospects to the east over Kent and Surrey, and terracing the hillside below it in order to contain a series of fountains, gardens and other attractions. The Palace itself was considerably enlarged in the process of being moved, with an arched roof throughout its length, a much larger transept, and supporting transepts and wings added at both ends. It was also five-tiered instead of three. Because it would require heat for its shrubs throughout the year, Paxton also introduced a bank of boilers, set into the hillside in a half-basement along the main axis of the building. These boilers could be serviced from a road running through the building, and the flues were led out underground to be discharged into chimneys at both ends of the Palace. The need for these chimneys, combined with the requirement for a large supply of water to service the lavish battery of fountains which he had installed, led Paxton to envisage two substantial towers which could perform both functions. It seems likely, however, that Paxton became anxious about the designs for these towers, which had been produced by his assistant, Charles H. Wild, and that he had turned to Brunel for advice about them. The subsequent involvement of Brunel in the building of the Crystal Palace towers provides a vivid cameo of his methods of work.[11]

Brunel confirmed Paxton's anxieties, observing that 'the attempt to support upwards of 500 tons at a height of more than 200 feet upon a cluster of slender legs with but a small base involves considerable difficulties'. He went on to point out that the twelve main legs of each tower should not also perform the function of water pipes, as Wild had envisaged; that it was necessary to provide horizontal bracing on each floor to prevent the legs from buckling; and that the water tank itself should be of wrought iron instead of cast iron, and that its weight should be carried directly on the tops of the columns rather than being transferred, as in Wild's plan, through supporting struts.[12] It is clear that, having been asked for his professional judgment, Brunel gave the problem his close attention. But he was concerned about the professional etiquette involved in his relations with Wild, whom he did not wish to appear to be displacing, so he wrote to Wild explaining how he had come to see his plans for the towers.[13] It seems that Wild had been absent from work on account of sickness, but that did not spare him from being cross-questioned by Brunel about the depth of the concrete foundations prepared for the towers and other technical details. Brunel urged Wild to consult the contractor who had laid the foundations, and to take further advice from Robert Stephenson. But then he rebuked Wild for reporting to Stephenson rather than himself: 'You must not forget that I was professionally applied to by the Directors of the Crystal Palace.' He was prepared to delay his report for a month to accommodate Wild, 'yet as a professional man I must not allow this desire to postpone my proceedings to the inconvenience of the Company'.[14] Brunel and Stephenson were soon in agreement, however, that the concrete used in the foundations was unsatisfactory, and that it would need to be replaced.[15] It was in these terms that Brunel reported to the directors at the end of November 1853, concluding with the remark that: 'In justice to my friend Mr Wild I wish to state that he has willingly adopted all my suggestions.'[16]

The directors decided that all Brunel's recommendations should be adopted, despite the expense and inevitable delays. They decided, moreover, that they would like Brunel to replace Wild as the engineer responsible for the towers. This is clear from an awkward letter in which Brunel tried to point out to Wild, as kindly as possible, that he was not up to the job,[17] and from a letter to Paxton a few days later in which Brunel in effect took charge of the operation.[18] But a further delay became inevitable when Paxton had second thoughts about the dimensions of the towers, and decided to increase the capacity of the tanks from 500 tons of water to 1500 tons. Brunel observed that this would involve a substantial increase in the strength of the towers, although there was no difficulty about this, apart from the expense.[19] Wild's slender towers, which can be seen in contemporary photographs to have been half-built, were promptly demolished,[20] and Brunel gave very close attention to the siting and construction of the new water towers. Laid on a 1 in 12 slope consisting of stiff London clay, the foundations would need to support around 2500 tons each, and these were provided in each case by a concrete ring with an outside diameter of 58 ft, laid in an excavation about 10 ft deep in the lower side of the hill. Upon this ring was built a substantial drum of brickwork, tapering slightly to a height of 18 ft, and on this stood twelve cast-iron foundation plates from which rose the cast-iron columns and panels, all carefully bonded and braced, which in turn carried the domed base of the water tank. Up through the centre of each tower rose the brick chimney, with the iron staircase turning around it. The chimney shaft went through the middle of the water tank to an ornamental cast-iron cap surmounting the pitched glass-covered roof over the tank. The two structures of the north and south towers were identical, adding impressive terminal features to the mass of the Crystal Palace, with which they harmonized in every respect.

Brunel proceeded to the construction of the towers with characteristically thorough preparation. He was ready to begin operations in August 1854, after the Queen had performed the official opening of the Palace on its new site, when he recommended that the contract should be awarded to Fox, Henderson & Co. Considering that they had been the major contractors for the original building, and for its move to Sydenham, it would have been difficult to imagine any other contractor better equipped to do the job. But Brunel had reservations about them, although he overcame these and expressed the belief that the directors should continue to show confidence in them:

> Besides this I believe you will get the work done much quicker by employing them. With all their faults, and no man I believe has had much greater experience than I have of the faults of Messrs Fox Henderson as contractors, yet I am bound to state that if properly looked after they have the ability and the desire to execute excellent work, and that the work of the towers which were pulled down confirms exactly this opinion.[21]

Brunel had every intention that the contractors should be 'properly looked after', and it was on his terms, with carefully graded penalty clauses written into the contract, that Fox Henderson got the job.

The contract had barely been signed before Brunel encountered an unanticipated problem in the shape of plans to build a new railway, to service the Palace, which would tunnel under the corner of the site on which the south tower would stand. He expressed his 'great astonishment' to Paxton and protested that: 'It will be quite out of the question building the tower till the tunnel is finished.'[22] Then Brunel consulted with 'my friend Mr Bidder', who was the engineer responsible for the tunnel, and was reassured that every effort would be made to prevent disturbance to the foundations of the tower, on the strength of which he was prepared to proceed with the work while monitoring the structure closely in order to register any sign of settlement.[23]

By November activity on the site was increasing and, as good as his word, Brunel was harassing the contractors with a close scrutiny: 'the castings are not as clean as I am accustomed to see from your works' being one of his gentler observations.[24] By the end of the month he was reporting to George Grove, secretary to the directors, that work was going ahead satisfactorily,[25] and by mid December he announced the completion of the massive concrete and brickwork bases of both towers, giving him confidence to

expect that the work would be finished by 1 May.[26] Brunel and his assistant
on the site, F. W. Shields,[27] both made visits to the ironworks in Birmingham
from which the bulk of the material had been ordered, and there was a
continuing barrage of supervisory comment to the contractors. If they
answered back, Brunel would subject them to what he called in another
context 'a crack of the whip': in one instance he rebuked Fox Henderson
with the observation that: 'probably a more strict adherence to the letter of
the contract on my part would secure more business-like proceeding on
your part. I shall try it'.[28] Nevertheless, he recommended prompt payment
to them for work completed.[29]

Another cause of complaint arose in March, when Brunel found fault
with the iron cement used as a sealant between the iron plates. He wrote
to the contractors:

> The iron cement joints turn out bad. What it arises from I have not yet discovered,
> but they have not hardened at all except on the skin. They will have to be cut
> out and remade. This must be attended to immediately, the work commenced
> and a clear admission on your part of your liability to make them good. I was
> particularly anxious that you should obtain information from experienced work-
> men either of your own or others as to the making of iron cement which is no
> longer so well understood as it used to be in my younger days, when millwrights
> used iron cement instead of fitted surfaces … and the sooner you get some old
> millwright to instruct you the better.[30]

There was a further rebuke in May when the contractors complained about
Shields for pointing out 'some most improper and unworkmanlike … soc-
kets', with the observation that they ought rather to be grateful to Shields
for allowing them to avoid possible 'serious consequences'.[31] And, as late as
September 1855, Brunel wrote a stiff letter to Sir Charles Fox objecting to
shoddy work which was causing leakages in the water towers, and requiring
it to be made good.[32] Yet it must be supposed that his bark was worse than
his bite, for within a few days he was prepared to express his entire
satisfaction with Fox Henderson to the directors of the Crystal Palace
Company: 'I never had a contract executed under me during which I had
less reason I may say less opportunity for complaining of or even of seeing
any loss of time.'[33] One may sympathize with contractors who had to deal
with him when he had *more* reason to complain.

The projected completion date of 1 May 1855 came and went, with Brunel
responding to an anxious enquiry from Paxton with the excuse that severe
winter weather conditions had caused the delay, but that work on the north
tower should be complete in two months, while that on the south tower
would take a little longer. Even this timetable proved to be optimistic, so
that the water pipes were not being tested until the end of July,[34] and only

in August did he feel able to report: 'All the frame work of both towers is completed and the tank of the North tower ready to be proved and that on the South is expected to be equally forward in the course of a week or ten days.'[35] But there were more problems with the final stages, especially with leaks in the tanks about which Brunel wrote to Fox, and also, at the beginning of 1856, with a fracture in the pipe: 'A most singular fracture has occurred in an elbow of a water pipe at the bottom of the South tower.'[36] All similar elbows were checked, and Fox Henderson were still being urged to make speed with replacements in May.[37] On the same day, however, Brunel recommended to Paxton that the Fox Henderson contract should be terminated, and that the remaining decorative work should be finished on a day-work basis.[38]

The towers were commissioned on 2 June 1856 and formally started to function sixteen days later with a grand ceremony of the turning on of the fountains in the presence of the Queen.[39] The enterprise neatly illustrates Brunel's tremendous attention to detail, his demand for perfection in workmanship, his need to have complete personal command over an operation, and his determination that assistants and contractors should do exactly what he wanted them to do. His shrewd assessment of the inherent weaknesses of the original designs for the towers, his eye for structural strength and integrity, and his precise judgments about the behaviour of sub-soils and cement mixtures, were all products of his well-honed engineering experience. But it was in his personal relationships that the project was most revealing, for he showed himself to be an autocratic leader, unwilling to delegate responsibility, and ready to assert himself vigorously in any matter on which he felt that his authority or his professional status was being challenged. Even Paxton, whom he recognized as a professional equal and his friend, did not escape his criticism when, presumably to avoid troubling Brunel, he consulted Shields on a technical detail: 'I should not act frankly towards you if I did not tell you that I strongly disapprove of your having submitted a letter and a professional opinion of mine to my assistant to report upon.'[40] Brunel was always very sensitive to issues of professional propriety, and this contributed to the very high standards which he practised himself and expected of others.

Brunel submitted a request for payment of £500 on account for professional services and expenses in June 1856,[41] and at the end of November that year he gave a full account to the company.[42] The water towers functioned efficiently at the Sydenham Crystal Palace, but they were never used on the scale intended by Paxton to supply his fountains. The Winter Garden and Leisure Park was not an unqualified success, and many of the fountains had fallen out of use long before the great fire of November 1936 which destroyed the Palace. The fire left Brunel's water towers intact, and it is was only the need for scrap metal at the beginning of the Second World War, together with the fear that they would provide landmarks for air attacks on London, which led to the decision to demolish them in 1940. Now all that remains are the well-preserved base of the south tower, incorporated into the Crystal Palace Museum, and the overgrown ruins of the north tower, felled with a charge of gelignite in 1941.[43]

At the same time as he was dealing with the Crystal Palace towers in the mid 1850s, Brunel was handling the construction of the *Great Eastern* and the Tamar Bridge, and a host of other commissions. Amongst these was a request from Prince Albert to build a bridge across the River Dee at the entrance to the royal estate at Balmoral. Although undoubtedly a comparatively minor work by Brunel's standards, this bridge is of historical interest for several reasons. For one thing, the silence concerning the bridge on the part of the standard biographers of Brunel is puzzling. His son Isambard makes no mention of it, although he makes several references to Prince Albert. Lady Noble tells a number of anecdotes about contacts between the Brunels and the Royal Family, but makes no reference to the Balmoral bridge. And Rolt, who did so much to introduce Brunel to a generation of industrial historians, likewise has nothing to say about this particular work, even though it survives in robust working order. Yet it was a remarkably prestigious commission, involving detailed personal discussion with the Prince, so the failure of previous biographers to mention it requires some explanation.[44]

The Balmoral bridge has been described as 'a single-span, wrought-iron, plate-girder bridge, slightly cambered ... Possibly the earliest wrought-iron girder bridge in Scotland'.[45] It consists of two riveted wrought-iron girders mounted between masonry piers giving a clear span of 125 ft: the width between the beams is 13 ft, with transverse girders decked with longitudinal planking of seasoned pine now covered with a layer of tarmac. The original timber deck was replaced in 1971, the new one being as far as possible identical to the one replaced. There are four small plates on the bridge, three of which survive, bearing the words: 'R. BROTHERHOOD   CHIPPENHAM WILTS 1856', but there is no indication of the fact that Brunel designed it. The design was a novel one in the 1850s, as the fabrication of large wrought-iron girders had only recently become feasible and engineers were still experimenting to discover the most effective way of using the material to combine strength with economy. The Balmoral design shows such economy in the shape of the upper flange of the girder, which is of slighter construction than those of previous arrangements used by Brunel. There is economy also in the diamond-shaped perforations in the girder web, although these may well have been an aesthetic concession to it being a public road bridge for a particularly sensitive location. Brunel used a similar design for girders in India and Australia. It represents the most practical shape evolved by him in wrought iron to deal with the compression strains in girder bridges.[46]

The first reference to the bridge in the private letter books was in July 1854 when, under the heading 'Balmoral Bridge', Brunel wrote to Colonel Charles Phipps, who was then Keeper of the Privy Purse to Queen Victoria:

> Dear Sir, The information sent is deficient in one or two important points and to save you trouble I send you a list of inquiries in a shape that may be sent direct to the party on the spot. It appears to be a case of some difficulty requiring consideration and if the matter does not press for immediate decision, I mean if a month or six weeks delay would not be too great, I will take the means of making myself acquainted with all the circumstances either through my own eyes or the eyes of those whose business it is to see for me. In the meantime a reply to the enclosed would be useful.[47]

The additional note asked for information on five points, including the height of floods in the river and the availability of timber and building stone in the neighbourhood.

In the event, Brunel did not rely on others to see for him but went to study the site himself. The evidence for this visit is an undated letter in the Royal Archives at Windsor, probably at the time of a journey to Scotland in the summer of 1854. Previous trips to Scotland are recorded in the desk diaries for 1851 and 1852, but sadly this source deteriorates in quality in 1853 and provides no clues of subsequent visits.[48] But the recipient of the letter in question, probably Phipps, has written on it 'To be kept at Balmoral' and the first part of it reads as follows:

> Dear Sir, On my return to Ballater today I found that unless I seized immediately on a pair of horses and commenced my return to Aberdeen I should be detained at least two days by reason of the demand for horses for Her Majesty and suite. I was therefore unable to profit by your obliging offer to enable me to show Mrs Brunel some of the beauties of Balmoral.[49]

Since Ballater is the town closest to Balmoral, it appears that Brunel and his wife stayed there during a short visit to the district before deciding to avoid the problems arising from the forthcoming visit by the Queen, so that they made a hurried departure, doubtless to keep pressing business engagements. But Brunel was there long enough to assess the situation of the proposed bridge at Balmoral, and to offer advice on the condition of other bridges in the area.[50]

In the following November Brunel wrote again to Phipps:

Dear Sir, Will you have the goodness to lay the accompanying sketches and the statement relating to the Dee Bridge before His Royal Highness and to let me know whether they meet with His Royal Highness' approval and whether any further explanation is desired or any alteration suggested by the Prince.[51]

The accompanying notes provided a choice of two designs:

In the designs indicated in the accompanying sketches the roadway of the bridge is assumed to have a clear width of gravelled road of 10 feet with a high wooden curb and a narrow footway of about 2 feet in width on each side. This would afford considerably greater accommodation to passengers than the present suspension bridge, and would appear to be more than ample for the traffic of the country ... The possible load in the present case is assumed to be 86 tons or about 1200 people. No. 2 [this should read No. 1] is constructed upon the principle of the Royal Albert Bridge at Plymouth which in a large structure has the advantage of giving the required strength with the minimum amount of material but in a comparatively small bridge like the present the framework of the roadway itself forming a large proportion of the whole the economy of material in the superstructure becomes of less value.

There are also several mechanical contrivances necessary to provide against the effect of expansion and contraction which in a large work barely affects the total cost but which are felt in the cost of a small one. Still it is a good bridge in a mechanical point of view. A material objection however exists to its adoption in the present case. Consisting as it does of many small parts it must be put together on a stage, and as it cannot be floated into place as at Plymouth, this stage must be erected in the bed of the river. This could be attended with considerable expense which would fully counterbalance the economy in the amount of material in the bridge itself and would be attended with some risk in the event of floods. I should therefore recommend the design shown in sketch No. 2. It happens that the span of this bridge taken in connection with the width of the roadway required and the possible load to be provided for is just within the convenient limits of a wrought iron girder of good construction of the depth of the parapets. If well made and with the improvements which a considerable experience in the making of such girders has suggested this would be the cheapest and most easily erected bridge that I can suggest and, if the appearance is not considered objectionable, I should strongly recommend it.

Such a work executed in the best possible manner might be contracted for including erection with the roadway over it complete for £2000 exclusive of the masonry and approaches which could be better executed by local contractors. The masonry in granite to the extent shown on the sketch ought not to cost £400.[52]

The drawings to which these notes refer do not survive, but the sketches from which they were made are available in the sketch books, where there are indeed two designs (although wrongly numbered in the transcription above), one bearing a striking resemblance to the Tamar Bridge and the other being clearly the design chosen for the existing bridge. There are also two pages in the calculation books devoted to Brunel's calculations for the plans.[53]

Among other matters raised by this correspondence, it is safe to infer that the idea for the Balmoral bridge emanated from Prince Albert, and that he gave his close personal attention to the project. The Prince had made the acquaintance of Brunel several years before. He had launched the *Great Britain* in 1843, only three years after arriving in Britain to marry Queen Victoria, and he had had further dealings with the engineer on the organizing committee for the Great Exhibition of 1851. It is clear from the last letter quoted above, moreover, that he had already given permission for the Tamar Bridge to be named after himself. It was natural enough, therefore, for the Prince to turn to Brunel for help in the improvement of the Balmoral estate, of which he and the Queen had purchased the lease in 1848, and to which they both devoted a great deal of attention thereafter. It was the sort of royal appointment which Brunel could hardly have refused, even though he was at that time heavily involved in the enormous task of building the *Great Eastern*, along with the multitude of other engineering commitments which he already had in hand.[54]

Brunel wrote to Phipps again in May 1855 to report progress. It is apparent that the wrought-iron girder design had been accepted because Brunel passed on the tenders received for the construction of such a bridge, and recommended acceptance of that for £1650 submitted by Rowland Brotherhood of Chippenham:

> Brotherhood whose tender is the lowest is a very respectable man ... He does a great deal of work of this description for railways and has always given me satisfaction. I understand from him that he is anxious to extend his business northwards and he is therefore likely to do it well.[55]

Brotherhood duly received the contract and proceeded to construct the iron girders for the bridge. Meanwhile, the masonry work for the abutments and approaches proved to be more troublesome than Brunel had anticipated, and delayed the completion of the work by a year or more. There were two substantial abutments of rough-hewn blocks of local granite, and this part of the work was the responsibility of Dr Andrew Robertson, who combined the posts of factor and doctor at Balmoral. In a letter addressed to him in April 1856 Brunel asked: 'Are the piers finished yet for the Balmoral Bridge? The bridge has of course been long finished and is becoming an inconvenience to the manufacturers.'[56] By September, he found it necessary to write again, this time to Phipps:

The iron work of the Dee bridge has been completed and tested some nine or ten months since but there does not appear from Dr Robertson's account any prospect of the abutments and approaches being sufficiently advanced to receive it until after the winter. The contractor is in consequence long in arrears of his payments besides having to give a large space in his premises to the bridge. He has pressed me to procure a payment on account and I think that £1000 at least should be advanced to him in the usual manner in such cases, on account of work executed.[57]

The original of this letter in the Royal Archives was marked, presumably by Phipps: 'will send him £1000. The Bridge may come in November. He had better provide carriage and workmen to put it up. Answered September 12'. Brunel, who must have received a letter in these terms, responded a few days later, giving the address of Brotherhoods for payment but pointing out: 'I am almost afraid it is too late in the season for him to commence. I have written to him however to proceed, if he possibly can.'[58] At the same time, a note to Brotherhood observed: 'It will be an advantage to the Queen that the bridge should be put up before next summer.'[59] Brotherhood did not need any encouragement to dispatch the ironwork which had been cluttering his site for so long. There is no account of how the task was performed, but it can reasonably be assumed that the girders were trans-ported in sections by rail to Banchory, the Deeside Railway having been opened from Aberdeen to that town, thirty miles from Balmoral, in Sep-tember 1856.[60] From there they must have made the last stage by road, to be assembled on the site by Brotherhood's team.

There must have been further delays, however, in this assembly because it was not complete until the autumn of 1857, by which time there had occurred the first hints that all was not well with the project. Colonel Phipps must have communicated clear misgivings on the part of the royal family to Brunel, producing the following response:

> I am much disappointed at your report of the appearance of the bridge at Balmoral. I confess I had hoped for a very different result and thought that at all events the perfect simplicity of the construction and absence of any attempt at ornament would secure it from being in any way unsightly or offensive, which I think is always a great first step, but I fear your expression of not extremely ornamental implies something very much the reverse.
>
>   As regards the elasticity I trust that it is not felt to an extent that is unpleasant as it is unavoidable ... But with regard both to the appearance and the stiffness, I will take an early opportunity of seeing it myself.[61]

Four days later he wrote again to Phipps to advise him on painting the bridge, and recommending 'some simple sober but warm brown tint' with a suitable contrast in shades between the underside and the outside. He added a postscript: 'The bridge near Plymouth which will hereafter bear the name of H. R. Highness was safely floated into place early last month. It was a work of considerable difficulty but everything combined to assist and the result was very satisfactory.' [62]

Whether or not Brunel managed to find 'an early opportunity' to see the finished bridge himself is not recorded, but in the circumstances of his commitments elsewhere this seems unlikely, and in any event there was little that could be done about it. It is clear that the royal family – or perhaps, more particularly, the Queen – did not like the appearance of the bridge and grumbled about its springiness under the carriages. On the latter point, the continued existence of the bridge has confirmed Brunel's opinion that there was no need for concern. But the appearance was another matter, and there seems to be little doubt that Brunel's royal patrons did not appreciate the unadorned iron girder bridge which had appeared on their doorstep. The view of functional elegance and perfect simplicity presented by Brunel has a striking modernity in its resemblance to aesthetic judgments about works of engineering which have been widely accepted in the twentieth century. But in the mid nineteenth century the engineer had to reckon with very different aesthetic sensibilities. This brings us back to the discussion of Brunel's style. The Balmoral bridge represents the mature functionalist style of Brunel's later years, and this was in sharp contrast with the 'Romantic Gothic' style adopted by the Royal Family in their reconstruction of Balmoral Castle and elsewhere. It was unfortunate for Brunel that in this respect the tide of public taste, dictated by John Ruskin and other advocates of the Gothic Revival, was running against the functionalist tradition. But the incident provides a significant clue to the puzzle of why Brunel's association with the bridge was allowed to fall into limbo by his biographers.

Queen Victoria provided oblique confirmation of the suggestion that the Balmoral bridge was not to her taste. In her *Leaves from the Journal of Our Life in the Highlands*, in which she tended to rhapsodize about all things Scottish, she described the 'Opening of the New Bridge over the Linn of Dee'. This was dated 8 September 1857, just a few weeks before Brunel felt obliged to respond to the complaints he had received about his bridge:

> At half past one o'clock we started in 'Highland State' – Albert in a royal Stuart plaid, and I and the girls in skirts of the same – with the ladies (who had only returned at five in the morning from the ball at *Mar Lodge*) and gentlemen, for the *Linn of Dee*, to open the new bridge there. The valley looked beautiful. A triumphal arch was erected, at which Lord Fife and Mr Brooke received us, and walked near the carriage, pipers playing – the road lined with Duff men. On the bridge Lady Fife received us, and we all drank in whiskey 'prosperity of the bridge'.[63]

There is a poignant contrast between the festivities marking the completion of this bridge, built for the Earl of Fife some twelve miles upstream from Balmoral, and the complete and ominous silence in the Queen's account regarding the Brunel bridge which was completed about the same time. The royal displeasure may not have been made public, but it was clearly communicated to Brunel and may well have influenced his son in choosing to make no mention of the bridge in his biography. The habit of ignoring it in accounts of the engineer's achievements was thus established.

It took some time to sort out the financial complications of the Balmoral bridge. Brunel wrote to Colonel Phipps in the spring of 1858 to present additional claims made on the contract by Brotherhood. He admitted that he had been too preoccupied with other business to attend to this, but on due consideration he supported Brotherhood's claim as reasonable even though 'his contract did not provide for any such additional claim', the main justification being the great inconvenience to which the contractor had been subjected through no fault of his own.[64] The claim was for an additional £167, and a further letter from Brunel to Phipps in the autumn led to a final agreement on these terms.[65] A paper in the Royal Archives under the heading 'I. K. Brunel in re R. Brotherhood's account of Dee Bridge' summarizes the costs of the bridge: to the 'contract price' of £1650 is added £167 as 'Amount of Extras Admitted by Mr Brunel'. Against this total of £1817 is set £1000 as 'Instalment on account paid Sept 20 1856', with the figure of £817 as 'Leaving Due'.[66] There is no mention here or elsewhere in the Royal Archives of any request for payment of professional fees having been received from Brunel, and it seems likely that he never submitted any such statement. It is possible, of course, that he was paid out of another account, but he does appear to have been somewhat irregular in any requests for payment, and it could be that he was influenced by the disappointment of his clients into choosing not to submit a personal account. But a memorandum by Dr Robertson, dated 1877, asserts that the bridge 'cost over £3000', so there may be more to be told.[67]

The Balmoral bridge was an important part of the 'improvement' of the Deeside estate as a royal residence, by altering the course of a public road which would otherwise have infringed the privacy of the Royal Family. It was erected efficiently and elegantly by Brunel and his contractor, but they received little thanks or recognition for their labours. The reason appears to have been that the bridge did not coincide with the fashion for ornamentation which was growing strongly in the 1850s. The taste of Queen Victoria especially was largely determined by this fashion, and it is clear that she simply did not like the functional iron girders of the bridge. Engineers met considerable criticism in the 1860s on account of their functional designs, particularly bridges. Even the editor of the *Engineer* wrote in 1866: 'A bridge, in addition to doing duty in an engineering sense, should convey a feeling of satisfaction to all who behold it, simply as a study of art giving gratification from its fitness and beauty, instead of creating disgust by its insufferable ugliness.'[68] A modern reader would not dissent from these sentiments, and Brunel would have had no trouble in accepting them. But in the end matters of beauty and ugliness are in the eyes of the beholder, and the dominant aesthetic fashions of the period placed the functional engineer, operating under constraints of economy and efficiency, at a particular disadvantage. The reputation of Brunel's Balmoral bridge was a victim to the vagaries of public taste for engineering styles.

10

The Professional Man

The engineering profession had emerged in Britain in the second half of the eighteenth century, when pioneers like John Smeaton had first identified themselves as 'civil' engineers, distinct from their military colleagues, and had made themselves available for the construction of the canals, roads, bridges, mills, ports and lighthouses required by a society undergoing rapid industrialization. Like architects and surveyors, and other men possessing distinctive skills appropriate to this new society, the engineers formed a natural 'professional' group, anxious to assert its integrity and indispensability. Engineers generally offered their services to a client in return for a salary, but the more talented members of the profession quickly established the practice of providing advice, designs and supervision of projects without committing themselves to the full-time employment of any single client. From Smeaton onwards, such 'consultant engineers' became the leaders of the new profession, and even though some like I. K. Brunel disliked the title, with its somewhat 'hands off' implications, the comparative independence of consultancy meant that it became the aspiration of every ambitious young engineer. So while Brunel preferred to represent himself as 'chief engineer', in fact it was by virtue of acting as a consultant engineer that he managed to perform the prodigious amount of work which he did. This, however, involved employing a large staff in order to divide the work into manageable units, and it was here that Brunel's professional consciousness was of particular value to him in establishing programmes and maintaining standards.[1]

Smeaton had set up the Society of Civil Engineers in 1771 as a select dining club for senior engineers, but it was not until 1818 that the profession began to assume a permanent institutional shape with the establishment of the Institution of Civil Engineers which, under the benign presidency of Thomas Telford, grew rapidly in the 1820s and achieved its royal charter in 1828. Brunel was recruited in 1830 as a young man of twenty-four, on the strength of his apprenticeship with his father, and he remained a committed member of the institution to his death. He attached great importance to the professional status of engineering, and worked throughout his engineering career to maintain what he considered to be 'gentlemanly' standards of professional conduct. The concept of the 'gentleman engineer' was not a precise one, but it was significant in mediating collective modes of correct performance to a body of men which, by the circumstances of its origin, was somewhat inchoate.[2] Brunel's insistence on such conduct amongst his team can be demonstrated from a study of his correspondence in the private letter books, which record the outgoing letters from his office and illuminate many aspects of his relationships with his peers, his staff, and those who served him professionally as contractors or in various other capacities. The sequence of fifteen letter books begins in 1834, but entries were only made systematically from 1836, when Joseph Bennett became Brunel's chief clerk, a position which he held to the end of Brunel's life. There is little to be said about Bennett, although Brunel came to depend heavily upon him in all routine secretarial matters, and it seems probable that he was writing with some satisfaction in his own choice of Bennett when he advised the promoters of the incipient South Devon Railway in 1836 that success would depend most upon the character of the secretary they chose:

> Nothing can be more erroneous than to suppose that a clerk is all that is required. A Secretary must in fact be able to assist the Directors in all their decisions and must be able to command such confidence on the part of the Directors in his judgment and opinions as will allow him to act frequently upon his own responsibility. I should go so far as to say that an inefficient Secretary might be more injurious to a Company even than an inefficient Engineer.[3]

A well-run office was an essential tool for Brunel in order to fulfil the ambitious programme of transport and civil engineering which developed rapidly from 1833, and Bennett played an important but self-effacing role in the perfection of this instrument.

By 1836 Brunel had settled at 18 Duke Street, Westminster, convenient for Parliament and Whitehall, in the house which remained his home and his office for the rest of his life. From here he administered the team of assistants, resident engineers, draughtsmen, clerks and pupils, which he assembled to undertake the many complex engineering operations in which he became involved as a professional consulting engineer. His first assistant engineer with the GWR was W. H. Townsend, a Bristol land surveyor who had initially been responsible for the mineral tramway known as the Bristol & Gloucestershire Railway. He had been a potential rival to Brunel as Engineer to the GWR, but he had agreed instead to act as Brunel's assistant surveyor. From the first, Brunel was impatient with Townsend's lax time-keeping habits, and he soon faded from the scene.[4] Amongst other early recruits were William Gravatt, who had worked with the Brunels on the Thames Tunnel, and who was given the responsibility for surveying the route for the Bristol & Exeter Railway, and J. W. Hammond, who became Brunel's most trusted assistant on the GWR works and his chief assistant until his death in 1847. Each major project required at least one resident engineer and sometimes also an assistant engineer and a surveyor. As in every year from 1836 Brunel had something like a dozen such projects (he listed eleven in his journal on Boxing Day 1835), his staff must regularly have been between thirty and forty strong. This does not include the local services employed on his behalf such as contractors and their workers, or members of important subsidiary staffs such as those of the GWR engineering workshops under Daniel Gooch.

Because Brunel conducted so many of his transactions with his staff by face-to-face contact in the course of his extensive travelling away from Duke Street, the record of his correspondence is an inadequate base from which to form a precise picture of this intricate team, but it is fortunate that at one point of time a circular letter was recorded which Brunel sent to all members of his staff. This was in 1850, when Bennett passed on a notice inviting designs for a competition, presumably in connection with preparations for the Great Exhibition the following year.[5] There is a list of thirty-three names of the people to whom it was addressed: R. P. Brereton, T. A. Bertram, R. Brodie, T. E. Blackwell, B. H. Babbage, A. J. Dodson, G. J. Darley, C. E. Gainsford, W. Glennie, J. B. Hannaford, J. Hewitt, R. W. Jones, S. Jones, M. Lane, E. F. Murray, P. J. Margary, S. Powers, W. Peniston, W. G. Owen, C. Richardson, H. Savage, C. Turner, R. Varden, W. Warcup, R. J. Ward, P. P. Baly, R. Beamish, W. Bell, O. C. Edwards, L. C. Fripp, J. Gibson, J. H. Hainson and G. F. Okeden. It is not clear why there are two alphabetical sequences here, and it cannot be assumed that all of them were in full-time employment with Brunel at that time: Beamish had retired from Marc Brunel's service on the Thames Tunnel a decade earlier, although he had returned in the late 1840s to assist Brunel with the Gloucester & Dean Forest Railway, and by 1850 Babbage was probably preparing to emigrate to Australia. It should also be remembered that 1850 would not have been a particularly good moment in Brunel's fortunes: some of his earlier projects were running down, and the phenomenal boom of the mid 1840s in railway construction was over. There are many indications of financial anxiety in the correspondence about this time, as in the following letter of 1849: 'These are *very* economical times. I foresee an extreme probability of the GWR Directors calling upon me to make an almost clean sweep of all expenses on the Wilts & Somerset ... no body must *rely* upon employment after this quarter.'[6] On the other hand, J. B. Hannaford and five other members of the drawing office staff who did not appear on the list, were dismissed shortly after the invitation was circulated.[7] So our estimate of the average size of Brunel's senior staff is almost certainly of the right order of magnitude. While only a few of his staff, including Gooch and Froude, went on to achieve distinguished careers for themselves as engineers, Brunel made sure that they were in general men of considerable ability.

With such a large and constantly changing body of assistants, it was inevitable that Brunel should have had some discipline troubles, but the surprising thing is probably that they were no greater. Brunel's admirers are almost certainly correct in claiming that he was skilful in selecting the right sort of people to help in his work. His chief assistants normally had his full confidence, although even J. W. Hammond, who was responsible for supervising the London end of the GWR works, did not escape some sharp words from him: 'When I refer to our "angry discussion" I meant simply and truly that I was angry, and if I failed to make you sensible that I was angry I must be a much milder and gentler being than I thought.'[8] The point at issue was Hammond's slowness in fulfilling Brunel's instructions to despatch some railway waggons to South Devon, but as Hammond was then acting for Brunel on the difficult and protracted task of reconstructing the south entrance lock to Bristol Docks, there may have been other causes of irritation. Moreover, as Hammond died the following year, it is possible that his reactions had already slowed below the hundred per cent efficiency required by his chief. He was succeeded by Robert Pearson Brereton, who served diligently and efficiently as Brunel's chief assistant. He had joined Brunel's staff in 1836, and lost an eye in an explosion while working on the GWR. He was sent to Italy in 1845 to help Brunel sort out some embarrassing complications which had arisen in the construction of the Genoa to Turin Railway, and he was described by Brunel as: 'my assistant, a peculiarly energetic persevering young man'.[9] He went on to work on the Royal Albert Bridge, and eventually it was on his shoulders that there fell the task of sorting out the complex affairs of the office after Brunel's premature death.

The disciplinary cases which are recorded in the private letter books reveal a lot about Brunel's methods of handling his staff. The case of William Gravatt is particularly interesting because Gravatt had been a close colleague of Brunel on the Thames Tunnel, and had been entrusted with the preliminary survey for the Bristol & Exeter Railway, a job which he performed very well.[10] But at the end of 1839 Gravatt made some complaints to the directors, and Brunel retorted with a substantial letter in which he urged Gravatt to reconsider his position and warned him: 'I tell you that I think you would be committing a most unprofessional act, sacrificing your duty to the Company, to me and to yourself, entirely to feelings, feelings which I ... consider quite improper to be indulged in.'[11]

There is no indication of the point at issue, but by the middle of the following year the position had deteriorated as Brunel wrote a strong letter accusing his assistant of betraying him. It begins 'My dear Gravatt', but in the copy at least the words 'My dear' are ostentatiously crossed out, and it goes on:

> It appears that you entertain views and opinions differing very much from my own on important engineering questions which have been discussed and which have been settled as following part of the plan of construction of the Bristol & Exeter Railway. In this there might be nothing extraordinary but that connected as we *have been* as intimate friends of long standing, acting as my assistant in this course for four or five years, constantly at my side when these subjects have been discussed in public or at the board, that you should never have hinted to me that you differed and that I should hear of it now for the first time and indirectly is extraordinary ... Is this the conduct of a friend, of a gentleman, of a subaltern trusted and confided in by the man above him? [12]

Brunel called a special board meeting to sort out the problem and the directors of the B & ER expressed their confidence in him suggesting that Gravatt should be given a much more limited role in the works.[13] But tension continued between the two old friends, because within a few months another row blew up when Brunel wrote to his assistant regarding 'the deplorable state' of the B & ER bridge near the Bristol terminus, and the following week he asked Gravatt to resign: 'It has been with great reluctance and regret that I have come to the conclusion that I now communicate to you. I feel that I cannot with justice to myself or to the Company take upon myself the responsibility of continuing to conduct the works through you as my Assistant.'[14] Gravatt refused to go quietly and made counter-charges which the board decided to investigate, much to Brunel's annoyance. The incident may have contributed to the souring of Brunel's relationship with the B & ER directors, because shortly after he withdrew as engineer to the railway. More especially, it reflects oddly on his attitude towards somebody who was, after all, an old personal and family friend, and suggests that there was more to the dispute than appears from Brunel's letters. The closest these get to describing the point at issue is when Brunel observes that: 'all the bridges [on the B & ER] are built much lower than the standard long since fixed for the Great Western'. We know that Gravatt had his own views about bridges, favouring a very low angle in the arch; and we know, also, that Brunel had trouble with at least one such bridge, over the Parrett at Bridgwater, for which Gravatt was almost certainly responsible. It is possible, therefore, that a genuine difference of professional opinion embittered what had previously been an intimate personal relationship, but the episode serves as a useful indication of Brunel's decisiveness.[15]

Another assistant engineer, J. H. Gandell, came under suspicion of having been involved in some improper speculation with GWR property at the temporary station of Faringdon, while the railway was under construction through the Vale of White Horse. Brunel wrote demanding that he choose between his profession and the business of the speculator, in which: 'you will make *more money* and run less risk of *losing credit*'.16 Gandell did not improve his ways to Brunel's satisfaction, particularly when it emerged that he had been suspected of misappropriating company supplies, on which charges his explanation failed to convince Brunel, who dismissed him.17 The perception of professional standards was closely related to mid nineteenth-century notions of gentlemanly behaviour, and Brunel always required a high degree of such conduct from his assistants: 'I should look much more for these qualifications [those required to serve the company] in a moderate degree in a gentlemanly and trustworthy young man than for any scientific or ingenious person who might be disposed to act too much on his own responsibility.'18 He expected them to be courteous and tactful towards proprietors and directors, firm and distant towards contractors, fair and just towards subordinates, and he did not hesitate to reprove assistants who fell below these standards. One assistant to feel his lash on these points was R. M. Marchant, who had taken a high-handed attitude towards a subordi-nate called Hulme. Brunel defended the latter as 'by Birth and Education and feeling a Gentleman in every sense of the word', and went on to criticise Marchant: 'When a man complains of want of courtesy he should himself be most gentlemanly and courteous in his language which you are *very far* from being in your note to me.'19 The unusual feature of this relationship was that Marchant appears to have been a relative of Brunel, being the offspring of one of his mother's many sisters, so that he was allowed more than normal latitude. But a further scene in this family drama occurred in 1851 when Marchant emerged briefly as Brunel's adversary in the altercation over the Mickleton Tunnel near Chipping Campden, for which he was the contractor. He had entered a disastrous partnership and failed to complete the tunnel on time, as a result of which Brunel raised a large band of railway navvies to evict him from the site.20

Despite his insistence on 'gentlemanly conduct', Brunel was very conscious of the fact that it could be abused. He explained to a grandparent in 1841 that: 'A short time back after repeated warnings to your grandson I was compelled to dismiss him from the Company's service as his excessive idleness not only rendered him useless but infected others.'21 And some years later, in the same vein, he wrote to his resident engineer on the Chepstow Bridge to enquire about a junior assistant, C. Smith, who had requested a testimonial: 'I have an impression – if it is wrong correct me –

that he is one of those who gets *up late,* go to their work at *gentlemanly hours* – and from whom it is difficult to get any real *work*'.[22] It was clearly possible to be too much of a 'gentleman' to suit Brunel, but in most respects he placed great emphasis on the qualities of integrity, reliability and courtesy which he identified with the concept. He had a particular dislike of vagueness and imprecision. Writing to an assistant in 1857 he said: 'You are getting very loose I won't say careless but very *imprecise* – when it is a question of calculation ... Your reasoning is (excuse me so describing it) Irish – it is loose and imprecise to a degree that makes it untrue.'[23]

Another temptation of gentlemanly life against which Brunel kept a watchful eye was the appeal of sporting activity. He delivered a strong reprimand to an assistant in 1853, following some remarks from directors of the railway:

> as to the apparent want of energy and activity on your part in attending to the Company's works ... contrasted with an alleged devotion to amusement and amongst other things to cricket ... I don't know why you should be less of a slave to work than I am, or Mr Brereton, or any of my assistants in town. It would rather astonish anybody if Mr Bennett should be a frequenter of Lord's cricket ground or practice billiards in the day time, and I don't know why a man having the advantages of country air and very light work should indulge them ... You must endeavour to remove any such grounds of observation.[24]

But the assistant so admonished managed to repair his damaged reputation, for exactly five years later Brunel invited him to be his resident engineer on the Bristol & South Wales Junction Railway, holding out the prospect of good cricket in the Bristol area:

> I want a man acquainted with tunnelling and who will with a moderate amount of inspecting assistance look after the Tunnel with his *own eyes,* for I am beginning to be sick of Inspectors who see nothing, and resident engineers who reside at home ... The country immediately north of Bristol I should think a delightful one to live in – beautiful country – good society near Bristol and Clifton etc. I can't vouch for any cricketing but I should think it highly probable.[25]

Charles Richardson accepted the post after some hesitation and was still engaged in it at the time of Brunel's death.

Nor had Brunel any objection to sport or recreation at the proper time and place. He defended one of his assistants vigorously against the charge of some directors that he kept boxing gloves in his room:

> I confess if any man had taken upon himself to remark on my having gone to the Pantomime, which I always do at Christmas, no respect for Directors or any other officer would have restrained me. I will do my best to keep my team in

order but I cannot do it if my Master sits by me and amuses himself in touching them up with his whip.[26]

On occasion, Brunel's defence of his assistants became almost a censure of those who ventured to express criticism. When J. Crosthwaite, a vocal member of the Liverpool faction which held an important group of GWR shares, was critical of one Andrews of the 'locomotive department', Brunel spoke out in his defence: 'I have a high opinion of Andrews' integrity, good intentions, and abilities but his temper is the most singular I ever had to deal with.' He then carried his defence into a rebuke of Crosthwaite: 'Upon my word you are the perfection of a contented proprietor – your property is at 75 per cent premium – and the higher it gets the more you grumble. I begin to suspect that like a horse's bite it is a proof of love.'[27]

It is not possible fully to reconstruct the relationship between Brunel and all his assistants, but a few instances provide interesting examples of how he treated them and of how they responded to his treatment. William Froude had been in his service for some time by 1844, when he asked for leave to look after his sick father. Froude was one of a highly talented family, and his ailing father was Archdeacon of Totnes. Brunel was unhappy about the request. He replied by saying that it would be very inconvenient for the company, but told him to take off six months during which he must make a resolution, 'as one would a religious vow if you ever make one', to have nothing to do with business 'except such as *I* may trouble you with'.[28] A year later he offered Froude the post of resident engineer on the North Devon Railway and he wrote gratefully when Froude accepted: 'I have been compelled to the destruction of my comfort to undertake a great deal more than I can possibly attend to with credit or satisfaction to myself – and but for your help on the North Devon I should have dropped a huge stitch in my work.'[29] Unfortunately, there was a major breakdown on the North Devon project for which Froude felt responsible and offered to forego his salary, but Brunel refused to accept this arrangement:

> You did your best and the utmost I can say now that I am no longer afraid of annoying you is that you made a great mistake in not perceiving the danger sooner – quite a strange unaccountable mistake but from that very circumstance it is one of those which no one could impute to anything but a very singular accident … You must have the goodness therefore to send me your statement for your own salary.[30]

Froude fulfilled other commissions for Brunel, including various theoretical and experimental tasks, after one of which Brunel commented:

> I deny altogether the very foundation of your theory now that you lay it bare – the rate of expansion will *not* be infinite in the case you assume … I feel I

may be altogether writing nonsense – one sadly loses the habits of mathematical reasoning. The subject is one of great importance to me just at present and I should like you to pursue it.[31]

Froude subsequently advised Brunel on the laws of motion of ships in connection with the construction of the *Great Eastern*, by which time he had embarked on innovative work in using testing tanks for ship designs, for which technique he became widely known and respected.[32] The friendly and fatherly nature of Brunel's attitude towards him certainly owed much to his recognition of Froude's intellectual distinction.

Brunel devoted a lot of his own time to detailed calculations of stresses in bridges, the strengths of various forms of construction, and similar matters of practical engineering importance, and he encouraged his assistants to do the same. One assistant who was employed for several years specifically to make calculations and experiments was William Bell. When Brunel advertised a post for 'superintendence of mechanical constructions' in 1846, Bell applied and Brunel wrote to one of his referees: 'Is he industrious and intelligent and secondly is he a willing man or one of those who fancy themselves not sufficiently appreciated – of the latter class I have always a great dread'.[33] The reply must have been favourable to Bell, because he got the job and was attached to the work on the south entrance lock at Bristol Docks, and was plied by Brunel with calculations on rivetting, testing cylinders under stress, and other matters, so that he made a valuable contribution to Brunel's technical grasp of the possibilities of using wrought iron in large structures. By the end of 1849 there was little left for him to do in Bristol, although Brunel retained him to continue some calculations and later wrote him a good reference:

[Bell] has been known to me for about ten years – I have a high respect for his integrity and zeal in the service of his employers. He is a very well informed young man in his profession and particularly also in those branches requiring mathematical knowledge which are too often neglected. He has been engaged on docks works as well as railway construction and if I had an opportunity I should employ him myself.[34]

Eighteen months later, Brunel offered Bell a job on the South Devon Railway, and he subsequently conducted complicated mathematical calculations with Froude in connection with the *Great Eastern*, and contributed the chapter on Dock Works towards Isambard's biography of his father.[35]

Of all Brunel's assistant engineers, the one who probably gave him most help was Daniel Gooch. Gooch came from a north country family of engineers but was an enthusiastic supporter of the broad gauge as a means of achieving high-speed passenger services on the railways. He approached

Brunel in July 1837 in response to information that he had received that Brunel was looking for a locomotive engineer on the GWR. He was then a young man of twenty-one. Brunel made a characteristically rapid assessment of Gooch's abilities and appointed him as the first locomotive superintendent of the railway in August. He started work immediately and demonstrated his value by coaxing the motley collection of locomotives at his disposal when the railway opened into tolerable performance. Then he went on to build his own steam locomotives and equipped the GWR with a superlative stock of high performance express engines which made a tremendous contribution to the success of Brunel's railway system. There is no doubt that Gooch felt warmly about Brunel, regarding him as 'my oldest and best friend' when IKB died in 1859. Gooch confided to his diary the splendid tribute to his former chief which has been much quoted subsequently: 'By his death the greatest of British engineers was lost; the man of the greatest originality of thought and power of execution, bold in his plans but right.'[36] In view of this categorical affirmation, it is curious that there was no corresponding expression on Brunel's side. He was certainly grateful to Gooch, because he thanked him cordially for his services on several occasions, gestures which were treasured by Gooch and recorded in his diary. But Brunel's references to Gooch in his general correspondence give no hint of any intimacy, and tend rather to suggest mild criticism and a sense of distance. The following remark in a letter to Saunders, the GWR company secretary, is typical. It is overtly about economies in coke, but is actually more concerned with what was perceived as an attempt by Gooch to disparage the quality of Bristol coke: 'You and I have often talked about Gooch's defects. If he has an object to gain he goes about it indirectly. He does not and never did like the Bristol coke department.'[37] Brunel was never less than supportive of his locomotive superintendent, but there is no evidence that, in his relations with Gooch, he ever lowered the veil of aloofness by which he tended increasingly to distance himself from his staff.

It is clear from these exchanges between Brunel and his assistant engineers that, with the possible exception of Froude, who became a friend of the family, he kept his distance. There was never any doubt about who was the chief, and his staff generally maintained a very respectful attitude towards him. The fact that he could, when he wished, be remote and even forbidding is well illustrated by John Brunton's picture of him. Brunton had been summoned by Brunel to attend at his Duke Street office at 6 o'clock one morning, without receiving any indication of the purpose of the errand. But as a junior engineer, working for one of Brunel's contractors on railways in the West Country, he held the chief in considerable awe and duly presented himself:

A footman in livery opened the door, and told me in reply to my enquiry that Mr Brunel was in his office room expecting me. I was ushered into the room blazing with light, and saw Mr Brunel sitting writing at his desk. He never raised his eyes from the paper at my entrance, I knew his peculiarities, so walked up to his desk and said shortly 'Mr Brunel I received your telegram and here I am'. 'Ah', was his reply, 'here's a letter to Mr Hawes at the War Office in Pall Mall, be there with it at 10 o'clock.' He resumed his writing and without a further word I left his office.[38]

This introduction led to Brunton's commission to build the Renkioi Hospital for British soldiers in the Crimean War. But it shows that, even when doing a service, Brunel knew how to stand upon his dignity. When he was involved in more routine business, especially with contractors, he could be quite ruthless in insisting on the meticulous details of agreed specifications. This quality derived partly from his habitual attention to detail which constantly surprised careless contractors, who found that their client knew more about the materials at their disposal than they did themselves, and were subsequently obliged to replace brickwork, ironwork, and other features. But Brunel did not always get it right, as the long-running saga between the contractor David McIntosh and the GWR demonstrated: in this case Brunel persistently refused to accept that the contractor had fulfilled his obligations, but the company was eventually obliged to settle, after both Brunel and McIntosh were dead, in favour of the contractor.[39]

How much were Brunel's assistants paid? There seems to have been no standard practice, the salary varying roughly according to the seniority of the post, the magnitude of the job, and the wealth of the company involved. The latter point was a particularly important variable: although Brunel employed all his own assistants, he expected to reimburse himself for their salaries and expenses from the companies on which he used them. The lowest salaries recorded as having been offered to assistants were early in his career, when W. G. Owen was offered £150 p.a. as a 'sub-assistant engineer', and William Glennie was offered the same terms as assistant engineer to be responsible for the Box Tunnel.[40] A more normal salary for an assistant engineer with Brunel was the £300 plus horse allowance accepted by John James on the Oxford & Rugby Railway.[41] T. E. M. Marsh had his salary reduced to £300 in 1849, and 'as the branch to which you are attending is fast diminishing in quantity I cannot ensure you a long continuance at that salary'.[42] H. S. Bush was offered £350 with a prospect of increase to £400 as resident engineer on the Cornwall Railway in 1858,[43] but on the same day Brunel named the scale £300 to £450 apologetically to C. Richardson for taking on the Bristol & South Wales Junction Railway – although, as we have seen, he offered the prospect of beautiful countryside and cricket as compensation for the low salary.[44] The following day he offered the post of resident engineer on a small Welsh branch line to Captain McNair at £225.[45] The work on Plymouth Docks undertaken by Brunel in the early 1850s must have been more remunerative, as he offered his assistant S. Power an increase to £500 to take it on.[46] At the upper end of the salary scale for Brunel's assistants, W. A. Purdon was offered a twelve-month engagement to investigate the possibility of an East Bengal Railway at one thousand guineas and expenses in 1855.[47]

Although expenses were normally allowed in addition to the basic salary, Brunel kept a strict eye on this expenditure, as is shown by his reprimand to T. Bratton, his assistant on the Oxford, Worcester & Wolverhampton Railway in 1852. He took Bratton to task for charging the *inside* fare on a coach as his travelling expenses when he actually rode *outside*, pointing out that he was on his honour to make a true return and that this device was '*simply not truth*'. Finally, he observed that the unfortunate assistant: '*should travel outside – inside is by day – in England – only fit for women and invalids*'.[48] As a matter of course, Brunel's appointments carried the condition of instant dismissal if he chose to exercise it, and the knowledge of this gave particular significance to any action or lack of action likely to incur the displeasure of the chief.

If Brunel appeared anxious to restrict expenditure on salaries to the minimum, this does not seem to have been the case with pupils, where he deliberately charged high fees in order to discourage the numerous applicants who wrote seeking positions in the office of the successful engineer for their sons or protégés. Brunel's attitude towards such pupils was ambivalent. He did not wish to be bothered with them and made it quite clear that he did not intend to devote any time specifically to them. But he acknowledged a professional duty to have a few such men in his entourage and laid down strict conditions on which he would agree to tolerate them. Early in his independent career he wrote to one parent: 'I do take pupils – or rather I have been driven to take them – I have no room now and I shall have none for twelve months – my terms are 600 guineas ... P.S. I would not take a pupil without six months notice'.[49] Within a few years the range of fees had been raised: 'the premium would depend entirely upon his [Brunel's] opinion of the qualifications of the young man ... the premium would vary from £600 to £800 according to the age and term of pupilage'.[50] By 1842 he was charging £800 for a four year apprenticeship, although the following year he accepted a youth for £700 to cover three years.[51] Then a year later he answered an enquirer: 'I diminish the applications by asking what I consider a large premium – £1000 ... and I do not profess to give in return anything whatever but the opportunities which my office affords to an industrious intelligent young man.'[52] The fullest statement of Brunel's conception of the role of his pupils occurs in a letter of 1846:

I take pupils but rather as the exception than the rule: that is, I do not seek it and rather raise difficulties than encouragement, and amongst other difficulties which I create is the premium I charge. I don't know whether it is high compared with what others charge but I know I should think it a great shame if I were a father wanting to put my son with an engineer. I charge £1000: that is to say £550 on entering and £150 a year for three years, and one year for nothing making in all four years during which time I profess to take no trouble whatsoever about the youth. He has all the opportunities which my office of course give him, and if he turns out well gets employed in responsible situations which improve him. Do not be induced to expect more for your son but at the same time I can not deprive myself of the opportunity of saying that it would at all times and therefore in so important a matter as your son's welfare afford me *great pleasure* to forward any views you may have.[53]

The need for pupils to have the qualities of gentlemen was stressed by Bennett, conveying Brunel's terms to an applicant. He pointed out that it was desirable:

that the young man shall be of gentlemanly habits as well as of good and gentlemanly connections, and that he shall have had a good education and that either by his special education and his tastes, or by his natural turn and ability he shall give sufficient reason to suppose that he will succeed in the profession.[54]

It seems likely, given these stringent conditions, that the number of pupils in Brunel's office can rarely have exceeded two or three at any one time, and those whose parents or guardians were able to have paid the fees would have been affluent members of the 'gentlemanly' classes.

Brunel's insistence on himself as a 'professional man', which appears in his attitude towards pupils and in many other aspects of his business, derived from his pride in his practice of engineering. He seems always to have taken great pleasure in his intimacy with other engineers, and attached more importance to his membership of the Institution of Civil Engineers than to his Fellowship of the Royal Society. Although he never found time to present a paper to the institution, he was a regular attender at meetings and eventually became a vice president. It is clear from his patchy correspondence with his fellow engineers that he was often in face-to-face communication with them. With Robert Stephenson in particular, the greatest of his peers and in many respects his greatest rival, Brunel appears to have maintained a strong friendship and even affection. Only hints of this appear in the letter books, but the impression is reinforced from some surviving comments. In 1844 Brunel wrote arranging to meet Stephenson in south Devon in order to consider Admiralty objections to coastal railways which had been encountered by both engineers. He joked ironically that the objection probably sprang from a fear that the object of coastal walling was 'to prevent poor shipwrecked mariners from climbing up it'.[55] And replying a few months later to a report that Stephenson had been offended by the hostility of some officers of the GWR, Brunel wrote:

> I will not conceal from you that the GWR Co. consider the act of the Birmingham Co. in going to Parliament for a parallel line of ten miles as one of the most unprovoked and unmitigated pieces of hostility committed in all this bitter season of warfare, but in the midst of all this warfare we have all sought to avoid anything like personal hostility.[56]

At this time the Gauge War was coming to its climax, but a few years later Brunel was still able to write: 'Excepting on one or two well known points of difference Stephenson and I generally agree perfectly.'[57]

In later years the two men enjoyed being consulted together on engineering matters as they contrived to go off to various parts of the country in order to give advice, both Manchester and Glasgow Waterworks schemes benefiting from their collective wisdom.[58] They also supported each other in public on a number of important occasions, Brunel backing Stephenson on the controversy about the collapse of the Dee Bridge in Chester, and attending the construction of the Britannia Bridge over the Menai Straits, while Stephenson turned out to support Brunel in the difficult weeks when the *Great Eastern* was being launched. The engineer-turned-commentator F. R. Conder recounted several delightful anecdotes about the leading engineers with whom he had been associated, including the story of Brunel, Robert Stephenson and Joseph Locke travelling together in a railway train. Stephenson was wearing a plaid, fashionable at the time and draped carefully round his shoulders. Brunel took a fancy to the plaid, and made a wager that he would be able to put it on properly at the first attempt by the next station: if he failed, he undertook to pay Stephenson £10, but if he won he would get the plaid. Then, while Stephenson and Locke continued their conversation, Brunel 'sat in a brown study, and said not a word' while observing every fold in the garment. By the time they reached the station, he was able to put it on confidently first try, and thus won the plaid. 'For many a day', said Condor, 'did he rejoice in its comfort', and he went on to describe the incident as 'a playful instance of the concentrated meditation which Mr Brunel gave to any subject on which he fixed his thoughts'.[59]

Brunel's correspondence is peppered with letters to other engineers, sometimes rather impatient, as when discussing procedure on a joint arbitration commission on fen drainage with Sir John Rennie;[60] and sometimes expressing robust disagreement, as when criticizing the idea of cash prizes suggested by William Cubitt to the Great Exhibition Buildings Committee of which they were both members.[61] But he seems to have accepted readily Joseph Paxton's elegant design for the Crystal Palace, despite having his own ideas for an appropriate Exhibition building, and in later years he gave Paxton advice and practical engineering assistance with the construction of two water towers when the building was removed to Croydon.[62] There are also letters to J. M. Rendel, C. B. Vignoles, Joseph Locke, James Nasmyth, William Armstrong and John Scott Russell. Some of these are just arrangements for meetings or simple requests for information, while others express opinions about fellow engineers.[63] Occasionally there is a longer letter, such as the glowing testimonial which helped Joseph Bazalgette to be appointed to the post with the Metropolitan Board of Works which revolutionized the sewage disposal system of London.[64] Central to this web of friends and professional contacts was membership of the Institution of Civil Engineers for which Brunel's loyalty never faltered, despite disagreements with its officers. He declined invitations to join other associations which he thought would compete with or injure the Civils, and for this reason he observed the foundation of the Institution of Mechanical Engineers with some suspicion. He acknowledged the achievements of 'our Respected Grandfather' George Stephenson, whom the Mechanicals had been established to honour,[65] but replied coolly to the letter inviting him to join the Mechanicals:

> I beg to record my thanks to Mr McConnell and the other members of the Committee of the proposed Institution of Mechanical Engineers for the honour they have done me. Will you oblige me by informing me whether the Institution is proposed to be of a local character or as an Institution for England generally, as in the latter case I fear it would tend to create a division in our Institution of Engineers and so far would I think be open to objection.[66]

For Brunel, the profession of engineer remained a unity, and he did not like any move to rend what he saw as a seamless fabric.

Success, when it came to Brunel as a professional man, came with remarkable rapidity. Even Brunel marvelled at the speed of the transition. Opening his journal at Christmas 1835, after a gap of two years which he acknowledged to have been 'the most eventful part of my life', he made a review of his commitments with the capital value of each item. First came: 'The Railway now is in progress. I am their engineer to the finest work in England – a handsome salary – £2000 a year – on excellent terms with my directors and all going smoothly.' He gave the capital for the GWR as £2,500,000. Next came Clifton Bridge – 'my first child, my darling, is actually going on' – at £70,000. Then followed Sunderland Docks, at £50,000; Bristol

Docks, at £20,000; the Merthyr & Cardiff Railway (Taff Vale), at £250,000; the Cheltenham Railway, at £750,000; the Bristol & Exeter Railway, at £1,250,000; the Newbury Branch, at £150,000; the Thames Suspension Bridge (the Hungerford Bridge, of which he said 'I have condescended to be engineer to this – but I shan't give myself much trouble about it'), at £100,000; and the Bristol & Gloster Railway, at £450,000. He added together these ten items, making a total of £5,590,000: 'A pretty considerable capital likely to pass through my hands – and this at the age of twenty-nine'.[67] Only a few months later, on 14 April 1836, he added a supplementary note:

> Since that time I have added to my stock in trade the Plymouth Railway, the Oxford branch and today somewhat against my will the Worcester & Oxford. Here's another £2,500,000 of capital – I may say £8,000,000 and really all very likely to go on. And what is satisfactory all reflecting credit upon me and most of them almost forced upon me ... Really my business is something extraordinary.[68]

For the rest of his career, Brunel was engaged simultaneously in a dozen or so major projects, the performance of which engaged the attention of the office team which we have been considering. The desk diaries kept in his office convey, at least for the central years of his career, from 1844 to 1853, a vivid picture of the complex and multifarious activity in which these commitments involved him. His days in the office were frequently broken into a series of half-hour consultations with staff, proprietors, and other people anxious to secure his attention, however briefly. This routine seems to have been abandoned in 1853, which may reflect the increasing obsession with the Great Ship project, or it may merely indicate a change in office practice. Another possibility is that, in the last six years of his life, Brunel's office became less efficient than it had been, and this may be related to his own heath and priorities or those of Joseph Bennett, who was presumably responsible for the desk diaries. Whatever the reason, the habit of keeping a detailed and annotated desk diary in the office lapsed, making it more difficult to follow the daily movements of the chief and his staff.[69]

It is impossible to determine with any precision the salary which Brunel derived from the large and varied range of commissions on which his office was engaged. The trustees of Clifton Bridge awarded him 5 per cent of the estimated cost of construction (£50,000), which was £2500, with £500 allowed for expenses and further allowances for assistant engineers.[70] As the construction was not completed by Brunel – even though the initial capital was spent – it is not clear how much of this reached him. On his own statement, quoted above, we know that the GWR gave him a 'handsome salary' of £2000 per annum.[71] When the main line was complete in 1843 the directors of the GWR considered the need for 'retrenchment of expenditure'

13. I. K. Brunel 'hung in chains': the famous photograph by Robert Howlett showing him standing in front of the chains designed to restrain the SS *Great Eastern* during her launch in 1857–58. (*Brunel University Library*)

14. The Crystal Palace as rebuilt at Sydenham, with Brunel's North Water Tower on the right.

15. The Balmoral Bridge, designed by Brunel to cross the River Dee at the entrance to Balmoral Castle in 1857. Queen Victoria was not pleased by its plain appearance, but it has proved to be a robust functional style of wrought-iron girder bridge. (*R. A. Buchanan*)

16. The SS *Great Eastern* under construction alongside the Thames at Millwall in 1857–58. (*Brunel University Library*)

17. The SS *Great Eastern* being prepared for her sideways launch into the Thames in 1857–58. (*Brunel University Library*)

20. A scene probably showing an episode in the attempt to launch the SS *Great Eastern* in November 1858: Brunel stands on the platform, with his dutiful assistants on either side. The figure on the left is possibly Captain Harrison. Photograph by Robert Howlett. (*Brunel University Library*)

19. Another photograph by Robert Howlett showing Brunel seated near one of the drums carrying the launching chains for the SS *Great Eastern* in 1857–58. (*Brunel University Library*)

20. A scene probably showing an episode in the attempt to launch the SS *Great Eastern* in November 1858: Brunel stands on the platform, with his dutiful assistants on either side. The figure on the left is possibly Captain Harrison. Photograph by Robert Howlett. (*Brunel University Library*)

16. The SS *Great Eastern* under construction alongside the Thames at Millwall in 1857–58. (*Brunel University Library*)

17. The SS *Great Eastern* being prepared for her sideways launch into the Thames in 1857–58. (*Brunel University Library*)

18. I. K. Brunel standing beside the launching chains of the SS *Great Eastern*: another photograph by Robert Howlett in 1857–58. (*Brunel University Library*)

21. Another episode during the launch of the SS *Great Eastern*. Brunel, on the right, is accompanied by colleagues, including (seated far left) Robert Stephenson. (*Brunel University Library*)

22. The last photograph of I. K. Brunel, taken on the deck of the SS *Great Eastern* as she was being prepared for her maiden voyage. Within a few hours of this picture being taken, in September 1859, Brunel was afflicted by the stroke which proved to be fatal. (*Brunel University Library*)

and reduced Brunel's salary to £1000 p.a., but they expected thereby to secure his continued attention for 'about one half of his time' to their business.[72] It seems reasonable to estimate that his annual income during the years of his greatest prosperity must have been at least £15,000, and that it may have been more in several years. These estimates receive confirmation from figures given in the letter books responding to enquiries from the Income Tax Commissioners. Income Tax had been introduced during the Napoleonic Wars, then phased out when peace was restored. It was reintroduced by Peel's Conservative administration in 1842, overtly as a short-term measure in the mid nineteenth-century reorganization of government, and was retained in subsequent budgets by Disraeli and Gladstone, with a rate for professional people of seven pence in the pound. As Brunel declared an income of £25,000 for 1846–47, and £18,500 for 1849–50, the government would have expected substantial sums from him, amounting to £730 and £540 respectively.[73] The sum to be taxed clearly varied considerably from year to year, but we can assume that all possible allowance was made in Brunel's office for necessary business expenses and payments to assistants and similar expenditure. Furthermore, Brunel appears to have been careless in his requests for payment, finding the subject undignified and disagreeable, and in at least two instances he chose not to request a salary: from the South Devon Railway, in the year when the atmospheric system was abandoned; and from the Balmoral Estate, when he became aware of the royal distaste regarding his bridge.[74]

Another insight into Brunel's finances is provided by a consideration of the numerous pass books issued by Drummond's Bank, who conducted most of Brunel's day to day business. Unfortunately, these are difficult to interpret, because of the large number of items about which it is impossible to be specific regarding their nature. However, taking 1842 as a specimen year, it is interesting to observe a number of features. In the first place, subscriptions to professional associations are prominent: £6 6s. 0d. to the Athenaeum Club on 1 January; £8 8s. 0d. to the Institution of Civil Engineers on 14 February; £10 10s. 0d. to the Reform Club on 28 April; and £5 5s. 0d. to the Royal Institution on 31 December. Insurance payments were made to Metropolitan Life, of £73 8s. 8d. on 28 July, and to Sun Fire, of £26 6s. 6d. on 3 June. Brunel paid four contributions of 'Assessed Tax' amounting to £44 17s. 1d. – substantially less than he was about to pay in Income Tax – but there were another three contributions amounting to £47 17s. 8d. towards Poor Rates. It is not possible to be certain which payments were salary payments to members of staff, but it seems likely that the £659 13s. 0d. paid to Hammond in three instalments was probably a salary of £600 plus £59 expenses. Similarly, the £265 paid to Bennett in six instalments was probably a salary of £250 plus some expenses. Two payments to Sir I. Brunel, amounting to £20, cannot be explained. For the rest, there are rents and water rates, gas bills and general office expenses, which are of no consequence for our purposes.[75]

One thing that emerges clearly from this survey of the finances of Brunel's professional business is that he should have been a wealthy man. His income was twenty times that of his senior assistants, and for twenty years he lived very comfortably, keeping a large establishment in London and a country estate, owning a carriage and horses as well as the personal carriage he designed for his professional travels, in which he could live and write – and smoke – while on his many journeys. His house was well endowed with furnishings, silverware, fine ceramics and works of art, all of which appear in the inventory which he commissioned in the last year of his life.[76] He spent most of what he earned in order to maintain himself and his family in a haute bourgeois, professional household, and he did so with some flair and ostentation. But he also invested heavily in some of the undertakings in which he was professionally engaged. It has been said of Brunel that 'he made it a principle throughout his life to invest in his own schemes and so to share their financial risks with others',[77] and although I have found no documentary confirmation for this assertion it seems likely that he did pursue such a rule. Daniel Gooch, who was in a position to know as well as most people, observed: 'He did not die a rich man, as if he was extravagant with shareholders' money he never asked others to take up a scheme which he did not himself largely embark in, and he thus lost a great deal of money.'[78] As Gooch, like Brunel, had invested in the Great Ship project, he would have known only too well how close that business came to complete disaster, and there is no doubt that Brunel lost heavily in it. But he also did well out of his railway investments, particularly in the 1840s, so on balance the practice of taking a share in the companies for which he was engaged was probably more rather than less remunerative. In the end, although not impoverished, Brunel did not leave great wealth to his family. His will, the effects of which were proved at under £90,000, left them in considerable comfort but with little margin for flamboyance.[79] For all his flair and vision as an engineer, Brunel did not make a huge fortune, although he did well by the standards of his times.

Brunel's devotion to his profession is manifest in all the arrangements of his office and his relationships with his peers, colleagues and subordinates. He applied almost all his immense energy throughout his adult life to the pursuit of his engineering commitments, refusing to be distracted by the temptations of a political or a social life, and finding little time for recreation, holidays or other activities. His success in creating and managing a large team in the office and in the field enabled him to fulfil the vision of engineering excellence which inspired him. His determination to exercise complete control over any engineering works which he undertook made it difficult for him to delegate responsibility to his team, so that they were expected to keep him fully informed about all matters of substance, and he maintained close personal supervision over all engineering activities. Incidentally, by maintaining rigorous professional standards for himself and his assistants he was able to assert a remarkable degree of independence in relation to the many boards of directors that he served. He thus did much to strengthen the role of the engineer as a professional consultant which had been established by Smeaton and confirmed by Telford and others. His forceful example helped to create the heroic image of the engineer of the Railway Age of early Victorian Britain. His limitations and prejudices, such as those in relation to technical education and state intervention to which we will return later, were those of his age, but it was Brunel's great distinction to have risen above these limitations and to have made the engineering profession one of the great creative forces of his generation.

11

Politics and Society

When Lady Gladwyn said of Marc Isambard Brunel that he was 'Typical of the French middle class, he remained reactionary all his life', she was making a fair summary of his political and social views. Always a royalist, although he switched his allegiance from the French to the British monarchy when the former was destroyed by the French Revolution, an ardent friend of aristocrats, and a paternalist in his social attitudes, he was never a man of progressive or liberal views. It is likely that his son assimilated these attitudes, and I. K. Brunel certainly had something of his father's deference towards the aristocracy and paternalism towards the lower classes. When Lady Spencer died in 1831, the younger Brunel noted in his journal: 'I have thus lost one of my best friends'.[1] This may suggest familiarity rather than deference, and was certainly combined in his case with a confident, even arrogant, professionalism. He never seems to have been ill at ease with those who could have been regarded by contemporaries as his social superiors. So while there is no doubt that the younger Brunel inherited a clear sense of social status, he was not, by the standards of his day, a snob.

There was also a strong link between Brunel's professionalism and his acceptance of the powerful middle-class consensus of the period in favour of economic liberalism. This consensus took several forms, affecting all political groups, and it can be conveniently expressed in the French term *laissez-faire*. It aspired to diminish the role of the state as far as possible, and to maximize that of the individual. The proper function of the state, according to economic liberalism, was that of the nightwatchman – essentially minimal, and concerned with the efficient protection of private property. It followed from this that the best sort of state was one which deliberately limited itself to providing the framework of law and order within which individuals, guided by the 'hidden hand' of private advantage, could work out whatever social arrangements suited their purposes. This model of the state had been advocated by the classical economists and utilitarians, and even those who adopted a more static, conservative, model of society found powerful pragmatic reasons for approximating to increasingly free trade policies in the 1820s.[2] The middling classes of British society in the nineteenth century generally found these assumptions congenial, and there can be little doubt that they had been fully incorporated into the young Brunel's view of life and social relationships by the 1830s.

A recent commentator has warned, however, that 'the Victorian state remains elusive', and 'it is vulgar error to see anything approaching unadulterated *laissez-faire* ... as the dominant belief of either classical economics or Benthamite utilitarianism'.[3] But even though all generalizations are unsatisfactory in plotting anything so complicated as mid nineteenth-century political and social attitudes, and even though the existence of many crosscurrents and contradictory tendencies must be recognized, the broad outlines of British mid century opinion, vulgar or sophisticated, approximated to a consensus in favour of economic liberalism. All political parties – Whig and Tory, Liberal and Radical – were affected by it to some degree. Reactionary conservative paternalists, of the sort which Marc Brunel might have approved, were largely dormant or defensive, whilst socialist collectivism was still only a cloud on the horizon, no bigger than a man's hand. The middle classes who benefited from the Reform Act of 1832 and the reform of municipal authorities in 1835, who devised the reform of the poor law and master-minded the repeal of the Corn Laws, were animated by ideas of economic and political liberalization, and these were the ideas embraced by the engineers and other new professional groups and adopted, in particular, by I. K. Brunel. Not that he allowed himself to become partisan about it: virtually his only act of political partisanship was his support for his brother-in-law Benjamin Hawes, who stood as a Radical candidate for the Lambeth constituency in the reformed House of Commons in the autumn of 1832. Thereafter he never permitted himself the luxury of overt political partisanship. While colleagues like Robert Stephenson, Joseph Locke and Daniel Gooch all found time to identify themselves with political parties and were elected to Parliament, Brunel steadfastly refrained from any such associations.

Nevertheless, the correlation between the period of vigorous Radical agitation, beginning with the Reform movement in the early 1830s and moving through the Anti-Corn Law League of the 1840s into the widespread adoption of Free Trade policies in the 1850s, with the period of Brunel's career as an independent engineer, is striking. Even though his participation in the political activity of 1832 was exceptional, it is worth a brief examination in order to illuminate our understanding of Brunel's political attitudes. In August 1832, he recorded in his journal: 'Have now for some time been entirely engaged in Electioneering'.[4] Hawes was formally selected as candidate at a meeting in Peckham shortly after, and the *Morning Advertiser* reported him as being: 'A thorough Reformer and unflinching economist, hoping to see all the institutions of the country put on a firm basis ... He stood with those who were not afraid to trust the people with knowledge and power'.[5] From a subsequent speech in the election it appears that reform of the church and the abolition of slavery figured prominently in Hawes' agenda.[6]

Many years after, William Hawes spoke warmly of Brunel's support for his brother in this election:

> He made friends and conciliated opponents among all classes of electors – especially among working men, large bodies of whom he met on several occasions – and among all shades of politicians; and to his energy, good judgment and skilful arrangement of electioneering details, which were not then so well understood as they now are, very much of the success achieved was due.[7]

Whatever his latent skills as a political organizer, at the beginning of 1833 Brunel recorded with apparent relief: 'Having got clear of Election ... I must now seriously attend to business'.[8] He still found time to walk to the House of Commons with Hawes the same day, when the latter was about to be sworn in, and some weeks later he went to the House again in the hope of hearing O'Connell speak.[9] As the eloquent spokesman for Irish nationalism, O'Connell might have expected some Radical sympathy, but on Brunel's account it was 'an extravagant flowery speech full of exciting false statements', so he was not greatly impressed. It is significant that this was a week after Brunel had been appointed engineer to the incipient GWR project, which launched him into a period of hectic activity from which, in a sense, he never emerged. His political career was thus short and vicarious, for never again did he give his support to a specific political party.

At a more general level of political association, however, Brunel's sympathetic identification with the aspirations of economic liberalism remained firm, and was expressed through his professional attitudes towards government activities such as railway inspection, and social policies such as urban improvement. He shared the deep suspicion of most engineers that the creation of the railway inspectorate represented an oblique attempt by central government to curb private initiative. The first inspectors – there were never more than two or three in Brunel's lifetime – were given powers under the Railway Regulation Act of 1840 and subsequent legislation to certify new lines as safe before they were allowed to carry passengers.[10] These minimal powers to ensure that the rapidly proliferating railway services of the 1840s were safe for the public were exercised with considerable care for the scruples of the railway companies and their engineers, but occasionally, as over Torksey Bridge built by John Fowler across the Trent in Lincolnshire, the inspectors could insist that changes should be made, and then Brunel joined his fellow engineers in complaining about their interference.[11] The superficial objection was that the inspectors did not understand the engineering technicalities, but as they were all military engineers with the Corps of Royal Engineers this could hardly be sustained, and the more profound objection was that their action was an intolerable interference by government in the affairs of private enterprise.

On this occasion, however, Brunel demonstrated that he was open to reasonable discussion, as he wrote to the inspector concerned, Captain J. L. A. Simmons RE, in February 1850, regarding the loading trials which had been conducted on Torksey Bridge:

> The general conclusion I have come to after all is, that we have not got the grievance against you which we supposed and that we must therefore live in hopes for another chance and manage better next time. Joking apart, I shall try and soften matters instead of urging them on as I had loudly declared I should, and will speak to Stephenson and others. I am bound to say that Stephenson was much more moderate than I.[12]

Shortly after he wrote to Fowler, reporting on the Torksey trials: 'the results seem to me to show that the bridge is safe enough under all probable circumstances, but at the same time I do not find it [to] comply with those conditions which I lay down for myself in the construction of similar bridges'.[13] The fact that both Stephenson and Brunel had come to the conclusion that cast iron was not suitable for general use in railway bridges meant that in this case, where Fowler had made use of cast iron, albeit very carefully, they were sympathetic to the inspector's caution and prepared to accept his ruling.[14]

The same issues had already been rehearsed at length in the Royal Commission that had examined the collapse of Robert Stephenson's iron bridge over the Dee at Chester in 1847. On that occasion Brunel had referred to the commissioners as 'despots',[15] and had submitted a substantial written statement arguing against government intervention:

> If the Commission is to enquire into the conditions '*to be observed*', it is to be presumed that they will give the result of their enquiries; or, in other words, that they will lay down, or at least suggest, 'rules' and 'conditions to be [hereafter] observed' in the construction of bridges, or, in other words, embarrass and shackle the progress of improvement to-morrow by recording and registering as law the prejudices and errors of to-day ... Devoted as I am to my profession, I see with fear and regret that this tendency to legislate and to rule, which is the fashion of the day, is flowing in our direction.[16]

However tortured the syntax of this observation, the sense of it is clear enough, and it associated Brunel firmly with the attitudes of economic

liberalism which were coming under anxious inquisition by officials vested
with responsibilities for the well-being of the community. Ironically, many
Radicals shifted their ground on this issue, as a measure of state intervention
came to seem the best way of guaranteeing free trade in a situation inviting
the development of monopolies. But Brunel remained with the ideological
rearguard, and for all his eloquence he could not stem the tide which he
saw was beginning to flow against his views.

Brunel carried his radical aversion towards government interference in
any sort of commercial relationship further than most of his colleagues
in one important respect. This was his view of patent law, an area of
government that caused widespread dissatisfaction in the eighteenth and
early nineteenth centuries on account of the inaccessibility and prohibitive
costs of the system. Whereas most critics wanted to reform the system,
Brunel adopted the more extreme abolitionist position which took *laissez-
faire* to the point of perversity. While other engineers, including such close
personal friends as Robert Stephenson, T. R. Guppy and even his own father,
had made full use of the patent system to protect their inventions and to
secure financial recompense for the investment of their time and talent,
Brunel steadfastly refused to take out any patents at all. He worked for many
years, as we have seen, to help his father to produce the 'gaz engine' under
the protection of his father's patent, but when this was finally abandoned,
in January 1833, he seems to have resolved that in future he would make
no further attempt to produce patentable inventions of his own. Parliamentary agitation brought minor reforms in 1835, 1839 and 1844, before the more
comprehensive renewal of the patent system in 1852, but these improvements
did not cause Brunel to modify his abolitionist posture.[17]

Brunel was always open to good ideas from other people, and showed
astonishing flexibility in adjusting to inventions such as the iron ship, screw
propulsion, the use of the 'wave line' in hull design, the atmospheric railway,
the electric telegraph, even the use of creosote as a wood preservative.
Inventors regularly pestered him with ingenious ideas. Although dismissive
of most of them, he was quick to recognize the merits of those which were
more promising. But he came to believe strongly that the patent system was
a check on enterprise, and as such he condemned it:

> I believe that the most useful and novel inventions and improvements of the
> present day are mere progressive steps in a highly wrought and highly advanced
> system, suggested by, and dependent on, other previous steps, their whole value
> and the means of their application probably dependent on the success of some
> or many other inventions, some old, some new ... Without the hopes of any
> exclusive privileges, I believe that a clever man would produce many more good
> ideas, and derive much more easily some benefit from them. It is true that he

will aim only at earning a few pounds instead of dreaming of thousands; but he will earn these few pounds frequently, and without interfering with his daily pursuits; on the contrary, he will make himself more useful.[18]

He maintained this position persistently to the end of his career, arguing trenchantly before a Select Committee of the House of Lords in 1851, and a meeting of the Society of Arts in 1856, that the present patent system rarely, if ever, benefited the genuine inventor, and acted most frequently as a hindrance to the adoption of good ideas and the promotion of further innovation.

The engineer's eloquence and personal experience were impressive, but not sufficient to persuade public opinion to abolish the system or even to adopt 'very cheap patents granted with great facility, to the poor illiterate workman, as well as to the rich manufacturer', which he was prepared to advocate as an alternative.[19] For a couple of decades it seemed as if the arguments in favour of abolition might be successful, with the *Economist* coming out strongly in support in the 1850s and 1860s.[20] The Patent Law Amendment Act of 1852, however, removed many of the previous objections to the system, making it more accessible and slightly less expensive, so that many more inventors made use of it. The onset of depression in the 1870s brought a check to the Free Trade ideology and reinforced support for patents as the best way of rewarding inventiveness. Brunel appeared unworried when others borrowed and even patented ideas to which he could have made a legitimate claim. Samuel Smiles regarded Brunel as less inventive than his father, but this is not proven: all that can be said with confidence is that he did not trouble to take out patents to protect his novel ideas.[21]

Brunel's views on patents and on government intervention were both put to the test by the introduction of the screw propeller in ships. Patents for the screw had been taken out in the 1830s by John Ericsson and Francis Pettit Smith. While Ericsson had despaired of arousing Admiralty interest and had emigrated to the United States, Smith had formed the Ship Propeller Company in 1839 to exploit his patent, building the 200 ton *Archimedes* to demonstrate its merits. Brunel was immediately impressed and recommended that the *Great Britain*, then being built in Bristol, should be adapted to screw propulsion. Although adopting Smith's system, he realized that much more work was needed to determine the best size, shape and fitting for the screw. This, however, required considerable expense and presented him with a potential delay in the completion of his new ship, so that it was a stroke of great good fortune for him that the Admiralty invited him to conduct tests on the screw for their own purposes. This he did, on the *Polyphemus* and the *Rattler*, and Andrew Lambert is almost certainly correct in recognizing that these tests provided vital information for Brunel in deciding on the design of the screw for the *Great Britain*. In effect, the Ship Propeller Company supplied essential development research free to both Brunel and the Admiralty before being itself forced into liquidation. Lambert is probably correct also in arguing that, despite its cautious initial response to the screw and its cynical use of the company, the Admiralty made the correct decision and began to re-equip the Navy for screw-propulsion. His argument is less satisfactory in relation to Brunel's attitude to the Admiralty. He blames Christopher Claxton for imputing animus against the government representatives on Brunel's part which was not present in reality. Although Claxton was certainly outspoken in his criticisms of Admiralty bureaucracy, and influenced the young Isambard Brunel in preparing his account of the episode for publication, there are plenty of anecdotes and comments on record by Brunel to show that he shared these views. The Admiralty was for him part of the necessary structure of government, but in dealing with it he never shook off his deep suspicion of government inefficiency which characterized the *laissez-faire* attitudes of his era, and in this he fully shared Claxton's views.[22]

When it came to warfare, even the strongest advocates of *laissez-faire* principles acknowledged that the state had a proper role in the defence of the realm, and Brunel was prepared to give his support to the government in its prosecution of the Crimean War against Russia in 1854–55. Even here, however, he chafed against the inefficiency of government departments. He had long been irritated by the Admiralty for what he regarded as its conservative attitudes on ship construction and propulsion. Now that he was prepared to put a flood of ideas about improved rifles, floating gun batteries and prefabricated hospitals freely at the disposal of the government, he found the in-built caution and bureaucracy of the Admiralty and other government departments very frustrating. His gun batteries, designed to be semi-submersible in order to present the smallest possible area as a target for enemy fire, were developed in considerable detail and submitted to the Admiralty, but they remained only intriguing ideas.[23]

His polygonally bored rifle was a more substantial invention, because he actually had at least one made and tested. In October 1852 he had written to the gunsmith Westley Richards: 'I have long wanted to try an experiment with a rifle, for the purpose of determining whether there is anything in a crotchet I have upon the subject.'[24] Brunel's 'crotchet' appears to have been a suspicion that the accuracy of a gun would be improved by imparting some spin to the shot, and he proposed to do this through a barrel of octagonal cross-section and with a twist increasing from breech to mouth. The rifle was presented by Brunel to his French friend D'Eichtal, who must have liked it because he later asked for another.[25] But Brunel took the idea no further, and when Richards later approached him in some embarrassment because Joseph Whitworth had taken out a patent for the idea, Brunel assured him that he had no intention of challenging 'my friend Mr Whitworth'.[26] The fact was, however, that this was an extremely important perception in the history of gunnery, and that Brunel allowed Joseph Whitworth to take all the credit for it, even though it is more than likely that it was his idea which stimulated the work of Whitworth in this field.

Thanks largely to the collaboration of Hawes, who was at the time of the Crimean War a member of the government as Under-Secretary at the War Office, Brunel managed to obtain official sanction for his innovative hospital scheme. Ironically, Hawes had incurred the hostility of Florence Nightingale for his lack of cooperation in the provision of medical facilities, but his support for his friend's scheme must stand to his credit in this respect. Brunel immediately undertook the design of an ingenious set of prefabricated buildings and arranged for their shipment to Turkey and for their erection there by his assistant, John Brunton. The buildings were designed as an interconnected series of wooden huts, with careful attention being given to heating, ventilation, drainage and sanitation throughout the complex. The site chosen by Dr Parkes, the able Medical Superintendent in the war, was at Renkioi, on the southern shores of the Dardanelles, and the whole operation was completed efficiently in time to come into service just as the campaign in the Crimea was ending. The buildings were thus not ready in time to make a significant contribution to the conduct of the war, but they provided valuable pioneering experience for subsequent hospital buildings and for the prefabrication of buildings in general. The design and construction of the hospital, with astonishing innovation and attention to detail, and almost incredible efficiency in shipping out the parts and assembling them promptly, provides in microcosm an outstanding example of Brunel's talents and methods of operation.[27]

In matters of social policy, in so far as he had any cause to become involved in them, Brunel showed a penchant for *laissez-faire* views and solutions derived from the same assumptions about government and the state which determined his economic and political opinions. His letter books and other papers are remarkably silent on the social cataclysm which afflicted Ireland in the 1840s, with the failure of the potato harvest in 1845 and the Famine the following year. They were at a distance from his main preoccupations in these years, but he did have Irish railway commissions, as we have seen, and these were interrupted by the Famine, so that comparative remoteness can be no excuse for indifference. It seems that Brunel shared the English economic liberal consensus in this affair as in others: the Irish were deemed to have brought the affliction on themselves, and were considered to be responsible for their own salvation, with the provision of government help in the crisis being judged likely to do more harm than good. Probably more than any other single issue, the Irish Famine demonstrated the moral bankruptcy of *laissez-faire* individualism.[28]

It was a bankruptcy which is visible with hindsight in many areas of mid nineteenth-century social policy, but in some cases the immediacy of the crisis was such that the inhibitions of economic liberalism had to be suppressed in order to introduce new remedies through communal action. The state, in fact, began to discover a new role as a humanitarian agency, to provide protection for women and children in factories and coal mines, to resolve problems of epidemic disease such as cholera, and to make sanitary provision for the new industrial towns. Historians have argued about whether this change was the result of a coherent policy of socialistic reform or the pragmatic response to a series of practical problems, but in either case the result was much the same.[29] As it moved slowly to tackle these problems, the state, through both national and local government, asserted new powers and established new agencies, and some of the strongest advocates of these innovations were men who had previously been Radical spokesmen. One such was Edwin Chadwick, a disciple of Jeremy Bentham and James Mill, who had been one of the architects of the utilitarian minimalist legislation which had produced the New Poor Law in 1834, but who was converted in the 1840s to more positively interventionist policies by the necessity for public health measures.[30] These were not matters to which, in the general run of things, Brunel devoted much attention. But when Chadwick wrote a pamphlet on the conditions of railway employees and circulated it to Members of Parliament and influential citizens, Brunel felt moved to make a rejoinder:

> I have read your pamphlet on the state of railway workmen with much interest. It is a subject on which I have myself thought a good deal, and many of the directors of companys I am engaged for have also turned their attention to it and made more exertions than you and probably others appear to think that directors generally do – indeed this is a common error into which the most praiseworthy redressors of wrong frequently fall – that of supposing that parties connected with the grievances and opportunity of profiting by them do not anxiously endeavour to remedy them. I should be *most happy* to join in any well directed efforts to remedy these very great and crying evils ... but I am finally convinced that any legislative interference in the shape of penalties upon those parties whose *friendly* and *cordial* assistance can alone afford any chance of success, will only aggravate the mischief without removing any of the original causes.[31]

Whether or not Chadwick had been soliciting Brunel's support personally in his campaign to ensure that railway employers would be liable for injuries

to their employees, he clearly received no help from this source. There is
no record of any subsequent communication between the two men on this
or any other matter. Chadwick, who had been moved by descriptions of the
appalling conditions under which the railway navvies worked on the Woodhead Tunnel, pressed the issue to a parliamentary debate and report, but
nothing was done about it. The gist of Brunel's attitude, which coincided
with that of the railway employers, is abundantly clear: the welfare of railway
workers was the business of the railways, and 'legislative interference' would
be counter-productive.[32]

Chadwick was also intensely interested in measures for improving water
supply and removing sewage waste in order to improve urban conditions
of life and eliminate cholera and other infectious diseases. In the process of
pursuing such policies in his usual ruthless and high-handed way, however,
he managed to antagonize many civic authorities and their engineers. From
a purely engineering point of view, Brunel participated in several water
schemes, designing the Clifton Water Works in Bristol and giving advice
on the major schemes for Manchester and Glasgow.[33] He also supported
Bazalgette's candidature for the post of engineer to the Metropolitan Board
of Works, and thus contributed to the huge sewer construction undertaking
which transformed the sanitary condition of London in the next two decades.
But the London scheme was one which became the subject of bitter conflict with Chadwick and his supporters, and the issues were discussed at
meetings of the Institution of Civil Engineers.[34] It is likely that Brunel shared
the antipathy of his colleagues towards what they saw as the extremely
interventionist measures of social improvement advocated by Chadwick.

Brunel's relations with the working classes reflect the assumptions and
prejudices of the Victorian bourgeoisie to which he belonged. The urban
proletariat was a new phenomenon, related to the rapid growth of towns
in response to industrialization. In so far as it represented the Victorian
form of the labouring underclass, depending for survival on employment
by the higher classes and carrying little political or social influence, it was
treated by these classes with a traditional mixture of disdain, condescension
and fear. Brunel had been born into the professional middle classes and he
inherited these attitudes towards his social inferiors, however much they
were diluted by his father's experience or his own humanitarianism. In
one-to-one relationships Brunel was generally open-minded and ready to
give a person the benefit of the doubt until he proved to be either incom-
petent or of an 'ungentlemanly' quality, but in relation to the 'great
unwashed' of the urban masses, his attitudes were mostly typical of his class.
Such people were necessary as labourers, either as railway 'navvies' or in
any other capacity, but this was a relationship properly governed by the

rules of the market, to be engaged or dispensed with according to the immediate needs of the employer and the conditions dictated by supply and demand. Any attempt to interfere with the dynamics of the free market process by collective bargaining for higher wages or better conditions of employment was anathema to the principles of economic liberalism, and was condemned by Brunel and all his engineering colleagues.

Adrian Vaughan is probably right in modifying Rolt's rosy picture of Brunel as a much-loved representative of the employers who could do no wrong in the eyes of his workers.[35] Although there is little record of labour disputes in the GWR under Brunel, this should be seen as indicating a strict sub-military discipline which became the general character of railway employment in the nineteenth century, rather than showing any particular affection towards Brunel. There are many hints of indifference or even harshness in Brunel's attitude towards the gangs of men employed on his building projects, as in respect to the deaths and injuries at work on the Box Tunnel, where many lost their lives. Such fatalities were widely accepted by employers at the time without incurring any liability on their part, although there is evidence of some of the new breed of railway contractors, including Thomas Brassey, exercising particular care over the safety of their workers.

For the most part, however, Brunel's attitude was that of his fellow engineers of the Railway Age and should not be regarded as a personal failure.[36] One curious indication of a degree of paternalism towards his workmen appears in a letter to Henry Wentworth Acland (1815–1900), the brother of Sir Thomas Dyke Acland the agricultural reformer, and himself a distinguished member of Oxford University. Brunel's writing is particularly scrappy and even more difficult than usual to read:

> I am very sorry I have not before heard of the very kind proceedings of the Oxford authoritites. Nothing would have given me more pleasure than to have shared as I should have done the gratification of our men in whose welfare I take a great interest, but I have engagements which I can not now put off. I thank you most sincerely for this [consideration towards] my respectable workmen, and I sincerely trust that they will display their gratitude. I would like to be allowed to join in the subscription – as 'a friend' of yours – not by name – and to be allowed on these conditions to send my £5.[37]

As the GWR line to Oxford was opened on 12 June 1844, it seems likely that these celebrations were related to that event and that the 'Oxford authorities' were putting on some junketings for the occasion. The point is slight but not insignificant: Brunel thought it worth thanking Acland on behalf of his men, in whose behaviour he showed less than complete confidence, and was prepared to make a modest and anonymous contribution himself.

The working classes were generally seen by the Victorian engineers as a largely homogeneous mass which could be 'tapped' for specific employment undertakings as and when required, but with no further commitment on the part of the employer. The existence of different grades of labourer, skilled and semi-skilled craftsmen, was only dimly appreciated, even by those employers who had most to gain from employment of these specific skills. These were the years, after all, in which the first British 'craft' unions emerged: the Amalgamated Society of Engineers was founded in 1851 and quickly established itself as a sound and cautious organization to promote the interests of skilled engineering craftsmen, and in the following decades it was joined by similar bodies for workers in the building trades and metal industries. These organizations pursued a policy of promoting themselves as responsible bodies which was eventually successful in moderating public opinion and securing legislative protection for their funds.[38] But some of the leading national engineers were vehement opponents of the unions in its early years: the anonymous 'Amicus' who wrote vitriolic letters to *The Times* during the engineering lock-out of 1851–52 turned out to be the son of William Fairbairn, and James Nasmyth claimed that his antipathy towards the trade unionists was one of the reasons for his early retirement from business in the 1850s.[39] All the available evidence suggests that the sympathies of Brunel would have been with his engineering colleagues on these issues, rather than with the trade unionists.

We can be even more certain regarding Brunel's attitude towards the mass working-class movement of his time in the shape of Chartism. The People's Charter, with its famous 'six points' calling for the ballot, universal manhood suffrage and other democratic proposals which would be regarded as moderate by twentieth-century standards, had been a product of the industrial unrest of the late 1830s.[40] It was presented as a petition to the House of Commons in 1838 and rejected, but by then there had developed amongst the hitherto largely inarticulate working class a strong sense of injustice and some momentum to achieve redress of grievances. The rejection of the Charter led to outbreaks of violence in various parts of the country. These were occasionally ugly but never really serious, although in so far as Britain had already achieved a remarkable degree of civil obedience without the apparatus of a police state, any disruption of law and order was potentially serious and the authorities rightly regarded it as such. Chartism simmered on through the 1840s, but appeared to be losing widespread support until Feargus O'Connor emerged and stimulated another wave of agitation that came to a crescendo in April 1848. Another petition was prepared for presentation to Parliament on 10 April, and the government became alarmed at the possibility of civil commotion, to counter which they called in the support of military units to be present in London, and summoned the special constabulary. These were citizens of standing who were prepared to assist the police in the maintenance of law and order. Brunel was amongst them.

We have already had cause to note Brunel's attitude towards the agitators in the Bristol Riots of 1831. On that occasion the sympathies of many middle-class citizens were confused, both by the dilatoriness of the military intervention in the disorder and by a widely felt hostility towards the local mercantile oligarchy. Although he appears to have enjoyed the excitement, Brunel was firmly on the side of the merchants and aldermen who were his personal friends. When it came to the crunch, radical sensibilities were in favour of law and order and against the mob. It is by no means certain that the same principles operated with as much force when the disorder took place in France, because as soon as the Chartist excitement subsided in 1848 Brunel rushed off to Paris with John Horsley to observe the course of the revolutionary activity which contorted French politics for most of that 'Year of Revolutions' and created the Second Republic. Their presence appears to have been welcomed by the revolutionaries, who greeted them as 'Citoyen Brunel' and 'Citoyen Horsley', even though the Britons seem to have been keener to pick up some furniture bargains than to take any active part in revolutionary proceedings.[41]

Back in London it was another story. Brunel had enrolled as a special constable for Westminster in the Chartist crisis, and was called upon to turn out for duty at the end of May, when the authorities remained nervous about the possibility of outbreaks of violence. Typically, Brunel chafed at having to take orders – and at having no orders to take. He wrote to the Hon. J. C. Talbot, who was in charge of the special constabulary in Brunel's part of Westminster:

> My Dear Talbot, I address you as our leader to beg of you to have some communication with some authority (if any exist of which there is no symptom) in order either to put an end to the farce which has been nightly acted in this district or ... that the childish proceeding which we are forced to take part in should be converted into a sensible and useful proceeding.[42]

It is not clear what particular 'proceedings' were intended, but by this time the crisis was effectively over and the special constabulary was about to be disbanded. What is clear from this letter is that Brunel was a firm supporter of law and order.

It is hardly necessary to add that Brunel gave no indication of sympathy with views of a more socialistic or communistic flavour, even though these were becoming widespread in Britain and on the Continent. After all, Karl Marx and Friedrich Engels had seized the opportunity offered by the

1848 revolutions throughout Europe to launch the *Communist Manifesto*.
Shortly afterwards Marx came to London as a political refugee and spent
the rest of his life there, studying in the British Museum Reading Room
and publishing *Das Kapital* in 1867. Engels, who worked in the 1840s as
agent for his father's textile mill in Manchester, had already written his
perceptive study of *The Working Classes in Manchester in 1844*, but it had
been published in German and did not become generally accessible to
English readers until much later in the nineteenth century. Neither Marx
nor Engels made any impression on the British working classes in their
lifetimes, and even less on the prosperous middling and professional
classes to which Brunel belonged. On the other hand, Brunel could not
have been completely immune to the work of such distinctively British
contributors to the communitarian ethic as Thomas Carlyle, John Ruskin,
and the self-styled 'Christian Socialists' consisting of clergy and laymen
who gathered around the Revd F. D. Maurice in 1848. It has to be admitted,
however, that there is a dearth of evidence regarding any interest by Brunel
in these writers.[43]

Of all the symbols of the spirit of the age in early Victorian Britain, one
of the most potent was the International Exhibition of Industry held in
Hyde Park in the summer of 1851. I. K. Brunel was intimately associated with
this event. The Great Exhibition has come to be regarded as the high-water
mark of the success of British industrialization, demonstrating the commanding lead established by British manufacturing industries and transport
systems over the rest of the world. It was the achievement of a small group
of men who represented the industrial leadership of the country, coordinated
by the Society of Arts and under the active patronage of Prince Albert. There
had been several precedents for the idea of the Exhibition. A series of eleven
expositions had been held in France between 1797, when they had been
established as an act of revolutionary self-confidence to demonstrate the
successes of French industry and craftsmanship, and 1849. Similar events
had been arranged in several British towns, inspired partly by the vogue for
'mechanics' institutes' in the 1820s and 1830s, but taken up with enthusiasm
by places such as Manchester and Birmingham as demonstrations of municipal enterprise from 1837 onwards. With these models in mind, and with
Prince Albert installed as President from 1842, the Society of Arts had begun
to consider the organization of a genuinely international festival of industry.
Henry Cole emerged as the able and persistent promoter of this scheme,
and when the Prince took it under his personal superintendence in 1849 it
began to take positive shape.[44]

A Royal Commission was appointed to pursue the plan to fruition,
consisting of a couple of dozen members representing the great and the

good of the nation, and Prince Albert became its chairman. In this capacity he spoke at civic banquets and money-raising meetings up and down the country, presenting his vision of the Exhibition with great clarity:

> Nobody ... who has paid any attention to the particular features of our present era, will doubt for a moment that we are living in a period of most wonderful transition, which tends rapidly to accomplish that great end – to which indeed all history points – the realization of the unity of mankind; not a unity that breaks down the limits and levels the peculiar characteristics of the different nations of the earth, but rather a unity the result and product of those very national varieties and antagonistic qualities.[45]

As far as Prince Albert was concerned, the Exhibition was intended to be the first great international celebration to display the results of modern industry and to demonstrate the inevitable progress towards international unity which he, like others of his confident early Victorian generation, took to be the necessary end-result of such industrial development. A recent commentator has suggested that it was not actually as simple as that, but that: 'the Exhibition was a protean event with numerous possible meanings'.[46] With its strong emphasis on educational improvement, particularly in industrial design, the Great Exhibition was organized 'less to demonstrate Britain's industrial success than to identify and rectify Britain's manufacturing deficiencies'.[47] But however diverse the objectives of the organizers, they produced the inspired management which, with a measure of good fortune, achieved huge success as an outstanding public spectacle.

The active officers of the Royal Commission were Henry Cole and John Scott Russell, and Cole in particular was assiduous in canvassing the provincial support which became such a remarkable feature of the Exhibition. He was a strong-minded and contentious man, and had previously taken a vigorous part in the 'Gauge War' against the broad gauge, but as his contributions had been largely anonymous it is not clear whether or not Brunel knew of this role.[48] There were serious difficulties to be overcome before the Exhibition could be safely established: funds had to be raised, a site determined, and possibly most critically, a suitable building design had to be chosen. Substantial financial guarantees were obtained from industrial and commercial interests; Prince Albert guided the Royal Commission to deciding on Hyde Park as the venue; and a Building Committee was appointed to choose the design. Brunel was invited to join this committee, and accepted at the end of January 1850. He had already made some acute observations on the system of classification proposed by the Society of Arts, which had originally promoted the Exhibition.[49] He was one of three engineers, the others being Robert Stephenson and the veteran

William Cubitt, who together with three architects and two aristocrats formed the committee.[50]

It is unlikely that Brunel spent a great deal of time on the Exhibition, although his desk diaries record several attendances at the committee and, as with any project to which he put even part of his mind, his presence was strongly felt.[51] His major role was in determining the visual impact of the Exhibition. The Building Committee was seriously late in deciding on the design for the structure to house the Exhibition, and the matter had still not been resolved by the summer of 1850. Designs had been invited from the public, and 245 had been received, but all had been rejected. Brunel then produced a design of his own, which was a large brick building with a cast-iron dome as its central feature. In mid May he described himself to one of the architects commissioned to work on the scheme as being 'brim full of the details of dome and specification – ready to pour upon you in a torrent'.[52] He also wrote to Cubitt requesting directions on how to proceed with arrangements for the dome.[53] The plan was well developed, but the initial response from the public was less than enthusiastic, and it seems unlikely that it would have been accepted. Then the design of Paxton for the glass and iron structure which became known as the Crystal Palace became available, and Brunel and his colleagues were quickly persuaded that it had outstanding merits. Brunel was helpful to Paxton with statistical details for his design, although he warned Paxton that 'I mean to try and win with our plan; but I have thought it right to give your beautiful plan all the advantages which it is susceptible of.'[54] He recognized the excellence of Paxton's design and there is no evidence that he persisted with his rival scheme. For his part, Paxton was anxious to acknowledge 'the kindness and liberality of Mr Brunel' as his sensational building was rapidly assembled from mass-produced parts and was opened to universal acclaim on 1 May 1851.

There were other matters about the Exhibition with which Brunel was concerned. He was influential in the composition of the display and the allocation of prizes. He approved the emphasis on making the Exhibition entirely voluntary, in the sense of not being dependent on state funding. He would have liked to make the prizes for exhibits non-pecuniary, being confined to the award of medals, but he was unable to achieve this fully. However, he spelt out his views to William Cubitt: 'The *opportunity of exhibition* I believe will be quite sufficient to induce all the competition we can desire. I think money prizes quite a mistake and medals or distinctions pretty nearly as bad. I hope you will hold the same views but I send you mine.'[55] Nevertheless, Brunel accepted the post of chairman and reporter of the jury for Class VII, on Civil Engineering, Architecture, and Building

Contrivances, and in this capacity he helped to dispense prizes, including one to Paxton for the Crystal Palace design, of which he spoke very warmly as being the building 'best adapted in every respect for the purpose for which it was intended'.[56] According to his son, Brunel also accepted 'a pecuniary acknowledgment for his services' at the close of the Exhibition, although this was 'much against his will', and he made sure that it was spent on the erection of model cottages for artisans at Watcombe, following a design approved by Prince Albert.[57] Then there was the presence of the railway locomotives at the Exhibition, with a massive GWR engine, Daniel Gooch's *Lord of the Isles*, dominating everything else and testifying to Brunel's achievements. Lady Noble drew attention to Brunel's dismissal of some of the electrical machines offered for exhibition as worthy only of being 'considered as toys'. He would have preferred all exhibits to be distinguished by their usefulness, but there is a real failure of perception here, which is strange in one who had so early appreciated the value of Michael Faraday's work, and the usefulness of the electric telegraph.[58]

Brunel thus joined in the national euphoria of the Great Exhibition in the summer of 1851. He was present at the opening on 1 May, when his desk diary records that: 'Mr Brunel went out at 10 a.m., returned at 20 minutes past 7 p.m.'. On 17 May, he 'went to the Exhibition buildings', and on 9 July he 'went to the Lord Mayor's Ball at Guildhall, given to the Queen in celebration of the Great Exhibition of 1851'. Then on 20 August, 'Mr Brunel went to the Exhibition Building accompanied by Master Brunel'.[59] To Brunel, as for so many others in that summer of confident achievement, the occasion represented a triumph for the unrestricted free enterprise of British *laissez-faire* industry. It was also both a strident declaration of British nationalism and a profound aspiration for peace and internationalism. And, with six million visitors, from all social classes and travelling from all parts of the country and beyond, it was the beginning of a revolution in leisure.[60] Britain was effectively demonstrating its success in becoming the workshop of the world, and Brunel found personal satisfaction in participating in a celebration to which he had made such a substantial contribution.

The Great Exhibition can also be seen as one of the great pivotal events of the nineteenth century. Although so much British industrial achievement seemed to have led up to the Exhibition and had been incorporated in its success, the pattern changed in subsequent years. There was no decline in British industrial activity, but the development of its rivals was swifter and rapidly appeared to overtake British achievements. Portents of this change were visible at the Exhibition, in American small arms produced with inter-changeable parts, and in the electrical gadgets that Brunel dismissed as toys. The rapid development overseas of new technologies and mass-production techniques put British industry at a disadvantage, and compelled it to make painful readjustments. Nationalism became more strident, and internationalism faded as a realistic prospect. And in attitudes towards education, in particular, the Exhibition brought a change of mood. A determination to improve British standards of design and industrial education had been, from the outset, a leading aim of the Society of Arts, and the slow success of this policy, with the investment of the profits of the Exhibition in a huge 'educational estate' in South Kensington and the gradual improvement in secondary and technical education, effected a profound social and cultural change in Britain. Brunel had little to do with this development. He contributed to the removal of the Crystal Palace to Sydenham, as already seen. And his abortive design for the building survived, at least in the minds of some of the organizers of the 1862 Exhibition which succeeded it, and to which the buildings bore a striking resemblance. These never won a fraction of the admiration bestowed upon the Crystal Palace, being blessed with the nickname of the 'Brompton Boilers'.[61] The very modesty of the success in 1862 served only to emphasise the way in which the Exhibition of 1851 was a one-off triumph, incapable of being reproduced. The deaths of Stephenson and Brunel, with that of Prince Albert himself, marked the end of an epoch as far as the outstanding performance of Great Britain was concerned.[62]

12

Victorian Family Man

It is not necessary to accept without qualification the stereotype of Victorian family life – stern father, submissive wife, family prayers, and children who were seen rather than heard – in defining certain typical characteristics, at least of middle-class families, of the early Victorian period. For one thing, the new middle classes, who were enjoying unprecedented prosperity as a result of industrialization, and who were beginning to exercise political influence in the reforms of the 1830s, tended to share many assumptions and attitudes. We have already considered their widespread support for economic liberalism, and the consequences of this for their political attitudes. They shared a similar set of social attitudes, and these did much to determine the quality of Victorian family life. Male dominance, for instance, was taken for granted: even the Queen, who gave her name to the period and who held a high view of her role as sovereign, submitted dutifully, if sometimes petulantly, to her husband in matters of family life.[1] Queen Victoria also demonstrated the possibilities of matriarchal authority in a paternalistic society, but then she spent the second half of her life as a widow, and left the family in no doubt that she expected to be obeyed. There is plenty of evidence of greater opportunities occurring for feminine independence and initiative in the nineteenth century, even though this fell far short of modern expectations and in the eyes of the law wives only gradually improved their status to become something more than mere chattels of their husbands. It is probably true to say that the lot of middle-class children also improved in the nineteenth century, but at the same time the traditional disciplines of childhood remained firm, with children being regarded as tokens of parental achievement, and as such expected to take over their father's responsibilities in commerce or industry or to follow them in the professions if they were boys, and to make suitable marriages if they were girls. Arranged marriages were common, although becoming increasingly irreconcilable with notions of Romantic love and free choice.

As his father was a French *émigré*, Brunel's family circumstances did not match this British model precisely, and the major influences on him as a boy were the extraordinary kindness and attentiveness of Marc Brunel as a father, and the close bond which existed between Marc and his wife Sophie. The young Brunel grew up in an intensely affectionate and supportive environment which allowed him plenty of scope to develop his talents, even though he then followed the convention of entering his father's profession. His elder sister Sophia was a lively girl who provided plenty of animation in the family, and went on to marry Benjamin Hawes, who became a close personal friend of the young Brunel. His second sister, Emma, was quieter and married a clergyman; the family records are curiously reticent about her.[2] There was also a wider family of some size. Brunel saw little of his father's family, although it seems that he did visit the parental farm in Normandy during his schooling in France. But his mother was the youngest of a very large family, and members of this family occasionally entered Brunel's life. He took on one young cousin as an engineering assistant: this was Robert Marchant, who proved to be unsatisfactory and quarrelled with Brunel, who reprimanded him.[3] One of the Marchant family kept a farm at Chilcompton, near Bath, and Marc and Sophie spent holidays there in 1841 and 1843 to give Marc a rest from his labours on the Thames Tunnel as it approached completion. It was when they were at Chilcompton in 1843, to the intense disappointment of Marc, that he came to miss the unscheduled visit of Queen Victoria and her Consort to the site of the Thames Tunnel.[4]

I. K. Brunel had thus the inestimable advantage of an outstandingly happy and secure family background. He did not succeed completely in replicating this experience in his own family, although by the standards of his times he achieved a very satisfactory and successful family life. Such was the degree of hyperactivity required both by the volume of business which came his way, and by his own meticulous standards of excellence and his reluctance to delegate, that it is remarkable he found as much time as he did to pursue the life of a family man. He accepted the conventional expectations of marriage and found sufficient time for a prolonged courtship before committing himself to wedlock. In 1827, at the age of twenty-one, he became emotionally attached to Ellen Hulme, whom he had known for seven years.[5] The origin of the relationship remains obscure, and it is difficult to believe that they saw much of each other because her family lived in Manchester, but Brunel kept up a correspondence for a further couple of years before bringing it to an end in April 1829. Ellen appears to have been a lively young lady who avoided giving direct answers to questions and indulged the 'shocking habit ... of quizzing', which Brunel found rather unnerving, possibly because it deprived him of the initiative.[6] The termination must have been reasonably harmonious because Brunel felt able to call on the family in Manchester in 1831.[7]

At this period of his life, when he felt particularly hard up and melancholy,

Brunel certainly observed the proprieties which required a young man to have sound economic prospects before making a proposition of marriage, so that he never reached this point with Ellen. The family chroniclers have been coy about her, volunteering no information, and she appears as only a shadowy figure in Rolt, who identifies her as belonging to 'the Manchester family whom he knew well'.[8] During Brunel's prolonged convalescence from the Thames Tunnel accident in 1828 he was grateful to John Hulme, who visited him regularly during the summer, 'talking over old times', reading books together, and reading more personal effusions.[9] When he called on the Hulmes in 1831, during his tour of northern England, he recorded that 'John is now established at Mansfield' but made no mention of Ellen.[10] There are later references to John in the private letter books, as he seems to have been employed for a time by Brunel. It seems likely that Ellen did not marry but that Brunel preserved a soft spot for her, because as late as 1858 there is a note in the letter books making arrangements for paying an annuity to Miss E. Hulme, whom he describes as having being born in November 1804, and her sister, born four years earlier:

> The arrangement I had wished to carry out was to have two separate annuities of £50 each and the balance invested in one on the survivor of the two; so that while they were both living they would get the three annuities amounting to £230 and I think that the survivor would get £180, which I thought a wise proposition.

Such a plan, which appears to have been carried out, suggests either that John was already dead or that the Misses Hulme had been otherwise left with limited resources. Brunel expected objections from Ellen – possibly more quizzing – and left the negotiations in the hands of the solicitors.[11]

On 10 June 1832, Brunel's private diary records an occasion when 'After lunch I went to Kensington – called on the Horsleys'. It seems likely that he was introduced to this talented artistic family by Benjamin Hawes. He immediately found their company congenial, as is demonstrated by references in his diary to attending concerts and other social activities at their home. There are also strong indications of his growing attachment to Mary, the eldest daughter of the family, although this did not blossom into a full courtship until 1836. Then in May of that year he 'made an offer' to her, which Mary accepted, and they were married in Kensington Church on 5 July 1836. There is little enough to be gleaned about the Horsleys from Brunel's diary entries,[12] but fortunately they were an articulate family who carried on a lively correspondence with each other, some of which has been published. From this and family memories it is possible to piece together the main story. Brunel was drawn to the Horsleys by their music and vivacity. The father, William, was a music master in Kensington, where the family lived in a pleasant house with a substantial garden in an area on the edge of Kensington Park then known as 'the Gravel Pits', 1 High Row (later, 128 Church Street). He had married Elizabeth Hutchins Callcott, and their children were Mary Elizabeth (1813–1881), Fanny (1815–1849), John (1817–1903), Sophia (1819–1894) and Charles (1821–1876). All the children were clever, with Sophia in particular having an exceptional musical talent, and John becoming an artist of considerable public reputation. Fanny and Sophia wrote animated letters to their governess-cousin Lucy Callcott, and these make up the bulk of the published correspondence.[13]

The family maintained a vigorous social life, with a strongly musical character, often performing concerts and presenting pantomimes and other amateur theatrical events. It was this activity which attracted to the household Felix Mendelssohn and other bright young talents, including Brunel. The girls kept up a lively gossip about family friends and musical events, and into this domestic, feminine, world, politics and national events rarely intruded. But their sheer good nature and capacity for fun and self-education is impressive, and they were shrewd observers of the comings and goings of their various gentlemen visitors. Brunel is reported as having been invited to dinner by their brother John (30 June 1833); Mary is described as having let her hair down to play 'Ghost' in the garden on a hot summer evening (15 July 1833); 'Isambard' is praised for taking them to the Zoo; they go down to Greenwich to visit the Tunnel with him; Brunel is noted as having been at dinner – 'he and Mary were of course a great deal together' and he 'mended a pair of compasses' (9 August 1834); and John is reported as going with him on a business trip to Merthyr, 'seeing works and the largest iron works in the [country]' (November 1834). Brunel is reported as coming to tea in June 1835, and three months later he came to dinner, 'the Rail Road Bill having passed'(6 September 1835). Then there was great excitement the next spring, when Fanny wrote to her aunt to report 'Mr Brunel's offer' (27 May 1836), and the younger girls and their mother all wrote to Mary on her honeymoon in North Wales. (9 July 1836)[14]

The woman who married Brunel in July 1836 was a person of statuesque beauty, as she appears in portraits by her brother and in the memory of her family. Her sisters had playfully called her the 'Duchess of Kensington' on account of her stately manners, but her family generally tended to denigrate her artistic talents in comparison with those of her siblings and other relatives. As the eldest child she seems to have assumed a leading part in all domestic arrangements, and her mother's loss of support in this respect soon became apparent after Mary's marriage, as her letter to her daughter on honeymoon is concerned largely with household details such as missing salt cellars. Mary promptly took charge of the Brunel household, which she appears to have run with exemplary efficiency, assimilating grandiose additions to the Duke Street premises, where the Brunels came to live in state above the office of the busy engineer.

Apart from a few fragments, such as a charming account by Brunel of the discomforts of a hotel where he was staying, told for the amusement of Mary, there is curiously little evidence of the relationship between husband and wife. Mary travelled occasionally with Brunel, accompanying him on one of his Italian expeditions, but she seemed happiest at home, where she showed every sign of being satisfied with the role of being an adornment in the social life of a successful professional man. Her family appear to remember her striking physical beauty; her liking for amateur theatricals, in which she liked to perform the more elegant roles; and her penchant for parading herself with fine gowns, expensive jewellery and liveried flunkeys. The most remarkable thing about her, however, is the lack of any written words to her husband, or to any body else. Her sisters were highly articulate, and wrote wonderful letters, but no communications from Mary appear to have survived. And apart from the frequently quoted letter about the discomforts of his hotel in Wootton Basset already mentioned, nothing survives of Brunel's letters to his wife. Some engineers enjoyed the companionship of very supportive wives: Trevithick's wife, for instance, ran his business during his long absences, and Brunel's own parents had a close and intense relationship. But Brunel and his wife never gave any indication that they had got less than they wanted or expected from their marriage.[15]

Mary Brunel bore her husband two sons and a daughter: Isambard (1837–1902), Henry Marc (1842–1903) and Florence Mary (1847?–1876). It is an interesting comment on Victorian sexual values that we have no precise date for the birth of Florence, even though the Brunel blood-line passed through her and not her two brothers. The elder son was born with a slight leg deformity which handicapped him in later life: he entered the legal profession and became an ecclesiastical lawyer. Henry followed his father and became an engineer, serving an apprenticeship with William Armstrong in Newcastle and eventually becoming a partner of Sir John Wolfe Barry. Isambard married Georgina Noble, a member of an important north-east England industrial family, but they had no children. Henry did not marry. Florence married a master at Eton College, Arthur James, and they had a daughter, Celia, who like her uncle married into the Noble family, and thus ensured the descent of the Brunels.[16]

It is hard to believe that Brunel, amongst all his demanding professional activities, found a great deal of time to spend with his family. But the fact that he was fond of children is apparent from the entries in his private diaries to attending to his nephew, the son of his sister and Benjamin Hawes,[17] and there is plenty of circumstantial evidence of visits to the circus and the pantomime at Christmas. Then there is the well-publicized incident of the swallowed half-sovereign arising from an entertainment for the children which involved a conjuring trick that went wrong. Interpolations in his desk diary for 1849 indicate that he took young Isambard with him for a busy four-day visit to South Wales, and that he spent some time flying kites with the children.[18] It is likely, however, he spent little time with his children, but that which he did devote to them would have been packed with his usual intensity, and the devotion of the sons to their father is left in no doubt from their determination to do justice to his memory when they came to prepare the book which became Brunel's first full biography. Henry wrote voluminous engineering notes for this project, which was mainly the work of his brother and was published in 1870. This work of filial piety, written when the young men were thirty-two and twenty-eight respectively, remains an invaluable source of information about the life of their father.

After leaving his parents' home in Chelsea in 1828, Brunel had not attempted immediately to make a permanent home for himself. He spent a lot of time with the Hawes family at Barge House in Lambeth, and established several short-term bases, including for a time an office at 53 Parliament Street. Shortly before his marriage in 1836 he had acquired 18 Duke Street, and in 1848 he negotiated possession of the adjacent house, No. 17. These were gracious houses, backing onto St James's Park. Duke Street has now disappeared under government offices, but ran parallel to Horse Guards Street, from Great George Street almost to Downing Street, in a socially select part of Westminster. Brunel allowed himself the pleasant diversion from his professional preoccupations of planning and furnishing this substantial property. The inventory compiled in 1858 gives a vivid indication of the opulence of the furnishings. The dining room had its 'richly carved sideboard with glass back in richly carved frame', its Venetian glass chandelier, Indian carpet and luxurious fittings; there were expensive carpets on the staircases; and the drawing room accommodated massive collections of the finest china and glass, with the silver and bronze ware and magnificent dinner services stored in the larder and butler's pantry. Then there was the substantial collection of paintings, the books, an organ and the grand piano, to which the inventory gives no cash value, although the valuation of the rest of the contents is given as £8326.[19] There was also a staff of maidservants, cooks and manservants, a butler and a liveried footman. Such a standard of living may have been modest in comparison with contemporary aristocratic households, but it was certainly well above the expectations of most Victorian middle-class families like those of the parents of both Brunel and his wife. Without any doubt, the Brunels had come up in the world.

John Horsley was a frequent visitor to the Duke Street establishment, where he participated in the theatrical, operatic and other cultural events staged in the house. He recalled many years after that 'The Duke Street house was unusually well fitted for performances of this kind [amateur theatricals], a noble staircase ascending from the entrance to the *piano nobile*, as the Italians call what we call the drawing room floor ... One of the drawing-rooms had a beautiful chamber organ in it ... that king of musical instruments.' [20] Brunel's sketch books preserve several pages of designs for wall fittings and other details, and among these one of the most revealing is his plan to have the main drawing room decorated by works of art commissioned from leading contemporary artists, all on Shakespearian themes. They included works by Landseer, Leslie, Callcott, Cope, Stanford, Lee, Egg and Horsley. The magnitude of the conception and the strict artistic conventions observed in carrying it out are highly indicative of the new affluence which was stimulating the professional classes at this time, enabling them to become patrons of the arts. The choice of commissions suggests a normative, not to say conventional, aesthetic standard. There was, for instance, no place for the Pre-Raphaelite Brotherhood among the selection of artists chosen by Brunel, although, to be fair, in 1848 this was still in its infancy, before its rapid rise to social acceptability. Perhaps unsurprisingly, J. M. W. Turner is not represented in the selection, even though his *Rain, Steam and Speed* of 1844 was an astonishingly early artistic tribute to transport technology, and to the GWR in particular. [21]

The other domestic concern which penetrated Brunel's professional activities in the later 1840s and 1850s was his aspiration to acquire a country estate and to endow it with buildings and gardens to his own design. This was an ambition shared by most of his successful contemporaries. It was becoming very common in this early Victorian period for leading engineers to equip themselves with impressive estates, sometimes with deer stalking, salmon fishing and grouse moors thrown in. Robert Stephenson, it is true, did not follow this trend, tending to direct his luxury consumption towards the purchase and fitting out of a yacht, *Titania*, instead. But then, he was a widower with no children for whom life at home had become distasteful, and the yacht provided an exhilarating substitute. With thoughts of his family and a stake in the countryside, Brunel followed a more typical course, and searched for an appropriate property. He settled for an estate at Watcombe, just north of Torquay in Devon, which he acquired in 1847.

After the first great wave of his railway construction had begun to subside, Brunel adopted a practice of taking a family holiday each summer. These holidays occasionally involved foreign trips, as to Italy in 1845, allowing him the opportunity to combine business with pleasure by visiting his Italian

projects, and Switzerland in 1846. But the dominant pattern which emerged
was that of choosing a convenient base in the west of England which would
permit him to continue supervising his business interests, with intermittent
visits to Duke Street, while his family remained on holiday. Such was the
case in 1842, when the family settled at Weston-super-Mare for August, and
in 1843, when Brunel was based in Clevedon for much of the summer. In
1847 the family discovered the charms of Torquay, and it was then that
Brunel made up his mind and bought the Watcombe estate.[22] There was
no house on the property, which consisted largely of a wooded south-facing
slope on the road to Teignmouth, but it allowed Brunel great scope for
planning the lay out of his garden. Much of his planting of trees, now come
to maturity, together with his garden walks, has miraculously survived,
although it has been neglected for many years. He also applied himself to
the design of a house, eventually settling for an Italianate villa with a
belvedere and a colonnaded terrace, but when he died work had only started
on the foundations, and the house was never built. The more modest house
which now stands on the site has nothing to do with Brunel or his family.[23]

Brunel was a demanding employer and professional leader who could be
overbearing and autocratic. Even though he could relax on terms of familiarity with his senior staff, as when they jocularly schemed to convert the
White Horse carved on the chalk downs at Cherhill into a steam locomotive,[24] he does not seem to have inspired the sort of intimate affection which
existed between Stephenson and some of his assistant engineers. It is significant that even Charles Macfarlane, who told the memorable story of his
winter journey with Brunel in 1829, when they travelled on outside seats on
coaches from Paris to London, admitted to a preference for the genial Marc
Brunel when the young Brunel introduced him to his family.[25] But despite
his easy assumption of authority, which induced a sense of remoteness,
I. K. Brunel had a need for close friends and confidants, and several such
figures played a part in his career. The first of these in his adult years was
Benjamin Hawes, the son of a successful Lambeth soap-boiler and himself
a businessman of Radical tendencies. Brunel supported his friend in the
election campaign of 1832. It was the marriage of Hawes to Brunel's assertive
elder sister Sophia which drew the two men together, and they became very
close friends during the years when Brunel was engaged on the Thames
Tunnel. The tenor of their relationship is indicated by the dedication of
Brunel's personal diary to his friend: 'My dear Benjamin, ever since I have
known you I have esteemed you. I know your faults, can avoid them and
now my attachment is as strong as true as perfect as I think is possible on
earth.' [26] The fact that the document was never delivered to Hawes (as far
as we can tell) does not invalidate the intensity of the sentiments expressed.

Brunel derived considerable moral support from Hawes at a difficult period of personal crisis in his life, and he was glad to be able to repay this debt by assisting Hawes in his election campaign. Although the careers of the two men diverged, with the election of Hawes to Parliament and the escalation of Brunel's professional activity, the families remained in close contact. Hawes also took an active part in promoting the Hungerford Bridge and the Renkioi Hospital, so that they never lost their working relationship, and Hawes survived to become Brunel's principal executor. William Hawes, the younger brother of Benjamin, also kept up a close personal relationship with Brunel and wrote a warm tribute which was incorporated in the family biography.[27]

Brunel found another congenial companion in John Horsley, later to become one of his other brother-in-laws (the third was Dr Seth Thompson, who married Mary's vivacious sister Fanny in 1841). The young Horsley responded eagerly to invitations from the dashing engineer to go travelling with him, as when they visited railway enterprises in South Wales in November 1834.[28] He was prepared to live roughly and to keep early rising hours with Brunel. We have it on Horsley's authority that 'his potency in SNORING was "prodigious"'.[29] We can only wonder what Horsley's sister made of this talent when she subsequently married him. Horsley was also delighted to accompany Brunel to Paris to witness the revolutionary activities taking place there in April 1848.[30] When Brunel was hard-pressed by the crises of the *Great Eastern* in the late 1850s, Horsley – who had recently undergone his own emotional traumas with the death of his wife and two children – drafted a letter, although he did not send it, urging his brother-in-law to seek the religious consolations in which he had found relief himself. Horsley survived, however, to provide the young Isambard with a long letter to include in the biography of his father, and thirty years later he was still alive to recall memories about Brunel, whom he regarded as one of the two great friends of his youth, the other being Felix Mendelssohn.[31]

Brunel acquired a circle of close friends as a result of his commitments in Bristol. He never had a home in the city, but a number of Bristol merchants and professional men were glad to entertain him on his frequent visits. Nicholas Roche was amongst the first to recognize the brilliance of the young man, and to promote his interests with fellow merchants in the Bristol Society of Merchant Venturers and elsewhere, which brought him commissions with the Bristol Docks Company and the Great Western Railway. But Roche soon retired from his active business interests in Bristol and went to live in Pembrokeshire, where Brunel was subsequently obliged to send him an apologetic letter because his surveyors on the South Wales Railway were cutting a slice through his estate.[32] The two Bristol men who

then became close friends of Brunel were Christopher Claxton and Thomas
Guppy. Captain Claxton, RN, had retired from active service in the Navy
and had taken a post as quay warden in Bristol Docks. In this capacity he
was able to give influential support to Brunel's attempts to improve the
conditions of the Bristol Floating Harbour, and then went on to become a
senior partner and adviser to Brunel in the construction of his two Bristol-
built steam ships. Brunel turned to him for practical help when the *Great
Britain* went aground in Dundrum Bay, and in later years Brunel sought
his advice on the tricky operations of floating bridge components into
position at Chepstow and Saltash – a function for which Robert Stephenson
also turned to him for help with similar tasks at Conway and Menai. Claxton
was also on hand to help with the *Great Eastern*, where he advised Brunel
on the launching procedure as well as on tidal and other constraints which
would affect the ship in the various harbours of the world which it was
intended to visit. It is clear that Brunel made a shrewd assessment of
Claxton's qualities from a comparison with a GWR director which he made
in his journal: 'Simmonds a hot tempered Tory – just such another as
K. Claxton – i.e. warm friend but changeable and very capable of being a
devil of an opponent.'[33]

Thomas Guppy was an engineer who ran a successful sugar-refining
business in Bristol with his brother. Their father, Samuel Guppy, had been
a prominent Bristol merchant with an interest in the copper trade, and their
mother, Sarah Maria Guppy, is credited with several inventions including
a copper sheathing nail which helped to limit the growth of barnacles on
ships.[34] Thomas Guppy was nine years older than Brunel, and became a
natural ally in his novel railway and ship-building enterprises. It was Guppy
who took up Brunel's daring suggestion to an early meeting of the directors
of the GWR that they should extend their service to New York by building
a steam ship to operate from Bristol, and together with Brunel and Claxton
he took a prominent part in the construction of the two Bristol-built ships.
With the *Great Britain* in particular he acted as resident engineer, working
in close and harmonious consultation with Brunel. The degree of harmony
is reflected in a series of letters written by Brunel to Guppy in 1838–40.[35]
They are written in a chatty and breezy style, such as IKB reserved for his
closest friends: 'You will find this a desperate long scrawl and rather over
much about self – but it's a recreation – next to a pleasant chat – after
nearly a dozen dull letters I have had to write about a fearfull heap of arrears
by my side'.[36] There is even a hint that the two wives enjoyed each other's
company: 'Mrs Brunel goes with me to Bristol next week and hopes
Mrs Guppy will be there – will she?'[37]

Most of the letters are concerned with railway and ship business, and often involve manoeuvres to outwit the 'Liverpool Party' among the GWR directors. But there is also intriguing discussion of a suggestion from Guppy that the two of them should establish a partnership, about which Brunel was slightly evasive.[38] Then, in response to surprising news that Guppy was planning to retire from business, Brunel wrote a long letter, ending:

> Do not but of course you will not decide hastily, and believe me though I fear but a very useless friend a very sincere one: and a grateful one for a succession of kindnesses and most useful support which I have experienced from you ever since you first laid hold of me in College Green in 1829, I think.[39]

The bundle of letters comes to a scrappy end soon after this, but the two men remained in close contact until 1849 when Guppy, apparently on medical advice because of symptoms of tuberculosis, moved to Naples, where he established a mechanical engineering workshop employing several hundred people, and built himself a villa where he lived on until 1882.[40]

Another group of friends were those whom Brunel came to know through the GWR. These included the chairman, Charles Russell, until his resignation in 1855 and suicide the following year, and the secretary Charles Saunders, who survived in office until 1863 and died soon after. Both gave Brunel close support in the early crises of the railway, but there does not appear to have been much personal intimacy between him and them.[41] Several of the leading officers of the GWR, most notably Daniel Gooch, who became the outstandingly successful locomotive superintendent of the railway, were men who had been appointed on his recommendation and who remained loyal and close to him. Gooch certainly numbered Brunel among his closest friends,[42] but the surviving letters from Brunel to Gooch are slightly formal and reserved, and it seems likely that Brunel was not completely relaxed with those whom he regarded as his juniors.[43] The same applies to those assistant engineers who ably carried out his instructions on the great railway building works such as Hammond, Babbage, Brereton and Froude, all of whom enjoyed Brunel's confidence in professional matters, but with whom he adopted a somewhat paternal attitude. He was probably most at ease with William Froude, because Froude was a man of independent means and quiet genius whose inspired understanding of the behaviour of ships at sea was much admired by Brunel.[44]

The most intimate friend of Brunel's mature years was Robert Stephenson. Like Brunel, Stephenson had been introduced to the engineering profession by a highly successful father, and both of them had built even greater fame on the achievements of their respective parents. In many professional matters, such as the gauge conflict and the atmospheric system, Stephenson and Brunel adopted antithetical positions and were strong rivals. But this rivalry never disturbed a close personal friendship which emerged when the two men were drawn together on railway affairs in the early 1830s, and by a shared loyalty to their profession and to the Institution of Civil Engineers. As with Guppy, a collection of about fifty letters survive, but in the case of Stephenson they are incoming letters rather than those written by Brunel. They begin with a friendly note from Stephenson in 1834: 'My Dear Sir, I was much pleased the other day on hearing the animated discussion on the second reading of your Bill.' [45] Later letters range over a variety of shared professional preoccupations. The two friends advised each other on assistant engineers; they undertook arbitrations for each other and together; they made reports together on water supply systems; and they attended each other's works on critical occasions to give advice and support. Very occasionally, a note of alarm and apology breaks into the correspondence, but this is hardly surprising considering the intense rivalry that developed between some of the enterprises for which they were responsible. Stephenson, for example, protests his innocence of any attempt to embarrass Brunel in a recent argument: 'Nothing would grieve me more than for you to believe that I have acted a double part respecting the extension of the West London.' [46] For his part, Brunel had observed of Stephenson: 'It is very delightful in the midst of our incessant personal professional contests, carried to the extreme of fair opposition, to meet him on a perfectly friendly footing and discuss engineering points.' [47] Brunel made three visits to Conway early in 1848 to advise his friend on the floating of the tubular bridge, and he turned up again in 1849 when the larger operation on the Britannia Bridge at Menai was starting. When he was unable to return the compliment at Chepstow Bridge in 1852, Stephenson apologized at some length:

Dear Brunel, The Ventilation Committee [of Parliament] have saddled Locke and myself with the arrangement of *Barry* v. *Reid* during the Easter recess and to superintend the alterations proposed to be made in the House of Commons to improve if possible its present insufferable stink. Can you imagine a more detestable task? I feel as Sergeant Murphy says 'like a cat in Hell without claws', but as we have undertaken it I am determined to stick to it. The time is short and the work to be done really very considerable, and this must be my excuse for not participating with your company. You have my kindest sympathy, but I think I hear you saying damn the fellow's sympathy I want none of it. Don't say so. I know too well what floating is, not to feel the advantage of a friend alongside one in such cases and believe me it is a source of sincere regret that I am not with you. Yours sincerely, Robert Stephenson. [48]

Stephenson amply repaid his debt later by attending Brunel at many of the critical moments in the saga of the *Great Eastern*, and when illness prevented him from doing so he always managed to write an encouraging note to his friend. It is a revealing tribute to the warmth of their personal friendship that the two men remained closely in touch during the last year of their lives, when they were both terminally ill. They spent Christmas together in Cairo in 1858, when Stephenson was on his last cruise on the yacht *Titania*, and Brunel was on his last family holiday.[49]

Several other personal friends of Brunel deserve to be mentioned. One of them, Adolphe D'Eichtal, is described by Lady Noble as 'his old French school friend',[50] and it seems as if he was one of the few contacts from his period in France (unless Ellen Hulme falls into this category) with whom he kept in touch in later life. Like John Hulme, D'Eichtal visited Brunel when he was recovering from the Thames Tunnel accident in 1828. The private letter books record a number of messages to him, mainly inconsequential, with informal answers to questions about railways and related matters.[51] Then there were Lord and Lady Spencer, of whom we have already noted Brunel recording that 'I have thus lost one of my best friends' when Lady Spencer died in 1831.[52] George John, the second Earl Spencer (1758–1834), was a cultured man, a Fellow of the Royal Society and of the Society of Antiquaries of London, who kept what has been described as 'the finest private library in Europe' at Althorp, his home in Northamptonshire. As First Lord of the Admiralty in Pitt's administration, he had befriended Marc in his early days in Britain, and was instrumental in securing the contract for the block-making machines. The Brunels were entertained on occasion at Althorp Hall, where Marc loved to browse in the library, and the family remained very grateful for this aristocratic recognition.[53]

Another friend was Lady Holland, the society hostess who condescended to make a journey by train, provided that Brunel would accompany her and hold her hand, which he gallantly agreed to do. Lady Holland had been a person of great notoriety in her day and an accomplished hostess who entertained leading politicians at her table. Although Lady Holland was elderly when Brunel knew her, Lady Noble was anxious to record this acquaintance, and to emphasize the social *cachet* which Brunel achieved by being cultivated by such a grand old lady: 'The adventure ripened into friendship, and the fascinating old lady seems to have afforded Isambard the one dazzling apparition in his austere life.'[54] Rolt carried the speculation further: 'It is obvious that Brunel found in this friendship something that Mary was never able to give him, and through his admiration for Lady Holland he may perhaps have realized the price he had paid for his lonely greatness, seeing, perhaps, in her ageing face the ghost of the might-have-been.'[55] But the search for a sexual *motif* in the life of I. K. Brunel is disappointing: it was certainly present, and demonstrated itself in his family life, but it was sternly controlled and subordinated to the objectives of his vision and his profession. Presumably stories about Lady Holland circulated in Brunel's family circles, but there is no documentary basis to suggest anything sensitive about his relationship with her.

Such was the vigour of Brunel's active life that it is easy to forget that he was never outstandingly robust. He had suffered serious internal injuries in the Thames Tunnel collapse of 1828, and had a whole series of lesser accidents. He records several bad falls from his horse in his diaries, and on at least one of these occasions he shook himself severely and damaged his knees.[56] Then there was the incident in the fire on board the *Great Western* when he fell down a hatchway in the smoke. In this instance it was fortunate that Claxton was standing in the engine room below and broke his fall.[57] Brunel did not usually make much fuss about his injuries, but he did tend to use his closest friends to unburden himself of these and other anxieties. In this vein, he wrote to Hawes in 1832 confessing his faults: 'I see them in crowds – they seem to me like a great field of weeds – with an unfortunate supply of huge thistles – towering above the whole. What is worse they decidedly increase – the few useful plants which were to be seen in fact dying away'.[58] Admittedly, this particular admission was never delivered, but he subsequently made Guppy a recipient of more specific confessions:

> I am not particularly well in body or mind. I don't get strong. I am still lame in the left foot and my back is weak. I don't write this letter without leaning back to rest and, in consequence I suppose of the state of my stomach, I am nervous anxious and unhappy, in fact blue devilish: an infinite number of things crowding before me requiring attention and thoughts, all in arrears. I am quite incapable of getting through them, everything seeming to go wrong ... I suppose I want a dose of salts. Yours very sincerely, I. K. Brunel.[59]

This was at a time when he was meeting great problems in the initial phases of operating the GWR, and when the injuries incurred on board the *Great Western* were still causing him physical discomfort, but he bounced back rapidly in the subsequent correspondence. It is worth recalling these moments of vulnerability behind the façade of calmness and decisiveness which always impressed his close companions.

There was an outbreak of communal anxiety about Brunel's health in the spring of 1843, when he swallowed the coin. In the course of entertaining his children with some conjuring tricks in the nursery, he managed to swallow a half-sovereign which lodged in his windpipe and threatened to choke him. It remained there for several weeks, and the problem of its removal taxed some of the leading medical brains of the time. The eminent surgeon Sir Benjamin Brodie was credited with having devised a long-handled pair of forceps to remove it: they became known as 'Brodie's

Forceps', even though Brunel himself probably designed them. Brodie conducted a tracheotomy with them, but failed to reach the coin. Brunel also
devised an apparatus for shaking the coin loose, but this did not succeed
either. As it happened, his father and mother were living at the Duke Street
house at the time of this domestic crisis, and it seems that Marc Brunel
produced the idea for strapping IKB to a board and jerking the coin free,
which, at last, produced the desired result. Brunel wrote to Claxton: 'I was
safely and comfortably delivered of my little coin'. The eminent historian
Thomas Macaulay is reputed to have rushed through the Athenaeum Club
shouting 'It's out!' Marc Brunel, who had been disconcerted at the coolness
of Mary towards Sophie and himself during these trying weeks, was happy
to report that all had returned to normal. It is clear, however, that Brunel
had one of his many brushes with death in the course of this episode.[60]

There are many indications of comparatively slight indispositions in the
life of Brunel. For example, at the end of October 1843, his desk diary
reported: 'Bad cold in bed all day'.[61] But such afflictions were mainly trivial,
and it was not until the mid 1850s that signs of more serious trouble began
to emerge. Then Dr Bright was called in for a consultation, and diagnosed
the renal condition of nephritis which came to bear his name as Bright's
Disease, and it was this which sapped Brunel's physical strength while the
struggles to launch and fit out the *Great Eastern* preoccupied the waking
hours of her designer. It is hardly necessary to add that the exhaustion from
the mental effort must to some degree have lowered his resistance to the
increasing physical weakness. His lifestyle – and particularly his excessively
heavy dependence on smoking cigars – cannot have helped either.[62] It is
probably true to say that Brunel drove his body cruelly and wore it out
prematurely: his great engineering achievements involved extreme costs of
physical well-being and health. While his professional skills and judgment
remained intact virtually to the end, his body collapsed under the pressures
placed upon it.

All Brunel's friends observed the rapid deterioration of his health during
the last months of his life, and several of them urged him, in one way or
another, to ease up the intense pressure which he imposed on himself to
complete the fitting out of the great ship. Typical among these was a letter
from A. Hill, of Plymouth Iron Works, Merthyr Tydfil, who after congra-
tulating Brunel on the successful launch at the end of January 1858, gave
him a warm and pressing invitation to have a holiday:

> It is said, that the bow is broken by being kept constantly strung and bent: but
> if occasionally relaxed, retains its elasticity. Your mind must want the relief of
> a little rest: cannot you *cut* anxiety, for a short time, and come here, to spend a
> week quietly with me: you shall [have] a comfortable warm bedroom (this snowy

weather), a library to yourself: my carriage and horses to take you about: and with all a *hearty welcome*. If by presenting my best respects to Mrs Brunel, you could prevail upon her, to accompany and take care of you; she shall be equally welcomed, and your visit would afford me much gratification.[63]

No reply is recorded.

One last attempt to recover Brunel's declining health was made under doctor's orders at the end of 1858 and beginning of 1859. He was sent on a prolonged holiday to Egypt. As he was able to take his family with him, this journey became the final episode of relaxation for Brunel as a Victorian family man. The journey involved a long coach trip across France, picking up Henry at Geneva on the way, and a rough passage in a small paddle-steamer on the Mediterranean. Christmas was spent in Cairo with Robert Stephenson and his party. Then the Brunels made a leisurely trip up the Nile, studying the relics on the way, after which they returned home through Italy and across Europe. We have several vivid insights into this expedition, mainly in the shape of diaries and scrap books kept by Henry Brunel. These include entries recording the captain of their boat falling overboard; Brunel and Henry socializing with other British visitors; taking pot-shots at a bottle in the river – 'my father fired but did not hit it. The pistol went off twice when he did not mean it …'; and all of them admiring the ancient ruins which they passed.[64] It was a period of unaccustomed relaxation from anxiety for Brunel, and there seems to be agreement amongst his family and friends that it did his health some good. But the grim realities of getting the *Great Eastern* seaworthy remained and closed in around him when the party returned home, with fatal results within six months.

When Brunel died in September 1859, much of the wealth which he had acquired during his professional career, and which he had invested in a fine house, a country estate, and a lifestyle for his family which was above the average level of bourgeois ostentation, had been greatly reduced. The failure of the *Great Eastern* as a business enterprise appears to have caused Brunel severe financial embarrassment, persuading him to have a detailed inventory of his Duke Street household made in November 1858. The eighty-three page notebook which contains this is a valuable source of information about the house, its contents, and the way in which it was managed.[65] But the household was still intact when he died, and although the will, proved at £90,000, was less than it might have been, the family were certainly not left penniless. In fact, substantial sums were left for Mary and the three children, with hardly any other provisions except for modest sums left to his mother-in-law and sister-in-law Sophia. Hawes and the family doctor, Seth Thompson, both brothers-in-law to Brunel, were the executors, along with Mary and Isambard Brunel.[66] The family were able to continue living in Duke Street, where Henry came to practise as an engineer after completing his apprenticeship with Armstrong in Newcastle. R. P. Brereton, who attended to the winding up of many of Brunel's professional commitments, also continued to operate from the ground-floor offices. The family eventually disposed of the Watcombe estate, although they maintained their close links with that part of Devonshire, living there for part of the year and keeping up a lively friendship with William Froude and his family.

The Brunel family became extremely protective of Brunel's reputation. They were particularly on their guard against John Scott Russell, who seemed ready to annex all credit for the *Great Eastern* as craftily as he had avoided all blame for its troubles. But suspicion fell on others who in any way denigrated the achievements of Brunel. Even the loyal Brereton was not above it, to judge from family comments on his paper on the Royal Albert Bridge, in which he claimed a share of the credit.[67] And when the Clifton Bridge, completed by his fellow engineers as a memorial to Brunel, was opened in December 1864, the family refused to attend the ceremony because they felt that Brunel's name did not figure with sufficient prominence.[68] This jealous concern for the reputation of the great engineer on the part of his family and subsequent biographers was understandable but probably unnecessary. His engineering works had already guaranteed that his reputation would be outstanding, and even though it is acknowledged that he made mistakes and that he occasionally acted hastily, stubbornly and irritably, there was never any professional impropriety or personal indiscretion to blemish his career. Despite the colossal pressure of professional commitments under which he habitually lived, he did not neglect his family and, in most respects, as we have seen, he admirably fulfilled the role of the Victorian *pater familias*. Indeed, in his anxiety to demonstrate the social status he had achieved by lavishing upon his family all the accoutrements of wealth, he lived out the conventional model of successful Victorian middle-class, professional *haute bourgeois* behaviour. Brunel's circle of acquaintances was perforce somewhat narrow: he was too heavily committed to his professional responsibilities to socialize freely; but within the limits imposed by these commitments he contrived to live a full and rewarding family life.

10. Parian statuette of Brunel.

13

The Heroic Age of British Engineering

Historians have found it difficult to appreciate the achievements of the engineers. There have been some distinguished exceptions, but to most mainstream British and American historians engineering has rarely seemed of central importance either to the narrative of past events or to their interpretation. For example, in his elegant essay of 1936, *Victorian England: Portrait of an Age*, the historian G. M. Young (1882–1959) contrived to write discursively about the cultural and intellectual developments of Britain in the nineteenth century without mentioning any engineers. Railways received incidental attention, mainly for their part in promoting government intervention in entrepreneurial activity, and both Faraday and Darwin received entries in the chronological table at the end of the book. This table recorded the publication of *The Origin of Species* in 1859, and listed the deaths in that year of John Austin, Leigh Hunt, De Quincey, Macaulay, D. Cox and H. Hallam – but not those of I. K. Brunel or Robert Stephenson.[1]

It is worth recalling the bias of this highly praised study of a generation ago, both because it should make us cautious about proclaiming finality for any of our historical judgments, and because it should be recognized that Young's attitude remains deeply entrenched in conventional historiography. The authoritative Ford Lectures, delivered at Oxford in 1960 by G. Kitson Clark, and published as *The Making of Victorian England*, contain many illuminating reflections on religion, radicalism and social class, but engineers and engineering are absent from its index and the discussion of railways is perfunctory.[2] The same bias pervades *Mid-Victorian Britain, 1851–1875* by Geoffrey Best, published in 1970. This contains much perceptive comment on life and leisure in the period, and includes a section on the impact of the railways, but makes no mention of the *Great Eastern* or her designer.[3] Even more recently, the solid contribution by K. Theodore Hoppen to the New Oxford History of England published in 1998 under the title *The Mid-Victorian Generation, 1846–1886*, has, for all its excellent qualities, little to say about the work of the engineers. I. K. Brunel achieves a single mention – as a patron of art.[4]

This professional myopia of historians regarding engineering matters is probably an aspect of the fact that they are generally more comfortable with documents than with artefacts, and even though many artefacts are profoundly revealing about the society which fashioned and used them, this physical or archaeological knowledge is still not welcomed as it should be by academic historians. It is as if the colossal technological achievements of industrialization and the transport revolution have been taken as given, without any need for explanation or analysis. There is, nevertheless, an important secondary tradition amongst historians which has attempted to correct the imbalance in the dominant interpretation. This has been formulated largely by economic and social historians, with the works of Sir John Clapham, David Landes, A. E. Musson and Eric Robinson deserving particular mention; but other historians, and outstandingly Jack Simmons with his work on railways, have joined in expounding the contribution of engineers to the shape and substance of modern society.[5] There have also been many specialist fields such as railway history and industrial archaeology which have been artefact-specific and which have flourished in the twentieth century.

An earlier tradition had elevated the engineering profession to heroic status. The initial responsibility for this development must lie with Samuel Smiles, but he was tapping a theme which was powerful in Victorian historiography and derived from the vision of Thomas Carlyle. It was Carlyle who gave general currency to the notion of hero-worship as a formative idea in history with his study *Heroes and Hero-Worship*. This was originally delivered as a series of lectures in May 1840, while Brunel was struggling to open the first stretch of the Great Western Railway from Bristol to Bath. Carlyle maintained that history was being transformed and moulded by the contributions of outstanding persons: that 'The History of the world is but the Biography of great men'.[6] With massive eloquence and robust intelligence he demonstrated that, far from being products of their times, individuals such as Mahomet, Dante, Shakespeare, Luther, Rousseau and Cromwell had transfigured the ages in which they lived. Most particularly, because his baleful but fascinating image resonated throughout the nineteenth century, the hegemony established by Napoleon Bonaparte at the beginning of the century had inspired belief in the power of outstanding men to bend their circumstances according to their own driving convictions. It is not clear how far Carlyle was prepared to see in these achievements a general power of human individuals to impress their personality upon their times, but certainly he did not include any engineers among his selected examples of heroism. This is a pity, because among his own contemporaries it was in fact the engineers who were producing the most dramatic visual changes in the environment with works of heroic scale and complexity. The power of steam, industrial productivity, improved roads and a network of canals, and – most particularly – the railways, were together transforming the fabric of society and creating a new way of life. But it took somebody with a more practical cast of mind than Carlyle to appreciate the heroic qualities of the engineers who masterminded this transformation.

Samuel Smiles may reasonably be regarded as the originator of the cult of the Heroic Engineers, although so far as I know he did not use the term himself. It was Smiles's search for exemplars of his individualistic ideal of 'self-help' which led him to adopt the careers of some of the leading engineers as worthy models for imitation, so that he wrote his *Lives of the Engineers* in 1862 and followed it up with other works on engineering biography.[7] Smiles was not an engineer himself, being a Scottish medical man turned journalist and railway administrator, but he approached his subjects with enthusiasm and undertook scholarly research on their life histories. The result was a series of studies with a strongly moralistic intention, because he was concerned to promote self-reliance and held up his subjects as models for emulation, especially by the young. But they were also eminently readable and, on the whole, accurate characterizations of some of the leading British engineers. In many cases they still provide excellent introductions to the lives of the engineers with whom he dealt.[8]

It is important to note that Smiles did not attempt to cover all the British engineers of his own time, if only to make the point that he did not include the Brunels in his selection. It is possible that he considered Marc Brunel as coming from a background which was beyond his terms of reference, although this seems unlikely because he held the French Huguenots in high esteem and wrote about them elsewhere, and in effect Marc joined their ranks as an émigré French Protestant even though he had been brought up a Catholic. The neglect of I. K. Brunel by Smiles is a different problem. There is plenty of evidence in incidental references to Brunel that Smiles regarded him with admiration, but Smiles was attached to the 'Narrow Gauge' interests and this might have inhibited him from tackling the champion of the 'Broad Gauge'. In any case, Smiles *did* write about the Brunels, in a lengthy review of the *Life* of Marc Brunel by R. Beamish, published in the *Quarterly Review* in 1862, which coincided with his *Lives of the Engineers*.[9] He was very complimentary of Brunel's talents as an engineer, although he regarded him as devoted to a form of gargantuanism: 'His ruling idea was magnitude; he had an ambition to make everything bigger than he had found it.' And this made him too expensive for Smiles: 'He was the very Napoleon of engineers, thinking more of glory than of profit, and of victory than of dividends.' These are interesting judgments, and even though they require some qualification they do not amount to a condemnation of Brunel, although they possibly compromise his candidature for a place among those most highly favoured by Smiles. But it seems most likely that, in the years immediately after Brunel's death, his family were less than helpful to Smiles at the time when he was collecting material for his *Lives*. As we have seen, the mild paranoia with which Brunel's family protected his reputation – and access to the necessary documents – could have made it too difficult and delicate a biography for an outsider such as Smiles to have undertaken in the early 1860s.[10]

Smiles's selection of engineers should thus not be seen as a complete pantheon of the Great Engineers of the period. His choice was very limited, being confined essentially in the *Lives of the Engineers* to Smeaton, Brindley, Telford, Rennie (senior), and the Stephensons (father and son). He subsequently wrote biographies of Boulton and Watt, and allowed Nasmyth to persuade him to write up the engineer's own notes on his career which then became an 'autobiography' of James Nasmyth.[11] Beyond this core selection there are as many again who would need to be included in any comprehensive assessment of the influential engineers of the period. In addition to the Brunels, such a supplementary list would need to include Sir John Rennie (junior), Charles Blacker Vignoles, George Parker Bidder, Sir William Cubitt, James Walker, Henry Maudslay, Joshua Field, Joseph Locke, and the Scottish Stevenson family of lighthouse builders.[12] However, such additions fill out Smiles's list rather than contradict his assumption that British engineering had been created by a small group of outstanding men: that is to say, it confirms the image which Smiles so successfully portrayed of a generation of heroic engineers by whose labours the face of the nation had been transformed.

Subsequent generations have given little attention to Smiles's special pleading, but they have also done nothing to modify his assertion of a special role for the engineers of his own time. Thus, when interest in engineering history revived in Britain in the 1950s, with the works of L. T. C. Rolt and a host of railway and canal historians and industrial archaeologists, it tended to confirm the view that all the Great Engineers had died – or at least had completed their major works – by 1860. This emphasis recognizes that British industrial and political superiority over the other nations of the world had reached its zenith in the mid nineteenth century, the Early Victorian period. This remarkable hegemony, moreover, was closely associated with the coming of the railways, and the railway engineers were thus crucial figures in the overall national achievement. Among this select body, even contemporaries had begun to speak of a 'Railway Triumvirate' consisting of Robert Stephenson, Joseph Locke and

I. K. Brunel.[13] Whereas Locke was the most prolific railway builder of the three, he has also come to be perceived as the least interesting in terms of technique and achievement, while Stephenson, with his superb locomotives and tubular bridges, and Brunel, with his broad gauge and great ships, have both come to be regarded as polymaths, bestriding the world of engineering with their outstanding prowess.

We do not need to argue further the case for Stephenson here, but so far as Brunel is concerned it is important to assess his stature as one of the greatest heroes of British engineering. In the first place, it should be observed that his reputation has endured well. The broad gauge has gone, having arrived too late to convince public opinion that it was necessary for a high-speed passenger transport service to adopt it on the rapidly expanding railway network, but the bulk of Brunel's dramatic civil engineering on the GWR survives, and with it the admiration of the passengers who use the route regularly. The Clifton Bridge and the Royal Albert Bridge, the great brick viaducts and the bridges over the Thames, are still in full working order. Many of his smaller bridges, including the girder bridge near the entrance to Balmoral Castle which incurred Queen Victoria's disapproval, also survive. One of the three great steam ships, the *Great Britain*, has almost miraculously been restored to the dry dock in which she was built in the 1840s, and has become a major tourist attraction and feature of urban renewal in the commercially obsolete Bristol City Docks. The visible, tactile evidence of our senses is thus able to validate the claim of Brunel's admirers that he should be regarded as one of the foremost – if not actually *the* foremost – engineer of all times. In his works Brunel is secure. He is, *par excellence*, an engineering hero.

In other respects, however, it is necessary to qualify any hero-worship. We have already observed that, in most social and political matters, Brunel was cautious in expressing opinions and strongly conformist in most of the views that he did express. Much the same can be said of his standpoint in matters of religion and science: he rarely stated an explicit view, unless it had some direct bearing on his professional judgment, but when he did it was usually in support of the conventional consensus. There are enough incidental references to going to church in his diaries and elsewhere to establish that he observed the proprieties of attendance at the Church of England when he was able to do so, and he certainly aimed at keeping Sunday free from professional commitments, even though he was prepared to make exceptions when he considered it was necessary.[14] As the putative lord of the manor in his Watcombe estate, moreover, Brunel accepted responsibility for the well-being of the local church and its minister, coming to his financial assistance on one occasion.[15] But on matters of personal faith he went on record in a frequently-quoted declaration to his son Isambard as being convinced of the power of prayer:

> Finally, let me impress upon you the advantage of *prayer*. I am not prepared to say that the prayers of individuals can be separately and individually granted, that would seem to me incompatible with the regular movements of the mechanism of the Universe, and it would seem impossible to explain why prayer should now be granted, now refused; but this I can assure you, that I have ever, in my difficulties, prayed fervently, and that – in the end – my prayers have *appeared* to me to be granted, and I have received great comfort.[16]

Rolt found 'a world of doubt' in that one underlined word 'appeared',[17] but I am not so sure. The reference to 'the regular movements of the mechanism of the Universe' speaks lucidly in support of the mechanical world view, post-Newton and famously expressed in Paley's image of the Divine Clock-maker, which was widespread in the early nineteenth century and would have seemed only common sense to Brunel. In so far as there is an element of doubt in his statement, it is the conventional doubt of Tennyson's *In Memoriam*, which enjoyed great popularity in the 1850s, including the approval of the very orthodox-minded Queen, and it is reasonable to assume that Brunel was very familiar with these sentiments. Yet by placing some sort of antithesis between his personal experience, which was clearly real and genuine to him, and the more formal expectations of religious belief, Brunel was surely in harmony with those doubts and reservations about formal religious observances which would shortly blossom into Victorian agnosticism and the rejection of religious formalism.

Brunel, of course, did not live long enough to need to take sides in this maturing controversy, dying as he did the month before the publication of *The Origin of Species*, with its profoundly disruptive implications for the conventional world-view of mid Victorian Britain. There is little evidence, indeed, that Brunel found much time for reading or writing anything that was not closely concerned with his professional commitments. He kept up to date on engineering matters and on aspects of science that interested him through attendance of his professional and scientific institutions, but it seems likely that the works of Carlyle and Ruskin passed him by, as did the flood of novels and poetry which adorned English literature in his lifetime. His patronage of the visual arts and of music is more securely established, but we should assume that, in the lack of contrary evidence, his general literary experience was slight and therefore likely to be conventional.

We do have two scraps of evidence, however, neither of which has been given attention before, which serve as straws in the wind to indicate Brunel's reactions to new religious attitudes. The first consists of a marginal note which he made in a book eventually sold from his son's library. The book was *The History of Civilization in England* by Henry Thomas Buckle (1821–1862), the first volume of which appeared in 1857. The copy from the library of Isambard Brunel, bearing his book-plate of an upturned spur and the words 'En Avant', was already a second edition, published in 1858, and an inscription on the fly-leaf, partly erased, reads: 'p. 791, mss note by my father'. The text bears signs of having been carefully and rather pedantically read by an owner who added many small pencil annotations in a neat script, ending on the last page with the note: 'Finished 2 October 1858'. It would seem that at some point in the following year his father looked at the book. Whether or not he read it is uncertain. But at least he read part of it, sufficient to disagree with the sentiments being expressed. This was in the final chapter, dealing with 'Proximate Causes of the French Revolution' (chapter 14), in which Buckle had outlined the intellectual background to the Revolution, giving an account of the utilitarian moral philosophy of Helvetius, according to which men seek pleasure and avoid pain, with everything else such as fame, friendship and maternal love being subordinated to this principle. Down the adjacent margin is scrawled, in the characteristic heavy pencil handwriting of I. K. Brunel 'all this is nonsense founded on the quibble on the word "pleasure" – *it pleases* some men to act rightly even to their own disadvantage – according to Buckle this is *selfish* indulgence – !!!' Against this Isambard has pencilled in a lighter hand: 'In this note, Mr B. does not subscribe to Helvetius' opinions. Does it please men to act *rightly* to their own *disadvantage*? Nothing but *advantage* can *in the end* come from doing right.' [18] It would be unreasonable to construct elaborate generalizations on the basis of this one comment, written in the last troubled year of his busy life, about Brunel's moral philosophy. But it is of interest, nevertheless; first, because he considered it worthwhile coming to grips with the text of this large and impressive volume; secondly, because he apparently misunderstands the passage to be conveying Buckle's own opinions, although the historian was careful to distance himself from the views of Helvetius which he expounds; and thirdly because Brunel seems to be making a reflection on his own life and motivation, by his clear implication that he has found satisfaction in sacrificing his own advantage in some circumstances. At least, this view goes some way to explaining the single-mindedness with which he devoted himself to the fulfilment of the *Great Eastern* project in the last years of his life.

The other scrap of evidence which throws some light on Brunel's view of life is in the correspondence between him and Robert Stephenson. We have already noted the warmth of this friendship, which increased as personal and professional adversity drew the two great engineers together. As they saw each other regularly, most of their correspondence consisted of hurried notes regarding meetings and professional commitments. But in January 1858 Stephenson wrote to Brunel from Newcastle to report on a visit he had made to a spiritualist séance. The subject had clearly been a matter of discussion between them, arousing their scepticism and even a degree of levity. Both are apparent in Stephenson's letter, which is worth quoting at some length:

> Dear Brunel, My Spirit rapping visit was unsatisfactory indeed I regarded it as a perfect failure altho I was induced from the apparent sincerity of the parties to promise that I would make another visit to another house, as they held out the prospect of my seeing two or three Ladies lift a table by their finger ends. They were very respectable people and doubtless believed all they said, but I stand amazed at their credulity, in short their credulity in my mind beats the spirits hollow. I could sooner believe in spirits than I could conceive such frustration of mind. The chief 'medium' as they call it was a tolerably good looking girl who talked sensibly enough, but all the party knew she was suffering from epilepsy and therefore had a diseased brain. During the evening she was thrown into hysterics because I ventured to say that I thought one of the knocks came from a part of the table where she was sitting. Notwithstanding this knowledge of the girl's condition, the whole company implicitly believed her when she informed them that she constantly conversed with spirits, some of them very recently removed from this state of existence. She frequently sees spirits hovering in the air and she also sees halos or luminous atmospheres around the bodies of her friends ... This will give you some notion of the kind of evening I had, and I must add one more anecdote. When we were about to leave the table, the master of the house proposed to us to have another bottle of wine. The most of the company declined, but the master said he would consult the spirits and did so in our presence in the most solemn manner – by looking earnestly down upon the table and by proposing himself in these terms – My dear spirit must we have any more wine? Whereupon three distinct knocks were heard under the table, which is always construed to mean yes. Whereupon we had another bottle of wine and I ventured to say I thought the party was getting more spirituous than spiritual. You must treat this as a private communication as I must meet the parties once or twice again. Yours sincerely, Robert Stephenson.[19]

The robust scepticism of the two friends in discussing spiritualism is a reassuring indication that they maintained a practical down-to-earth no-nonsense attitude towards religion.

As far as science was concerned, Brunel managed to preserve a sort of respectful distance. He was on terms of personal familiarity with such outstanding scientists of his day as Michael Faraday, Charles Babbage and John Herschel, and had been brought up to feel at home in the company of scientists and savants of all types. He was on sufficiently friendly terms with Faraday to drop in on him unannounced at his Chelsea home, and was occasionally asked to stay to dinner. He was also closely acquainted with the irascible mathematician Charles Babbage, a friend of the family, of whom he recorded in 1827: 'Mr Babbage and his little boy here poor man: he has lately lost his father, wife and three children, he seems to feel it much and is going abroad.' But three years later he was socializing with Babbage and others: 'Met Mr Babbage, Lubbock, Lardner, Peacock, Hume and Bayly at Clements. Dined at Mr Bayly's with astronomers. Herschel about undulation of chains ... cloudy night.' [20] Even though all these scientific contacts were generated by his father's professional standing, the young Brunel quickly demonstrated that he was able to hold his own in their company and established warm personal friendships with some of them. He was particularly grateful for the support of Babbage when, in 1832, he was in dispute with the distinguished astronomer Sir James South about an observatory that Brunel had built for him.[21] Incidentally, it is worth noting that, in contrast with the supposed conflict between science and religion which subsequently became widely assumed, most of these scientific friends were men of fairly conventional orthodoxy in their religious views, and it is tempting to see them as models for Brunel's own beliefs. Faraday, it is true, was a devoted member of a small Protestant sect, the Sandemanians, but Herschel and Babbage were men of more orthodox beliefs. Babbage made public his own religious position with his *Ninth Bridgewater Treatise* in 1837, and it seems possible that Brunel was sympathetic to the speculative numerological arguments that Babbage presented for proving the existence of God.[22]

Brunel was elected into membership of the Royal Society in 1830 at the age of twenty-four,[23] but this was again probably on account of his father and friends, and he never appears to have contributed much to the activities of that body. He did, however, attend some meetings of the British Association for the Advancement of Science, which had been established in 1831 and pursued an energetic policy of popularizing science through annual meetings in different provincial centres.[24] Brunel was present at the Bristol meeting in 1836, when he came into conflict with two groups of scientists regarding his steam ships and railway works. First, he disputed with the statistician Dr Dionysius Lardner, who took him to task about the implausibility of his projects for a transatlantic steam ship service and for the unprecedentedly long tunnel at Box. These debates have been amply chronicled, even though the details are elusive, and in both cases Brunel demonstrated the error of his opponent by the practical operation of his innovatory transport systems.[25]

The second area of dispute was potentially of more significance, because

Brunel came into controversy with one of the leading geologists of his day
at a time when that science was raising issues of profound intellectual
significance about the age and evolution of the world. The geologist involved,
admittedly, was not in the forefront of these revolutionary developments,
but he was a scientist of some stature nevertheless. He was Professor William
Buckland (1784–1856), canon of Christ Church, Oxford, and twice president
of the Geological Society. Buckland was well known for his vigorous expo-
sitory style, in lectures and in print, and he took a keen practical interest
in engineering which led him to become an active member of the Institution
of Civil Engineers, and a frequent contributor to its discussions. In this
capacity he threw serious doubt on Brunel's Box Tunnel project – not on
Lardner's objection to the life-threatening acceleration that on his calculations was likely to occur in it, but to the potential dangers of the unlined
tunnel as envisaged by Brunel. Buckland subsequently repeated the statement of his fears, and his objection drew a careful retort from the engineer:

> the inference unavoidably to be drawn from them [Buckland's notes] is that the
> back joints as we call them and other defects which exist originally or which show
> themselves after a time in this rock are not well known and tolerably well
> understood and guarded against by practical engineers and even by our workmen.
> In this opinion I assure you that you are mistaken. Ignorant as I may probably
> be myself of the science of geology, I cannot have been engaged for several years
> making very extensive excavations, probably the largest hitherto made, in this
> particular rock ... without acquiring a very intimate and practical knowledge of
> the structure and peculiarities of this particular mass of rock which is now in
> question; and I will say frankly what I feel on this point, which is that I ought
> now to possess a more thorough and practical knowledge of this particular rock
> and its defects and the best mode of remedying them than even you yourself with
> your immeasurably greater scientific knowledge of rocks generally and, not with-
> standing the heavy responsibilities which rest upon me, from all of which you
> gentlemen of science are happily for yourselves so free, I feel that as regards the
> works of the Box Tunnel everything necessary has been done to render them
> secure and that the doubts and fears you have so easily raised but which it might
> be more difficult again to set at rest, are entirely unfounded. In conclusion I must
> observe that no man can be more sensible than I am of the great advantage it
> would be to me as a civil engineer to be better acquainted with geology as well
> as with many other branches of science.[26]

Again, the practical success of the largely unlined tunnel was Brunel's
vindication, at least in the short term, even though caution eventually
prevailed upon the directors of the GWR to provide brick arches near the
portals of the tunnel which were most subject to frost action.[27]

These encounters with contemporary scientists demonstrate both Brunel's readiness to defer to scientific knowledge in general terms, and his conviction of his own superior judgment on practical matters. They also show his clear recognition of the distinction between science and engineering, especially in so far as the latter involved 'heavy responsibilities' which did not encumber the professional scientist. But he remained broadly sympathetic to the scientific endeavour, although it is a pity that we have no clues concerning his attitude towards the more conventionally shocking aspects of this tide which was swelling during his lifetime. These included uniformitarian theory in geology, derived from Charles Lyell's insistence that all the processes of geological change are of an ever-present rather than a 'catastrophic' nature; the emergence of speculation about the action of ice and the Ice Ages; and, most revolutionary of all, the turmoil in the life sciences about the differentiation of species and the process of change over time, which caused a famous controversy in 1844 with the publication of *Vestiges of Creation* by Robert Chambers (1802–1871).[28] Charles Darwin was effectively deterred from publishing his own disturbing views on these subjects by the savage response to *Vestiges*, so that the great Victorian debate over evolution was postponed for fifteen years, and did not begin until after Brunel's death. We have no way of knowing how he would have responded to this debate, but the indications, such as they are, suggest that he would have continued in his attitude of conservative conformity, modified on occasion by a robust pragmatism. In any event, it is not on his scientific or religious views that Brunel's claim to heroic stature rests. For this we must look elsewhere.

We have already assessed the singularity of Brunel's works, and on these alone his stature rests securely. But he was also an outstanding exponent of engineering professionalism, and he did as much as any individual could do to uphold the dignity of his profession. He demonstrated this in part by his membership of the Institution of Civil Engineers, which he joined in 1830, in the same year in which he joined the Royal Society. He found little time for the latter, but he was and remained to the end an enthusiastic member of the Civils. That is not to say he attended meetings regularly or even frequently, but among his manifold commitments he attended when he could, and often expressed his opinions in discussions. He never got round to submitting a paper himself, and occasionally had hard things to say to the general secretary, as in 1853 when he took Manby to task for promoting discussion of the Great Ship project.[29] But the institution bore him no grudge, choosing rather to honour him by electing him to Council and in time appointing him as vice-president. He could have succeeded Robert Stephenson as president in 1858, but asked for this honour to be held over on that occasion because of his professional commitments and failing health. Joseph Locke took his place, and had the melancholy task of presenting from the presidential chair a joint tribute to his two friends and rivals after their deaths in the autumn of 1859.[30]

When Brunel had joined the Civils, the institution had only recently received its charter, in 1828, and it still enjoyed the presidency of Thomas Telford, who died in 1834. Telford left the institution a substantial endowment of books, papers and property, and it matured rapidly as the major meeting place and professional club of the burgeoning engineering fraternity. The institution provided a focal point for the consensus of the British engineers at a time when the advent of the railways was bringing phenomenal growth to the profession, and it fulfilled its role effectively even though it failed to achieve control over entry to the profession and was obliged to accept the proliferation of engineering institutions which began with the formation of the Institution of Mechanical Engineers in 1848. Brunel responded cautiously to this initiative, fearing a threat to the seamless garment of the profession.[31] His fears were not unfounded, for with the support of George and Robert Stephenson, who became the first and second presidents respectively, and despite the initial localized character of the Mechanicals, with their headquarters in Birmingham, it quickly acquired the characteristics of a national body and provided a precedent for more than a dozen similar break-away associations before the end of the century. Brunel did not join the new institution, insisting to the end on the unique character of the Civils.[32]

The engineers were slow to establish procedures for the training and education of recruits to the profession. This was partly because of their failure to control entry to the profession, with the bullish nature of the open market for engineers created by the railway boom making it possible for anybody who could convincingly pretend to be an engineer being legally acceptable for the job. But it also derived from the fact that engineering was a new profession, and that the first two generations – roughly speaking, up to the death of Telford – were a mixed bag of men from a wide variety of backgrounds who had acquired such skills as they came to possess by their own efforts and by learning from practice. This fact rendered them curiously resistant to the ideas of engineering theory and academic learning. Engineering education made a formal start in the 1830s and 1840s, with professorial appointments at the Universities of London and Glasgow, but it was at first an uphill struggle with little success. It was only in the 1850s and 1860s, with the careers of men such as Rankine at Glasgow and Osborne Reynolds in Manchester, that a tradition of engineering education became firmly established in British universities, but their influence was not strongly felt until after the death of Brunel.[33]

Nevertheless, Brunel deserves some credit for the change in attitudes that made this development possible. His own training had benefited from the theoretical expertise which his father had acquired as a student in France, and the evidence of his calculation books demonstrates his reliance on mathematical competence in many of his crucial engineering decisions. Some of these decisions may seem faulty in the light of modern theory, but Brunel should properly be regarded as the most theoretically conscious engineer of his period, and time has justified most of his theoretical work. He was therefore not unsympathetic to the importance of theory in the training of engineers, and did what he could to impart his own expertise to assistants and pupils in his own practice. But he did nothing to promote university teaching of engineering, and he was sufficiently British in his prejudices to confess to an anxiety about continental theory, as he advised one young man:

> I must strongly caution you against studying *practical* mechanics among French authors: take them for abstract science and study their statics, dynamics, geometry etc etc to your heart's content but never even read any of their works on mechanics any more than you would search their modern authors for religious principles. A few hours spent in a blacksmith's and wheelwright's shop will teach you more practical mechanics. Read *English* books for practice. There is little enough to be learnt in them but you will not have to unlearn that little.[34]

This sums up very neatly the mid century British view of engineering education. It was suspicious of attempts to reduce practical skills to theoretical techniques, while leaving the way open for the acquisition of new theoretical skills as they become available. This was to be of special importance in the emergence about this time of new fields of engineering, involving electricity, organic chemistry and thermodynamics. Brunel himself was never accomplished in these new skills, but his readiness to assimilate the lessons of scientific experiment is apparent in his attitude towards the mathematical testing conducted by William Froude on ship models, his recognition of the potential of the electric telegraph, his use of new chemical preparations in preserving wood, and in many other ways. His appreciation of the importance of such work and his sympathy towards the theoretical understanding necessary for its application helped to prepare the ground for scientific engineering.[35]

In the final resort, however, it was Brunel's enthusiastic commitment to his chosen profession which was his greatest service to engineering. By a lifetime of devotion, he helped to establish engineering as a profession of social standing, fit for a gentleman; but at the same time he ensured that no 'gentleman' was able to regard it as an easy career option because he epitomized in his own conduct the dedication and hard work which was required for success in the profession. He and his immediate colleagues, such as Stephenson and Locke, joined a small profession struggling to establish its identity in a society undergoing vast and rapid changes. They left it with firmly established institutions and a high degree of respect in a society which was acknowledged to be the leading industrial and political nation in the world. It is paradoxical that the engineering profession in Britain did not manage to maintain this high profile and distinguished social standing achieved by Brunel's generation of heroic engineers. The number of professional engineers continued to grow substantially, from the 1659 in recognized institutions in 1860 to 40,375 in 1914, while the number of national institutions jumped from three to seventeen. But the status of the profession seemed to slide imperceptibly into the humdrum, at least in the eyes of its practitioners, who became very conscious of what they regarded as a decline in their social standing. This was doubtless attributable in part to the fact that engineering had become accepted as a feature of the everyday life of the nation, as demonstrated by their greater numbers and the proliferation of their institutions. What they gained in utility, however, they lost in romance: it became difficult to regard the man from the waterworks or gasworks, installing domestic equipment, as an heroic figure.

Where the engineering profession continued to build epic works, moreover, there were several disasters such as the collapse of the Tay Railway Bridge in 1879 and the sinking of the *Titanic* in 1912 which called into question the competence and reliability of the profession. And most influential of all the new factors framing the circumstances of the late Victorian period, the comfortable assumption of Britain being the 'workshop of the world', and acknowledged world leader in the construction of railways and major engineering works, suffered a prolonged process of deflation as rival nations underwent industrialization. The result was that the perceived status of engineering declined as one aspect of the comparative decline of Britain in relation to the rest of the industrialized world. The heroism of the mid century British engineers derived largely from the recognition by posterity that they lived in an heroic age for British leadership and the British economy. By their vision and their drive Brunel and his colleagues had helped to fashion this achievement, but with the loss of British leadership later generations of engineers had to accept a more prosaic role.[36]

There was, of course, more to it than that: Brunel and a handful of his colleagues possessed the qualities of personality which allowed them to take advantage of circumstances which were extraordinary, and the fact that they seized these advantages presented by their time with such commitment is evidence of outstanding features of character and ability. The situation called for heroic engineers, and the social structure enabled those with the talents to do so to respond. I. K. Brunel was such a man, grasping the opportunities of his circumstances to build the *châteaux d'Espagne* which inspired his imagination, with utter dedication and, ultimately, self-sacrifice. L. T. C. Rolt has argued eloquently that Brunel was a 'Renaissance Man': a man whose versatility, vision and genius distinguished him as one of those characters like Leonardo and Michaelangelo who flourished in the Renaissance but who managed to appear larger than life, with achievements which are relevant to all times.[37] It is an attractive image, but I consider that it is essentially flawed because it neglects the extent to which Brunel was a man of his times. It is a truism – *pace* Carlyle, who saw all his heroes as people who changed their environment rather than as men who belonged to their times – that all people in all stages of the history of the world are conditioned by the society into which they are born, and that their achievement, if any, consists in their ability to build on and transform these given conditions. The talents of Isambard Kingdom Brunel were such that they provided precisely the qualities necessary to perform what was required by a society in rapid transformation, and it was his great good fortune that, in his railway works and shipbuilding, he found the opportunity to fulfil his vision.

Once Britain had begun to yield its leadership in industrialization to other European nations and the United States of America, however, the achievements of Brunel and his engineering contemporaries could not be replicated in the public imagination, and came to assume in retrospect heroic grandeur. They were not tarnished by the decline of Britain, which, although comparative rather than real, was strongly felt as other nations acquired industrial prowess. It promoted what one acute modern commentator has called 'the decline of the industrial spirit' in British life. Whatever the degree of special pleading in Martin Wiener's argument, there can be no doubt that he struck a chord in observing the distinct rustication of English ideals after 1850, with industrial aspirations being demoted in favour of gentrification and the rural idyll. More people than ever worked in industry and lived in cities, but they had lost some of their former conviction that industrialization was synonymous with progress. Wiener cited Brunel as an example of this changing attitude, in choosing to send his sons to public school: 'Isambard Kingdom Brunel (1806–1859), the greatest engineer of his generation, sent two sons to Harrow, where they were hardly likely to follow their father's profession.'[38] The fact that Brunel's younger son, Henry, did just that, serving an engineering apprenticeship after leaving Harrow and becoming a distinguished engineer in his own right, does not diminish the main thrust of Wiener's argument: that English education failed to endorse the 'industrial spirit'. Posterity came to isolate the great engineers of Brunel's generation as self-made men who had seized the opportunities offered by a rapidly industrializing society to build railways and other large works, and had thereby won admiration as the figures of an Heroic Age. Engineering has remained important, and become even more important, in the last hundred and fifty years, as a means of underpinning the standard of living in modern societies. But for national ideals and aspirations British people have tended to look elsewhere.

So Brunel the engineer has come to be regarded as a national hero. However, it is necessary also to assess Brunel as a man, to see how he fulfils the heroic role that posterity has thrust upon him. There are interesting indications of his desire for the recognition of others in the revealing personal diary of his early years. He confessed that: 'My self conceit and love of glory or rather approbation vie with each other which shall govern me.'[39] Nevertheless, he established a strict discipline and daily regimen for himself that reveal his determination to give priority to the demands of his profession:

> First, rules as regards my health I will (if I can) go to bed at such time as to be able to rise early: for instance I think I *could* always go to bed at 12 or 1 and get up at 5 or 6 ... If then I rose early I would breakfast at 8 and eat a substantial one. I would then, when I wanted to, go to town pretty early. Oh that I had a gig or horse! I would dine at about 4.30 or 3.30 according to circumstances have tea at 8.30 and a *light* supper at 10.30 ... By rising early I can go below [in the Tunnel] to see the end of the night shift [and] give directions for the next; then attend to above ground matters etc and at 8 eat a hearty Breakfast.[40]

It is safe to assume that Brunel had already established a routine of this type as resident engineer on the Thames Tunnel, but his prolonged indisposition after the inundation of January 1828 gave him the opportunity to rationalize what was already emerging as his favoured pattern of work. He did not require much sleep, and by arranging a spartan routine of meals he managed to cram in work on his reports and abundant letters and memoranda, with slots allocated to reading and writing his journal, in addition to the multifarious tasks of running the engineering operation. In the event, he did not get the chance to apply this routine in the Thames Tunnel, on which work did not resume until he was otherwise engaged, but what we find expressed here is the determination of an ambitious young man to make the best and fullest use of his time in order to establish a reputation for himself.

The formula worked, as can be seen in the recollections of friends and assistants who accompanied him over the next three decades of frenetic activity. He directed all his operations at a high tempo: assistants were expected to be at work early, and to continue for long hours; clients were consulted at all hours of day and night; work on drawings could go on overnight on occasion; long journeys were regularly undertaken, usually on the outside of coaches before he had his own special coach made for his greater convenience. Despite his love of horses, and his hankering after a horse of his own, Brunel does not seem to have been a good horseman, with his diaries recording occasions when he fell off.[41] As the railway system grew, so it became available to help him to get around the country to supervise his own projects and to observe the work of others. His life was lived under pressure, and he conveyed the pressure to his team. But this seems to have been accepted in good part, as a consequence of working for a genius, and was made the more acceptable by the good humour of Brunel himself. St George Burke, his legal colleague in the early struggles for railway authorizations, wrote warmly of his cheerful zest, exemplified in his ingenious devices for waking Burke up in the morning: 'I believe that a more joyous nature, combined with the highest intellectual faculties, was never created.'[42] Similarly, George T. Clark, an early assistant engineer on the GWR who went on to become an ironmaster at Dowlais, wrote: 'His light and joyous disposition was very attractive. At no time was he stern, but when travelling or off work he was like a boy set free. There was no fun for which he was not ready.'[43] This was the image caught also in MacFarlane's lively portrait of 1829, when he joined Brunel on an eventful coach journey from Paris to London.[44] Likewise by those friends of his youth, William Hawes, younger brother of Benjamin, and John Horsley, his brother-in-law to be. Hawes wrote:

> The most striking feature in his character as a young man, and one which afterwards produced such great results, was an entire abnegation of self in his intercourse with his friends and associates ... His influence among them was unbounded, but never sought by him; it was the result of his love of fair play, of his uniform kindness and willingness to assist them, of the confidence he inspired in his judgment, and the simplicity and high-mindedness of his character.[45]

In the course of vivid evocations of Brunel's home and artistic talents, Horsley wrote: 'he was my most intimate friend'.[46]

Admittedly, most of these words of praise refer to Brunel in the 1820s and 1830s. All his close friends were well aware of the enormous demands that his professional commitments made upon him, and were particularly conscious of his increasing obsession with the Great Ship. They were worried about his physical and mental deterioration under the pressure of this responsibility, but unable to do anything about it except to urge him to slow down. The colleague of these later days who spoke most warmly of Brunel, both as a friend and as an engineer, was Daniel Gooch. Usually very taciturn, and regarded in a somewhat guarded way by Brunel himself, Gooch nevertheless confided to his diary the most telling and perceptive tribute to Brunel when he died:

On the 15 September 1859 I lost my oldest and best friend in the death of Mr Brunel ... By his death the greatest of England's engineers was lost; the man of the greatest originality of thought and power of execution, bold in his plans but right. The commercial world thought him extravagant, but altho' he was so, great things are not done by those who sit down and count the cost of every thought and act. He was a true and sincere friend, a man of the highest honour, and his loss was deeply deplored by all who have the pleasure to know him.[47]

Gooch paid off his personal debt to Brunel by turning the *Great Eastern* briefly into a viable economic proposition as a cable-laying ship, and by stepping into the chairmanship of the GWR and rescuing the company from the doldrums in which it had fallen.

By any reckoning, I. K. Brunel was a great engineer, perhaps the greatest. Without any generally agreed criteria for making such an assessment, however, this becomes a matter of individual preference, even though he had outstanding qualifications for such a judgment. He possessed a vision of great works, his 'castles in Spain', many of which he was able to translate into reality. He possessed the skills, the drive, and the organizational ability to see through enterprises that would have defeated most men. He was not always successful, but even his failures were impressive. His works astonished his contemporaries, and many of them survive to fascinate us today. But Brunel was also a great man, as testified by the witness of his many friends and admirers, and as with so many truly great men, his works assumed an epic, legendary quality, so that it often becomes impossible to separate historical fact from the wealth of legendary accretions. Epic stories of bravery and presence of mind in the Thames Tunnel, when the river broke through the shield, and in the construction of the Clifton Bridge, when he ferried a party across the precarious iron bar linking the two pier platforms, are well authenticated. So are his coolness of leadership in the Box Tunnel and in the dispute in the Mickleton Tunnel; in the many crises in the construction of his three great ships; and in the domestic crisis precipitated when he swallowed the half-sovereign which stuck in his wind-pipe. But I have found no documentary basis for the often-repeated story that Brunel aligned the Box Tunnel so that the rising sun shone through it on his birthday, even though careful examination shows that it could indeed do so, and it is certainly a good story.[48] Nor have I found any confirmation of the equally good story that an important cause of the 'atmospheric' failure on the South Devon Railway was that rats ate the grease on the seal and broke the vacuum. Such legends, however, confirm the larger than life quality of the figure to which they become attached.

Finally, we should consider how his society honoured Brunel for indications of his 'heroic' stature. Too much controversy had surrounded his works to make immediate recognition as a national hero possible at his death, and he did not share the acclaim of Robert Stephenson when he died a month after Brunel. Stephenson was given a burial in Westminster Abbey, the national shrine for heroes of all sorts. Brunel was laid to rest more modestly in the family tomb at Kensal Park, where his father had contributed to the project for a London necropolis. Neither of the great engineers would have attached much importance to the disposition of their bones, any more than they valued titular honours in their lifetimes, as it is probable that they both refused them. Both, however, accepted honorary degrees from the University of Oxford. Both of them, moreover, enjoyed a measure of royal approval, although it seems likely that Brunel dissipated some of this with the disagreement over the Balmoral bridge. And both of them had statues and figurines made in their honour. Brunel's family promoted a fund to provide a memorial window for him in Westminster Abbey. According to Lady Gladwyn, they did this by melting down the massive silver table-centre with which Brunel had been presented by the GWR. The result was an unimpressive piece of stained glass, now in the south aisle of the abbey. More significant, because it represented the committed respect of his peers, the Institution of Civil Engineers sponsored the completion of the Clifton Suspension Bridge. Even though, as we have seen, Brunel's family were disgruntled about the lack of emphasis on the Great Man, in fact there can be no doubt, from the bridge itself and from the inscription on it, that it has a powerful memorial purpose.[49]

I. K. Brunel came rapidly to receive from posterity the accolade of having been one of the greatest and most heroic of British engineers. This judgment does justice to the dynamic, effervescent personality, which inspired such loyalty and affection amongst his friends. He was a man motivated by a vision of creative imagination to transform the ability of people to travel. The vision matured in the space of a few years as a result of circumstances which brought him to Bristol and introduced him to novel and exciting opportunities that simply had not existed before. Brunel was never an easy man to live with. He was always restless, ebullient, challenging those around him to do what he wanted them to do. In many respects, he accepted the assumptions and prejudices of his own society without question, being a conformist in most matters of taste and belief. But in his engineering vision he was a driven man, and he devoted himself to the fulfilment of his objectives and thereby to the transformation of the way of living in modern societies. He was not so much a Renaissance Man as a man of his times, an eminent early Victorian, of the heroic age of British engineering.

Appendix

Inventory of Furniture
The Property of I. K. Brunel Esq

Nos 17 and 18 Duke Street Westminster, November 1858

The following notes are a summary of the main headings used in the eighty-three page reporter's notebook filled with information taken in this survey. There is a further notebook with twenty pages filled. Both documents are in the Bristol Collection, at DM 1285/ 2 and 3. The purpose of the survey appears to have been to assess the value of the Brunel household at a time when financial disaster threatened with the problems of the Eastern Steam Navigation Company. The inventory is useful because it gives an idea of the size and disposition of the household, excluding the engineering business accommodation on the ground floor, and of the considerable affluence of a well-established professional family. Brunel acquired No. 18 Duke Street in 1836, and added No. 17 in 1848. It seems likely that access was opened up between the two houses, as the inventory shows that they were clearly run as a single unit.

No. 17 House

- Governess' Room
- Closet adjoining
- Laundry
- Lumber Room
- Cook's Room
- Mr Isambard's Room
- Landing
- Schoolroom
- Red Room or Study
- Laundry
- Dining Room: contents include
  - A richly carved sideboard with glass back in richly carved frame £300
  - Chimney piece with marble figures £185
  - Venetian glass chandelier £48
  - Two Crystal Mirrors £350
  - Rich crimson silk curtains to windows £75
  - A Bronze Candelabra ... for gas £150

The Indian Carpet
- The Paintings in the Dining Room:
    - *Midsummer Night Dream* by Landseer
    - *Scene from Henry VIII* by Leslie
    - *Julliet* [sic] by Leslie
    - *Masquerade scene from Henry VIII* by Leslie
    - *Sauce and her Dog* by Callcott
    - *Death of King Lear* by Cope
    - *Macbeth* by Stanfield
    - *Forest Scene* by Lee
    - *Romeo and Juliet* by Horsley
- Stairs
    - The Brussels carpets and stair rods
- Summary valuation of contents of No. 17:
    Furniture: £2169
    Paintings: [no figure given]

No. 18 House

- Right Attic
- Left Attic
- Servants end room
- Manservant's room
- Housemaid's room (2 beds)
- Lady's Maid's room
- Laundry
- Mr H. Brunel's bedroom (Books – 258)
- Mrs Horsley's room
- Mrs Brunel's Bedroom (Books – 160)
- Spare Bedroom
- Mr Brunel's Dressing Room
- Breakfast Room
- Organ Room
- Drawing Room: contents include
    China
       Raphael ware
       Delf [sic]
       Chelsea
       Sevres
       Dresden
       Venetian glass vases
    Bronzes

- Staircase and Landing:
  - clock by 'Dent' in finely carved frame
  - The Wilton carpet and rods
- Stairs and Entrance
- Butler Pantry: contents include
  - Glass
  - Dresden Breakfast service
  - Gilt Lights
  - Plate
  - Silver Gilt
- Larder: contents include
  - Best Dinner Service –
    'Berlin – Flowers and Insects' 142 plates, 57 soup etc.
  - Best Dessert Service
  - Best Tea Service – Dresden
  - White and Gold Tea Service
  - White embossed Dinner Service
- Kitchen:
  - Coppers
- Servants' Hall – eight chairs
- The Paintings in No. 18 Drawing Room:
  - Italian composition by Sir A Callcott
  - [sixteen others by Callcott]
  - [two portraits by Horsley]

- The Paintings in the Organ Room:
  - *A Calm* by J. C. Horsley
  - *Two Gentlemen of Verona* by Egg
- The Painting on the Staircase:
  - Fresco – *Peace*
- The Paintings in the Study:
  - Portrait of Mr Brunel
  - Ditto Mrs Brunel
- The Painting in the Breakfast Room:
  - Portrait of Sir Isambard
- Summary Valuation of contents of No. 18:
  Furniture: £2438; Plate: £2886; Bronze: £833
  Paintings; Books (1280 vols); Organ; Grand Piano; all no value given.

11. The Engineering Projects of Isambard Kingdom Brunel.

Notes

Notes to Introduction

1. Lytton Strachey, *Eminent Victorians* (London, 1918).
2. Samuel Smiles, *Self Help* (1859); *Lives of the Engineers* (1862, reprinted Newton Abbot, 3 vols, with Introduction by L. T. C. Rolt, 1968). For a fuller discussion of Smiles's views of the Brunels, see below, Chapter 13.
3. See Derrick Beckett, *Brunel's Britain* (Newton abbot, n. d.), for a good survey.
4. R. A. Buchanan and Neil Cossons, *The Industrial Archaeology of the Bristol Region* (Newton Abbot, 1969), p. 49.
5. The National Portrait Gallery *Catalogue* gives details of the history and provenance of these portraits of the Brunels, except for the Wyatt portrait of Marc Brunel, which was reproduced in Sotheby's *Catalogue of British Paintings, 1500–1850* on 10 July 1996: I am grateful to Trevor Fawcett for this reference.
6. Cynthia Gladwyn, 'The Isambard Brunels', *Proceedings of the Institution of Civil Engineers*, 50 (1971), pp. 11; Charles MacFarlane, *Reminiscences of a Literary Life* (London, 1917), the final section of which, 'The Brunels, Civil Engineers', pp. 279–93, contains delightful character studies of both Marc and IKB.
7. Celia Noble, *The Brunels: Father and Son* (London, 1938), p. 260, speculated about the Brunelleschi connection; Gladwyn, 'The Isambard Brunels', p. 11, dismissed the speculation as 'an amusing little fantasy'.
8. Gladwyn, 'The Isambard Brunels', p. 12.
9. The Marochetti statue was erected as a memorial to IKB by the Institution of Civil Engineers. Some fine Parian ware representations of Brunel standing, arms folded, were also produced: at least one of these survives in my possession, a gift of Sir Arthur and Lady Elton.
10. Great Western Railway, *Minutes of Directors*, 15 October 1909: the collection subsequently passed to the British Rail Archives and then to the Public Record Office at Kew, where it is now accessible in sixty-three items under 'PRO RAIL 1149'.
11. See L. T. C. Rolt, *Landscape with Figures* (Stroud, 1992), pp. 133–42.
12. The Bristol Collection has been well catalogued and the University Library has prepared a brief Guide to the material: see also the Bibliography, below.
13. I. Brunel, *The Life of Isambard Kingdom Brunel, Civil Engineer* (London, 1870; reprinted Newton Abbot, 1970).

14. Ibid., p. 485.
15. Noble, *The Brunels* (1938).
16. Gladwyn, 'The Isambard Brunels', (1971).
17. L. T. C. Rolt, *Isambard Kingdom Brunel: A Biography* (London, 1957; paperback 1989, with Introduction by R. A. Buchanan).
18. Ibid., paperback p. xxiii.
19. Rolt, *Landscape*, pp. 133–42.
20. For published works, see Bibliography, below. The societies included the Brunel Society, established in Bristol in 1968: it published a useful series of *Newsletters* and stimulated research on the Brunels; in 1995 it merged with the Bristol Industrial Archaeological Society.
21. Adrian Vaughan, *Isambard Kingdom Brunel: Engineering Knight-Errant* (London, 1991).
22. Sir Alfred Pugsley, ed., *The Works of Isambard Kingdom Brunel: An Engineering Appreciation* (Institution of Civil Engineers and University of Bristol, 1976; and Cambridge, 1980).

Notes to Chapter 1: An Age of Revolution

1. D. Thomson, *Europe since Napoleon* (1957), remains an excellent introduction to these events, and Eric Hobsbawm, *The Age of Revolution: Europe, 1789–1848* (1962), provides useful background.
2. Edmund Burke (1729–1797) wrote *Reflections on the Revolution in France* in 1790; Thomas Paine (1737–1809) responded with *The Rights of Man* in 1792.
3. P. Mathias, *The First Industrial Nation* (London, 1969) is a good outline, and Sir John Clapham, *An Economic History of Modern Britain* (Cambridge, 1926), is still a superb basic study of this period of industrialization.
4. These National Census figures, which do not include Ireland, are given in P. Mathias, *First Industrial Nation*, table 1, p. 449.
5. Clapham, *Economic History*, p. 536: observed that the 1851 Census showed that half the population had become urban: 'a situation which had probably not existed before, in a great country, at any time in the world's history'.
6. Herbert Butterfield, *The Origins of Modern Science* (1949), did much to set the agenda for the modern understanding of the historical role of science, but many others have written on the subject. See, for instance, Owen Chadwick, *The Secularization of the European Mind in the Nineteenth Century* (Cambridge, 1975), and the brilliant essay by Stephen Toulmin and June Goodfield, *The Discovery of Time* (1965).
7. PLB 2B, pp. 299–302, 21 June 1842, has a long letter from IKB to William Buckland regarding the safety of the Box Tunnel: see below, Chapter 13.
8. Cynthia Gladwyn, 'The Isambard Brunels', *Proceedings of the Institution of Civil Engineers*, 50 (1970): the reference to Marc's religion is on pp. 6–7.
9. Ibid., p. 2: the name Isambard 'was evidently reserved for members of the family destined for the priesthood'. Lady Gladwyn also hints at medieval

precedents for 'Isambert' as the name for doughty priests and engineers in the family, ibid., pp. 12–13.

10. J. C. Horsley, *Recollections of a Royal Academician*, ed. Mrs Edmund Helps (London, 1903), p. 169.

11. Henry Marc Brunel, (1842–1903), contributed to the design of Tower Bridge and the distinctive cantilever Connel Ferry Bridge north of Oban. Many of his papers survive and provide a valuable addition to the Bristol Collection.

12. PLB 2C, pp. 78–84, 14 November 1842, IKB to B. H. Babbage: see below, Chapter 10.

13. See below, Chapter 2.

14. PriD, 26 December 1835.

15. PLB 6, pp. 65–69, 13 July 1848, IKB to Count St George.

16. TTJ 3, 27 January 1828: 'Very comfortable at the Albion: some pleasant company ... Strolled on the pier smoking my meerschaum before Breakfast.'

17. Celia Noble, *The Brunels: Father and Son* (London, 1938), pp. 149–53; L. T. C. Rolt, *Isambard Kingdom Brunel* (1957), p. 102 (paperback, p. 139).

18. PerD, pp. 11, 12 and 35; and see below, Chapter 11, for a discussion of the Ellen Hulme affair.

19. See below, Chapter 12.

20. TTJ 3, 20 June 1828.

21. I. Brunel, *Life of Isambard Kingdom Brunel* (1870), pp. 75–76 and 94–98.

22. PLB 2A, 3 December 1839, 23 July 1840 and 15 January 1841.

23. GWR 5, pp. 114, 192, etc; see below, Chapter 5.

24. I. Brunel, *Life*, p. 98.

25. Rolt, *Brunel*, (1957), p. 138 (paperback, p. 183); see also p. 324 (paperback, p. 419).

26. See below, Chapter 9.

27. See below, Chapter 10.

28. PerD, p. 3.

29. PriD, 5 December 1831.

Notes to Chapter 2: Apprenticeship

1. R. A. Buchanan, *The Engineers* (1989), gives a general account of this background. For French engineering, see Terry Shinn, 'From "Corps" to "Profession": The Emergence and Definition of Engineering in Modern France', in R. Fox and G. Weisz, eds, *The Organization of Science and Technology in France, 1808–1914* (Cambridge, 1980).

2. For the life of M. I. Brunel, see R. Beamish, *Memoir of the Life of Sir Marc Isambard Brunel* (London, 1862); and the more recent biography, P. Clements, *Marc Isambard Brunel* (London, 1970).

3. Clements, *Marc Isambard Brunel*, chapter 5. For George John, second Earl Spencer (1758–1834), see also DNB entry, and below, Chapter 12. The Block Mill still survives in the Naval Dockyard at Portsmouth, although nearly all the machines have been removed, some of them to the Science Museum and other collections.

4. Celia Noble, *The Brunels Father and Son* (1938), pp. 35–46, gives the family account of IKB's early education. Clements, *Marc Isambard Brunel*, p. 37 note 2, claims that he has been unable to locate birth certificates to give precise dates for the birth of IKB's sisters. According to Lady Gladwyn, 'The Isambard Brunels' (1971), p. 9, there were two more daughters who died at birth.

5. L. T. C. Rolt, *Isambard Kingdom Brunel*, p. 17 (paperback, p. 37).

6. Ibid. Maudslay's trainees included Nasmyth and Whitworth. IKB has been described as a pupil of Maudslay, but this is not strictly true, although he undoubtedly learnt much from visiting his workshop: see ESNLB, 1, p. 135, 24 March 1853, IKB to Messrs Maudslay & Field: 'you led me to hope that your firm with which all my early recollections of engineering are so closely connected and in whose manufactory I probably acquired all my early knowledge of mechanics, would be able and willing to enter into the project zealously.' This was in connection with IKB's plans for his Great Ship, but Maudslays did not respond positively to the flattery.

7. Breguet to MIB, 1 November 1821, quoted Rolt, *Brunel*, p. 18 (paperback, p. 38).

8. Noble, *The Brunels*, p. 46.

9. Clements, *Marc Isambard Brunel*, chapter 14, 'Isambard as Partner'.

10. MIB, Diary, 1823. Most of Marc's diaries are in the Institution of Civil Engineers archives. For the spelling of 'gaz' I have adopted the usage favoured by the Brunels, although the more conventional 'gas' appears in the patent.

11. IKB, PriD, 30 January 1833. Michael Faraday (1791–1867) made his reputation as a brilliant lecturer at the Royal Institution with the Friday Evening Discourses that he conducted between 1825 and his retirement in 1862 – he gave three on the Thames Tunnel between 1826 and 1828, as well as that on the gaz engine. See L. Pearce Williams, *Michael Faraday* (London, 1965), p. 331, where he mistakenly says that the tunnel was 'built under the direction of I. K. Brunel'.

12. There is a good account of the Gaz engine by C. Farrell, in *Gazetteer of the Brunel Society*, 2 (May 1977), pp. 9–12.

13. Clements, *Marc Isambard Brunel*, p. 257, gives the patent for marine steam engines as No. 4683 of 26 June 1822.

14. Documentary sources for the construction of the Thames Tunnel are found in (a) the archives of the Institution of Civil Engineers, which contain many records, correspondence, etc. including the diaries of Marc Brunel; and (b) the Bristol Collection, especially the three volumes of IKB's 'Thames Tunnel Journal' (TTJ), but also his Personal Diary (PerD).

15. For Beamish and Gravatt, see Clements, *Marc Isambard Brunel*, p. 130. There is a good obituary notice for Gravatt in *Proceedings of the Institution of Civil Engineers*, 26 (1866–67), pp. 565–75: see below, Chapter 10, for the subsequent quarrel between IKB and Gravatt.

16. There is a good account of IKB's energy and responsibility in Beamish, *Marc Brunel*, pp. 228–29: for the social life and flirtations, see the relevant entries in PriD and PerD for 1826–28.

17. Beamish, *Marc Brunel*, p. 241.

18. Ibid., pp. 257–59, for the Tunnel Dinner on 10 November 1827.

19. PerD, p. 6, 13 October 1827.

20. Beamish, *Marc Brunel*, p. 234.

Notes to Chapter 3: Castles in the Sky

1. IKB's diaries are in the Bristol Collection: see below, Bibliography, for details and notes on the coding.

2. TTJ, 12 February 1827.

3. TTJ, 16 October 1826.

4. TTJ, 9 March 1827. Sir William Congreve (1772–1828) was comptroller of the Royal Laboratory, Woolwich, and inventor of the rocket projectile named after him.

5. TTJ, 15 February 1828.

6. TTJ, 23 March 1828.

7. TTJ, 6 May 1828; 24 May 1828; and 14 June 1828.

8. TTJ, 12 July 1828.

9. TTJ, 21 July 1828.

10. TTJ, 13 August 1828.

11. TTJ, 6 October 1828.

12. Charles MacFarlane, *Reminiscences of a Literary Life* (London, 1917).

13. Ibid.: MacFarlane is described by the *DNB* as a 'miscellaneous writer'. His major work was a *Civil and Military History of England*, published in eight volumes, 1838–44. He died in 1858.

14. TTJ, 12 February 1829.

15. TTJ, 13 February 1829.

16. TTJ, 20–21 February 1829.

17. TTJ, 21 February 1829.

18. TTJ, 24 February 1829.

19. TTJ, 21 March 1829.

20. TTJ, 9 April 1829.

21. TTJ, 4 May 1829.

22. TTJ, 6 May 1829: Charles Babbage (1792–1871), Lucasian Professor of Mathematics at Cambridge and inventor of the 'difference engine', a mechanical calculating machine, parts of which were made by the engineer Joseph Clement until the project was abandoned in 1834. William Buckland (1784–1856) was Professor of Mineralogy at Oxford and President of the Geological Society in 1824 and 1840: he was also a keen member of the Institution of Civil Engineers.

23. PriD, 28 April 1824.

24. PriD, 24 August 1824.

25. PriD, 11 December 1824

26. PriD, 29 March 1829: for Augustus Charles Pugin (1762–1832), Gothic architect, see Clements, *Marc Isambard Brunel*, p. 79.

27. PriD, 22 April 1824.

28. PriD, 2 September 1824.

29. PriD, 9 September 1824.

30. PriD, 22 January 1825.

31. PriD, 22 April 1824.

32. PriD, 10 February 1825.

33. PriD, 7 September 1824.

34. PriD, 14 January 1826.

35. PerD, p. 3.

36. PerD, p. 3.

37. PerD, pp. 4, 11, and elsewhere.

38. TTJ, 6 May 1828.

39. PriD, 4 December 1831.

40. PerD, p. 28.

41. PerD, p. 35: Rolt speculated about the identity of Ellen Hulme but other biographers have offered no additional comments: perhaps it was too delicate as a matter of family concern to be discussed in public, but see below, Chapter 12.

42. Ibid.: the dating system indicates that it was the first day of the week (Monday) on 6 April 1829, and it was adopted throughout the rest of IKB's diaries.

43. Ibid., dated 7 2/8 32 (i.e. Sunday 2 August 1832).

44. Ibid.: for an account of the election, see Chapter 11 below.

45. There is a tantalizing possibility that the Hawes family kept papers connected with IKB, and that some of them might still survive.

46. PriD, March 1830

47. PriD, 16 September 1830.

48. PriD, 17 September 1830.

49. PriD, 26 March 1831.

50. PriD, 17 June 1831.

51. PriD, 30 October 1831.

52. PriD, 8 November 1830.

53. PriD, 5 December 1831.

54. PriD, 5 December 1831.

55. PriD, 17 December 1831.

56. PriD, 3 May 1832.

57. PriD, 3 January 1833.

58. PerD, p. 31, 15 June 1828.

59. PriD, 26 March 1830.

60. William Youatt, *The Horse ... with a Treatise on Draught* (1831; 2nd edn, 1843), 'On Draught', pp. 518–63. For the Newcastle & Carlisle Railway, see L. T. C. Rolt, *Isambard Kingdom Brunel* (1957, p. 47; paperback pp. 73–74).

61. Youatt, *The Horse*, p. 527.

62. W. Froehling, 'An Anonymous Publication of Isambard Kingdom Brunel', in *Transactions of the Newcomen Society*, 58 (1986–87), pp. 141–51. There is some correspondence between IKB and the Society for the Diffusion of Useful

Knowledge in the Library of University College, London. See also PLB, 2A, c. p. 50, 26 February 1841, IKB to Thomas Coates (Secretary SDUK) refusing an invitation to write an extended article.

63. PriD, 16 April 1830.
64. PriD, 18 August 1830.
65. PriD, 19 May 1831.
66. PriD, 6 November 1831.
67. PriD, 8 November 1831.
68. PriD, 21 April 1832.
69. PriD, 22 April 1832.
70. PriD, 25 April 1832.
71. Sir James South (1785–1867), astronomer, was a friend of Sir John Herschel and the Earl of Rosse.
72. PriD, 10 June 1832.
73. PriD, 30 January 1833.
74. PriD, 21 February 1833.
75. PriD, 7 March 1833.
76. PriD, 17 March 1833.
77. PriD, 14 April 1833.
78. PriD, 23 July 1833.
79. PriD, 24 August 1833.
80. PriD, 11 November 1833
81. PriD, 9 July 1833.
82. PriD, 10 July 1833.
83. PriD, 11 August 1833.
84. PriD, 27 August 1833.
85. PriD, 26 December 1835.
86. St George Burke, in I. Brunel *Life of Isambard Kingdom Brunel* (1870), pp. 75–78; and Rolt, *Brunel,* pp. 82–83; (paperback, pp. 116–17).

Notes to Chapter 4: Bristol

1. J. Latimer (1824–1904) was a celebrated chronicler of Bristol history: his book *The Annals of Bristol in the Nineteenth Century* (Bristol, 1887), is an excellent source of facts on Bristol for our period; but he was very critical of IKB – see p. 191, where he describes Brunel as: 'an inexperienced theorist, enamoured of novelty, prone to seek for difficulties rather than to evade them, and utterly indifferent as to the outlay which his recklessness entailed upon his employers'. Bryan Little, *The City and County of Bristol* (London, 1954), although now rather dated, remains a good work of general reference on Bristol. See also R. A. Buchanan and Neil Cossons, *Industrial Archaeology of the Bristol Region* (Newton Abbot, 1969).

2. I have not managed to find any reference in the private diaries either: nor in the diaries of Marc Brunel until the entry 'Isambard set off for Bristol' for 23

January 1830. But PerD, p. 31, mentions 'intend going to Redcliff [?] next week' under 8 June 1828.

3. The diaries of Marc Brunel (MIBD), at the Institution of Civil Engineers, mention this assistance.

4. PLB, 2A, circa p. 90, 11 January 1842, IKB to Gower: see below, Chapter 7.

5. Copies of the census notebooks are available in Bath City Library. I am grateful to my friends William and Pauline Hanna for pointing out this reference to me.

6. The *Prospectus* is mounted at the beginning of the 'Proceedings of Trustees, 1830–1900' of the Clifton Suspension Bridge, housed in the Bristol Collection under DM484.

7. See, for instance, B. W. E. Alford, 'The Economic Development of Bristol in the Nineteenth Century: An Enigma?' in Patrick McGrath and John Cannon, eds, *Essays in Bristol and Gloucestershire History* (Bristol, 1976), pp. 252–83; and Kenneth Morgan, 'The Economic Development of Bristol, 1700–1850', in Madge Dresser and Philip Ollerenshaw (eds), *The Making of Modern Bristol* (Bristol, 1996).

8. See the view presented by W. E. Minchinton, 'Bristol: Metropolis of the West in the Eighteenth Century', *Transactions of the Royal Historical Society*, fifth series, 4 (1954), pp. 69–89.

9. R. A. Buchanan, 'Construction of the Floating Harbour', *Transactions of the Bristol and Gloucestershire Archaeological Society*, 88 (1969), pp. 184–204.

10. For a discussion of the rise and decline of industries in Bristol, see Buchanan and Cossons, *Industrial Archaeology of the Bristol Region*.

11. Recorded in 'Proceedings of Trustees'. The SMV is well treated in Patrick McGrath, *The Merchant Venturers of Bristol* (Bristol, 1975), although he does not have much to say about the Suspension Bridge, see ibid., pp. 434–35.

12. 'Proceedings of Trustees', minute for 18 March 1831. See also PriD, 15 March 1831, where IKB mentions going over to Blaise Castle to 'talk over the old fool' – i.e. Davies Gilbert.

13. 'Proceedings of Trustees', minute for 20 April 1831.

14. The letter of 27 March 1831 is quoted in full by Celia Noble, *The Brunels: Father and Son* (London, 1938) p. 109, but I have not seen the original. PriD, 26 March 1831, records: 'Attended Committee. Unanimous in favour of Egyptian'. L. T. C. Rolt, *Isambard Kingdom Brunel* (London, 1957), p. 56 (paperback, pp. 84–85), follows Noble. For a general account of the Clifton Bridge, see Sir Alfred Pugsley, 'Clifton Suspension Bridge', in A. Pugsley, ed., *The Works of Isambard Kingdom Brunel* (Bristol and London, 1976), pp. 51–68. See also G. Body, *Clifton Suspension Bridge: an Illustrated History*, (Bradford-on-Avon, 1976).

15. Quoted in Rolt, *Brunel*, p. 58 (paperback, p. 87).

16. Latimer, *Annals*, p. 133, castigated Brunel for his extravagance, and for littering the landscape with these useless towers.

17. Susan Thomas, *The Bristol Riots* (Bristol Historical Association, 1974), p. 1.

18. Ibid., p. 26.

19. Mark Harrison, *Crowds and History: Mass Phenomena in English Towns, 1790–1835* (Cambridge, 1988), p. 64. This is the best recent account of the Bristol Riots, although concerned to set them in an unnecessarily opaque theoretical context.

20. Latimer, *Annals*, pp. 206–18, has a useful account of the riots, but does not mention Brunel in this context.

21. PriD, II.3.i, p. 174, 30 October 1831: 'the 14th' was the detachment of troops under Colonel Brereton.

22. CSB 'Proceedings of Trustees', minute for 15 June 1831.

23. PriD, 3 November 1833: 'Poor Mr Roch dangerously ill'. He recovered, but retired to Wales.

24. For a summary of port improvements, see R. A. Buchanan, *Nineteenth-Century Engineers in the Port of Bristol* (Bristol Historical Association, 1971). Also see Charles Wells, *A Short History of the Port of Bristol* (Bristol, 1909).

25. Brunel's Report of 1832 is in *Bristol Dock Company Minutes*, 8 September 1832. This and other archival material relating to the Port of Bristol is now in Bristol City Archives. For a detailed analysis of the 1832 Report, see R. A. Buchanan, 'I. K. Brunel and the Port of Bristol', in *Transactions of the Newcomen Society*, 42 (1969–70), pp. 41–56.

26. IKB's *Report*, 31 January 1842, printed by the BDC.

27. Buchanan and Cossons, *Bristol Region*, p. 33 and plate 35.

28. G. Farr, *The Steamship Great Western* (Bristol Historical Association, 1963).

29. G. Farr, *The Steamship Great Britain* (Bristol Historical Association, 1965); see also Ewan Corlett, *The Iron Ship* (Bradford-on-Avon, 1975).

30. W. G. Neale, *At the Port of Bristol*, 1 (Bristol, 1968), pp. 5–8.

31. IKB's *Report* to the BDC, June 1844.

32. PLB, 3, pp. 57–58, 3 June 1844, IKB to Claxton.

33. The standard work on the early history of the GWR is E. T. MacDermot, first published in 1927 and revised by C. R. Clinker, *History of the Great Western Railway*, 3 vols (1964).

34. See below, Chapter 6.

35. *Bristol Times*, 18 August 1849.

36. *Bristol Times and Mirror*, 28 January 1871.

37. PriD, 30 August 1833, p. 90, describing members of the London Committee of the GWR.

38. I have found no record of the Lardner v. Brunel debate at the British Association.

39. Great Western Steamship Company Report to the AGM on 1 March 1838: I am grateful to my friend David K. Brown for drawing my attention to this reference. See also the chapters by Denis Griffiths in Denis Griffiths, Andrew Lambert, and Fred Walker, *Brunel's Ships*, (Chatham Publishing/National Maritime Museum, 1999), chapter 1, 'Formation of the GWSS Company'; chapter 2, 'The Genesis of the *Great Western*'; chapter 5, 'The GWSS Company Works'; and chapter 7, 'The Steamship *Great Western*'.

40. R. A. Buchanan and M. W. Doughty, 'The Choice of Steam Engine Manufacturers by the British Admiralty, 1822–1852', *Mariner's Mirror*, 64 (1978), pp. 327–47.

41. Frustrated in this attempt to accompany the *Great Western* on her first voyage, it is curious to note that IKB made no voyages on any of his three ships.

42. There is a sequence of fifty-one numbered letters from IKB to Guppy (although sixteen are missing) in the Brunel Collection in Bristol, under 'Letters and Documents', DM 1306/VII.

43. See the chapters by Professor Lambert in Denis Griffiths et al., *Brunel's Ships*, chapter 3, 'Brunel, the Navy and the Screw Propeller', and chapter 8, 'HMS *Rattler*: Brunel's Warship in Service, 1845–56'. Francis Pettit Smith (1808–1874) was knighted for his invention of the screw propeller in 1871.

44. PLB, 3, pp. 238–39, 11 December 1844, IKB to Hunt.

45. Buchanan and Cossons, *Bristol Region*, p. 49; and Corlett, *Iron Ship*. The ship was returned to the dry dock in which she had been built in Bristol City Docks in 1970 on 19 July, the date favoured by IKB for such manoeuvres.

46. For the later career of the *Great Britain*, see Corlett, *Iron Ship*.

47. PLB, 7, p. 236, 1 June 1850, IKB to the Rev. E. Banks. For this and the Clifton Water Works, see R. A. Buchanan, 'Brunel in Bristol', in McGrath and Cannon, eds, *Essays in Bristol and Gloucestershire History*, pp. 246–49.

48. PLB, 10, pp. 59–63, 16 November 1854, IKB to John Yates, in the course of complaining about a newspaper article on the SS *Great Eastern* project, which had 'failed to do justice to the spirited merchants of Bristol' by ignoring their contribution to transatlantic steam navigation – and, by implication, ignoring the contribution of IKB himself.

Notes to Chapter 5: The Great Western Railway

1. The main documentary sources for the contribution of IKB to the GWR are well known. They are the Private Letter Books (PLB) in the Bristol Collection, the GWR Letter Books in the PRO Collection (GWRLB), Parliamentary Papers for the many government committees and enquiries (PP), and accounts gathered by I. Brunel in his *Life* of his father (1870; reprinted 1970). The standard modern work remains E. T. MacDermot, *History of the Great Western Railway*, 2 vols (1927), with a revised edition by C. R. Clinker, 3 vols (1964), which quotes at length from IKB's reports to the directors on the gauge and other matters. Unless stated otherwise, MacDermot has provided the source for the basic facts in this chapter.

2. PriD, 1 March 1833, quoted Celia Noble, *The Brunels: Father and Son* (1938), p. 247.

3. PriD, 7 and 9 March 1833: on the latter date IKB wrote 'dined at Mr Roche's from his account I only gained my appointment by one vote this was going too close – must be more active another time. Cave was against me for Green who was my only dangerous opponent'.

4. For a good general account of railway development, see J. Simmons, *The*

Railways of Britain (London, 1961; 2nd edn. 1968). See also Harold Perkin, *The Age of the Railway* (1970).

5. The phrase 'the finest work in England' was used to describe the GWR by IKB in PriD, 26 December 1835, reflecting on the remarkable nature of his commitments: the passage is quoted at length in L. T. C. Rolt, *Isambard Kingdom Brunel* (1957), p. 84 (paperback, p. 119).

6. MacDermot, *History of GWR*, i, p. 4.

7. I. Brunel, *Life*, quotes St George Burke QC on IKB: 'In his cross-examinations he was generally a match for the most skilful counsel, and by the adroitness of his answers would often do as much to advance his case as by his examination in chief … He was almost as much of a diplomatist as an engineer', pp. 93–94. See also ibid., pp. 75–78, for Burke's description of IKB's character.

8. MacDermot, *History of GWR*, i, p. 80, describes IKB's negotiations with Robert Gordon, squire of Kemble, in order to secure passage through his estate for the Cheltenham line. See also PLB 1, 2 February 1836, IKB to W. H. Townsend, conveying instructions for dealing with the Revd Proctor Thomas about the route across his property.

9. MacDermot, *History of GWR*, i, p. 5: I have not located the original source of the letter to Hammond, although several letters in GWRLB relate to staff appointments and related business – e.g. Hammond's appointment as resident engineer on the London end: IKB to the directors, 7 January 1836. Notice of the appointment of Bevan and Harrison as sub-assistants is given at the same time, while William Gravatt was also appointed as a resident engineer. Three days earlier, on 4 January 1836, IKB recommended to the Bristol Committee the appointments of T. C. Bell at £200 p. a., and H. Babbage, Thomas George and Samuel Jones at £150 p. a.

10. Report, IKB to the directors of the GWR, 15 September 1835.

11. IKB's Reports to the directors of the GWR on the gauge and other matters are quoted at length in MacDermot, *History of GWR*, i, pp. 17–19 (15 September 1835); pp. 35–39 (15 August 1838), etc.

12. See below, Chapter 8, for a discussion of these locomotives.

13. PLB, 2A, pp. 46–48, 2 January 1841, IKB to D. Gooch.

14. MacDermot, *History of GWR*, i, pp. 309–28. The most serious problem seems to have been that of maintaining the insulation of the electric wires.

15. Jack Simmons, ed., *The Birth of the Great Western Railway: Extracts from the Diary and Correspondence of George Henry Gibbs* (Bath, 1971), p. 42: the entry is from Gibbs's diary for 13 July 1838.

16. The GWR Letter Books, vols 2–7 in the PRO RAIL 1149 series, contain some delightful notes by IKB to Robert Stephenson regarding the naming of the locomotives which the GWR was gratefully receiving from the Tyneside firm: see, for instance, GWRLB 5, p. 200, 30 July 1839, IKB to Messrs Stephenson & Co.

17. PriD, 25 March 1833.

18. There are many outline plans for stations in the sketch books. Temple Meads

has received special attention, both on account of its survival, as a prime feature of industrial archaeology, and because of its unusual hammer-beam roof: see R. A. Buchanan and Neil Cossons, *Industrial Archaeology of the Bristol Region* (Newton Abbot, 1969), pp. 211–13.

19. PLB, 8, pp. 99–101, 13 January 1851, IKB to M. D. Wyatt.

20. Sir Daniel Gooch, *Memoirs and Diary*, ed. Roger Burdett Wilson (1972), p. 40.

21. Keith Falconer and John Cattell, *Swindon: The Legacy of a Railway Town* (HMSO for the Royal Commission on the Historical Monuments of England, 1995), p. 36.

22. L. T. C. Rolt, *Isambard Kingdom Brunel* (1957), p. 140 (paperback, p. 186).

23. PLB, 3, pp. 36, 171–72 and 197, 10 May, 28 October and 8 November 1844, IKB to Roche and Brodie.

24. PLB, 9, pp. 339–40, 30 May 1854, IKB to J. Hooper: he goes on to hold out the prospect of helping 'the duke of Beaufort with any plans in this direction', which seems to be an early hint of the 'direct' South Wales route through Badminton.

25. The image of the 'web' is IKB's: see his reference to dropping 'a huge stitch in my work', PLB, 4, pp. 127–29, 26 July 1845, IKB to William Froude, regarding the North Devon Railway.

26. For IKB and the Gauge Commission, see I. Brunel, *Life*, pp. 117–22.

27. Cross-examined by the opposition counsel before the parliamentary committee for the first GWR Bill, George Stephenson defended IKB's route: 'I can imagine a better line, but I do not know of one': quoted Rolt, *Brunel*, p. 78 (paperback, p. 111).

28. For IKB's timber bridges, see L. G. Booth, 'Timber Works', in Sir Alfred Pugsley, ed., *The Works of Isambard Kingdom Brunel* (1976), pp. 107–35. See also John Binding, *Brunel's Cornish Viaducts* (Penryn, 1993).

29. The collapse of the Dee Bridge led to the government enquiry and to the *Report of the Commission on the Application of Iron to Railway Structures*, Parliamentary Papers (1849), c. 1123, xxix: evidence was taken from IKB and other leading engineers.

30. The Britannia Bridge has been the subject of scholarly consideration in N. Rosenberg and W. G. Vincenti, *The Britannia Bridge: The Generation and Diffusion of Technological Knowledge* (Boston Massachusetts, 1978). The bridge was destroyed by an accidental fire in the 1970s.

31. R. A. Buchanan, 'The Cumberland Basin, Bristol', *Industrial Archaeology*, 6 (1969), pp. 325–33, gives the history of this bridge.

32. MacDermot has useful accounts of both bridges: *History of GWR*, i, pp. 295 and 298–99, on Chepstow; and ii, pp. 141–45, on the Royal Albert Bridge at Saltash: see also R. P. Brereton, 'The Centre Pier of Saltash Bridge', in *Proceedings of the Institution of Civil Engineers*, 21 (1861–62), pp. 268–92, and John Binding, *Brunel's Royal Albert Bridge* (Truro, 1999).

33. R. A. Buchanan and Stephen K. Jones, 'The Balmoral Bridge of I. K. Brunel', *Industrial Archaeology Review*, 4, (1980): see also below, Chapter 10.

34. For the dinner table silver, see Cynthia Gladwyn, 'The Isambard Brunels' (1971), p. 14, referring to 'a gigantic, tremendously ornate, table-centre of silver gilt, presented with lesser companion pieces by the Great Western Railway Company'.

Notes to Chapter 6: Overseas Projects

1. For this reliance on British engineering, see R. A. Buchanan, 'The Diaspora of British Engineering', *Technology and Culture*, 27 (1986), pp. 501–24. This chapter draws on my Presidential Address to the Newcomen Society in 1983: 'The Overseas Projects of I. K. Brunel', *Transactions of the Newcomen Society*, 54 (1982–83), pp. 145–66. I am grateful to the editor for his agreement to me using the material here.

2. R. C. Cox, *Engineering Ireland, 1778–1878*, Exhibition Catalogue, School of Engineering, Trinity College Dublin, 1978.

3. PLB, 2C, pp. 230–31, 27 October 1843, IKB to J. Samuda. The fact that IKB had made at least one earlier visit to Ireland appears from PriD, 18 September 1830, where he records making a journey to Cork 'by Severn steam boat' with some 'dreadful weather'.

4. PLB, 3, pp. 202–3, 16 November 1844, IKB to W. Johnson, asking for help with Irish survey.

5. PLB, 3, pp. 177–78, 4 November 1844, IKB to B. Gibbons.

6. PLB, 3, pp. 213–14, 26 November 1844, IKB to B. Gibbons.

7. See above, Chapter 4; and especially PLB, 5, pp. 69–75, 10 December 1846, IKB to C. Claxton.

8. PLB, 9, p. 235, 10 November 1853, IKB to S. Hughes.

9. PLB, 10, p. 145, 15 May 1855, IKB to the Hon. T. Ponsonby.

10. K. A. Murray, 'Bray, Brunel and All That', *Journal of the Irish Railway Record Society*, 5 (1960), pp. 207–27. I am grateful to Stephen Jones for drawing my attention to this reference.

11. See E. T. MacDermot, *History of the Great Western Railway*, (1964), i, pp. 295–96.

12. For the Italian background, see D. Mack Smith, chapter 21, 'Italy', in *The New Cambridge Modern History*, x (Cambridge, 1964); and Derek Beales, *The Risorgimento and the Unification of Italy* (London, 1981).

13. The process culminated in 1870, when control of Rome was secured: 'A "geographical expression" had come to life. With the acquisition of Rome, the *risorgimento* seemed, for the time being, to be complete', Mack Smith, 'Italy', p. 576.

14. It is ironic that the most reactionary regime in Italy had so many industrial 'firsts', and that a British engineer such as Guppy, who had worked with IKB in Bristol, chose to move his business to Naples when his health dictated a warmer climate in 1848.

15. I have found no evidence of Cavour's involvement in IKB's projects, but circumstantial evidence makes it seem very probable.

16. PLB, 2A, pp. 80–83, 28 August 1841, IKB to Edwin Gower.

17. PLB, 2A, pp. 90–95, 9 December 1841, IKB to Edwin Gower.

18. PLB, 2A, pp. 97–99, 11 January 1842, IKB to Edwin Gower.

19. PLB, 2C, pp. 20–30, 20 July and 29 July 1842, IKB to W. Johnson.

20. M. Moseley, *Irascible Genius: A Life of Charles Babbage, Inventor* (London, 1964). Ms Moseley is inaccurate in her comment on B. H. Babbage: 'In 1840 Herschel, who had been pupil and then Assistant to Mark Isambard Brunel [sic!] on the Great Western Railway, was taken by Brunel to Italy to make surveys for the projected Genoa-Turin railway', ibid., p. 167.

21. PLB, 2C, pp. 1–7, 14 May 1842, IKB to President and Members, Royal Railway Society.

22. PLB, 2C, pp. 20–26, 25 July 1842, IKB to B. H. Babbage, 'No. 4'.

23. PLB, 2C, pp. 42–43, 15 August 1842, IKB to B. H. Babbage, 'No. 5'.

24. PLB, 2C, pp. 78–84, 14 November 1842, IKB to B. H. Babbage, 'No. 7'.

25. PLB, 2C, pp. 147–48, 12 March 1843, IKB to B. H. Babbage, 'No. 9' (pencilled in).

26. PLB, 2C, pp. 151–61, 20 March 1843, IKB to B. H. Babbage, 'No. 10'; also 23 March ('No. 11') and 7 April 1843 ('No. 12', from J. Bennett to B. H. Babbage).

27. PLB, 2C, pp. 182–83, 7 July 1843, IKB to W. Coffin; p. 186, 12 July 1843, IKB to C. B. Vignoles.

28. PLB, 2C, pp. 212–13, 25 September 1843, IKB to B. H. Babbage (practice of numbering discontinued).

29. The report is copied in PLB, 2, pp. 229–54: it is undated and out of sequence.

30. PLB, 2C, p. 290, 26 January 1844, IKB to Edwin Gower.

31. PLB, 3, pp. 88–89, 16 July 1844, IKB to B. H. Babbage.

32. PLB, 3, pp. 104–5, 26 July 1844, IKB to B. H. Babbage.

33. PLB, 3, p. 115, 14 August 1844, IKB to B. H. Babbage.

34. PLB, 3, pp. 253–54, 20 December 1844, IKB to B. H. Babbage.

35. PLB, 4, pp. 3–11, 4 March 1845, IKB to Count Pollan.

36. PLB, 4, pp. 98–101, 10 June 1845, IKB to B. H. Babbage.

37. PLB, 4, pp. 122–23, 17 July 1845, IKB to Count Pollan; also IKB to B. H. Babbage, 9 July 1845.

38. PLB, 4, pp. 111–12, 2 July 1845, IKB to B. H. Babbage: 'I am very anxious to come by the Coast and Genoa to show that beautiful country to Mrs Brunel.'

39. PLB, 4, pp. 151–52, 18 November 1845, IKB to Count Pollan.

40. PLB, 4, p. 166, 16 December 1845, IKB to R. P. Brereton.

41. For IKB's official resignation, see PLB, 4, pp. 166–68, IKB to Count Pollan: he submitted a final account to the Sardinian government, for the balance of £2610 1s. 10d. in February – see PLB, 4, p. 221, 27 February 1846, IKB to Count Pollan.

42. PLB, 4, pp. 158–60, 2 December 1845, IKB to directors of the Maria Antonia Railway: he suggested a two year term for Babbage's contract, and recommended the adoption of the atmospheric system of propulsion, although he recognized that, in the interests of standardization with other sections of the north-south line, locomotives would be more appropriate.

43. PLB, 4, pp. 161–62, 3 December 1845, IKB to Maria Antonia Railway.

44. PLB, 4, pp. 229–32, 11 March 1846, IKB to B. H. Babbage.

45. PLB, 4, pp. 271–74, 15 June 1846, IKB to W. Marsh.

46. PLB, 4, pp. 287–88, 14 July 1846, R. P. Brereton to B. H. Babbage.

47. PLB, 4, pp. 298–99, 11 August, 1846, R. P. Brereton to B. H. Babbage.

48. PLB, 5, p. 24, 8 October 1846, IKB to J. L. Gooch; p. 142, 12 March 1847, J. Bennett to J. L. Gooch.

49. A complete tracing of Florence Station was sent in June 1847; IKB was also concerned with stations at Prato and Pistoia.

50. PLB, 5, pp. 215, 30 June 1847, R. P. Brereton to B. H. Babbage.

51. PLB, 5, pp. 248–51, 6 September 1847, R. P. Brereton to B. H. Babbage.

52. PLB, 5, pp. 341–42, 4 February, 1848, IKB to B. H. Babbage.

53. PLB, 6, pp. 50–51, 13 June 1848, IKB to Bonfil (Count St George).

54. PLB, 6, pp. 65–69, 13 July 1848, IKB to Count St George.

55. PLB, 6, pp. 86–87, 3 and 17 August 1848, IKB to W. Marsh: the settlement was for £1028 12s. 10d.

56. PLB, 9, pp. 188–89, 13 September 1853, IKB to H. E. Goode; pp. 227–28, 7 November 1853, IKB to A. S. Lee; and p. 240, 14 November 1853, IKB to W. Johnson.

57. PLB, 9, pp. 190–93, 17 September 1853, IKB to Mr Landfear.

58. PLB, 2, pp. 381–404, 30 November 1855, IKB to Grand Trunk Railway of Canada; and PLB, 10, p. 221, 8 December 1855, IKB to E. S. Betts. See also PLB, 10, pp. 301–2, 24 October 1856, IKB to H. W. Blake, when IKB refused to give advice on the GTR.

59. PLB, 10, pp. 333–34, 5 August 1857, IKB to C. H. Gregory: amongst other works, Doyne designed the elegant iron-arch bridge over the South Esk at Launceston, Tasmania.

60. Michael Satow and Ray Desmond, *Railways of the Raj* (London, 1980), pp. 9–19, gives a useful summary of these pioneering operations.

61. See *John Brunton's Book* (Cambridge, 1939), p. 82.

62. PLB, 10, p. 213, 3 November 1855, J. Bennett to W. A. Purdon.

63. PLB, 10, pp. 309–10, 26 January 1857, IKB to W. A. Purdon.

64. PLB, 10, pp. 377–82, 18 January 1858, IKB to J. F. Leith – a copper-plate copy at the end of this volume, setting out his terms.

65. PLB, 11, pp. 11–13 and 22–24, 4 and 19 February 1858, IKB to J. F. Leith.

66. PLB, 11, pp. 83–84, 16 September 1858, J. Bennett to J. Brunton.

67. PLB, 11, pp. 101–2, 9 November 1858, IKB to W. A. Purdon.

68. PLB, 11, pp. 224–25, 20 August 1859, IKB to W. A. Purdon.

69. I. Brunel, *Life of Isambard Kingdom Brunel* (1870) p. 91; also PLB, 11, p. 233, J. Bennett to James Fergusson, nominating Brereton to attend the board of the Eastern Bengal Railway 'relative to engineering matters'.

70. For the general situation in Australia in the mid-nineteenth century, see G. Blainey, *The Rush that Never Ended: A History of Australian Mining* (Melbourne, 1963).

71. For details of IKB's Australian projects, I am indebted to Peter S. Staughton

of Melbourne for letting me have a copy of his notes on 'Victorian Railways'. According to these, the Saltwater Bridge was completed in December 1858 and tested the following month. Brunel had been appointed to succeed Captain Douglas Galton RE as Inspecting Officer to supervise contracts in Britain in December 1856.

72. PLB, 11, p. 125, 25 November 1858, IKB to E. Barnard.

73. PLB, 11, p. 256, 10 November 1859, J. Bennett to E. Barnard.

74. PLB, 11, p. 296, 11 October 1859, J. Bennett to Gooch (presumably Daniel).

75. PLB, 11, pp. 271–73, 14 November 1859, Executors of IKB to Duke of Newcastle.

76. I am grateful to Ken G. McInnes, Chairman of the Engineering Sub-Committee of the Victorian Division of the Institution of Engineers, Australia, for introducing me to this site in 1981.

77. E. Corlett, *The Iron Ship* (Bradford-on-Avon, 1974), pp. 242–47, records the *Great Britain* making thirty-four round voyages from Liverpool to Melbourne between 1852 and 1876.

78. Babbage advised on the water-supply of Blackpool as an Inspector for the Board of Health in 1849. There is an article on B. H. Babbage in the *Australian Dictionary of Biography*.

Notes to Chapter 7: Disasters

1. L. T. C. Rolt, *Isambard Kingdom Brunel* (1957) p. 104 (paperback, p. 141), describes the first hazardous crossing of the Avon Gorge. For the coin-swallowing incident, see below, Chapter 12.

2. Ibid., p. 117 (paperback, p. 157).

3. R. B. Wilson, ed., *Sir Daniel Gooch: Memoirs and Diary* (Newton Abbot, 1972), pp. 33–39. When Gooch was critical of Brunel's locomotives he received an angry rebuke, but on consideration IKB left Gooch to get on with his improvements: 'His good sense told him that what I said was correct and his kind heart did me justice', p. 35.

4. E. T. MacDermot, *History of the Great Western Railway* (1964), ii, chapter 6, pp. 103–36, gives an unadorned account. After receiving surprisingly little specialist attention for many years, two monographs appeared on the atmospheric system within a year: C. Hadfield, *Atmospheric Railways* (Newton Abbot, 1967), and F. M. Clayton, *The Atmospheric Railways* (Lichfield, 1966). See also R. A. Buchanan, 'The Atmospheric Railway of I. K. Brunel', *Social Studies of Science*, 22 (1992), pp. 231–43, on which I have drawn extensively in this text: the paper was originally presented to the ICOHTEC Symposium on 'Failed Innovations' at Hamburg in 1989.

5. Robert Stephenson expressed his objections fairly but forcibly in his *Report of the Atmospheric Railway System* to the directors of the Chester & Holyhead Railway, published in London, 9 April 1844. There is a copy in the Bristol Collection, annotated by IKB, but otherwise the archival material on the atmospheric system is disappointing.

6. See Jack Simmons, *The Railways of Britain* (2nd edn, London, 1968), p. 17.

7. PLB, 2, pp. 261–67, 19 August 1844, report to the directors of the South Devon Railway.

8. The point was made forcefully by Stephenson, *Report of the Atmospheric Railway System.*

9. PLB, 2, pp. 316–22, 19 August 1848, report to the directors of the South Devon Railway, recommending abandonment of the atmospheric system; it is also given in the appendix to Clayton, *The Atmospheric Railways*, pp. 135–38.

10. The engine makers included James Watt and Maudslays, so it is unlikely that there were any serious faults in the machinery.

11. The electric telegraph was first used on railways by IKB: Paddington was connected with West Drayton in 1838, and the telegraph was extended to Slough in 1842, being responsible for the arrest of a suspected murderer in 1845: see MacDermot, *Great Western Railway*, i, pp. 320–28. Railways were slow in adopting it for general signalling because of problems with insulating the wires and other difficulties, see Sir John Clapham, *An Economic History of Modern Britain: The Railway Age* (Cambridge, 1926), pp. 395–96: 'Even the Great Western moved slowly: it did not lay wire through the Box tunnel until 1847'; and there were serious and inexplicable delays in installing it between the South Devon engine houses, where it would have been very useful.

12. Jack Simmons, *The Victorian Railway* (London, 1991), p. 73. The story about the Devon rats is typical of many IKB stories: it is probably true, but I can find no documentary basis for it.

13. The South Devon Railway directors were happy to retain Brunel as their engineer, and the chairman, Thomas Gill MP, in particular remained in favour of the atmospheric system, holding out for it and eventually resigning in protest against the decision of his colleagues. IKB appears to have requested no fees from the company until the line was complete.

14. R. B. Wilson (ed.), *Sir Daniel Gooch: Memoirs and Diary* (Newton Abbot, 1972), p. 47.

Notes to Chapter 8: The Great Ship

1. The Family view of the controversy is given in I. Brunel, *Life of Isambrard Kingdom Brunel* (1870), and L. T. C. Rolt, *Isambard Kingdom Brunel* (1957), while Russell's point of view is given by George S. Emmerson, *John Scott Russell* (1977). I tried to take a median position in 'The *Great Eastern* Controversy: A Comment', *Technology and Culture*, 24 (1983), pp. 98–106, and this is still my point of view. See also my paper, 'The First Voyage of the SS *Great Eastern*' in *Proceedings ICOHTEC Symposium* (Vienna, 1991); and George S. Emmerson, *The Greatest Iron Ship: SS Great Eastern* (Newton Abbot, n.d., but 1981). There is ample documentary material of various sorts in the Bristol Collection, and I have relied heavily on the six volumes of letter books of the Eastern Steam Navigation Company (ESNLB).

2. PLB, 9, pp. 261–62, 22 November 1853, IKB to C. Manby; see also pp. 257–59, 21 November 1853: there is a report in *Proceedings of the Institution of Civil Engineers*, 13 (1853–54), pp. 1–63, of a paper by A. Henderson 'On the Speed and Other Properties of Ocean Steamers', but this was on 8 November so it could not have been the immediate cause of IKB's agitation – JSR took part in the discussion, but not IKB.

3. PLB, 10, pp. 58–59, 16 November 1854, IKB to John Scott Russell.

4. PLB, 10, pp. 59–63, 16 November 1854, IKB to John Yates.

5. The letters of Brunel's assistant Bradford Leslie from Glasgow and Liverpool (where he was also supervising work on the railway bridge for Victoria, Australia) are in the Bristol Collection: it is unusual for such incoming letters to survive, but this series of thirty-one letters were written between 19 December 1856 and 7 August 1857.

6. For Yates's response to IKB on this issue, see below notes 20 and 21.

7. ESNLB, 3, pp. 416–29, 7 October 1856, IKB to Directors, estimates the labour force at '1000 to 1200 men', in the course of a long proposal for managerial reorganization.

8. *The Times*, 21 September 1859.

9. PLB, 12, p. 14. This volume, the last in the series, is devoted to notes compiled by I. Brunel and Henry Brunel in preparation for writing the biography of their father: this passage appears to have been recorded from an interview with IKB.

10. The series of sketch books contain many images of the ship and its equipment; see, for instance sketch book, 1852–54, p. 9.

11. For Charles Geach, see the obituary notice in *Proceedings of the Institution of Civil Engineers*, 14 (1854–55), pp. 148–51; also Rolt, *Brunel*, pp. 243–44 (paperback, p. 316); Emmerson, *Russell*, pp. 79f.

12. ESNLB, 2, pp. 341–61, October 1855: Memorandum by IKB.

13. ESNLB, 2, pp. 298–99, 5 October 1855, 'Memoranda for my Own Guidance'.

14. See for example ESNLB, 1, pp. 104–7, 5 October 1853(2?), IKB to G. B. Airey, proposing an observatory on board; and ESNLB, 1, pp. 237–42, IKB to C. Piazzi Smyth at the Royal Observatory in Edinburgh (with references to 'spinning discs', p. 324, and even 'gravity is eliminated', p. 327).

15. ESNLB, 1, pp. 259–64, 16 August 1854, IKB to Yates.

16. PLB, 10, p. 234, 9 January 1856, IKB to Russell.

17. ESNLB, 2, pp. 267–68, 2 October 1855, IKB to Russell.

18. The Hollingworth Collection is a small collection of papers, mostly associated with John Scott Russell and the *Great Eastern*, in the University of Bath Library: this is a typed copy of a letter dated 28 August 1856 from Russell to the directors of the ESNC.

19. ESNLB, 3, p. 291, 25 June 1856, IKB to John Yates.

20. ESNLB, 3, pp. 451–52, 3 October 1856, John Yates to IKB: this appears to be a response to IKB's attempt to define managerial responsibilities on the project:

see also Yates to IKB, 7 October 1856; IKB to Directors, 7 October 1856; and Yates to IKB, 13 October 1856.

21. ESNLB, 3, pp. 452–54, 7 October 1856, Yates to IKB.

22. ESNLB, 5, p. 359, 22 December 1857, Yates to IKB: I have searched the files of the *Builder* for this advertisement, but without success; I have also failed to find it in the *Engineer*. The letters appear in ESNLB, 5, pp. 322–73, December 1857 and January 1858.

23. Rolt, *Brunel*, p. 277–78 (paperback, pp. 359–60).

24. It is possible that Thomas Wright of Notting Hill was the articulate and intelligent mechanic who wrote some excellent accounts of working-class life in Victorian England under the pseudonym 'A Journeyman Engineer', such as *The Great Unwashed* (London, 1868).

25. Joule's letter of 21 December 1857 does not appear to have received any special acknowledgment from IKB, so it is possible that they were not personally acquainted.

26. Some degree of personal acquaintance does appear to exist between IKB and Thornton.

27. ESNLB, 5, pp. 322–23, 17 December 1857, IKB, 'Memorandum of a Verbal Report'.

28. Tangye Brothers claimed that 'we launched the *Great Eastern* and she launched us', but I have found no specific mention of the firm in the Letter Books: see Richard Tangye, *'One and All': An Autobiography* (London, 1889), pp. 61–66, with the quotation on p. 65.

29. PLB, 11, pp. 110–12, 6 November 1858, IKB to Thomas Brassey.

30. *The Times*, 10 August 1859.

31. *The Times*, 19 September 1859.

32. There are several full newspaper reports of the Weymouth inquest: see especially *The Times*, 13, 18, 19 and 20 September 1859, with leading article on 21 September when there is also a full report; and *Morning Chronicle*, 19, 20 and 21 September 1859.

33. *Morning Chronicle*, 21 September 1859.

34. *Morning Chronicle*, 20 September 1859.

35. *The Times*, 21 September 1859.

Notes to Chapter 9: Other Significant Works

1. PriD, 26 December 1835: the last entry in the second of two foolscap volumes, DM 1306 II.3.ii; See also Rolt, *Isambard Kingdom Brunel* (1957), pp. 84–86 (paperback, p. 119), quoting the passage.

2. This section draws on my essay 'The Engineering Style of I. K. Brunel', in *Polhem*, 15 (1997), which was a paper delivered to the ICOHTEC Symposium at the SHOT Conference in Uppsala in August 1992. For the 'Egyptian thing', see IKB's excited letter of March 1831 to Benjamin Hawes, quoted above, in Chapter 2.

3. The frieze was designed for IKB by his friend (and later brother-in-law) John Horsley, who described it in I. Brunel, *Life of Isambard Kingdom Brunel* (1870), p. 56.

4. Augustus Charles Pugin (1762–1832) was a fellow-Frenchman and contemporary of Marc Brunel. His son, Augustus Welby Northmore Pugin (1812–1852), collaborated with Sir Charles Barry on the new Palace of Westminster. Both were closely associated with the Gothic Revival in Britain.

5. John Latimer, *Annals of Bristol in the Nineteenth Century* (Bristol, 1887), p. 281: 'an engine house of somewhat fantastic design', with a footnote on its removal in 1864 after a suggestion that 'it should be converted into a church for the use of sailors and bargemen'.

6. For an account of the ships and bridges, see above, Chapters 5 and 6.

7. The two brick piers are still clearly visible at either end of the Charing Cross Railway Bridge.

8. For the fulminations of William Morris about the Forth Bridge, see Thomas Mackay, *The Life of Sir John Fowler* (London, 1900), p. 314.

9. This section draws on my article, with Stephen K. Jones and Ken Kiss, 'Brunel and the Crystal Palace', in *Industrial Archaeology Review*, 17 (1994). The conservatory at Chatsworth, completed in 1840, had been built by Paxton in collaboration with Decimus Burton.

10. The destruction of this portico became a *cause célèbre* in the development of industrial archaeology: see R. A. Buchanan, *Industrial Archaeology in Britain* (Harmondsworth, 1972).

11. Patrick Beaver, *The Crystal Palace* (Chichester, 1970), gives a general account of the development of the Sydenham site.

12. PLB, 9, pp. 201–7, 1 October 1853, IKB to Sir Joseph Paxton.

13. PLB, 9, pp. 209–11, 8/9 October 1853, IKB to C. H. Wild. Charles Heard Wild had been associated with the original Crystal Palace from the outset, working under William Cubitt and alongside Matthew Digby Wyatt and Owen Jones. With the removal of the building to Sydenham, Wild had become one of the principal officers responsible for the reconstruction.

14. PLB, 9, p. 234, 9 November 1853, IKB to Wild.

15. PLB, 9, pp. 243–45, 14 November 1853, IKB to R. Stephenson; pp. 246–48, 15 November, IKB to Wild.

16. PLB, 9, pp. 271–79, 22 November 1853, IKB to Directors of the Crystal Palace Company.

17. PLB, 9, pp. 266–67, 25 November 1853, IKB to Wild.

18. PLB, 9, pp. 279–80, 30 November 1853, IKB to Joseph Paxton.

19. PLB, 9, pp. 302–3, 8 February 1854, IKB to Joseph Paxton.

20. Beaver, *The Crystal Palace*, p. 79: P. H. Delamotte photographed the work at Sydenham from 1851 to 1854, but unfortunately he does not appear to have covered IKB's work.

21. PLB, 10, pp. 20–24, 4 August 1854, IKB to Joseph Paxton.

22. PLB, 10, pp. 32–33, 28 September 1854, IKB to Joseph Paxton.

23. PLB, 10, pp. 42–43, 21 October 1854, IKB to Joseph Paxton.

24. PLB, 10, p. 50, 3 November 1854, IKB to Fox Henderson.

25. PLB, 10, p. 71, 30 November 1854, IKB to George Grove, later to become Sir George Grove, editor of the *Dictionary of Music and Musicians* and first Director of the Royal College of Music.

26. PLB, 10, pp. 79–81, 13 December 1854, IKB to Directors the Crystal Palace Company.

27. F. W. Shields subsequently recalled his experience of putting in the foundations of the water towers using Portland cement, which was 'much preferable to Roman cement, and should be used whenever a first-rate concrete was required', in Daniel Miller, 'Structures at Sea', *Proceedings of the Institution of Civil Engineers*, 22 (1863), p. 443.

28. PLB, 10, pp. 100–1, 1 February 1855, IKB to Fox Henderson.

29. £3000 on 18 January 1855 and £4000 on 13 February 1855.

30. PLB, 10, pp. 131–32, 21 March 1855, IKB to Fox Henderson.

31. PLB, 10, pp. 153–54, 26 May 1855, IKB to Fox Henderson.

32. PLB, 10, pp. 200–2, 24 September 1855, IKB to Charles Fox.

33. PLB, 10, pp. 203–7, 28 September 1855, IKB to George Grove.

34. PLB, 10, pp. 164–65, 30 June 1855, IKB to Joseph Paxton, urging that proper testing procedures be followed.

35. PLB, 10, pp. 185–86, 3 August 1855, IKB to Joseph Paxton.

36. PLB, 10, pp. 240–41, 30 January 1856, IKB to Joseph Paxton.

37. PLB, 10, p. 268, 2 May 1856, IKB to Fox Henderson.

38. PLB, 10, p. 269, 2 May 1856, IKB to Joseph Paxton.

39. Graham Reeves, *Palace of the People* (Bromford, 1986), p. 29.

40. PLB, 10, pp. 168–69, 7 July 1855, IKB to Joseph Paxton.

41. PLB, 10, p. 269, 2 May 1856, IKB to Joseph Paxton.

42. PLB, 10, p. 304, 20 November 1856, J. Bennett to George Grove.

43. The museum is on Anerley Hill, near the Boundaries Gate and Crystal Palace Parade.

44. This section draws on my article with Stephen K. Jones, 'The Balmoral Bridge of I. K. Brunel', *Industrial Archaeology Review*, 2 (1980).

45. John R. Hume, *The Industrial Archaeology of Scotland*, ii, *The Highlands and Islands* (London, 1977), p. 93, where a misprint attributes the construction of the bridge to 'A. Brotherhood'.

46. See Fig. 1 in Buchanan and Jones, 'The Balmoral Bridge of I. K. Brunel'.

47. PLB, 10, pp. 14–15, 25 July 1854, IKB to Col. Phipps.

48. The deterioration may reflect a general over-burdening of IKB's office staff.

49. Royal Archives, Windsor, PP Balmoral 2/174. I am grateful for the gracious permission of Her Majesty the Queen to quote from this collection where appropriate.

50. He gave sound advice about the small suspension bridge half a mile downstream from the Balmoral site, as being: 'perfectly safe for all ordinary loads'.

51. PLB, 10, pp. 70–73, 30 November 1854, IKB to Phipps.

52. Ibid.: a long note appended to the letter of 30 November.

53. Sketch book, 8, pp. 25–28, 14 November 1854, entry under 'Dee Bridge'; the adjacent entry under 'Balmoral Bridge', pp. 29–30, 28 November 1854, consists of two empty pages.

54. Work had begun on the *Great Eastern* in February 1854.

55. PLB, 10, p. 147, 15 May 1855, IKB to Phipps: at £1650 the Brotherhood tender compared favourably with those of John Scott Russell at £1956 and W. G. Armstrong at £2318: seven tenders are recorded in Royal Archives, PP Balmoral 2/192.

56. PLB, 10, p. 206, 16 April 1856, IKB to Dr Andrew Robertson.

57. PLB, 10, p. 289, 5 September 1856, IKB to Phipps; also Royal Archives, PP Balmoral 2/192.

58. PLB, 10, p. 290, 15 September 1856, IKB to Phipps.

59. PLB, 10, p. 294, 22 September 1856, J. Bennett to Brotherhood.

60. The Banchory to Aboyne stretch of the railway was opened in 1859.

61. PLB, 10, pp. 340–41, 2 October 1857, IKB to Phipps: the words 'not extremely ornamental' require placing in quotation marks to make the passage read easily.

62. PLB, 10, pp. 342–43, 6 October 1857, IKB to Phipps.

63. Queen Victoria, *Leaves from the Journal of Our Life in the Highlands* (London, 1868), p. 159: there are cuttings in the Royal Archives describing the opening of this Linn of Dee bridge, one of which, dated 14 September 1857 and possibly from *The Times*, describes it as 'a new Gothic bridge'. This contrasts with the description of the completion of the Balmoral bridge in the *Aberdeen Journal* for 2 September 1857: 'The bridge, which was designed by Mr Brunel, is constructed on the principle of the tubular bridge across the Menai Strait.'

64. PLB, 11, pp. 34–35, 22 March 1858, IKB to Phipps.

65. PLB, 11, pp. 115–17, 18 March 1858, IKB to Phipps: a letter of 24 November (p. 123) confirms payment.

66. Royal Archives, PP Balmoral 3/255.

67. Royal Archives, Add Q3/108, subsequently dated 1877: this sum presumably included the work on the abutments and approaches supervised by Robertson.

68. *Engineer*, 21 (4 May 1866), p. 315, 'The Architecture of Bridges': there are comments in the same vein in the issues for 7 April 1865 and 27 July 1866; also in *Engineering*, 1 (11 May 1866), p. 309.

Notes to Chapter 10: The Professional Man

1. The material for this chapter appeared as 'I. K. Brunel, Engineer' in Sir Alfred Pugsley, ed., *The Works of Isambard Kingdom Brunel* (1976). For a general review of the circumstances in which British engineering developed, see R. A. Buchanan, *The Engineers* (1989), chapters 1–3; also Garth Watson, *The Civils: The Story of the Institution of Civil Engineers* (1988).

2. R. A. Buchanan, 'Gentlemen Engineers: The Making of a Profession', *Victorian Studies*, 26 (1983), pp. 407–29.

3. PLB, 1, p. 79, 28 March 1836, IKB to Thomas Gill.

4. Townsend was employed for a time on the B&ER survey: see PLB, 1, p. 50, 2 February 1836, IKB to W. H. Townshend (sic), concerning a route modification near Wellington in the property of the Revd Mr Proctor Thomas, 'who is a Gentleman perfectly to be relied upon'.

5. PLB, 7, p. 133, 5 and 6 March 1850, J. Bennett to staff.

6. PLB, 6, pp. 271–72, 4 May 1849, IKB to W. W. Briston. Briston has not been identified.

7. PLB, 7, p. 160, 25 March 1850, J. Bennett to J. R. Hannaford and others.

8. PLB, 5, pp. 52–53, 27 November 1846, IKB to J. W. Hammond; see also 22 and 30 November.

9. PLB, 4, pp. 151–52, 18 November 1845, IKB to Count Pollon. The lost eye is marked by a black eye-patch worn by Brereton in the portrait of him at Brunel Technical College, Bristol, and it is reproduced in the charming mural decorating the Hayward Room on the SS *Great Britain*.

10. For William Gravatt (1806–1866), see the obituary notice in *Proceedings of the Institution of Civil Engineers*, 26 (1866–67), pp. 565–75.

11. PLB, 2A, pp. 4–8, 3 December 1839, IKB to W. Gravatt.

12. PLB, 2A, pp. 31–34, 23 July 1840, IKB to W. Gravatt.

13. PLB, 2A, 4 August 1840, IKB to Directors of B & ER.

14. PLB, 2A, pp. 61–65, 4 and 15 June 1841, IKB to W. Gravatt.

15. PLB, 2A, pp. 74–78, 19 July 1841, IKB to Bardham (for Board of B & ER); also 22 July 1841. The *PICE* obituary, see note 10 above, referred to Gravatt as 'in the strictest sense, a remarkable man, peculiar to a degree which may fairly be described as extraordinary'. He died on 30 May 1866. There is an interesting account of the 'Somerset Bridge' over the River Parrett at Bridgwater in Brian J. Murless, *Bridgwater Docks and the River Parrett*, Somerset County Library (1983): I am grateful to my brother, Sandy Buchanan, for drawing my attention to this reference.

16. PLB, 2B, pp. 26–28, 13 January 1840, IKB to J. H. Gandell.

17. PLB, 2A, pp. 17–19, 4 March 1840, IKB to J. A. Gandell: also 16 March and 2 November 1840: on two subsequent occasions, 12 May 1841 and 9 September 1844, IKB refused to provide a testimonial for Gandell.

18. PLB, 5. pp. 259–60, 13 May 1846, IKB to W. M. Bennett.

19. PLB, 5, pp. 146–49, 26 and 29 March 1847, IKB to R. M. Marchant: the reference to 'Hulme' strikes a chord, being almost certainly IKB's Mancunian friend John Hulme, whom he appears to have employed in an engineering capacity.

20. L. T. C. Rolt, *Isambard Kingdom Brunel* (1957), pp. 157–58 (paperback, p. 207): the incident is sometimes referred to as the 'Battle of Mickleton Tunnel'; see also Terry Coleman, *The Railway Navvies* (Harmondworth, 1968), pp. 110–14; David Brooke, *The Railway Navvy* (Newton Abbot, 1983), pp. 98–100; and David Brooke, 'The "Great Commotion" at Mickleton Tunnel, July 1851', *Journal Rail and Canal Historical Society*, 30 (July 1990), pp. 63–67. Regarding Marchant, see PLB, 8, p. 306, 16 February 1852, IKB to R. M. Marchant, where

IKB objects to being blamed for RMM's business failure: 'As long as you wish to abuse me you must have the goodness to do it in some other way than by writing to me as I shall return your letters unread.'

21. PLB, 2B, p. 188, 3 June 1841, IKB to Robert Bird.

22. PLB, 7, pp. 67–68, 29 December 1849, IKB to W. J. Owen.

23. PLB, 10, pp. 338–39, 28 September 1857, IKB to G. J. Darley.

24. PLB, 9, pp. 185–86, 14 September 1853, IKB to C. Richardson.

25. PLB, 11, pp. 80–82, 14 September 1858, IKB to C. Richardson: according to his obituary notice in *Proceedings of the Institution of Civil Engineers*, 123 (1895–96), pp. 417–19, Charles Richardson was a man of 'great physical strength and activity': he 'made the first cricket bat with a cane-spliced handle, and invented and made a catapult for bowling a cricket ball'; he went on to become engineer to the Severn Tunnel and made a fortune out of manufacturing bricks at Cattybrook which were used to line the tunnel.

26. PLB, 2B, pp. 256–58, 19 January 1842, IKB to C. A. Fripp, a director of the GWR.

27. PLB, 3, pp. 100–2, 26 July 1844, IKB to J. Crosthwaite.

28. PLB, 3, pp. 48–49, 28 May 1844, IKB to W. Froude.

29. PLB, 4, pp. 125 and 126–27, 22 and 26 July 1845, IKB to W. Froude.

30. PLB, 4, pp. 168–70, 19 December 1845, IKB to W. Froude: the breakdown appears to have been concerned more with inter-company politics than with any engineering failure. See David St J. Thomas, *A Regional History of the Railways of Great Britain*, i, *The West Country* (Newton Abbot, 1960), pp. 92–94; also E. T. MacDermot, *History of the Great Western Railway* (1927), ii, pp. 84–86.

31. PLB, 5, p. 157, 7 April 1847, IKB to W. Froude: the subject matter is not explained.

32. ESNLB, 4, pp. 98–101, 4 January 1857, W. Froude to IKB, and further letters in May 1857: see also David K Brown, 'William Froude and "the Way of a Ship in the Midst of the Sea"', in R. Angus Buchanan, ed., *Engineers and Engineering* (Bath, 1996), pp. 179–209.

33. PLB, 4, p. 181, 6 January 1846, IKB to the Revd Corrie.

34. PLB, 9, pp. 7–8, 23 April 1852, IKB to Trustees of the Clyde Navigation: the 'ten years' was somewhat hyperbolic.

35. PLB, 9, p. 216, 20 October 1853, J. Bennett to W. Bell, offering work on the South Devon at £250: 'Mr Brunel is sorry to offer you so small a salary but the circumstances of the case define this'; see also ESNLB, 4, pp. 343–47, 8 May 1857, W. Froude to IKB, relating to work by Bell. There is a curious letter of IKB to W. Glennie, in charge of work at the Saltash Bridge (PLB, 10, pp. 217–18), referring to the dismissal of a person called Bell for drunkenness, but from the circumstances this could not have been William Bell, who went on to write chapter 7, 'Railway Bridges and Viaducts', and chapter 14, 'Dock and Pier Works' for I. Brunel, *Life of Isambard Kingdom Brunel* (1870).

36. R. B. Wilson, ed., *Sir Daniel Gooch: Memoirs and Diary* (Newton Abbot, 1972; first partially published in 1892), pp. 75–76: see also below, Chapter 13.

37. PLB, 2A, pp. 106–9, 6 December 1842, IKB to Saunders.

38. John Brunton, *John Brunton's Book*, introduced by J. H. Clapham (Cambridge, 1939), p. 47.

39. David Brooke, 'The Equity Suit of *McIntosh* v. *The Great Western Railway*: The "Jarndyce" of Railway Litigation', *Journal of Transport History*, third series, 17 (September 1996).

40. PLB, 1, p. 19, 16 January 1836, IKB to W. G. Owen, with a prospect of rising to £300; and also pp. 126–28, 3 March 1836, IKB to William Glennie. There is a series of three slim index-books in the Bristol Collection under the heading 'Payments to Assistants/General Statements', with entries arranged more or less alphabetically, but it is difficult to extrapolate annual salaries from these figures.

41. PLB, 4, p. 204, 31 January and 5 February 1846, J. Bennett to John James: 'Banbury would be the best place for you to reside at.'

42. PLB, 7, p. 48, 10 December 1849, IKB to T. E. Marsh: Marsh subsequently established his own practice in Bristol, and his name appears on the Halfpenny Bridge replacement of 1877 in Bath.

43. PLB, 11, p. 79, 14 September 1858, IKB to H. S. Bush.

44. PLB, 11, pp. 80–82, 14 September 1858, IKB to C. Richardson.

45. PLB, 11, p. 82, 15 September 1858, IKB to Captain McNair.

46. PLB, 9, pp. 9–10, 24 April 1852, IKB to S. Power: see also PLB, 10, p. 323, IKB to S. Power, providing him with a very warm testimonial. Samuel Power (1814–1871) had, unusually for a British engineer, a distinguished classical and medical education at Trinity College Dublin before entering the profession: see the obituary notice in *Proceedings of the Institution of Civil Engineers*, 33 (1871), pp. 236–41.

47. PLB, 10, p. 213, 3 November 1855, J. Bennett to W. A. Purdon. Wellington Purdon (1815–1889) worked on the Woodhead Tunnel under Vignoles and then Locke, before being taken on by IKB to build his Wexford line, and then to survey the line for the East Bengal Railway: see the obituary notice in *Proceedings of the Institution of Civil Engineers*, 97 (1889), pp. 408–13.

48. PLB, 8, p. 270, 7 January 1852, IKB to T. Bratton.

49. PLB, 1, p. 159, 3 October 1836, IKB to Henry Sale of Merthyr.

50. PLB, 2A, pp. 18–19, 17 October 1839, J. Bennett to Messrs Maurice and Jamieson.

51. PLB, 2A, p. 100, 28 February 1842, IKB to a solicitor regarding Edmund Le Fallais; and PLB, 2C, p. 273, 11 December 1843, IKB to Captain Wormeley.

52. PLB, 3, pp. 223–24, 5 December 1844, IKB to Bryman Bryman.

53. PLB, 4, pp. 246–47, 17 April 1846, IKB to J. A. Whitcombe.

54. PLB, 9, pp. 267–9, 4 November 1853, J. Bennett to Charles Foster Gower.

55. PLB, 3, p. 11, 2 April 1844, IKB to R. Stephenson.

56. PLB, 3, pp. 225–26, 6 December 1844, IKB to R. Stephenson.

57. PLB, 5, p. 127, 18 February 1847, IKB to B. Hawes.

58. PLB, 9, pp. 8 and 12–15, 24 April and 5 May 1852 for Manchester Water Works; and PLB, 10, pp. 30, 32, and 84–85, 28 September and 28 December 1854, for Glasgow Water Works.

59. F. R. Conder, *The Men Who Built Railways*, ed. J. Simmons (London, 1983),

pp. 136–37; first published anonymously in 1868 as *Personal Reflections of English Engineers.*

60. PLB, 4, p. 103, 12 June 1845, IKB to Sir John Rennie, and subsequently.

61. PLB, 7, pp. 143–45, 11 March 1850, IKB to William Cubitt, and pp. 220–21, 16 May 1850 etc.

62. PLB, 9, pp. 201–7, 1 October 1853, IKB to Sir Joseph Paxton; for IKB's idea of a domed structure for the Exhibition, see IKB to Cubitt, 16 May 1850; also above, Chapter 9.

63. PLB, 2B, pp. 30–33, 27 January 1840, IKB to R. Bright, and pp. 33–36, 27 January 1840, IKB to P. Prothero: both letters express IKB's criticisms of Rendel.

64. PLB, 10, p. 235, 10 January 1856, IKB to J. W. Bazalgette.

65. PLB, 3, pp. 139–40, 4 September 1844, IKB to G. Hudson.

66. PLB, 5, p. 98, IKB to Archibald Slate.

67. PriD, 26 December 1835, listed his active projects and their capital value in ten items: IKB was then at 53 Parliament Street, about to move to Duke Street.

68. PriD, 14 April 1836, appears as an addendum to the previous entry (note 67 above): IKB, now at 18 Duke Street, marvels at the addition of three more items to his portfolio.

69. The twenty-five desk diaries (DD) acquired by the Bristol Collection at the Christie's Sale in November 1996 consist of an intermittent and varied series of volumes covering the years 1833–59: they are at their most useful for the middle years, 1845–53.

70. Details of IKB's contract with Clifton Suspension Bridge Trustees are given in the 'Proceedings of Trustees', 1, for 20 April 1831, where a pencil note suggests that he should be paid in yearly instalments of £800.

71. PriD, see note 67 above.

72. The GWR considered a policy of financial retrenchment in 1843: see John Cattell and Keith Falconer, *Swindon: Legacy of a Railway Town* (HMSO, for the Royal Commission on the Historical Monuments of England, 1995), p. 30, quoting PRO RAIL 250/3.

73. For IKB's Income Tax returns see PLB, 2A, for 2 August 1843, July 1847, and 8 September 1850. The reintroduction of Income Tax in the 1840s is discussed in K. Theodore Hoppen, *The Mid-Victorian Generation, 1846–1886*, New Oxford History of England (Oxford, 1998), pp. 127 and 150–51.

74. See above, Chapter 9, for a discussion of the Balmoral bridge.

75. There is a series of passbooks in the Bristol Collection for IKB's account with Drummond Bank covering most years from 1835 to 1856: this appears to cover most of his general business in these years, but he also had accounts with the West of England Bank and others.

76. The Inventory of 17/18 Duke Street conducted in 1858 records these items: for a discussion of the contents, see below, Chapter 12 and the Appendix.

77. Rolt, *Brunel*, p. 322 (paperback, 416).

78. Wilson, *Sir Daniel Gooch, Diary*, p. 76.

79. For a discussion of IKB's will, see below, Chapter 13.

Notes to Chapter 11: Politics and Society

1. PriD (II.3.i), 9 June 1831. For the quotation from Lady Gladwyn, see above, Chapter 2.

2. Boyd Hilton, *Corn, Cash, Commerce: The Economic Policy of the Tory Governments, 1815–1830* (Oxford, 1977), describes this pragmatic attitude towards Free Trade.

3. K. Theodore Hoppen, *The Mid-Victorian Generation, 1846–1886* (Oxford, 1998), pp. 91 and 92.

4. PriD (II.3.i, p. 338), 11 August 1832.

5. *Morning Advertiser*, 4 September 1832, 'Lambeth Election': cutting in PriD, 11 August 1832.

6. *The Globe*, 14 September 1832: cutting in PriD.

7. William Hawes, quoted in I. Brunel, *Life of Isambard Kingdom Brunel* (1870), p. 502.

8. PriD (II.3.ii), 1 January 1833.

9. PriD (II.3.ii, p. 34), 5 March 1833 and 13 March 1833.

10. R. A. Buchanan, 'Engineers and Government in Nineteenth-Century Britain', in Roy MacLeod, ed., *Government and Expertise* (Cambridge, 1988), p. 49.

11. For Torksey Bridge, see Thomas Mackay, *Life of Sir John Fowler* (1900), pp. 95–102; the railway inspector's criticism of the bridge was the subject of earnest discussion at the Institution of Civil Engineers in 1850, see *Proceedings of the Institution of Civil Engineers*, 9 (1849–50), pp. 181–82 and 233–87.

12. PLB, 7, pp. 111–12, 11 February 1850, IKB to Captain Simmons RE.

13. PLB, 7, pp. 128–131, 5 March 1850, IKB to John Fowler.

14. Captain Simmons, subsequently Sir John L. A. Simmons (1821–1903), became a firm friend of John Fowler: see T. Mackay, *The Life of Sir John Fowler* (1900), p. 96.

15. PLB, 5, pp. 285–86, 14 October 1847, IKB to W. Cubitt.

16. Quoted in I. Brunel, *Life*, p. 486.

17. For the patent system, see H. I. Dutton, *The Patent System and Inventive Activity during the Industrial Revolution, 1750–1852* (Manchester, 1984): this is a sound but narrow study of patents as economic history. For a more comprehensive historical background, at least up to the nineteenth century, see Christine MacLeod, *Inventing the Industrial Revolution: The English Patent System, 1660–1800* (Cambridge, 1988). For Gaz, see above, Chapter 3, and PriD (II.3.ii), 30 January 1833.

18. Quoted in I. Brunel, *Life*, p. 491; see also PLB, 8, pp. 164–73, n.d. but May 1851.

19. Quoted in I. Brunel, *Life*, p. 491.

20. Dutton, *The Patent System.*, pp. 28–29.

21. See 'The Brunels', *Quarterly Review* (1862), pp. 1–39, confidently attributed to S. Smiles.

22. See the account of his relations with the Admiralty regarding the introduction of the screw in I. Brunel, *Life*, chap. 10; and Andrew D. Lambert, chaps 3 and

8 in Denis Griffiths, Andrew Lambert and Fred Walker, *Brunel's Ships* (Chatham, 1999); also Andrew Lambert, 'The Royal Navy and the Introduction of the Screw Propeller, 1837–1847' in Stephen Fisher, ed., *Innovation in Shipping and Trade*, Exeter Maritime Studies, 6 (Exeter, 1989), pp. 61–88.

23. I. Brunel, *Life*, pp. 454–61: see also PLB, 12, pp. 65–122, for summary of papers, and PLB, 10, pp. 237–38, 14 January 1856, IKB to Viscount Palmerston, urging the Prime Minister to take rapid action in order to 'permit of its being brought into practical operation this season'.

24. The correspondence with Westley Richards is collected in I. Brunel, *Life*, pp. 449–52.

25. PLB, 11, pp. 61–62, 22 May 1858, IKB to Westley Richards, ordering another gun for D'Eichtal, like the one he had made two years before.

26. PLB, 12, pp. 1–13, on the octagonal rifle: there is a hint that Isambard and Henry Brunel were providing Armstrong with material which he could use in his feud with Whitworth.

27. I. Brunel, *Life*, pp. 461–73, remains the best summary of the Renkioi Hospital: it is derived from the report by Dr Parkes and other material compiled in: 'Minute Book: Draft History of PS *Great Western*, SS *Great Britain* and PS *Great Eastern*', which is bound like a letter book in the Bristol Collection. See also David Toppin, 'The British Hospital at Renkioi, 1855', *Arup Journal*, 16 (1981), and John Brunton, *John Brunton's Book*, pp. 44–81. The Royal Commission on the Historical Monuments of England (RCHME), in its recent survey *English Hospitals, 1660–1948*, ed. by Harriet Richardson (London, 1998), gallantly includes a section on the Renkioi Hospital, pp. 90–91. On the polygonal rifle-barrel see L. T. C. Rolt, *Isambard Kingdom Brunel* (1957), p. 217 (paperback, p. 282, where 'Robert Whitworth' is corrected to 'Joseph Whitworth'); see also PLB, 9, pp. 125–26, 7 February 1853, IKB to Westley Richards, 'I want a rifle barrel made octagon shaped inside ... Can you make me such a barrel for an experiment?' (a note in the margin adds 'copied for Sir W. Armstrong 12 Nov 62 I. B.', so it seems that Isambard Brunel was providing Armstrong with material to use against his rival: see note 26, above).

28. On the Irish Famine, see C. Woodham-Smith, *The Great Hunger* (1962).

29. Oliver MacDonagh, *A Pattern of Government Growth* (London, 1961), developed this argument in relation to the Irish Passenger Acts designed to encourage emigration from Ireland.

30. S. E. Finer, *The Life and Times of Sir Edwin Chadwick* (London, 1952), demonstrates that Chadwick's consistent pursuit of the objective of efficiency caused him to make this transition.

31. PLB, 4, pp. 224–28, 7 March 1846, IKB to E. Chadwick.

32. See the account of Chadwick's campaign to make railway employers liable for the injuries of their employees in Terry Coleman, *The Railway Navvies* (Harmondsworth, 1968), pp. 139–50.

33. See above, Chapter 4, for Clifton Water Works.

34. PLB, 10, p. 235, 10 January 1856, IKB to J. W. Bazalgette. It is something of a

surprise to find a chapter in Finer, *Sir Edwin Chadwick*, on 'The Engineers', containing a swingeing denunciation of the 'Institute [sic] of Civil Engineers' for their successful obstruction of Chadwick's schemes, but IKB is not mentioned in this context.

35. A. Vaughan, *Isambard Kingdom Brunel: Engineering Knight-Errant* (London, 1991), pp. xi.

36. Rolt, *Brunel*, p. 138 (paperback, p. 184), justifies the loss of life on railway works: 'Such prodigious feats are never accomplished without risk and sacrifice.'

37. IKB to H. W. Acland, 13 June 1844: the letter is bound in MS Acland d. 66, 37326, 'Letters from Engineers', in the Bodleian Library, Oxford. I am grateful to Dr Julian Acland for helping me in its interpretation.

38. R. A. Buchanan, 'Trade Unions and Public Opinion, 1850–1875' (unpublished PhD thesis, University of Cambridge, 1957), chapter 2.

39. Nasmyth's evidence to the *Royal Commission on Trades Unions*, 10th Report, Parliamentary Papers 1868, 39, questions 19, 222 and 19, 223, in which he claims that his annoyance at trade union intervention caused him 'in defence of my own happiness' to abandon his business entirely. See J. A. Cantrell, *James Nasmyth and the Bridgewater Foundry* (Manchester, 1984), p. 224; S. Smiles, *James Nasmyth: An Autobiography* (London, 1885), gives a more anodyne account of his retirement.

40. E. Royle, *Chartism* (Harlow, 1980), provides a useful general survey: 'Much of the industrial strife of the late 1830s and early 1840s can be traced to depression and attempts to reduce wages' (p. 4).

41. Celia Noble, *The Brunels, Father and Son* (1938), pp. 184–85.

42. PLB, 6, pp. 41–44, 31 May 1848, IKB to the Hon. J. C. Talbot: IKB had recently acquired No. 17 Duke Street, next door to No. 18, from Talbot.

43. For Marx in Britain, see Isaiah Berlin, *Karl Marx* (Oxford, 1939).

44. John Timbs, *The Year Book of Facts in the Great Exhibition of 1851* (London, 1851), gives a useful account of the origins and development of the Exhibition. See also Jeffrey A. Auerbach, *The Great Exhibition of 1851: A Nation on Display* (New Haven, 1999).

45. Quoted in Timbs, *Book of Facts*, p. 20.

46. Auerbach, *Great Exhibition*, p. 2.

47. Ibid., p. 10.

48. Sir Henry Cole (1808–1882), KCB 1875, wrote under the pseudonym 'Vigil', *Inconsistencies of Men of Genius Exemplified in the Practice and Precept of I. K. Brunel, Esq., and in the Theoretical Opinions of Charles Alexander Saunders* (1846), in which he described IKB as 'an eccentric genius': see Rolt, *Brunel*, pp. 154–55 (paperback, pp. 203–4).

49. PLB, 7, pp. 37–41, 30 November 1849, IKB to John Scott Russell, 'Society of Arts: National Exhibition for 1851: Suggestions'; 30 January 1850, IKB to Russell, accepting nomination.

50. Auerbach, *Great Exhibition*, p. 41, for composition of the Building Committee.

51. DD, 1850, 12 and 13 February, 2 March (with Scott Russell), 9 April, 3 June

(Building Committee) 26 June (Fox); DD, 1851, 1 January (at Hyde Park), 18 February (ditto).

52. PLB, 7, p. 222, 19 May 1850, IKB to C. H. Wild.
53. PLB, 7, pp. 220–21, 16 May 1850, IKB to W. Cubitt.
54. Timbs, *Book of Facts,* p. 33.
55. PLB, 7, pp. 143–45, 11 March 1850, IKB to W. Cubitt.
56. Noble, *The Brunels,* p. 199, for IKB on the Crystal Palace.
57. I. Brunel, *Life,* p. 448 note 1.
58. Noble, *The Brunels,* p. 200.
59. All entries are from the desk diaries, dates as cited.
60. Auerbach, *Great Exhibition,* p. 137.
61. Ibid., p. 215, for reference to the 'Brompton Boilers', with illustration, p. 217.
62. Ibid., p. 205, for the reproduction of the painting by 'John Colcott [sic] Horsley': 'A Portrait Group of Queen Victoria and her Children', which he dates as 'circa 1865' even though the size of the Prince of Wales and the lack of any regal mourning makes 1855 or even 1851 more likely.

Notes to Chapter 12: Victorian Family Man

1. Queen Victoria's attitudes are clearly conveyed in her *Leaves from the Journal of Our Life in the Highlands* (London, 1868), although it should be remembered that Albert was already dead when she published these, so that there is an element of retrospective submission about them. For a recent overview of Victorian gender relationships, see Leonore Davidoff and Catherine Hall, *Family Fortunes: Men and Women of the English Middle Class, 1780–1850* (1987). Peter Gay, *The Bourgeois Experience: Victoria to Freud,* i, *Education of the Senses* (New York and Oxford, 1984), provides a more penetrating psychoanalytical insight into Victorian society.

2. See above, Chapter 2, for family details. Sophia was described by Lady Noble, *The Brunels, Father and Son* (1938), as 'a remarkably talented woman who understood her father's and her brother's plans and was called by Lord Armstrong "Brunel in petticoats"' (p. 45). As William (Lord) Armstrong could only have known her as the mature Lady Hawes in the 1840s and 1850s, this seems a rather odd remark to have made. Sophia married Benjamin Hawes in 1820. Emma married a clergyman, the Revd Frank Harrison, and seems usually to have been referred to disparagingly as 'poor Emma' or in similar terms by the family.

3. See above, Chapter 10, for the dispute with Marchant: he was also the contractor in dispute with IKB at the Mickleton Tunnel dispute in 1851. According to a note on 'The Pedigree of the Mudge Family' received from Mr Frank D. Smith of Bolton, Thomas Mudge (1760–1843) the London clock maker, had married Elizabeth Kingdom, sister of IKB's mother, and their daughter Sarah had married William Marchant, who farmed at Chilcompton. Robert Mudge Marchant CE was the son of this union, and thus a second cousin to IKB.

4. Paul Clements, *Marc Isambard Brunel*, pp. 241 and 249.

5. PerD, p. 11: see also above, Chapter 3, and below, Appendix.

6. PerD, p. 35, 6 April 1829: the reference to 'quizzing' is on p. 32.

7. PriD, II.3.i, 4 December 1831.

8. L. T. C. Rolt, *Isambard Kingdom Brunel* (1957), p. 90 (paperback, p. 124).

9. TTJ, 3, DM 1306/I.3.iii, 6 May 1828 and subsequently.

10. PriD, 4 December 1831, note 7 above.

11. PLB, 11, pp. 1–2, 20 January 1858, IKB to E. W. Field: the addition is obscure because of a third sum – 'the balance' – which is not specified. IKB was anxious to refrain from direct negotiation with the Hulmes because 'I am rather in disgrace'. Ellen is not mentioned in IKB's will. John Hulme is referred to in PLB, 5, pp. 146–47, 26 March 1847, IKB to R. M. Marchant, where IKB claims to have known Hulme for 'upwards of thirty years'.

12. PriD, 26 May 1832, p. 319, and 10 June 1832, have brief references to visits to the Horsleys; there are also references to meals at the Horsleys in 1834 and 1835.

13. Rosamund Brunel Gotch, ed., *Mendelssohn and his Friends in Kensington: Letters from Fanny and Sophy Horsley Written 1833–36* (Oxford, 1934). There are other letters by the Horsley young ladies that I have not traced: see Celia Noble, *The Brunels, Father and Son* (1938), p. 201, for a reference to a letter of Sophie at the time of the opening of the Great Exhibition on 1 May 1851.

14. All citations are from Gotch, *Mendelssohn and his Friends*. Some original items are in the Bristol Collection, such as Mrs Horsley's letter to her daughter on honeymoon, 9 July 1836 – DM 1284.

15. For Mary Brunel, see Noble, *The Brunels*, pp. 134–35, and Cynthia Gladwyn, 'The Isambard Brunels' (1971), pp. 13–14. Lady Noble would have had strong personal memories of her grandmother, who died when she was ten.

16. Lady Noble's book, *The Brunels: Father and Son*, is richly embellished by information from the family tradition, without other documentary basis: she quotes in full, with illustrations, the letter written by IKB to Mary from a hotel in Wootton Bassett, ibid., pp. 159–61.

17. PriD, 21 April 1832: 'Rode to Zoological Gardens to meet Ben & little ones', and elsewhere.

18. DD, 13 July 1849: this is one of several additions in indelible pencil, apparently drawn in part from the infant Isambard's own diary – see the entry for 30 July 1849 – 'Papa flew our kite'.

19. The inventory of 1858 is reproduced in outline in the Appendix below.

20. J. C. Horsley, *Recollections of a Royal Academician* (London, 1903), pp. 194–95. The Duke Street houses were completely demolished to make space for government offices later in the nineteenth century.

21. Sketch books, 23, pp. 9–10, give drawings of picture arrangements; the main items are listed in the inventory of 17–18 Duke Street taken in November 1858, see Bristol Collection DM 1285/2, and the Appendix.

22. The family 'holidays' in 1842 and 1843 are marked in the DD for those years, and further expeditions may be inferred from this source for 1844 (the West Country), 1845 (Italy), 1846 (Switzerland), 1847 (Torquay), 1848 (Torquay), 1849 (Devonshire), 1850 (Torquay), 1851 (Devonshire), 1852 (the Continent, 'accompanied by Mrs Brunel and his eldest son'), and 1853 (Watcombe).

23. For Watcombe, see Noble, *The Brunels*, pp. 194–95; more recently, some exciting work of archaeological rediscovery has been done on the gardens by G. Tudor, *The Brunels in Torbay*, Torquay Natural History Society (1989). The quotation is from Rolt, *Brunel*, p. 236 (paperback, p. 306).

24. An account of the projected White Horse jape can be found in I. Brunel, *Life of Isambard Kingdom Brunel* (1870), pp. 95–96, where it appears in a statement by George T. Clark, a former assistant of IKB, who had gone on to prosper at Dowlais Iron Works: 'It was, of course, not intended to carry this joke into execution, but Brunel often alluded to it, and laughed over the sensation it would have created.'

25. Charles MacFarlane, *Reminiscences of a Literary Life* (London, 1917), the text having been written shortly before the author's death in 1858; see especially pp. 279–93.

26. PerD, 8 April 1829.

27. The close family links survived IKB's death: see HMB Private Journal, 12 January 1862, 'Uncle Benjamin was very lively and agreeable' at a dinner engagement, although it is recorded on 20 May that 'Uncle Benjamin was buried'. See also the tribute to IKB by William Hawes in I. Brunel, *Life*, pp. 500–5.

28. DD 1834: a loose pages lists jobs to be done in South Wales: see also Horsley, *Recollections*, pp. 177–78.

29. Horsley, *Recollections*, p. 178.

30. Ibid., pp. 94–100: see also Noble, *The Brunels*, pp. 184–85.

31. Ibid., p. 169. See Rolt, *Brunel*, p. 280 (paperback, pp. 362–63), for Horsley's letter urging IKB to consider his ultimate destiny.

32. PLB, 3, p. 36, 10 May 1844, IKB to N. Roche; 8 November 1844, IKB to Roche, 'A singular chance or fatality has carried my levels almost thro' your house'; and 28 October 1844, IKB to R. Brodie, 'Try and keep the line a little farther from Mr Roche's'.

33. For Claxton, see *Brunel Society Gazette*, 4, January 1989, pp. 12–18 by Geoff Mead; and PriD, II.3.ii, p. 90, 30 August 1833, describing a member of the London Committee.

34. Notes on the family of T. R. Guppy in the Bristol Collection.

35. About fifty letters from IKB to Guppy survive in the Bristol Collection at DM 1306/VII.

36. Guppy Letters, no. 6, IKB to Guppy, 19 May 1838.

37. Guppy Letters, no. 17, IKB to Guppy, 3 October 1838.

38. Guppy Letters, no. 8, IKB to Guppy, 1 June 1838.

39. Guppy Letters, no. 28, IKB to Guppy, 3 January 1840.

40. Guppy obituary notice, *Proceedings of the Institution of Civil Engineers*, 69 (1882), pp. 411–15.

41. About thirty letters from IKB to Saunders survive in the Bristol Collection, but all are dated 1854 and deal with railway business: sequence of 'bonded' letters in folder under DM 1713.

42. Gooch expressed a warm regard for IKB in his memoirs: see R. B. Wilson, ed., *Sir Daniel Gooch: Memoirs and Diary* (Newton Abbot, 1972), especially pp. 75–76.

43. See above, Chapter 10.

44. For a recent study of Froude, see David K. Brown, 'William Froude and "the Way of a Ship in the Midst of the Sea"', in R. A. Buchanan, ed., *Engineers and Engineering* (Bath, 1996), pp. 179–209.

45. There are fifty-six letters in the Bristol Collection from Robert Stephenson to IKB under DM IX, X: this is no. 1, 15 March 1834.

46. Stephenson Letters, no. 28, n.d. but 1847.

47. I. Brunel, *Life*, p. 485: the quotation is particularly interesting because it purports to come from IKB's 'private journals' for 5 May 1846, but no such documents are known to have survived: it is possible that they were destroyed by the family (but if so, why?), and it is also possible that they are still in the possession of the family.

48. Stephenson Letters, no. 37, 7 April 1852.

49. The surviving records are tantalizingly silent about what took place at this Christmas in Cairo, but the best account is probably that of Henry Brunel, HMB Private Journal, Saturday 25 December 1858: 'Being Christmas I went to Church in the morning with my mother. In the afternoon we took a drive. In the evening all the Stephenson party, viz. Mr S., Mr and Mrs Perry, Miss Bidder, Mr Rouse and Captain Peri[?] came to dinner with us': The 'Miss Bidder' is Liza, daughter of the engineer George Bidder, who made some good sketches of Egyptian scenes which survive in the Bidder family.

50. Noble, *The Brunels*, p. 146.

51. The octagonal-barrelled gun ordered from Westley Richards, PLB, 9, 7 February 1853, was for D'Eichtal: see also the repeat order, PLB, 11, pp. 61–62, 22 May 1858, IKB to Westley Richards.

52. PriD, 9 June 1831: see above, Chapter 11.

53. MIB Diaries, 22 April 1829; PriD 18 March 1830, referring to a 'Spencer Soirée'.

54. Noble, *The Brunels*, pp. 149–53.

55. Rolt, *Brunel*, p. 102 (paperback, p. 139).

56. PriD, 13 May 1831, and again 11 March 1833.

57. Rolt, *Brunel*, p. 195 (paperback, p. 255): this event occurred on 31 March 1838.

58. PerD, 'codicil' of 2 July 1832 to his letter to Hawes.

59. Guppy Letters, no. 5, IKB to Guppy, 11 May 1838.

60. The story of the swallowed coin has been well told by Noble and Rolt, but for a detailed treatment see Michael Williams's feature in *Brunel Society Gazette*, September 1980, pp. 1–7.

61. DD 29 October 1843.

62. Noble, *The Brunels*, p. 190, describes IKB's cigar case, containing fifty cigars.

63. *Great Eastern* Correspondence, friends and colleagues, DM 1306/XI.20, no. 26, A. Hill to IKB, 2 February 1858.

64. HMB Diary 1859, entries for 1 January, 2 January and 3 January, and also HMB Private Journal and associated documents from the expedition.

65. Inventory, Bristol Collection, DM 1285/2; see also Appendix.

66. The will was proved on 10 October 1859, registering 'Effects under £90, 000'. I am grateful to Rod Knight, Group Manager to the Court Service, Principal Registry of the Family Division, for providing me with a copy of this interesting document.

67. HMB Private Journal, 5 March 1862: Henry made an urgent visit to consult Froude in Oxford when he heard about Brereton's paper, but he appears to have been reassured. The paper appeared as R. P. Brereton, 'The Centre Pier of Saltash Bridge', in *Proceedings of the Institution of Civil Engineers*, 21 (1861–62), pp. 268–76.

68. HMB Letter Book, 5, p. 270, 29 November 1864 (05270), HMB to W. Froude: 'the whole thing feels quite independent of any question of honouring his memory'.

Notes to Chapter 13: The Heroic Age of British Engineering

1. G. M. Young, *Victorian England: Portrait of an Age* (London, 1936).

2. G. Kitson Clark, *The Making of Victorian England* (London, 1962).

3. Geoffrey Best, *Mid-Victorian Britain, 1851–1875* (New York, 1972).

4. K. Theodore Hoppen, *The Mid-Victorian Generation, 1846–1886* (Oxford, 1998): the IKB reference is on p. 410.

5. Sir John Clapham, *An Economic History of Modern Britain: The Early Railway Age, 1820–1850* (Cambridge, 1926); David Landes, *The Unbound Prometheus* (Cambridge, 1969); A. E. Musson and Eric Robinson, *Science and Technology in the Industrial Revolution* (Manchester, 1969); and Jack Simmons, *The Railways of Britain* (London, 1961).

6. Thomas Carlyle, *On Heroes and Hero-Worship, and the Heroic in History* (1840; Everyman edn, 1908), p. 236.

7. Samuel Smiles, *Lives of the Engineers* (1862; reprinted Newton Abbot, 3 vols, with Introduction by L. T. C. Rolt, 1968); also *Industrial Biography* (London, 1878), and *Self Help* (London, 1859).

8. R. A. Buchanan, 'The Lives of the Engineers', in *Industrial Archaeology Review*, 11 (1988), pp. 5–15, explores this theme further; see also Adrian Jarvis, *Samuel Smiles and the Construction of Victorian Values* (Stroud, 1997), for a perceptive but somewhat combative interpretation.

9. 'The Brunels', *Quarterly Review*, 112 (1862), pp. 1–39, attributed to S. Smiles.

10. See above, Chapter 12.

11. S. Smiles, ed., *James Nasmyth, Engineer: An Autobiography* (London, 1885).

12. There are good modern biographies of a few of these engineers: see particularly K. H. Vignoles, *Charles Blacker Vignoles: Romantic Engineer* (Cambridge, 1982); Craig Mair, *A Star for Seamen: The Stevenson Family of Engineers* (1978); and E. F. Clark, *George Parker Bidder: The Calculating Boy* (Bedford, 1983).

13. The 'Railway Triumvirate': Terry Coleman, *The Railway Navvies* (Harmondsworth, 1968), p. 116, attributes this term to the obituary for Joseph Locke in *The Times*, 21 September 1860: 'In common with the most fortunate of his profession he enjoyed golden opportunities, and in conjunction with Stephenson and Brunel more particularly, he may be said to have completed the triumvirate of the engineering world.'

14. There are occasional references to church attendance in IKB's diaries: see PriD for 12 February 1832, 22 April 1832 and 10 June 1832. From DD it is apparent that he normally kept Sunday free from professional commitments, although he would sometimes see a colleague or make a journey on a Sunday if it was sufficiently important to do so.

15. PLB, 11, pp. 137–38, 1 December 1858, IKB to R. T. Lingwood, re 'Darby and St Mary Church', offering to settle 'the liabilities incurred by our late Vicar' at Watcombe.

16. The personal letter, IKB to I. Brunel, 2 February 1858, is still in the possession of the family: Lord Gladwyn sent it to the Archivist at Bristol to be transcribed in February 1997. Even by IKB's standard, it is extremely difficult to read, but the passage quoted agrees with the interpretation of Celia Noble, *The Brunels, Father and Son* (1938), pp. 236–37, who gives the letter in full.

17. L. T. C. Rolt, *Isambard Kingdom Brunel* (1957), pp. 324–25 (paperback, pp. 419–20).

18. The copy of H. T. Buckle, *The History of Civilization in England* (London, 1857), 1, was shown to me by a friend who had bought it in a second-hand bookshop: the marginal inscriptions have been transcribed as quoted by myself: I am very grateful to Dr Mark Gray for bringing the book to my attention.

19. R. Stephenson to IKB, 17 January 1858, Bristol Collection DM 1306/xi. 20. xliii: the letter is one of ten in a blue envelope marked 'Robt Stephenson: Letters of the Time of the Launch 1857–58'. The mid nineteenth-century vogue for mesmerism, spiritualism and related phenomena is well treated in Alison Winter, *Mesmerized: Powers of Mind in Victorian Britain* (Chicago, 1998).

20. There are several references to Faraday (e.g. 22 January 1825 – 'nothing particular') in the private diaries., and in TTJ, 6 May 1829, IKB records having dinner with him. The quotations are from TTJ, 15 October 1827; and PriD 18 August 30. For Babbage, see Philip Morrison and Emily Morrison, eds, *Charles Babbage and his Calculating Engines* (New York, 1961), where on pp. 88–89 Babbage is quoted from his *Life of a Philosopher*, describing a visit to the Thames Tunnel in 1827 when IKB narrowly averted a disaster; also pp. 113–19, where Babbage describes speed trials conducted by him for IKB on the GWR.

21. For the problem with Sir James South and his observatory in Kensington, see above, Chapter 3.

22. Charles Babbage, *The Ninth Bridgewater Treatise: A Fragment* (1837). Babbage seems to have been stirred into writing this tract by an assertion of Whewell, one of the eight scholars who had been commissioned to demonstrate 'the Power, Wisdom and Goodness of God, as manifested in the Creation' under the terms of the will of the Earl of Bridgewater in 1829. Whewell had denied that 'the mechanical philosophers and mathematicians of recent times' could make any useful contribution to this discussion, and Babbage set out to prove him wrong.

23. I. Brunel, *Life of Isambard Kingdom Brunel*, (1870), p. 516n.

24. J. Morrell and A. Thackray, *Gentlemen of Science* (Oxford, 1981).

25. Lardner was a scientist and mathematician who made a significant contribution to railway statistics, but his 'refutation' of the practicability of transoceanic steam traffic led to him receiving the scorn of his engineering contemporaries and the abuse of engineering historians.

26. PLB, 2B, pp. 209–302, 21 June 1842, IKB to Revd Dr Buckland (the last entry in the volume).

27. The Box Tunnel lining was the subject of occasional anxiety to the directors of the GWR and parts of it were subsequently lined with brick; see Rolt, *Brunel*, p. 139 (paperback, p. 185).

28. R. Chambers, *Vestiges of the Natural History of Creation*, published anonymously in 1844.

29. PLB, 9, pp. 257–59 and 261–62, 21 and 22 November 1853, IKB to C. Manby; also see above, Chapter 8.

30. Locke's tribute to Brunel and Stephenson at the Institution of Civil Engineers, *Proceedings of the Institution of Civil Engineers*, 19 (1859–60), pp. 1–2; quoted I. Brunel, *Life*, p. 517.

31. PLB, 5, p. 98, 6 January 1847, IKB to Archibald Slate: see also above, Chapter 10.

32. R. A. Buchanan, *The Engineers* (1989), chapters 4–6, on institutional proliferation. A good general account is provided by W. H. G. Armytage, *A Social History of Engineering* (1961). A more recent work, with a promising title, is Maxine Berg, *The Machinery Question and the Making of Political Economy, 1815–1848* (Cambridge, 1980), but the author is not very interested in the professional engineers and persists in referring to their institutions as 'institutes', pp. 152–55.

33. Buchanan, *The Engineers*, chapter 9, on education and training.

34. PLB, 6, p. 150, 2 December 1848, IKB to P. J. Palmer.

35. As a non-engineer I am not able to assess the technical and scientific merits of IKB's many calculation books and similar data: but see T. M. Charlton, 'Theoretical Work', in Sir Alfred Pugsley, ed., *Works of Isambard Kingdom Brunel*, (1976), chapter 9.

36. Buchanan, *The Engineers*, for the subsequent history of the engineering profession.

37. Rolt, *Brunel*, p. 321 (paperback, p. 415)

38. Martin J. Wiener, *English Culture and the Decline of the Industrial Spirit, 1850–1980* (Cambridge, 1981), p. 19. Wiener's thesis has been widely challenged, as by W. D. Rubinstein, *Capitalism Culture and Decline in Britain, 1750–1990* (London, 1993).

39. PerD, p. 3.

40. PerD, pp. 18–19.

41. Falls from horses are recorded in PriD, 13 May 1831 and 3 September 1832 – 'broke a gig shaft with my left leg – which was thereby somewhat damaged'.

42. Burke, quoted in I. Brunel, *Life*, p. 75.

43. Clark, quoted ibid., p. 97.

44. Charles MacFarlane, *Reminiscences of a Literary Life* (London, 1917), pp. 279–93.

45. William Hawes, quoted I. Brunel, *Life*, p. 500.

46. Horsley, quoted ibid., p. 507.

47. Sir Daniel Gooch, *Memoirs and Diary*, ed. R. B. Wilson (Newton Abbot, 1972), p. 76.

48. The alignment of the Box Tunnel has been the subject of serious discussion in the *New Civil Engineer* and elsewhere. I am grateful to my friend James Richard for making calculations which convinced me that the alignment on 9 April would permit the sun to be visible through the tunnel soon after dawn on a fine day.

49. Cynthia Gladwyn, 'The Isambard Brunels' (1971), p. 14, refers to: 'a gigantic, tremendously ornate, table-centre of silver gilt, presented with lesser companion pieces by the Great Western Railway'.

Bibliography

Manuscripts and Primary Documents

The University of Bristol Library: Special Collections

The Brunel Collection (referred to throughout as the 'Bristol Collection') has been built up since the 1950s to become the largest single repository of material on I. K. Brunel and his family. There is a brief introductory 'Guide' published by the library, and G. Maby has prepared a typescript 'Index'. The main items in the Collection are:

Private Letter Books (PLB): fifteen volumes of out-going letters from IKB's office, from 1836 to 1860; the folio volumes are numbered 1–12, but 2A, 2B, and 2C are additional. They are roughly chronological, but there is some overlap, especially in the early volumes, and vol. 12 consists entirely of notes assembled by Isambard and Henry Brunel for the *Life* of their father.

Large Sketch Books (LSB): a series of twenty folio volumes, the first (1852–54) being unnumbered, but then running 1–19, with three volumes missing (14, 16, 18). Generally chronological, but tending to concentrate on topics (e.g. Watcombe in vol 2, Paddington in vol 3, the Great Ship in vols 0 and 7).

Small Sketch Books (SSB): an incomplete series of thirty-three small format notebooks (vols 2, 4, and 7–21 are missing), containing much rougher drawings than LSB.

GWR Sketch Books (GWSB): a further series of twenty-one books of drawings, with ancillary volumes.

Calculation Books (CB): several volumes, usually associated with a particular project.

Desk Diaries (DD): an incomplete series, 1833–1859, with 1837, 1838, 1839, 1840 and 1841 missing: Letts style printed diaries, filled in unevenly with office engagements and other notes: those at the beginning and end of the series are disappointingly thin, but those from 1842 to 1854 are very informative. Some years (1834, 1842 and 1845) have two such diaries, but they are not well kept.

Personal Diary (PerD): kept by IKB in 1827–29.

Private Diaries (PriD): kept by IKB during two periods, each covered by two volumes: first, from 1824 to 1826; and second, from 1830 to 1833 (with brief additions in 1835, 1839 and 1840).

Thames Tunnel Journals (TTJ): kept by IKB from October 1826 to September 1829, in three folio vols.

Correspondence: there is a large collection of miscellaneous incoming letters, but they are not generally well arranged. There is a bundle of fifty-six letters from Robert Stephenson, written between 1834 and 1858; a group of twenty-nine letters from W. G. Armstrong (1850–54); a series of fifty-one letters from T. R. Guppy (mainly 1838–40), with about twelve missing; and a series of thirty from Bradford Leslie (1856–57), reporting on work in ironworks which he was supervising for IKB.

Clifton Suspension Bridge (CSB): reported in a folio volume, 'Proceedings of Trustees, 1830–1900'. There are also two Letter Books, and a book of CSB Committee Minutes (1831–39) with its own 'Letter Book, 1830–57'.

The SS *Great Britain* is not well covered, but there is the 'Log Book' of its fourth voyage.

HMS *Rattler* is covered in two slim folio volumes of calculations and drawings.

The SS *Great Eastern* is well treated in six folio volumes of 'Eastern Steam Navigation Letter Books' (ESNLB) running from 1852 to 1859; supplemented by a large collection of 'Correspondence with Friends and Colleagues' (forty-eight items, including letters from William Froude and Robert Stephenson); Letters on 'Inventions Offered for Use on the *Great Eastern*', a 'Calculation Book', and several miscellaneous documents such as applications for jobs on the ship.

There are volumes on 'Payments to Assistants', 'Parliamentary Accounts' of sums received from railway companies, and many sheets of 'Miscellaneous Accounts'; and the 'Inventory of Furniture Etc. of the Property of I. K. Brunel Esq.' summarized in the Appendix. There are also a set of bank passbooks.

Marc Isambard Brunel is represented by a few letters to his son in the 1820s and 1830s.

Henry Marc Brunel is represented by a very large collection of papers, most of which deal with his career and personal life after 1860, and do not concern us here: but his diary for 1858, 1859 and 1860–61; his 'Private Journal' for 1862; his 'Journal' of the trip to Egypt in 1858–59; and his early 'Letter Books' and the 'Summary of his Career', written for his brother, are valuable.

The Public Record Office

The PRO at Kew holds the collection of sixty-three items deposited with the GWR by the descendants of IKB early in the twentieth century: they were handsomely bound by the board of directors in their present form. Many of the volumes are of government and other official papers, but items 2–7 are a fine set of GWR Letter Books (GWRLB) from 1835 to 1843. Also items 8–10 contain the mind-boggling collections of 'Facts' in which IKB delighted. All held at PRO, RAIL 1149. The Family Record Centre at Myddelton Street, Islington, holds microfilm of Census returns.

Bodleian Library Oxford

IKB letter in the Acland Collection relating to the railway extension to Oxford.

Bristol City Archives

These acquired the large collection of documents from the Port of Bristol Authority (PBA) which include the original manuscript copies of IKB's Reports on the Floating Harbour.

Institution of Civil Engineers

The Institution Library holds extensive material relating to Marc Isambard Brunel, particularly his diaries and papers regarding the Thames Tunnel. Much of this is stored in the special archive created by the institution for some of its most valuable records.

University of Bath Library

The Hollingworth Collection, deposited in the library, contains a series of copy-letters relating to the building of the *Great Eastern*: chiefly important because it includes letters of John Scott Russell to IKB of which the originals have disappeared.

University College London

UCL holds a small collection of manuscript letters relating to IKB's publication on 'The Horse'.

University of Melbourne Archives

The papers of Messrs Gibbs, Bright & Co. which owned the *Great Britain* when it was operating on the Australian run, were deposited here and contain some interesting details.

The Royal Archives, Windsor

Correspondence and documents relating to the Balmoral Bridge.

Parliamentary Papers, Newspapers, Periodicals, etc.

As cited in the text.

Printed Works

All works published in London unless stated otherwise.

Adelman, Paul, *Victorian Radicalism: The Middle-Class Experience, 1830–1914* (1984).

Alford, B. W. E., 'The Economic Development of Bristol in the Nineteenth Century: An Enigma?', in McGrath, P., and Cannon, J., eds, *Essays in Bristol and Gloucestershire History* (Bristol, 1976).

Armytage, W. H. G., *A Social History of Engineering* (1961).

Auerbach, Jeffrey A., *The Great Exhibition of 1851: A Nation on Display* (New Haven, 1999).

Babbage, Charles, *The Ninth Bridgewater Treatise: A Fragment* (1837).

Ball, Adrian, and Wright, Diana, *SS Great Britain* (Newton Abbot, 1981).

Beales, Derek, *The Risorgimento and the Unification of Italy* (1971).

Beamish, Richard, *Memoir of the Life of Sir Marc Isambard Brunel* (1862).

Beaver, Patrick, *The Big Ship: Brunel's Great Eastern – A Pictorial History* (1969).

—, *The Crystal Palace: A Portrait of Victorian Enterprise* (Chichester, 1986).

Beckett, Derrick, *Brunel's Britain* (Newton Abbot, 1980).

Berg, Maxine, *The Machinery Question and the Making of Political Economy, 1815–1848* (Cambridge, 1980).

Berlin, Isaiah, *Karl Marx* (Oxford, 1939).

Bessborough, Earl of, ed., *Lady Charlotte Guest: Extracts from her Journal, 1833–1852* (1950).

Best, Geoffrey, *Mid-Victorian Britain, 1851–1875* (New York, 1972).

Binding, John, *Brunel's Cornish Viaducts* (Penryn, 1993).

—, *Brunel's Royal Albert Bridge* (Truro, 1999).

Binnie, G. M., *Early Victorian Water Engineers* (1981).

Blainey, G., *The Rush that Never Ended: A History of Australian Mining* (Melbourne, 1963).

Body, G., *Clifton Suspension Bridge: An Illustrated History* (Bradford-on-Avon, 1976).

Booth, L. G., 'Timber Works', in Pugsley, Sir Alfred, ed., *The Works of Isambard Kingdom Brunel* (1976), pp. 107–35.

Brereton, R. P., 'The Centre Pier of Saltash Bridge', in *Proceedings of the Institution of Civil Engineers*, 21 (1861–62), pp. 268–76.

Briggs, Asa, *Victorian People: Some Reassessments of People, Institutions, Ideas and Events, 1851–1867* (1954).

Brooke, David, 'The Equity Suit of *McIntosh* v. *The Great Western Railway*: The "Jarndyce" of Railway Litigation', *Journal of Transport History*, third series, 17 (1996).

—, 'The "Great Commotion" at Mickleton Tunnel, July 1851', *Journal of the Rail and Canal Historical Society*, 30 (1990), pp. 63–67.

—, *The Railway Navvy: 'That Despicable Race of Men'* (Newton Abbot, 1983).

Brown, David K., 'William Froude and "the Way of a Ship in the Midst of the Sea"', in Buchanan, R. Angus, ed., *Engineers and Engineering* (Bath, 1996).

Brunel, Isambard, *The Life of Isambard Kingdom Brunel, Civil Engineer* (1870; reprinted Newton Abbot, 1970).

Brunton, John, *John Brunton's Book*, ed. Sir John Clapham (Cambridge, 1939).

Buchanan, R. A.,'Brunel in Bristol', in McGrath, P., and Cannon, J., eds, *Essays in Bristol and Gloucestershire History* (Bristol, 1976).

—, ed., *Engineers and Engineering* (Bath, 1996).

—, 'Engineers and Government in Nineteenth-Century Britain', R. M. MacLeod, ed., *Government and Expertise* (Cambridge, 1988), pp. 41–58.

—, 'Gentlemen Engineers: The Making of a Profession', *Victorian Studies*, 26 (1983), pp. 407–29.

—, 'I. K. Brunel and the Port of Bristol', *Transactions of the Newcomen Society*, 42 (1969–70), pp. 41–56.

—, *Industrial Archaeology in Britain* (Harmondsworth, 1972).

—, *Nineteenth-Century Engineers in the Port of Bristol* (Bristol, 1971).

—, 'The Construction of the Floating Harbour, *Transactions of the Bristol and Gloucestershire Archaeological Society*, 88 (1969), pp. 184–204.

—, 'The Cumberland Basin, Bristol', *Industrial Archaeology*, 6 (1969).

—, 'The Diaspora of British Engineering', *Technology and Culture*, 27 (1986).

—, 'The Engineering Style of I. K. Brunel', *Polhem*, 15 (1997).

—, *The Engineers: A History of the Engineering Profession in Britain, 1750–1914* (1989).

—, 'The First Voyage of the SS *Great Eastern*', *Proceedings of the International Committee for the History of Technology Symposium* (Vienna, 1991).

—, 'The *Great Eastern* Controversy: A Comment', *Technology and Culture*, 24 (1983), pp. 98–106.

—, 'The Lives of the Engineers', *Industrial Archaeology Review*,11 (1988).

—, 'The Overseas Projects of I. K. Brunel', *Transactions of the Newcomen Society*, 54 (1982–83), pp. 145–66.

—, 'The Wives of the Engineers', *Engineers and Engineering* (Bath, 1996).

Buchanan, R. A., and Cossons, Neil, *The Industrial Archaeology of the Bristol Region* (Newton Abbot, 1969).

Buchanan, R. A., and Doughty, M. W., 'The Choice of Steam Engine Manufacturers by the British Admiralty, 1820–1852', *Mariner's Mirror*, 64 (1978), pp. 327–47.

Buchanan, R. A., and Jones, Stephen K., 'The Balmoral Bridge of I. K. Brunel', *Industrial Archaeology Review*, 4 (1980).

Buchanan, R. A., Jones, Stephen K., and Kiss, Ken, 'Brunel and the Crystal Palace', *Industrial Archaeology Review*, 17 (1994).

Buchanan, R. A., and Williams, Michael, *Brunel's Bristol* (Bristol, 1982).

Butterfield, H., *The Origins of Modern Science, 1300–1800* (1949).

Cannadine, David, 'Present and Past in the English Industrial Revolution, 1880–1980', *Past and Present*, 103 (1984), pp. 131–72.

Cantrell, J. A., *James Nasmyth and the Bridgewater Foundry* (Manchester, 1984).

Carlyle, Thomas, *On Heroes, Hero-Worship and the Heroic in History* (Everyman edn, 1908).

Cattell, John, and Falconer, Keith, *Swindon: The Legacy of a Railway Town* (1995).

Chadwick, O., *The Secularization of the European Mind in the Nineteenth Century* (Cambridge, 1975).

Charlton, T. M., 'Theoretical Work', in Pugsley, Sir Alfred, ed., *The Works of Isambard Kingdom Brunel* (1976), chapter 9.

Checkland, S. G., *The Rise of Industrial Society in England, 1815–1885* (1964).

Clapham, Sir John, *An Economic History of Modern Britain: The Early Railway Age, 1820–1850* (Cambridge, 1926).

Clark, E. F., *George Parker Bidder: The Calculating Boy* (Bedford, 1983).

Clark, G. Kitson, *The Making of Victorian England* (1962).

Clements, Paul, *Marc Isambard Brunel* (1970).

Clinker, C. R., *Paddington, 1854–1979: An Official History of British Rail Western Region* (Weston-super-Mare, 1979).

Coleman, Terry, *The Railway Navvies* (Harmondsworth, 1968).

Conder, F. R., *The Men Who Built Railways* (a reprint of *Personal Recollections of English Engineers*, published anonymously in 1868), ed. Simmons, Jack (1983).

Corlett, Ewan, *The Iron Ship: The History and Significance of Brunel's 'Great Britain'* (Bradford-on-Avon, 1975).

Cottrell, A. E., *The History of the Clifton Suspension Bridge* (Bristol, 1928).

Cox, R. C., *Engineering in Ireland, 1778–1878* (Dublin, 1978).

Davidoff, Leonore and Hall, Catherine, *Family Fortunes: Men and Women of the English Middle Class, 1780–1850* (1987).

Dumpleton, Bernard, and Miller, Muriel, *Brunel's Three Ships* (Melksham, 1974).

Dutton, H. I., *The Patent System and Inventive Activity during the Industrial Revolution, 1750–1852* (Manchester, 1984).

Emmerson, George S., *John Scott Russell: A Great Victorian Engineer and Naval Architect* (1977).

—, 'L. T. C. Rolt and the *Great Eastern* Affair of Brunel versus Scott Russell', *Technology and Culture*, 21 (1980), pp. 553–69.

—, 'The *Great Eastern* Controversy: In Response to Dr Buchanan', *Technology and Culture*, 24 (1983), pp. 107–13.

—, *The Greatest Iron Ship: The SS Great Eastern* (Newton Abbot, 1981).

Engels, F., *The Condition of the Working Classes in England in 1844*, English edn, with introduction by Chaloner, W. H. and Henderson, W. O. (1958).

Falconer, Jonathan, *What's Left of Brunel* (Shepperton, 1995).

Falconer, Keith, see Cattell, John.

Farr, G., *The Steamship Great Britain* (Bristol, 1965).

—, *The Steamship Great Western* (Bristol, 1963).

Farrell, Christopher, 'The Brunels and their Gaz Engine', in *Brunel Society Newsletter*, 2 (May 1977).

Finer, S. E., *The Life and Times of Sir Edwin Chadwick* (1952).

Fox, R., and Weisz, G., eds, *The Organization of Science and Technology in France, 1808–1914* (Cambridge, 1980).

Fry, P. S., 'Brunel's Crimean Hospital', in *Brunel Society Gazetteer*, 2 (September 1984).

Gay, Peter, *The Bourgeois Experience: Victoria to Freud*, i, *Education of the Senses* (New York and Oxford, 1984).

Gibbs, George Henry, see Simmons, Jack, ed, *The Birth of the Great Western Railway*.

Gladwyn, Cynthia, 'The Isambard Brunels', *Proceedings of the Institution of Civil Engineers*, 50 (September 1971), pp. 1–14.

Gooch, Sir Daniel, see Wilson, R. B., ed., *Memoirs and Diary*.

Gotch, Rosamund Brunel, *Mendelssohn and his Friends in Kensington* (Oxford, 1934).

Griffiths, Denis, Lambert, Andrew, and Walker, Fred, *Brunel's Ships* (1999).

Hadfield, Charles, *Atmospheric Railways: A Victorian Venture in Silent Speed* (Newton Abbot, 1967).

Harrison, Mark, *Crowds and History: Mass Phenomena in English Towns, 1790–1835* (Cambridge, 1988).

Hawke, G., *Railways and Economic Growth* (Cambridge, 1970).

Hay, Peter, *Brunel: His Achievements in the Transport Revolution* (Reading, 1973).

Hilton, Boyd, *Corn, Cash, Commerce: The Economic Policies of Tory Governments, 1815–1830* (Oxford, 1977).

Hobsbawn, E. J., *The Age of Revolution* (1962).

Hoppen, K. Theodore, *The Mid-Victorian Generation, 1846–1886* (Oxford, 1998).

Horsley, John Callcott, *Recollections of a Royal Academician* (1903).

Hume, John R., *The Industrial Archaeology of Scotland*, 2 vols (1977).

Jarvis, Adrian, *Samuel Smiles and the Construction of Victorian Values* (Stroud, 1997).

Joyce, Patrick, *War, Society and Politics: The Culture of the Factory in Later Victorian England* (1982).

Lambert, Andrew, 'The Royal Navy and the Introduction of the Screw Propeller, 1837–1847', Fisher, Stephen, ed., *Innovation in Shipping and Trade*, Exeter Maritime Studies (1989), pp. 61–88.

—, see also Griffiths, Denis et al.

Landes, David, *The Unbound Prometheus* (Cambridge, 1969).

Latimer, J., *The Annals of Bristol in the Nineteenth Century* (Bristol, 1887).

Little, Bryan, *The City and County of Bristol* (1954).

McCord, Norman, *The Anti-Corn Law League, 1838–1846* (1958).

MacDermot, E. T., *History of the Great Western Railway*, 2 vols (1927–31); revised edition by Clinker, C. R., in 3 vols (1964).

MacDonagh, Oliver, *A Pattern of Government Growth* (1961).

MacFarlane, Charles, *Reminiscences of a Literary Life* (1917).

McGrath, P., *The Merchant Venturers of Bristol* (Bristol, 1975).

Mackay, Thomas, *The Life of Sir John Fowler* (1900).

MacLeod, Christine, *Inventing the Industrial Revolution: The English Patent System, 1660–1800* (Cambridge, 1988).

MacLeod, Roy, ed, *Government and Expertise: Specialists, Administrators and Professionals, 1860–1919* (Cambridge, 1988).

Mair, Craig, *A Star for Seamen: The Stevenson Family of Engineers* (1978).

Mathias, P., *The First Industrial Nation* (1969).

Mead, Geoff, 'Christopher Claxton', *Brunel Society Gazette*, 4 (January 1989), pp. 12–18.

Minchinton, W. E., 'Bristol: Metropolis of the West in the Eighteenth Century', *Transactions of the Royal Historical Society*, fifth series, 4 (1954), pp. 69–89.

Morgan, K., 'The Economic Development of Bristol, 1700–1850', in Dresser, Madge, and Ollernshaw, Philip, eds, *The Making of Modern Bristol* (Bristol, 1996).

Morrell, Jack, and Thackray, Arnold, *Gentlemen of Science: Early Years of the British Association for the Advancement of Science* (Oxford, 1981).

Morrison, Philip and Emily, eds, *Charles Babbage and his Calculating Engines: Selected Writings by Charles Babbage and Others* (New York, 1961).

Mosse, John, 'Bristol Temple Meads', *Bristol Industrial Archaeology Society Journal*, 4 (Bristol, 1971).

Murless, Brian J., *Bridgwater Docks and the River Parrett*, Somerset County Library (1983).

Murray, K. A., 'Bray, Brunel and All That', *Journal Irish Railway Record Society*, 5 (1960).

Musson, A. E., and Robinson, Eric, *Science and Technology in the Industrial Revolution* (Manchester, 1969).

Nasmyth, James, *James Nasmyth, Engineer: An Autobiography*, ed. Smiles, S. (1883).

Neale, W. G., *At the Port of Bristol*, 1 (Bristol, 1968).

Noble, Celia Brunel, *The Brunels, Father and Son* (1938).

Noble, Sir Humphrey, *Life in Noble Houses* (Newcastle, 1967).

O'Callaghan, John, *The Saga of the Steamship Great Britain* (1971).

Perkin, H., *The Age of the Railway* (1970).

—, *The Origins of Modern English Society, 1780–1880* (1969).

Pudney, John, *Brunel and His World* (1974).

Pugsley, Sir Alfred, ed, *The Works of Isambard Kingdom Brunel: An Engineering Appreciation* (1976, and Cambridge, 1980).

Reeves, Graham, *Palace of the People*, Bromford Library Service (1986).

Richardson, Harriet, ed., *English Hospitals, 1660–1948*, RCHME (1998).

L. T. C. Rolt, *George and Robert Stephenson: The Railway Revolution* (1960).

—, *Isambard Kingdom Brunel* (1957); Penguin paperback with Introduction by R. A. Buchanan (Harmondsworth, 1989).

—, *Landscape with Figures: The Final Part of his Autobiography* (Stroud, 1992).

—, *Victorian Engineering* (1970).

Rosenberg, N., and Vincenti, W. G., *The Britannia Bridge: The Generation and Diffusion of Technological Knowledge* (Boston, Massachusetts, 1978).

Rowland, K. T., *The Great Britain* (Newton Abbot, 1971).

Royle, Edward, *Chartism*, Seminar Studies in History (1980).

Rubinstein, W. D., *Capitalism, Culture, and Decline in Britain, 1750–1990* (1994).

Russell, John Scott, *The Modern System of Naval Architecture* (1865).

Simmons, Jack, ed, *The Birth of the Great Western Railway: Extracts from the Diary and Correspondence of George Henry Gibbs* (Bath, 1971).

—, *The Railways of Britain* (1961; 2nd edn, 1968).

—, *The Victorian Railways* (1991).

—, see Conder, above, *The Men Who Built Railways*.

Smiles, Samuel, *Industrial Biography* (1878).

—, *James Nasmyth: An Autobiography* (1883).

—, *Self Help* (1859).

—, 'The Brunels', *Quarterly Review* (1862), pp. 1–39.

—, *The Lives of the Engineers* (1862; ed. Rolt, L. T. C., 3 vols, Newton Abbot 1968).

Smith, D. Mack, 'Italy', chapter 21, *The New Cambridge Modern History*, x (Cambridge, 1964).

Spratt, H. P., *Outline History of Transatlantic Steam Navigation* (HMSO, 1950).

Strachey, Lytton, *Eminent Victorians* (1918).

Tames, Richard, *Isambard Kingdom Brunel* (Aylesbury, 1972).

Tangye, Richard, *One and All : An Autobiography* (1889).

Thomas, David St J., *A Regional History of the Railways of Great Britain*, i, *The West Country* (Newton Abbot, 1960).

Thomas, Susan, *Bristol Riots* (Bristol, 1974).

Thompson, E. P., *The Making of the English Working Class* (1963).

Thomson, David, *Europe since Napoleon* (Harmondsworth, 1957).

Timbs, John, *The Year Book of Facts in the Great Exhibition of 1851* (1851).

Toppin, David, 'The British Hospital at Renkioi 1855', *Arup Journal*, 16 (1981).

Torrens, H. S., *Men of Iron: The History of the McArthur Group* (Bristol, 1984).

Totterdill, John W., 'A Peculiar Form of Construction', *Journal of the Bristol and Somerset Society of Architects*, 5 (1961), pp. 111–12.

Toulmin, Stephen, and Goodfield, June, *The Discovery of Time* (1965).

Tudor, Geoffrey, *The Brunels in Torbay* (Torquay, 1989).

—, 'To the Spanner Born', *Times Higher Education Supplement*, 19 August 1988.

Vaughan, Adrian, *Isambard Kingdom Brunel: Engineering Knight-Errant* (1991).

Victoria, Queen, *Leaves from the Journal of Our Life in the Highlands* (1868).

'Vigil', *Inconsistencies of Men of Genius* (1846).

Vignoles, K. H., *Charles Blacker Vignoles: Romantic Engineer* (Cambridge, 1982).

Walker, Charles, *Thomas Brassey: Railway Builder* (1969).

Watson, Garth, *The Civils: The Story of the Institution of Civil Engineers* (1988).

Wells, Charles, *A Short History of the Port of Bristol* (Bristol, 1909).

Whitley, H. S. B., 'Timber Viaducts in South Devon and Cornwall, GWR', *Railway Engineering*, October 1931.

Wiener, Martin J., *English Culture and the Decline of the Industrial Spirit, 1850–1980* (Cambridge, 1981).

Williams, L. Pearce, *Michael Faraday* (1965).

Williams, Michael, 'Brunel and the Swallowed Coin', *Brunel Society Gazette*, September 1980.

—, see Buchanan and Williams, *Brunel's Bristol*.

Wilson, Roger Burdett, ed, *Sir Daniel Gooch: Memoirs and Diary* (Newton Abbot, 1972).

Winter, Alison, *Mesmerized: Powers of Mind in Victorian Britain* (Chicago, 1998).

Woodham-Smith, Mrs Cecil, *The Great Famine* (1955).

Wrigley, E. A., *Continuity, Chance and Change: The Character of the Industrial Revolution in England* (Cambridge, 1988).

Young, G. M., *Victorian England: Portrait of an Age* (1936).

Index